T0180761

Communications
in Computer and Information Science　1877

Rationale

The CCIS series is devoted to the publication of proceedings of computer science conferences. Its aim is to efficiently disseminate original research results in informatics in printed and electronic form. While the focus is on publication of peer-reviewed full papers presenting mature work, inclusion of reviewed short papers reporting on work in progress is welcome, too. Besides globally relevant meetings with internationally representative program committees guaranteeing a strict peer-reviewing and paper selection process, conferences run by societies or of high regional or national relevance are also considered for publication.

Topics

The topical scope of CCIS spans the entire spectrum of informatics ranging from foundational topics in the theory of computing to information and communications science and technology and a broad variety of interdisciplinary application fields.

Information for Volume Editors and Authors

Publication in CCIS is free of charge. No royalties are paid, however, we offer registered conference participants temporary free access to the online version of the conference proceedings on SpringerLink (http://link.springer.com) by means of an http referrer from the conference website and/or a number of complimentary printed copies, as specified in the official acceptance email of the event.

CCIS proceedings can be published in time for distribution at conferences or as postproceedings, and delivered in the form of printed books and/or electronically as USBs and/or e-content licenses for accessing proceedings at SpringerLink. Furthermore, CCIS proceedings are included in the CCIS electronic book series hosted in the SpringerLink digital library at http://link.springer.com/bookseries/7899. Conferences publishing in CCIS are allowed to use Online Conference Service (OCS) for managing the whole proceedings lifecycle (from submission and reviewing to preparing for publication) free of charge.

Publication process

The language of publication is exclusively English. Authors publishing in CCIS have to sign the Springer CCIS copyright transfer form, however, they are free to use their material published in CCIS for substantially changed, more elaborate subsequent publications elsewhere. For the preparation of the camera-ready papers/files, authors have to strictly adhere to the Springer CCIS Authors' Instructions and are strongly encouraged to use the CCIS LaTeX style files or templates.

Abstracting/Indexing

CCIS is abstracted/indexed in DBLP, Google Scholar, EI-Compendex, Mathematical Reviews, SCImago, Scopus. CCIS volumes are also submitted for the inclusion in ISI Proceedings.

How to start

To start the evaluation of your proposal for inclusion in the CCIS series, please send an e-mail to ccis@springer.com.

Pablo H. Ruiz · Vanessa Agredo-Delgado ·
Alicia Mon
Editors

Human-Computer Interaction

9th Iberoamerican Workshop, HCI-COLLAB 2023
Buenos Aires, Argentina, September 13–15, 2023
Revised Selected Papers

 Springer

Editors
Pablo H. Ruiz ⓘ
Universidad Nacional Abierta
y a Distancia - UNAD
Popayán Cauca, Colombia

Alicia Mon ⓘ
Universidad Nacional de La Matanza
Buenos Aires, Argentina

Vanessa Agredo-Delgado ⓘ
Universidad del Cauca
Popayan Cauca, Colombia

Corporación Universitaria Comfacauca
Unicomfacauca
Popayan Cauca, Colombia

ISSN 1865-0929   ISSN 1865-0937 (electronic)
Communications in Computer and Information Science
ISBN 978-3-031-57981-3   ISBN 978-3-031-57982-0 (eBook)
https://doi.org/10.1007/978-3-031-57982-0

Preface

To celebrate the ninth year of the event, the ninth Ibero-American Workshop on Human-Computer Interaction (HCI), organised by the National University of Matanza and the HCI-COLLAB network, was held in Buenos Aires, Argentina in 2023. Year after year, this event has brought together many researchers, exhibitors and interested parties from different parts of the world, allowing the community around the topic of Human-Computer Interaction to grow more and more, strengthen its ties, manage new projects and work together. The ninth version of this workshop was held in person, with some presentations of virtual articles, which allowed participation in the presentations and attendance at the keynote lectures, workshops and various presentations and activities that took place during the event.

Human-Computer Interaction (HCI) refers to the design and use of interactive computer systems, focusing on the interaction between humans and computers. Its main goal is to create effective and efficient interfaces that allow users to interact intuitively and comfortably with computer systems.

In this sense, this book brings together a set of papers that were presented at the workshop, with topics related to HCI such as: Emotional Interfaces, Usability, Video Games and Gamification, Computational Thinking, Internet of Things (IoT), Software Engineering, ICT in Education, Augmented and Mixed Virtual Reality for Education, Adaptive Instructional Systems, Accessibility, Artificial Intelligence in HCI, Industry 4.0 and HCI, Infotainment Systems, Intelligent Systems, Collaborative Work and Learning, Cognition, and Interaction, among others.

The IX Ibero-American HCI Workshop (HCI-COLLAB 2023) received 84 papers, of which 23 were accepted to be part of this book. The double-blind reviews were carried out by at least 3 national and international reviewers per submission.

We thank the members of our Programme Committee for their work and contribution to the success of our workshop, each of the authors for their contributions, the organizers and Springer, who in recent years have allowed us to gather the best papers in the published proceedings in the CCIS series, and to continue to promote the visibility of the event every year.

February 2024

Pablo H. Ruiz
Vanessa Agredo-Delgado
Alicia Mon

Organization

Program Committee members

Laura Aballay	Universidad Nacional de San Juan, Argentina
Anas Abulfaraj	DePaul University, USA
Silvana Aciar	Universidad Nacional de San Juan, Argentina
Thiago Adriano Coleti	Universidade Estadual do Paraná, Brazil
Vanessa Agredo Delgado	Corporación Universitaria Comfacauca, Colombia
Raúl Antonio Aguilar Vera	Universidad Autónoma de Yucatán, Mexico
Sergio Albiol	Universidad de Zaragoza, Spain
Deema Alsekait	Princess Nourah Bint Abdulrahman University, Saudi Arabia
Sílvia Amélia Bim	Universidade Tecnológica do Paraná, Brazil
Leandro Antonelli	Universidad Nacional de La Plata, Argentina
Jeferson Arango López	Universidad de Caldas, Colombia
Rafael Araújo	Universidade Federal do Uberlândia, Brazil
José Guadalupe Arceo Olague	Universidad Autónoma de Zacatecas, Mexico
Gabriel Avila	Institución Universitaria Politécnico Grancolombiano, Colombia
Sandra Baldassarri	Universidad de Zaragoza, Spain
Thiago Barcelos	Instituto Federal do São Paulo, Brazil
Susana Bautista	Universidad Francisco Vitoria, Spain
Beatriz Beltran	Benemerita Universidad Autónoma de Puebla, Mexico
Alejandro Benito Santos	Universidad de Salamanca, Spain
Javier Berrocal	Universidad de Extremadura, Spain
Manuel Bolaños	Universidad de Nariño, Colombia
Clodis Boscarioli	Universidade Estadual do Oeste do Paraná, Brazil
Juliana Braga	Universidade Federal do ABC, Brazil
Juliana Bueno	Universidade Federal do Paraná, Brazil
Marta Cecilia Camacho	Institución Universitaria Colegio Mayor del Cauca, Colombia
Héctor Cardona Reyes	Centro de Investigación en Matemáticas A.C., Mexico
Alexandre Cardoso	Universidade Federal do Uberlândia, Brazil
Oscar Carrillo	CPE Lyon, France
Pedro Castillo Valdivies	Universidad de Granada, Spain
Thais Castro	Universidade Federal do Amazonas, Brazil

Silvio Cazella	Universidade Federal do Ciências da Saúde de Porto, Brazil
José María Celaya Padilla	Universidad Autónoma de Zacatecas, Mexico
Eva Cerezo	Universidad de Zaragoza, Spain
David Céspedes Hernán	Benemérita Universidad Autónoma de Puebla, Mexico
Mario Chacon	Instituto Tecnológico de Costa Rica, Costa Rica
Cecilia Challiol	Universidad Nacional de La Plata, Argentina
Esteban Clua	Universidade Federal Fluminense, Brazil
César Collazos	Universidad del Cauca, Colombia
Gustavo Eduardo Constain Moreno	Universidad Nacional Abierta y a Distancia, Colombia
André Constantino	Instituto Federal do São Paulo, Brazil
Omar Correa	Universidad de las Ciencias Informáticas, Cuba
Laura Cortes	Universidad Militar Nueva Granada, Colombia
Rosanna Costaguta	Universidad Nacional de Santiago del Estero, Argentina
Mayela Coto	Universidad Nacional de Costa Rica, Costa Rica
Ticianne Darin	Universidade Federal do Ceará, Brazil
Marcelo De Paiva Guimar	Universidade Federal do São Paulo, Brazil
Horacio Del Giorgio	Universidad Nacional de La Matanza, Argentina
Saul Delabrida	Universidade Federal do Ouro Preto, Brazil
Juan Ruben Delgado Contrera	Instituto Tecnológico y de Estudos Superiores de Monterrey, Mexico
Gloria Díaz	Institución Universitaria, Colombia
Ana Grasielle Dionisio Correa	Universidade Presbiteriana Mackenzie, Brazil
Carlos Domínguez	Tecnológico Nacional de México, Mexico
Rodrigo Duarte Seabra	Universidade Federal de Itajubá, Brazil
Rubén Edel Navarro	Universidad Veracruzana, Mexico
Maria Amelia Eliseo	Universidade Presbiteriana Mackenzie, Brazil
Nancy Estevez	Centro de Neurociencia de Cuba, Cuba
Habib Fardoun	King Abdulaziz University, Saudi Arabia
Valeria Farinazzo Martins	Universidade Presbiteriana Mackenzie, Brazil
Alejandro Fernández	Universidad Nacional de La Plata, Argentina
Leandro Florez	Universidad Antonio Jose Camacho, Colombia
Hugo Franco	Universidad Central, Colombia
Ismar Frango Silveira	Universidade Presbiteriana Mackenzie, Brazil
Bruno Gadelha	Universidade Federal do Amazonas, Brazil
Jesus Gallardo	Universidad de Zaragoza, Spain
Carlos Eric Galván Tejada	Instituto Tecnológico y de Estudios Superiores de Monterrey, Mexico
Jorge Galván Tejada	Universidad Autónoma de Zacatecas, Mexico

Hamurabi Gamboa Rosales	Universidad Autónoma de Zacatecas, Mexico
Alfredo García	Benemérita Universidad Autónoma de Puebla, Mexico
José García Alonso	Universidad de Extremadura, Spain
María Isabel García Arenas	Universidad de Granada, Spain
Alicia García Holgado	Universidad de Salamanca, Spain
Francisco José García Peñalvo	Universidad de Salamanca, Spain
Pablo García Sánchez	Universidad de Granada, Spain
Juan Enrique Garrido	Universitat de Lleida, Spain
Isabela Gasparini	Universidade do Estado de Santa Catarina, Brazil
Rosa Maria Gil	Universitat de Lleida, Spain
William Giraldo	Universidad del Quindío, Colombia
Maria Clara Gomez Alvarez	Universidad de Medellín, Colombia
Marc Gonzalez	Faculdade de Engenharia do Sorocaba, Brazil
Pascual González	Universidad de Castilla-La Mancha, Spain
Victor González	Instituto Tecnológico Autónomo de México, Mexico
Yesenia Nohemi González	Intituto Tecnológico de Apizaco, Mexico
Juan Manuel González Callero	Benemerita Universidad Autónoma de Puebla, Mexico
Claudia González Callero	Benemérita Universidad Autónoma de Puebla, Mexico
Carina González Gonzál	Universidad de La Laguna, Spain
Toni Granollers	Universitat de Lleida, Spain
Beatriz Grass	Universidad de San Buenaventura, Colombia
Ricardo Gutiérrez	Universidad Militar Nueva Granada, Colombia
Francisco Luis Gutiérrez Vela	Universidad de Granada, Spain
Elaine Harada Teixeira de Oliveira	Universidade Federal do Amazonas, Brazil
Oscar Henao	Universidad Tecnológica de Pereira, Colombia
Carlos Henrique da Silva	Instituto Federal do São Paulo, Brazil
Eduardo Hideki Tanaka	Instituto de Pesquisas Eldorado, Brazil
Antonia Huertas	Universitat Oberta de Catalunya, Spain
Julio Hurtado	Universidad del Cauca, Colombia
Jorge Ierache	Universidad Nacional de La Matanza, Argentina
Javier Jiménez	Universidad CESMAG, Colombia
Ivette Kafure	Universidade do Brasilia, Brazil
Andre Kawamoto	Universidade Federal Tecnológica do Paraná, Brazil
Avanilde Kemcinzki	Universidade do Estado de Santa Catarina, Brazil
Agustín Lagunes Domínguez	Universidad Veracruzana, Mexico
Carlos Lara-Alvarez	Centro de Investigación en Matemáticas, Mexico
Germán Ezequiel Lescano	Universidad Nacional de Santiago del Estero, Argentina

Alejandra Beatriz Lliteras	Universidad Nacional de La Plata, Argentina
Adriana Lopes Damian	Universidade Federal do Amazonas, Brazil
Víctor López-Jaquero	Universidad de Castilla-La Mancha, Spain
Maria Dolores Lozano	Universidad de Castilla-La Mancha, Spain
Huizilopoztli Luna García	Universidad Autónoma de Zacatecas, Mexico
José Antonio Macías Iglesias	Universidad Autónoma de Madrid, Spain
Natasha Malveira Costa Valentim	Universidade Federal do Paraná, Brazil
Cristina Manresa Yee	Universidad de las Islas Baleares, Spain
Samuel Marcos Pablos	Universidad de Salamanca, Spain
Anna Beatriz Marques	Universidade do Ceará, Brazil
Daniela Marques	Instituto Federal do São Paulo, Brazil
Mayra Nayeli Márquez Specia	Benemérita Universidad Autónoma de Puebla, Mexico
Erika Martínez	Benemérita Universidad Autónoma de Puebla, Mexico
Ramon Mas	Universidad de las Islas Baleares, Spain
Eleandro Maschio	Universidad Tecnológica Federal do Paraná, Brazil
Ecivaldo Matos	Universidad Federal do Bahía, Brazil
Alejandro Mauricio Gonzále	Universidad Autónoma de Zacatecas, Mexico
Nuria Medina	Universidad de Granada, Spain
Amanda Melo	Universidade Federal do Pampa, Brazil
Alfredo Mendoza Gonzál	Universidad Autónoma de Zacatecas, Mexico
Ricardo Mendoza Gonzál	Instituto Tecnológico de Aguascalientes, Mexico
Ana Isabel Molina	Universidad Castilla-La Mancha, Spain
Alicia Mon	Universidad Nacional de La Matanza, Argentina
Maria Fernanda Montoya	Universidad Tecnológica de Pereira, Colombia
Arturo Moquillaza	Pontificia Universidad Católica del Perú, Peru
Antonio Mora García	Universidad de Granada, Spain
Marcelo Morandini	Universidade do São Paulo, Brazil
Fernando Moreira	Universidade Portucalense, Portugal
Lourdes Moreno	Universidad Carlos III, Spain
Arturo Moreno	Universidad Autónoma de Zacatecas, Mexico
Mario Moreno Rocha	Universidad Tecnológica de la Mixteca, Mexico
Jorge Alejandro Morgan Benita	Universidad Autónoma de Zacatecas, Mexico
Roberto Muñoz	Universidad de Valparaíso, Chile
Freddy Muñoz	Fundación Universitaria de Popayán, Colombia
John Edison Muñoz Cardona	Universidad de Waterloo, Canada
Jaime Muñoz-Arteaga	Universidad Autónoma de Aguascalientes, Mexico
Juan Manuel Murillo Rodríguez	Universidad de Extremadura, Spain
Diego Navarro	Blekinge Institute of Technology, Sweden

Sergio Ochoa	Universidad de Chile, Chile
Manuel Ortega Cantero	Universidad de Castilla-La Mancha, Spain
Beatriz Pacheco	Universidade Paulista, Brazil
Patricia Paderewski	Universidad de Granada, Spain
Natalia Padilla Zea	Universidad Internacional de la Rioja, Spain
Philippe Palanque	Université Toulouse III, France
Marisa Panizzi	Universidad Nacional de Hurlingham, Argentina
Vania Paula de Almeida	Universidade Federal do São Carlos, Brazil
Freddy Paz	Pontificia Universidad Catolica del Perú, Peru
Carlos Pelaez	Universidad Autónoma de Occidente, Colombia
Victor Penichet	Universidad de Castilla-La Mancha, Spain
Victor Peñeñory	Universidad de San Buenaventura, Colombia
Francisco Perales	Universidad de las Islas Baleares, Spain
Roberto Pereira	Universidade Federal do Paraná, Brazil
Byron Peréz	Universidad Militar Nueva Granada, Colombia
Jose Andres Perez Bertozzi	Universidad de Costa Rica, Costa Rica
Blanca Nydia Perez Camacho	Benemérita Universidad Autónoma de Puebla, Mexico
Jorge Perez Medina	Université Catholique de Louvain, Belgium
André Pimenta Freire	Universidade Federal do Lavras, Brazil
Juan David Pinto	Universidad del Cauca, Colombia
Julio Ponce	Universidad Autónoma de Aguascalientes, Mexico
Patricia Pons	Instituto Tecnológico de Informática, Spain
Renata Pontin de Mattos Fortes	Universidade do São Paulo, Brazil
Taciana Pontual	Universidade Federal Rural de Pernambuco, Brazil
José Antonio Pow-Sang	Pontificia Universidad Catolica del Perú, Peru
Yuliana Puerta	Universidad Tecnológica de Bolívar, Colombia
Caroline Queiroz Santos	Universidade Federal dos Vales do Jequitinhonha e Mucuri, Brazil
Daniela Quiñones	Pontificia Universidad Católica de Valparaíso, Chile
Gabriel Mauricio Ramirez Villegas	Universidad de Medellín, Colombia
Leonardo Ramón	Universidade Federal do Piauí, Brazil
Alberto Raposo	Pontificia Universidad Católica de Río de Janeiro, Brazil
Paulo Realpe	Universidad Antonio Jose Camacho, Colombia
Miguel Redondo	Universidad de Castilla-La Mancha, Spain
Oscar Revelo	Universidad de Nariño, Colombia
Alessandra Reyes-Flores	Universidad Veracruzana, Mexico
Kamila Rios H. Rodrigue	Universidade do São Paulo, Brazil

Oscar David Robles Sanchez	Universidad Rey Juan Carlos, Spain
Virginia Rodés Paragarino	Universidad de la República, Uruguay
Bruno Rodrigues	Universidade Presbiteriana Mackenzie, Brazil
Andrés Rodríguez	Universidad Nacional de La Plata, Argentina
Raul Eduardo Rodríguez Ibañez	Universidad Simón Bolivar, Colombia
Maria Francesca Roig	Universidad de las Islas Baleares, Spain
Mario Rossainz	Benemérita Universidad Autónoma de Puebla, Mexico
Pablo Ruiz	Corporación Universitaria Comfacauca, Colombia
Cristian Rusu	Pontificia Universidad Católica de Valparaiso, Chile
Guillermina Sánchez Román	Benemérita Universidad Autónoma de Puebla, Mexico
Vagner Santana	Universidade Federal do ABC, Brazil
Pablo Santana Mansilla	Universidad Nacional de Santiago del Estero, Argentina
Cecilia Sanz	Universidad Nacional de La Plata, Argentina
Wilson Javier Sarmiento	Universidad Militar Nueva Granada, Colombia
Juliano Schimiguel	Universidade Cruzeiro do Sul, Brazil
Milene Selbach Silveira	Pontífice Universidade Católica do Rio Grande do Sul, Brazil
Ramiro Serrano Vergel	University of Michigan, USA
Tiago Silva da Silva	Universidade Federal do Estado de São Paulo, Brazil
Soraia Silva Prietch	Universidade Federal do Mato Grosso/Rondonópolis, Brazil
Antonio Silva Sprock	Universidad Central de Venezuela, Venezuela
João Soares Neto	Universidade Federal do Recôncavo da Bahia, Brazil
Andrés Solano	Universidad Autónoma de Occidente, Colombia
Andrés Solis	Corporación Universitaria Comfacauca, Colombia
Roberto Solis Robles	Universidad Autónoma de Zacatecas, Mexico
Christian Sturm	Ingolstadt University of Technology, Germany
Ingrid Teixeira Monteiro	Universidade do Ceará, Brazil
Diego Torres	Universidad Nacional de La Plata, Argentina
Pablo Torres Carrion	Universidad Técnica Particular de Loja, Ecuador
Andrea Vázquez Ingelmo	Universidad de Salamanca, Spain
Klinge Villalba Condori	Universidad Católica de Santa María, Peru
Angela Villarreal	Universidad Nacional Abierta y a Distancia, Colombia
Maria Lili Villegas	Universidad del Quindío, Colombia
Eva Villegas	Universitat Ramon Llull, Spain

Jorge Vitor	Universidade Federal do Rio Grande do Sul, Brazil
Marisol Wong Villacres	Escuela Superior Politécnica del Litoral, Ecuador
Luciana Zaina	Universidade Federal do São Carlos, Brazil
Sergio Zapata	Universidad Nacional de San Juan, Argentina

Academic Committee President

Alicia Mon	Universidad Nacional de la Matanza, Argentina

Program Committee President

César Alberto Collazos	Universidad del Cauca, Colombia

Editorial Committee

Pablo H. Ruiz	Universidad Nacional Abierta y a Distancia - UNAD, Colombia
Vanessa Agredo-Delgado	Corporación Universitaria Comfacauca Unicomfacauca and Universidad del Cauca, Colombia
Alicia Mon	Universidad Nacional de la Matanza, Argentina

Contents

A Case Study on Teaching HCI to Interactive Art Practitioners (and Learning from Them)

Andres Rodriguez[1,2(✉)] and Alejandro Fernandez[1,3]

1 LIFIA, Facultad de Informática, UNLP, La Plata, Argentina
{andres.rodriguez,alejandro.fernandez}@lifia.info.unlp.edu.ar
2 MAE, UNTREF, Buenos Aires, Argentina
3 CIC, Buenos Aires, Argentina

Abstract. The fields of HCI and interactive art have long maintained an increasingly fruitful relationship of dialogue, exchange, cross-pollination, and complementation. From an art perspective, HCI knowledge and strategies deliver novel tools for offering experiences to the public and open new possibilities for artists to investigate and experiment. From the HCI perspective, artists contribute new representations and experimentations of forms of interaction, as well as bring closer the crossover of knowledge areas that are often far from the HCI radar.

This paper reports on an exploratory experience of teaching HCI concepts to interactive arts practitioners. The experience sought to promote a vibrant connection between both realms. We seek to understand the potential mutual influences between Interactive Art and HCI. We aim to identify the aspects of HCI that can benefit the artist's work and, in that process, recognize the insights that can be captured for the HCI agenda.

Keywords: HCI Teaching · Experiential learning · Interactive art

1 Introduction

The arts and sciences are two drivers of culture. Before the Renaissance, they were difficult to distinguish clearly. However, after that period the West embarked on a race of specialization that so profoundly divided art from science that they seemed to generate two irreconcilable cultures for a long time. Today we live in an exciting era, with intertwined visions between art and science that sometimes make it difficult to distinguish between techno-scientific work and artistic speculation [1]. There exists an increasing level of artistic activity using computers, the Internet, and the whole techno-scientific toolkit (see, for example, the artworks based on plants screaming and in the inter-species convergence [2, 3]). This situation suggests that it is impossible to understand the future of the arts without paying attention to science and technology, in the same way, that art cannot be disregarded when exploring new horizons of the socio-technical system.

While some artists assimilate the computer to their traditional media (treating it like a sophisticated brush or a fancy camera), many others recognize this machinic element as the tip of a techno-cultural iceberg leading to a post-human era. At the same time,

P. H. Ruiz et al. (Eds.): HCI-COLLAB 2023, CCIS 1877, pp. 1–15, 2024.
https://doi.org/10.1007/978-3-031-57982-0_1

research on the quest for a human-computer *integration*, that subsumes the human-computer interaction approach [4], gets meaning and a source of inspiration from those artistic adventures.

The fields of HCI and interactive art have long maintained an increasingly fruitful relationship of dialogue, exchange, cross-pollination, and complementation. From an art perspective, HCI knowledge and strategies deliver novel tools for offering experiences to the public and open new possibilities for artists to investigate and experiment. From the HCI perspective, artists contribute new representations and experimentations of forms of interaction, as well as bring closer the crossover of knowledge areas that are often far from the HCI radar.

This paper reports on an exploratory experience of teaching HCI concepts to interactive arts practitioners. The experience sought to promote a vibrant connection between both realms. In reporting the experience, we seek to understand the potential mutual influences between Interactive Art and HCI. We aim to identify the aspects of HCI that can benefit the artist's work and, in that process, recognize the insights that can be captured for the HCI agenda. The artistic reflection and exploration presented in this work, as part of that dialogue HCI-Interactive Arts, seeks not only to contribute to the detection of the limits of that interaction but fundamentally to call attention to and question the use and exploitation of the body for the benefit of that interaction, as a kind of physiological extractivism in favor of a technification without limits.

This article is organized into four parts. After presenting the background of the investigation, we describe the Case Study that is the center of the work. Next, we discuss some lessons learned and end with the conclusions.

2 Background

Art and HCI have different objectives and approaches. However, they share several aspects that build a close relationship between the two, and that can benefit both. The evolution of HCI is often described in three waves (although some authors propose a fourth, based on entanglement, [5]). After the first wave, centered on human factors, a second one emerged, concerned with well-established, well-defined communities of practice (the workplace). The third wave then broadened and intermixed contexts such as private and professional life [6]. Within this wave, the relational turn [7], the embodiment [8], and the sensorial computing [9] have a strong relationship with the work presented in this article.

While HCI can assist artists (with evaluation methods, design principles, or information about human behavior), HCI concerns in interactive art go beyond the traditional perspective. For example, artists are not as concerned with task analysis, error prevention, or task completion times as they are with issues such as enjoyment, play, and long-term engagement. Meanwhile, HCI's concerns about experience design and understanding user engagement are especially relevant to interactive art. The artist is concerned with how the artwork behaves, how the audience interacts with it (and possibly with each other through it), and ultimately with the participants' experience and degree of engagement. In a sense, these issues have always been part of the artist's world, but in the case of interactive art, they have become more explicit and prominent within the entire canon of concern.

Interaction is relevant to the core of both interactive art and HCI. When designers and artists are sensitive to the unique effects of each type of interaction, they can choose the most appropriate for their purpose and provide richer user experiences. Revisiting interactivity with an emphasis on user participation, social interaction, and multi-sensory effects can not only enhance storytelling but ultimately improve the entire interactive art and HCI experience. Research in the intersection of art and HCI requires focusing on issues that are partly new to HCI research, for example, the user research processes typical of participatory design (traditionally, the creative process of art has been a secretive and private endeavor, only contacting the audience when it is released).

In the third wave of HCI, embodied cognition has become a theoretical foundation for research. As Dourish stated, the history of interaction design shows a progression toward greater use of the body and a greater understanding of its importance [8]. From the original command line interfaces (CLI) to today's ubiquitous tangible user interfaces (TUI) to graphical user interfaces (GUI). Theories of embodied and enactive cognition deny mind-body dualism and expand the design space for interaction to consider the whole body. With this embodied interaction, representations of computing and inter-actions with computing can be achieved through perception, planning, and performing actions with the body, which is the artists' area of expertise. HCI researchers can learn how artists see and interpret objects in the world and how they interact with the world [10].

Penny [11] argued that contemporary art strategy should shift from a "represen-tational" model to a "performative" one. Therefore, applying embodied interaction to interactive art offers a new paradigm of aesthetic practice involving behavioral design. Theories of embodiment raise new issues for artists and researchers to consider in their interaction design [12]. First, users can learn by doing. They think by gestures and movements and easily identify constraints and implicit problems. Second, users can act through an artifact rather than acting on it. They perceive the artifact as an exten-sion of their body rather than as an independent object. This explains the increased importance of emotions and affects in interaction design [13]. Third, users can easily perceive the state and response of other users, as suggested by distributed cognition the-ory [14]. Embodiment facilitates learning by participating in a community of practice and enhances coordination based on peripheral participation. Fourth, embodiment brings the previously unavailable opportunity to integrate the physical and digital worlds. This integration creates malleable materials and experiences.

The importance of the pedagogical strategy of learning by doing and its reflective component in teaching interaction design has been opportunely pointed out by Klemmer et al. [12]. They note the convenience of including in the courses the embodied aspects of learning, situated reasoning, thinking through the prototyping, and the implicit risk in action. All of these are natural components of an interactive art studio. The Experi-ential Learning Framework has been proposed by Kolb (later revised by Morris) as a systematic way to achieve this objective of learning by doing [15]. This framework is based on five themes: "learners are involved, active participants; knowledge is situated in place and time; learners are exposed to novel experiences, which involve risk; learning demands inquiry to specific real-world problems; critical reflection acts as a mediator of meaningful learning" [15]. The framework organizes the teaching into four stages: a contextually rich concrete experience, critical reflective observation, contextual-specific abstract conceptualization, and pragmatic active experimentation. This organization into stages of doing and reflecting are aligned with the basic mechanism of reflective design [16] and can contribute to facilitating the inclusion of HCI/UX knowledge in the practice of the interactive artist.

Reflecting on HCI teaching practices is not new to the community. For several years now, a community of practice on the subject has been developing with the endorsement of SIGCHI [17]. Among others, this community considers answering questions such as what it means to teach HCI, and what the most impactful and effective ways to learn HCI are [18]. This community offers lines of contributions that are relevant to the work presented here but, at the same time, presents gaps to be filled. On the one hand, different pedagogical approaches to engage students and deepen their understanding of HCI concepts, skills, and methods have been proposed. On the other, teaching HCI skills to different populations (e.g., training sketching and graphic design skills to computer science students [18]). However, in all cases, it is about teaching HCI to populations that will use that knowledge in traditional professional development for the field. The literature has identified several lessons from artistic research from which HCI can benefit, for which joint and reciprocal actions are necessary, such as teaching topics from one of these areas of knowledge to practitioners from the other [13].

3 Case Study

3.1 Goals and RQs

Stimulating the creativity of interaction designers is a recurring concern on the HCI agenda. For this, it is necessary to understand the designer's creative processes of both those that use creativity "without borders" (as is the case with art) and of those that show some restrictions for the development of innovations (such as "boundary conditions" or "edge cases" found in science and technology). For example, Fisher observed how the study of optical illusions could provide information on the process of visual perception and how the errors induced by these illusions effectively stimulate creativity [19].

In HCI and UX Design, user-centered methods are essential. For example, they are essential in adapting the conceptual model of the system to the user's mental model [20]. In Interactive Art, artists can also benefit from knowing the abilities and limitations of their audience or public to make decisions informed by that knowledge. However, due to the nature of their work, they rarely seek to satisfy people's needs or demands. An observation of how artists use that knowledge in their work can spark new and interesting ideas for HCI and UX. Benford's discussion of user interfaces that make people uncomfortable shows something to be learned from the art: making the user comfortable is not the only option, and it may not always be the best [21]. That work shows the cyclical way in which he draws on HCI and psychology to create art and then gains insights that can, in turn, contribute to HCI. In the same sense, the work of Subversive Ergonomics shows questions about the habitual "trainer" approach in Human Factors to offer the "normal user" an experience of discomfort or disability [22].

These relationships between interactive art, audience engagement, and UX design make up a significant and fruitful area of research. Studying at such a crossroads can benefit both interactive digital arts and HCI. From the artist's perspective, it can lead to a better-informed use of the perception and cognition of the artwork and its context by the human participant. This does not necessarily imply that artworks are created to meet consumer demands but rather that the artist will have a greater ability to challenge perception and cognition, to disturb, to alarm, or to confuse participants. Or to relax them, to please them, or to influence them if that is her choice. From the perspective of the interaction designer, there is a growing interest in fostering and even exploiting the creativity that users put into play. This exploitation can manifest itself through increased engagement and interest through the provision of more creative experiences. After much debate, the notion of UX (adding hedonic aspects to pragmatic usability) seems to have reached that privileged place. For good experience design, HCI might have something to learn from the artists [23].

Therefore, we sought to provide answers to two main research questions:

- **RQ1. What lessons can HCI give to Interactive Art?** Can interactive artists incorporate HCI knowledge into their work process?
- **RQ2. What insights can HCI get from the work of Interactive Art practitioners?** Can knowledge relevant to the HCI agenda be found in interactive art?

3.2 Method

Context. The Case described here corresponds to the last module of a set of 3 included in a Master's program in Interactive Arts offered by the National University Tres de Febrero in Argentina[1]. Modules are titled Digital Design (DD), Programming Interactive Sensory Environments 1 (PISE1), and Programming Interactive Sensory Environments 2 (PISE2). DD and PISE1 must be taken in the first year, PISE2 in the second one. This set of modules was designed from two premises: a) provide HCI content with an increasing progression of embodiment, b) use an experiential learning approach.

DD is an introductory programming module for artists. Processing[2] is used as a programming language and platform. Practice and assignments are organized around the study of optical illusions to present visual perception from an artist-friendly point of view and the development of a simple interactive application. This course takes advantage of the Processing low threshold of access to introduce GUI-based interfaces. During the second semester, students take PISE1, an advanced programming course for artists with a focus on computer vision (CV) and gestural interactions. These two modules serve as an introduction to basic HCI experiential teaching strategies. With this background students address the course that is the focus of this article in the third semester: PISE2.

PISE2 focuses on teaching haptic and enactive interactions (EI). It is organized around the idea of Umwelt and sensory substitution and augmentation to experiment with creating and prototyping integrated multi-sensory interactions [24–26]. Sensory substitution and augmentation involve offering information to the user through an unusual sensory modality, for example, converting visual data into tactile stimuli. These types of strategies are essential for the creation of EI. For the course's final project, students self-organize in groups (minimum of three members, maximum of four). Their assignment

---

[1] https://maestriaae.net/.
[2] http://processing.org.

is to design an EI with sensory substitution to provide the user one of the following: *"visual perception through hearing"*, *"visual perception through touch"*, *"embodied perception of some remote physical environment or some digital environment"*, *"multisensory enactive interaction"*. The group's design must be developed into an interactive prototype. The course is organized into ten weekly meetings with a studio format, lasting four hours each.

The course is organized at micro and macro levels following the Experiential Learning process as revised by Morris [15]. Students go through the four phases throughout the course and within each meeting.

Contextually Rich Concrete Experience. For students to realize that knowledge is situated in context, the course is run as a studio where students build their final project from the first day, working in groups. The classroom provides the necessary tools and materials for the work. However, the students usually also bring their own tools and take the sketches and prototypes home to continue working. This work experience in real situations of ideation, construction, and evaluation provides the appropriate context so that the IE design experience is concrete, rich, situated, and specific to the environment of each group.

Critical Reflective Observation. To contribute to experiential learning, reflective observation must be critical: students must take the stance of challenging the adequacy of abstract conceptualizations (new or preexisting) against what they experience in the real world (since the problems are context-specific). In this sense, at the macro level, the assignments have pedagogical objectives that are communicated at the beginning. Still, they are open-ended, and teachers accept the natural impulse of artists to guide their work also based on their motivations (which can change during the course). In this context, students need to critically review all the knowledge conceptualized from the dissertations of each of the topics (Haptics, Umwelt, Sensory substitution, etc.). It is not enough to understand themes and concepts. Students must incorporate them into their practices through critical observation and reflection. This requires a setting where students feel comfortable with the ambiguity and uncertainty that the project goes through until its completion.

Context-Specific Abstract Conceptualization. This is probably the most important stage for our goals. We intend that students can conceptualize what they have learned in a way that is beneficial to their artistic practice. To do this, this conceptualization must be approached in a context-specific manner. All the HCI knowledge that is provided is adapted in each course to the path that the different projects take. For example, in some past courses, projects quickly became organized around vibrotactile interactions and wearable devices. In these cases, the conceptual dissertations were organized around practical constructions of the "sketching haptics" style [27] that enabled students to jump to the abstract concepts of haptic interaction from the specific context of each group. We try to get students to conceptualize the HCI approaches fully but in their own way, thus reinforcing their own active experimentation.

Pragmatic Active Experimentation. A key benefit of context-specific abstract conceptualizations is that they enable students to act pragmatically, basing their actions on active experimentation to find a new concrete experience. It implies proving if the conceptualization they arrive at can be applied or not to their new concrete experiences.

All experiential learning takes students out of their comfort zone so that they realize that conditions change, sometimes very discretely, through time and place. To do this, they need to experiment actively, push to the limit of the newly acquired knowledge through concrete experimentation, and continually evaluate their practice against the assignment's goals, their own goals, and the criticisms of other students. Each meeting ends with instances of critique. The course is organized to guarantee at least three cycles of iteration, testing, and critique for each project.

Over 100 students have taken the course (N = 101, cisgender women = 44, cisgender men = 53, transgender women = 4) with diverse backgrounds (architecture, visual and electronic arts, design, computer science, and engineering). All of them were active practitioners in their areas of expertise at the time of classes. The participants are mostly from Argentina (approximately 50%) with a wide variety of other origins: Brazil, Chile, Colombia, Ecuador, Spain, Italy, Mexico, and Venezuela. The average age is 32.1 years (SD = 5.09).

We use participant observation as a research tool during the studios. This method requires two complementary activities to be done by the researcher: observing everything that happens and participating in the activities of the study population [28]. Therefore, the first author (with a design background) performed as Participating Observer (PO) in the role of an external design consultant for each group. Meetings between each group and the PO were video audio recorded. The PO took personal written notes. At the end of each edition of the course, we did an analysis of the data collected to create a record with the *People-Activities-Time-Space* Model (PATS) [28]. This model records "who", "how many" and performing "what roles" are there (People); "what" is going on, "what" are the predominant activities, "what situations are frequent" (Activities); "when" and for "how long" they are carrying out each activity (Time); "what" the place is like and the "which objects" they are managed (Space).

3.3 Results

Along the instances of the course, 29 projects were completed. Table 1 presents the list with titles and a brief description. We now briefly describe two of those projects.

Project 16. Sending Hugs

In this project, the students began with a phenomenological analysis of the hug, far beyond the mere instrumentality of the act of hugging and based on the experience they lived during the confinement during the COVID pandemic. At that moment the hugs ceased to exist temporarily, so they asked themselves "What would we give to recover the old hugs". This way of approaching the work, apparently far from the instructions of the course, is an approach that is repeated in all the projects and shows the natural rebellion, the defiant attitude, the critical position that is common in artistic work.

After that, the analysis of the lost experience of the hug was translated into usual interaction design practices: identify who hugs, when they do it, what does the act of hugging consist of, how does it end, and how can it be stored in virtual memories? This analysis, so typical of the specifications of the "empathizing" stages of design thinking, continued with a decomposition of possible elements to integrate into a "machine to store and receive hugs", the configurable parameters, the possible forms of storage and transmission, etc.

The initial sketches to define the shipping scenario, which they themselves defined as "a WhatsApp of hugs", soon led to formal explorations and construction techniques. In all the steps, it was obvious to see how each member of the group sought to experience in their own body what would be a desired and desirable experience.

Fig. 1. Sending hugs project. Left: final prototype of vest. Right: "Whatsapp of hugs" proposal

The discussion around the haptic stimulation format to provide in the "delivery" of the virtual hug was very interesting. They began with extensions of the small exercises shown in the vibrotactile actuation course with ERM motors. However, they quickly abandoned those actuators because they did not believe in the ability of this technology to deliver "the wealth of stimuli that a good hug deserves" (sic). They then began to explore pneumatic actuation by adapting tire-inflating-style pumps, which they continued to use until the closure proposal.

The final prototype (see Fig. 1) and its presentation accompanied by a video[3] is a perfect combination of "Ode to the Hug" artwork and the typical demonstration of an interaction design proposal.

Project 23. Olorin

The students sought a multisensory interaction: centered on olfactory interaction and supported by visual and haptic perception. They raised a speculative design on devices to bring calm through the recording, storage, and reproduction of aromas of loved ones. The work was approached with a process much closer to design thinking, with the exploration of possible requirements among the other students of the course and the compilation of previous proposals in the technological field on the registration or reproduction of aromas (see Fig. 2).

They quickly zeroed in on possible alternatives to increase engagement with the scents generated. The device ceased to be the center of the work to become "the experience". They explored a thousand and one technological ways to generate aromas (they even cannibalized an electronic nebulizer). Finally, they opted for a playful experience,

---

[3] See the video at https://youtu.be/cKap-G3E0zE.

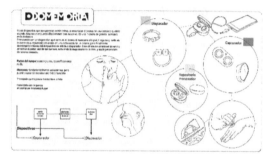

Fig. 2. Olorin project. Initial approach for an automatic memory device

which in part arose as an opportunistic design. They found a portable electronic lemon-shaped aromatizer and with that discovery, they triggered several alternatives of pendant dolls, leading to the birth of Olorín.

Fig. 3. Olorin project. Visual journey of the project

This project was the clearest case of something that was repeated in more than half of the jobs: to commit to something and feel like your own, you need to interact (and play) with it all the time. Members of this group (and many others) once they reached a prototype state with a certain functionality, they spent almost the entire class individually interacting with that design (see Fig. 3). The combination of smells, toy appearance, and large hand-sewn arms made Olorín the "pet" of that course.

Table 1. Projects developed.

ID	Title	Description
1	Granny	Playful adaptation as a puppet of the Enactive Torch
2	Nightmare catcher	Parody of the dream catcher
3	Haptic mouse	Vibrotactile augmented mouse
4	Border area	Perceiving in the body the sensations of a migrant
5	Body clapping	Feeling in the body a received applause
6	Touching the soul	Device for visually sensing another person's heart rate
7	Sphaira	Playful object with different vibrotactile responses
8	Haptic image	Device that turns vision into touch
9	Sonar for the blind	Vibrotactile transduction of physical obstacles
10	Color by heat	Vest to convert color into thermal stimulus
11	Sneakers for the blind	Decoding the ground into vibrotactile signals
12	Characters on the fingers	Glove for turning audio into vibrotactile
13	4.7k haptic beam	Turns light into caressing the skin
14	Empatheia vibratio	Installation for the campaign about legal abortion
15	Remote caresses	Wearable to generate haptic stimuli at a distance by internet
16	Sending hugs	Vest to send and receive hugs by internet
17	Good waves	Vibrotactile augmented emojis
18	Andres's bar	Virtual bar with haptic vests
19	Hapticode	Turning air gestures into vibrotactile stimuli
20	Cafunet	Speculative Design of Cranial Tactile Stimulation
21	Aquae vivae	Speculative design of sexual tactile stimulation
22	Neon veil	Haptic Neon Veil
23	Olorin	Wearable multi-sensory toy
24	Podal landscape	Foot tactile stimuli pathways
25	Pulsotron	Heartbeat pen drives
26	Affection lollipop	Lollipop with vibrotactile stimuli
27	Bat cave	Installation to explore a bat cave
28	Caresses from far away	Device for exploring remote affective touch
29	Hold my gaze	A sustained gaze gets warmth and tactile stimulation

4   Lessons Learned

This work aimed to answer two separate research questions: **RQ1. What lessons can HCI give to Interactive Art?** and **RQ2. What insights can HCI get from the work of Interactive Art practitioners?** During this exploration, our first finding is that the answers to each of these questions have a flip side that contributes to answering the other. The relationship that emerges from our explorations between Interactive Art and HCI is one of mutual potential influence. The very process of teaching HCI topics to interactive art practitioners sheds light on possible agenda items for HCI research or joint research between both fields. For interactive digital art, the experience and feelings of the public are key factors, but it's not about how a work looks or sounds; it is about what the public experiences while interacting with the artwork. It is therefore not surprising that the growing body of practice-based research in interactive digital art is pushing the boundaries of our knowledge about what is known as UX Design as the practitioner side of HCI [34] . Among the topics of an investigation that relates HCI, digital art, and the experience of the participants, we can ask several questions on which there are no agreed or complete answers: when is something attractive? What makes it attractive? What impact does familiarity have? What are the appropriate methods for evaluating interactive experiences? HCI and interactive digital art have a lot to offer each other, but what exactly can be transferred in each direction?

Digital art is increasingly interactive. Part of this is based on interactions that evolved from computer games and device use. Much of it is aimed at engaging the audience in some form of interactive experience that is a key element in the aesthetics of art. Problems related to HCI could be considered as important to the creation of interactive art, as are problems related to paint colors. Concerns related to experience design, user or audience understanding, and engagement are especially relevant. But it is also important to know about haptic sensations and perceptions, the sciences that explain them and the technologies that stimulate them, their integration into UX design.

Below we detail the main lessons that intertwine potential learning and mutual pollination between HCI and Interactive Art that this work yields.

4.1 The Designer's Experience Matters

Some interactive artworks put into play two experiences. That of the public or audience and that of the artist as performer. In some cases, they are simultaneous; in other cases, the performance of the artist gives way to that of the public or vice versa. Despite the HCI mantra "know thy user" [29] (sometimes translated as "the designer is not the user"), we can learn much from the artist's first-person experience as a performer. It can open spaces for methodological innovations in the exploratory phases with techniques such as body-storming or design with the body [30].

4.2 Engagement, Multimodality, Usage Time, and Boredom All Compete in the Same League

What shape can the interaction have to make it more interesting or challenging from the user's point of view? Is there any modality or combination of modalities that have a predictably greater capacity for commitment? An artist can watch the audience interact with her work and find out if her work generates high or low engagement. However, the assumption that someone who interacts for long periods of time with artwork is more engaged than someone who jumps in and out quickly does not seem like an appropriate strategy. It is equivalent to doing a test with users presenting prototypes and just asking:

do you like it? To further understand the relationship of both with the work, some specially designed methods to obtain information in HCI may be necessary, such as questionnaires, interviews, focus groups, etc. Do these practices make sense in art?

However, if we assume that when we talk about attractive interaction in art, we are talking about a similar phenomenon in HCI, we could get information for the exploratory phase of UX design. For example, we could analyze the way artists manage to dissociate their authorial character from their performative capacity when analyzing options at the stage of sketches and prototypes. Artists tend to assume forms of evaluation in the first person that refer to the dialectic of sketching proposed by Goldschmidt (see that-see how) [31]. This approach could give rise to new evaluation methodologies for embodied and enactive designs. Part of this challenge has been undertaken, for example, by the work of Kristina Höök on designing with the body [30].

Familiarity with an artwork sometimes decreases engagement. For example, the initial pleasure and excitement of a simple, well-designed interaction can turn to boredom after 100 repetitions. The audience may come to want the system to do something different. At HCI we know that a user's level of expertise changes with time of use, and UX design must consider the skills and knowledge of all users, from beginners to experts. But becoming an expert relies, among many things, on system consistency (getting the same output for the same input ever). So, what about the hedonic, emotional aspects of the UX? Of course, some artworks change their behavior over time, but a change in behavior implies at least the possibility of a change in the level of engagement. From the art, some frameworks have been developed to keep and increase the engagement along the interaction with the artwork. They could provide good inspiration for new UX design methodologies [32].

4.3 You can't Evaluate What You can't Measure. And You Cannot Measure What is not Defined

Is it possible to fully understand the audience interaction experience? Does it make sense to ask for a verbal articulation of feelings? Is memory reliable? Are there any objective UX measures? Evaluation methods are the answer to these questions. For this to be possible, two tasks are necessary: understanding the UX and making it manageable and measurable. Although there have been substantial advances, we still do not have a widely agreed upon definition of UX [23]. The development of evaluation methods based on the practice of the UX concept can be a valid path toward a better understanding of the UX. "UX is what we measure" could be one approach while there is no accepted definition of UX. However, this approach requires some reflection on evaluation needs and practices. By discussing the notions implicit in the requirements and evaluation methods, we can better articulate what the user experience really should be. Works from HCI and arts are trying to build a comprehensive notion [33, 34].

5   Conclusion and Future Work

In this exploratory work, we presented evidence that the relationship between HCI and Interactive Art can be mutually fruitful. We have described an investigation that explores the possibilities of enlightening the artistic work with the pedagogical practice from HCI, which at the same time allows extracting elements of interest for research in the creation of interactive technologies.

The relationship between experience design, the user or audience understanding, and engagement constitutes a particularly relevant and enriching intersection for both Interactive Art and HCI.

In Interactive Art we can expect an informed use of the perception and cognition of the audience and its context. This does not mean that the artwork is made to please or meet the demands of the users. Rather it implies that the artist will be better able to challenge perception and cognition, disturb, alarm, or confuse the participants (see for example [22]), as well as relax or please them if that is their choice (see for example, [35]).

In HCI, UX, and the design of interactive technologies, the search for creative user behavior based on a better understanding of the creative process delivered by interactive arts can occupy a relevant place not only for the development of creativity support tools (see for example, [36]) but also to explore new relationships with agency systems such as the new Generative Artificial Intelligence.

The current wave of HCI oriented towards corporeality, social interaction, and experience design gives a fertile field for the conscious incorporation, adaptation, and appropriation of the creative techniques offered by Interactive Art.

To deepen this line of work, we will undertake two simultaneous actions. On the one hand, sustaining the continuity of the MAE courses that gave rise to this work will allow the exploratory research begun to be furthered. At the same time, we are planning reciprocal actions to those described here with the participation of Interactive Art practitioners as lecturers in a new postgraduate career in HCI recently started at the UNLP College of Informatics.

References

1. Wilson, S.: Information Arts. Intersection of Art Science and Technology. The MIT Press, Cambridge (2002)
2. Khait, I., et al.: Sounds emitted by plants under stress are airborne and informative. Cell **186**(7), 1328–1336 (2023). https://doi.org/10.1016/j.cell.2023.03.009
3. Cantera, A.L.: Biopoéticas: convergencias artísticas interespecie. J. Artistic Res. **27** (2022)
4. Mueller, F.F., et al.: Next steps for human-computer integration. In: CHI 2020, pp. 1–15 (2020). https://doi.org/10.1145/3313831.3376242
5. Frauenberger, C.: Entanglement HCI the next wave? ACM TOCHI **27**(1), 1–27 (2020). https://doi.org/10.1145/3364998
6. Bødker, S.: When second wave HCI meets third wave challenges. In: NORDCHI 2006, pp. 1–8. ACM, New York (2006). https://doi.org/10.1145/1182475.1182476
7. Gunkel, D.J.: The relational turn: third wave HCI and phenomenology. In: Filimowicz, M., Tzankova, V. (eds.) New Directions in Third Wave Human-Computer Interaction: Volume 1 - Technologies. HIS, pp. 11–24. Springer, Cham (2018). https://doi.org/10.1007/978-3-319-73356-2_2
8. Dourish, P.: Where the Action Is: The Foundations of Embodied Interaction. MIT Press, Cambridge (2004)

9. Varsani, P., Moseley, R., Jones, S., James-Reynolds, C., Chinellato, E., Augusto, J.C.: Sensorial computing. In: Filimowicz, M., Tzankova, V. (eds.) New Directions in Third Wave Human-Computer Interaction: Volume 1 - Technologies. HIS, pp. 265–284. Springer, Cham (2018). https://doi.org/10.1007/978-3-319-73356-2_15

10. Fishwick, P.A.: Software aesthetics: from text and diagrams to interactive spaces. Int. J. Arts Technol. 1(1), 90–101 (2008). https://doi.org/10.1504/IJART.2008.019884

11. Penny, S.: Towards a performative aesthetics of interactivity. The Fibreculture J. 19 (2011)

12. Klemmer, S.R., Hartmann, B., Takayama, L.: How bodies matter: five themes for interaction design. In: Proceedings of the 6th Conference on Designing Interactive Systems, pp. 140–149 (2006). https://doi.org/10.1145/1142405.1142429

13. Jeon, M., Fiebrink, R., Edmonds, E.A., Herath, D.: From rituals to magic: interactive art and HCI of the past, present, and future. Int. J. Hum. Comput. Stud. 131, 108–119 (2019). https://doi.org/10.1016/j.ijhcs.2019.06.005

14. Hutchins, E.: Cognition in the Wild. MIT Press, Cambridge (1995)

15. Morris, T.H.: Experiential learning–a systematic review and revision of Kolb's model. Interact. Learn. Environ. 28(8), 1064–1077 (2020). https://doi.org/10.1080/10494820.2019.1570279

16. Schon, D.A.: The reflective practitioner, New York (1968)

17. Churchill, E.F., Bowser, A., Preece, J.: Teaching and learning human-computer interaction: past, present, and future. Interactions 20(2), 44–53 (2013). https://doi.org/10.1145/2427076.2427086

18. MacDonald, C.M., et al.: Teaching and learning human–computer interaction (HCI): current and emerging practices. Front. Comput. Sci. 5, 1188680 (2023). https://doi.org/10.3389/fcomp.2023.1188680

19. Fischer, G.: Turning breakdowns into opportunities for creativity. Knowl.-Based Syst. 7(4), 221–232 (1994). https://doi.org/10.1016/0950-7051(94)90033-7

20. Norman, D.A.: The Psychology of Everyday Things. Basic Books (1988)

21. Benford, S., et al.: Sensible, sensable and desirable: a framework for designing physical interfaces. Technical report equator-03-003, Equator (2003)

22. Benavidez Ortiz, P.: Ergonomias subversivas. Sistema Enactivo de Percepcion de la Discapacidad. Master's thesis, Universidad de Tres de Febrero (2020)

23. Hassenzahl, M., Burmester, M., Koller, F.: User experience is all there is. i-com 20(3), 197–213 (2021). https://doi.org/10.1515/icom-2021-0034

24. Visell, Y.: Tactile sensory substitution: models for enaction in HCI. Interact. Comput. 21(1–2), 38–53 (2009). https://doi.org/10.1016/j.intcom.2008.08.004

25. Froese, T., McGann, M., Bigge, W., Spiers, A., Seth, A.K.: The enactive torch: a new tool for the science of perception. IEEE Trans. Haptics 5(4), 365–375 (2011). https://doi.org/10.1109/toh.2011.57

26. von Uexkull, J.: Andanzas por los mundos circundantes de los animales y los hombres. Editorial Cactus, Buenos Aires (2016)

27. Moussette, C.: Simple haptics: sketching perspectives for the design of haptic interactions. Ph.D. thesis, Umeå Universitet (2012)

28. Guber, R.: La etnografía: método, campo y reflexividad. Siglo XXI Editores, Buenos Aires (2019)

29. Hansen, W.J.: User engineering principles for interactive systems. In: Proceedings of the November 16–18, 1971, Fall Joint Computer Conference, pp. 523–532 (1971). https://doi.org/10.1145/1479064.1479159

30. Hook, K.: Designing with the Body: Somaesthetic Interaction Design. MIT Press, Cambridge (2018)

31. Goldschmidt, G.: The dialectics of sketching. Creat. Res. J. 4(2), 123–143 (1991). https://doi.org/10.1080/10400419109534381

32. Bilda, Z.: Designing for audience engagement. In: Candy, L., Edmonds, E. (eds.) Interacting: Art, Research and the Creative Practitioner, p. 346. Libri Pub. Limited (2011)
33. Law, E., Bevan, N., Gristou, G., Springett, M., Larusdottir, M.: Meaningful Measures: Valid Useful User Experience Measurement-VUUM Workshop 2008, Reykjavik. COST Action (2008)
34. Candy, L., Ferguson, S.: Interactive Experience in the Digital Age: Evaluating New Art Practice. Springer, Cham (2014). https://doi.org/10.1007/978-3-319-04510-8
35. Duarte, Y.: Pellizcar (el cuerpo) para despertar (la mente). Master's thesis, Universidad de Tres de Febrero (2021)
36. Shneiderman, B., et al.: Creativity support tools: report from a US National Science Foundation sponsored workshop. Int. J. Hum.-Comput. Interact. 20(2), 61–77 (2006). https://doi.org/10.1207/s15327590ijhc2002_1

A Multidisciplinary Approach to Developing a Digital Game to Enhance Social Cognition Skills in Adolescents with ASD

Leonardo Veríssimo[1] , Natália Becker[1] , André Andriotti[2] ,
Carlos de Oliveira[2] , Rafael J. Pezeiro[2] , Claudionor Domingues[2] ,
and Valéria Farinazzo Martins[2,3(✉)]

[1] Human Developmental Sciences Graduate Program, São Paulo, Brazil
natalia.becker@mackenzie.br
[2] Faculty of Computing and Informatics, São Paulo, Brazil
valeria.farinazzo@mackenzie.br
[3] Graduate Program in Applied Computing – Professional, São Paulo, Brazil

Abstract. Autism spectrum disorder (ASD) is characterized by problems with social interactions and communication, and restricted or repetitive behaviors. Upon reaching adolescence, individuals with ASD are often faced with a broader environment and more complex relationships. It is important, therefore, to find ways to develop and improve the social cognition skills of these individuals. Here we describe the development process of a digital game for training social cognition in adolescents with autistic spectrum disorder. All phases of development are presented in this work. This project involved an interdisciplinary team of seven people from the areas of computer science and psychology, as well as undergraduate and graduate students, researchers, and a person with autism. The project involved the use of speech recognition and interaction design for mobile devices. The results are presented in this article and were validated, informally, by a researcher in Psychology, a researcher in the area of Human Computer Interaction and an autistic Psychologist.

Keywords: Serious Game · Digital Game · ASD · Autism · Social Cognition · Adolescence

1 Introduction

Autism spectrum disorder (ASD) is a developmental disorder which affects an individual's social skills related to interaction and social communication, which include emotional reciprocity, non-verbal communication and the ability to maintain healthy relationships (Grossard et al. 2017).

Health professionals have sought to create different types of tools and therapeutic methods to help individuals with ASD develop these skills. One of the methods that has been frequently adopted in educational and therapeutic areas is the use of serious games. One of the objectives of these games is to simulate real-life experiences in order

P. H. Ruiz et al. (Eds.): HCI-COLLAB 2023, CCIS 1877, pp. 16–28, 2024.
https://doi.org/10.1007/978-3-031-57982-0_2

to provide practical learning to the user (Da Rocha, Bittencourt and Isotani, 2015). This approach is widely used in the health area for the treatment of patients with developmental disorders, including ASD. Individuals with ASD tend to engage effectively with technology (Zakari, Ma and Simmons 2014) As a result, the use of this approach has been recommended in training for individuals with ASD to enhance their social skills.

Arenales-Loli (2013) argues that the use of toys is essential in clinical practice to achieve therapeutic progress with children, while for adults, since the beginning of psychoanalysis, the use of language has proved to be beneficial. However, adolescence represents a gap between these two stages of life, and the resources used with children and adults may not be effective with adolescents, who do not want to play with toys, but they may not have the necessary articulation required for the psychotherapy through speech that is typically used with adults. Therefore, the author suggests the use of games, especially board games, in view of the exchanges that takes place in this environment in respect of dialogue, body posture; facial expressions; frustrations and achievements.

Gikovate and Figueiredo (2022) address the relationship between autism and social cognition and point out that health professionals often mistakenly assume that people with autism do not desire social interaction. As a result, they do not provide training to acquire or improve these skills. The authors point out that it is the condition itself, combined with social isolation, which frequently result in people with poor social skills. However, it is possible, and necessary, to provide training to people with ASD to help them improve these skills.

Thus, the focus of this study is the development of a digital game, based on the construct of social cognition, for clinical use by psychologists to teach and develop these skills in autistic adolescents.

This study is organized as follows: Sect. 2 comprises a theoretical foundation on the concepts of ASD and social cognition, in addition to related subjects; Sect. 3 describes the developmental methodology, and the different stages necessary for fulfilling the research objective; Sect. 4 looks at game development and its different stages, namely: requirement analysis, design and implementation; and Sect. 5 contains some final considerations in respect of the work.

2 Theoretical Foundation

2.1 Autistic Spectrum Disorder (ASD)

Autism (from the Greek autos = oneself) emerged in the scientific context with the discoveries of Leo Kanner and Hans Asperger in 1943 and 1944. Initially, it was closely associated with schizophrenia and other disorders, but it came to be considered as a distinct pathology in the 1980s with the arrival the third edition of the Diagnostic and Statistical Manual of Mental Disorders (DSM-III). In DSM-IV it was classified into several types of syndromes and disorders, and with the arrival of the DSM-V it became an "umbrella" term where these disorders and syndromes with similar symptomatology were grouped (Gikovate and Figueiredo, 2022).

ASD has the following essential characteristics: difficulties in social communication, restricted and repetitive patterns of behavior, and heightened sensory sensitivity. Therefore, studies relating to ASD have historically run in parallel with training in social skills. Something that hinders the process are myths related to the development of social skills, and even the misconception that individuals with autism are not interested in relating.

DSM-5 presented ASD in a bidirectional way, placing it within two large groups of symptoms: "criterion A" - referring to impairments in communication and social interaction and "criterion B" - referring to restricted and repetitive patterns of behavior, interests or activities. In addition to these two large groups, in order to arrive at a diagnosis, it is necessary that the symptoms have been present in the person's life since childhood (criterion C); they should cause damage to functional life, be it professional, social or academic (criterion D); and not have any other explanation related to some type of syndrome, intellectual development or other clinical picture. The way of classifying the level of support was also changed in DSM-5, namely: level 1 - requiring support; level 2 - requiring substantial support; and level 3 - requiring substantial support. These core criteria remain the same in the DSM-5-TR (APA 2014; APA 2023).

2.2 Social Cognition

Social cognition is a set of skills related to processing emotional and social information. It also refers to the mental operations that underlie and are necessary for social interactions. It is useful in encoding and interpreting social cues, generating behaviors and reactions that are appropriate to the context, person and mental state (Mecca, Dias and Berberia, 2016).

This construct is present in a human's life from the first moments of life. In early childhood, the first social contacts take place, which are fundamental for the development of the individual. Naturally, the first traits involving social competence are rudimentary and, with the passage of physiological maturation and environmental stimulation, become more complex. In this initial period, it is recognized that the relationship with the mother and/or caregiver is of great importance. During childhood, many skills will be developed such as the identification of basic feelings, shared attention, the elaboration of more complex feelings, theory of mind, and symbolization, among others. Adolescence naturally brings the need for maturation of the individual, especially in the social aspects. During this period and into young adulthood, many challenges will have to be faced. Finally, in adulthood and old age, there can be a reduction in social cognition parallel with physiological decline, especially with regard to the intensity of affective responses (Figueiredo, 2022).

Social cognition involves different anatomical areas of the brain and a variety of neurotransmitters. This highlights its complexity and involvement in diverse skills and abilities in an individual's life. Mecca, Dias and Berberia (2016) point out that there is no consensus on the number of areas and domains that comprise this construct, but that among the different areas, there is a triad of skills (or areas): perception of emotions; theory of mind (ToM) (or mental state attribution) and attribution bias. The authors mention that another area, called social perception, has also been introduced and become recognized as an important factor in social cognition.

Mecca, Dias and Berberia (2016), in a later study, present a summary of domains that comprise the construct of social cognition: affiliation and social motivation, agent recognition, perception of biological movement, recognition of action and imitation, social attention, emotion recognition, empathy, social learning, theory of mind, social perception and attribution style.

The environment and culture profoundly impact individual learning and, therefore, cannot be disregarded. Moreover, the functioning of the individual is complex and involves many relationships. It is possible, by way of introduction, to highlight four important environments/relationships, namely: the family environment, the school environment, the social environment and the emotional environment. These domains are exercised with varying degrees of functionality depending on the training and skills developed. They can be considered functional when these domains produce a welcoming, healthy, productive environment with evolving interactions (Figueiredo, 2022).

2.3 Related Works

Some studies focused on social cognition training in adolescents were identified in the literature. A study carried out by researchers in North America sought to map how autistic people and their families used their free time. The study reported that most of the analyzed group (a total of 103 participants meeting the research criteria) spent time watching TV or using the computer, and were normally accompanied by their mothers, or remained alone. There was little evidence of other social interactions with factors such as family income and geographic location (areas classified as dangerous) markedly reducing this social interaction (Orsmond, 2011).

Given this situation, some initiatives were developed to train a range of skills in people with ASD. One of these resources was the Treatment and Education of Autistic and Related Communication Handicapped Children (TEACCH) program. A meta-analysis of 13 studies in which 172 individuals were exposed to TEACCH found that it had a small or negligible effect on motor, verbal, cognitive, communication, and daily skills. Gains in respect of social and maladaptive behavior were larger, but the study acknowledged that its findings should be considered exploratory as they were based on limited data (Virues-Ortega, et al. 2013).

Two other important studies, both produced in Sweden, sought to evaluate social skills training (SST) applied over a short period (Olssen et al., 2017) and over a long period (Jonsson et al., 2019). The results of the first study indicated that short-term training produced learning, but that it was not retained in the long term, while the second study reported that skills taught over a long period were maintained. However, although the second study reported the most promising results, the authors reached the conclusion that the effectiveness of the training was not statistically significant.

Another strategy used in social cognition training is virtual reality. In a study carried out with a group of autistic people in transition to adulthood, the participants obtained a considerable acquisition of ToM, increased recognition of emotions, and improvements in social and occupational functioning in everyday life, and these effects were long-lasting (Kandalaft, et al., 2013).

A systematic review of Brazilian literature found that the most common strategies used for teaching social cognition in autistic adolescents and adults is Discrete Trial Teaching (DTT) or naturalistic teaching. The DTT model dates back to the end of the 1980s and is based on a "one to one" intervention, with only the therapist and the patient. In this method instructions, resources and training are carried out to subsequently generalize the behavior. The results presented in review demonstrated the effectiveness of the training, with an emphasis on the acquisition of greater autonomy by patients (Carmo, et al. 2021).

There are few instruments that specifically target social cognition training for autistic people, sometimes because of the complexity of creating realistic everyday the difficulty of creating situations and sometimes because there is disagreement regarding evidence-based criteria to prove the effectiveness of the training. The aforementioned model, using virtual reality, showed good evidence of learning. The form of training used was an interaction between two characters, in multiple environments (an office building, a pool hall, a fast-food restaurant, a technology store, an apartment, a coffee shop, an outlet store, a school, a campground and a park). In each scenario, specific training was given based on predetermined skills. Following the training, the participants presents increased scores in tests that evaluated social cognition (Kandalaft, et al. 2013).

Thus, this study aligns with that of Kandalaft et al., (2013) in that it uses a series of everyday scenarios encountered by autistic people for the training of social cognition: however, rather than virtual reality, a game based on questions and answers using voice recognition was used.

3 Development Methodology

This project has been under development since August 2022, and involves a team made up of four students from the Computer Science course, as part of their graduation course completion work, a researcher in computing (more specifically in human-computer interaction), a psychologist completing his master's from the Graduate Program in Developmental Disorders and a researcher in the field of psychology - both researchers are from the same graduate program, giving the project an interdisciplinary character.

In order to achieve the general objective of this project – the development of a game to train adolescents with ASD in social cognition using scenarios in which social interaction takes place - the following steps were undertaken:

- A bibliographic survey on the topics involved, focusing on ASD and the main skills needed by autistic adolescents.
- A study of technologies related to voice recognition and the programming languages required for the construction of the digital game.
- Frequent meetings of the interdisciplinary team so that the stages of the application development could be discussed and validated.
- The conception and development (analysis, design and implementation) of a game to train the social skills of autistic people by capturing audio and sounds.
- Tests of the application by the researchers in order to reach the established minimum requirements.
- An evaluation of the usability of the developed game, carried out by specialists.

4 Game Development

4.1 Game Description

The project consists of a game for mobile devices aimed at autistic teenagers whose objective is to help players interact with the outside world, have access to everyday situations and learn how to deal with these situations, in a fun and practical way. To accomplish this, several scenarios and situations are presented in which the player will have to interact verbally, through voice recognition, obtaining feedback for each chosen answer. A "tips" menu was also developed that will always be available for the user to access and read about how to behave appropriately in each of the scenarios in the game. Moreover, the player's name and the therapist's e-mail are registered at the beginning of the game, so that the professional can follow the patient's progress and develop appropriate intervention strategies.

The scenarios are the everyday environments experienced by teenagers and reflect practical aspects of life, being: going to a restaurant (snack bar), going to a birthday party, an online interaction, a classroom interaction, and a shopping trip.

The main skills that are practiced (and which are described in more detail below) are: negotiation, skills, assertiveness, social motivation, empathy, social communication, emotional state recognition, shared attention, civility skill; interpretation of metaphors, self-regulation, and non-verbal communication.

The methodology for the development of this game is based on an iterative approach to software system development, combining top-down and bottom-up development characteristics. This generates versions (or prototypes) that are successively refined until a level of maturity is reached that fulfills the initially identified requirements. (Sommerville, 2011). In this type of approach, the success of the project depends on the designers knowing who their users are, the team working together and that the various versions are created and tested quickly. The stages of the game development are presented below.

4.2 Requirements Analysis

The requirements analysis determines the functionality and constraints that are needed in the system before starting to develop it. In this way, the implementation phase has clear objectives to determine where to begin the software construction, as this stage also determines the priority of each requirement. Among the functional requirements determined by the developers together with the experts are:

- The psychology professional should be able follow the patient's progress in the game.
- The game must have an avatar representing the person who interacts with the player.
- In the game, the avatar must communicate with the player through a pre-processed voice.
- The player should respond to the questions using their voice, although there are options for written responses on the screen.
- The player must be able to press a button (in respect of one of the possible responses) after three failed voice recognition attempts.

- If the player selects an incorrect answer, the game should provide appropriate and motivating feedback, and allow the player to try one again.
- The game must retain a history of the responses of the player.
- The game must provide a report of answers to the psychology expert.

The non-functional requirements for the game are:

- The game should be developed in such a way as to guarantee the best user experience for someone on the autism spectrum.
- The group should decide on the visual identity of the game.
- The game must support voice recognition.
- The game will be developed for mobile devices.
- The game requires internet access.
- Throughout the development of the project, meetings were held between all members every fortnight, with the aim of sharing the progress of the work, discussing any issues, and deciding on the next steps to be taken.

4.3 Project

Taking into account the results of the requirement analysis and the priority in which each functionality must be implemented, the design phase began, in which the appropriate tools, platforms and teams were defined to ensure efficiency and effectiveness in relation to the development of the product. In light of this, it was decided that the project should be developed on the Unity Engine game development platform, using the C# and SQLite programming languages; a voice detection algorithm was also developed, using the libraries provided by the language itself to implement such functionality. For this purpose, the "Mobile Speech Recognizer" asset was integrated into the prototype (Zmudzinski 2016), which allows voice recognition to work with mobile devices in a simple way. In brief, this tool uses the voice recognition engine of the device's operating system and communicates through Unity scripts, sending objects of a string data type.

Following this, the development group was divided into two teams with two members each: the design team and the development team. The first was responsible for planning and building screens using the Figma tool for each game feature, while the second was assigned to implement them using the Unity platform.

Figures 1, 2 and 3 (Fig. 1, Fig. 2 and Fig. 3) below show some of the screen models designed for the application. They were conceived in collaboration with the experts to validate the visual components on a mobile device.

Fig. 1. Templates of the menu and selected scenario screens

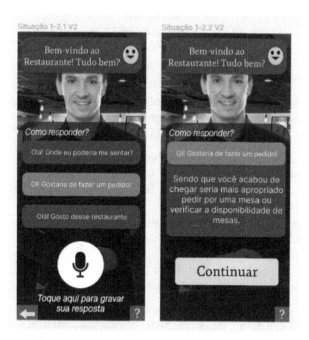

Fig. 2. Templates of the status and feedback screens

Fig. 3. Templates of the tips screen

4.4 Implementation

In the implementation stage, the development team was responsible for building a working prototype based on the complete product. For this, regular meetings were essential for the definition and validation of tasks, which are detailed below:

- Define and test the speech recognition algorithm.
- Refine the prototype to represent one of the game's scenarios.
- Build the functionality for pressing the button after three failed voice recognition attempts.
- Define how and which data will be stored.
- Configure the local database.
- Integrate the database into the prototype.
- Implement the Figma tool design into the prototype.
- Implement the narration of one of the statements.

Figure 4 shows the development environment and one of the implemented screens. It should be noted that during the development of each task, different tests were carried out in order to ensure the quality of the product and prevent possible errors in the system. Figure 5 shows the first functional version of the game.

At the beginning of the game, there is a menu screen, where the user can choose between starting to play, accessing a menu of social communication tips or asking for help if the player wants to see a tutorial about the game. It should be noted that the options

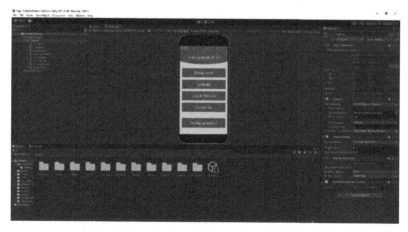

Fig. 4. Prototype development screen in the Unity Engine.

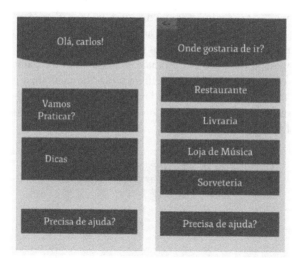

Fig. 5. Menu and scenario selection screens from the first working version of the game.

for tips and help are still under development, as is a registration screen to register the player's name and the professional's e-mail.

When selecting the "Let's Practice?" button, the player advances to the select scenario screen (Fig. 6), where it is possible to choose which scenario to interact with, in addition to the help button.

After the player selects a scenario, they are directed to the situation screen, with which they will have to interact verbally (or by touch, if voice recognition fails three times) in different contexts, with three possible responses to each situation. After choosing one of the options, feedback is given to the user, so that they can learn from their decisions.

The visual design and the development design were decided through meetings, including the color palette of the menus and options, the scenarios and how they should

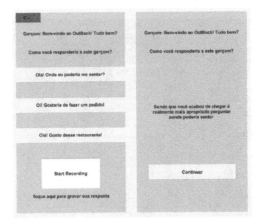

Fig. 6. Status and feedback screens from the first functional version of the game.

behave - considering their essential role in engaging the user. Blue was chosen because it has come to be the color associated with autism and the idea of fostering friendship and acceptance for individuals on the autism spectrum.

During development, the need to introduce a "mascot" in the game was identified, so that the player could be guided by something more "human" than just lines of text. The first versions of the mascot is illustrated in Fig. 7. Subsequently, the mascot shown in Fig. 8 was chosen by the team by voting on nine examples generated by the artificial intelligence DALLE-E 2 (OpenAI 2022).

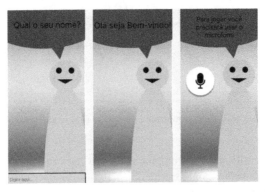

Fig. 7. Initial instruction screens showing the first version of the mascot design (a. What is your name? b. Hello, welcome. c. To play you need to use the microphone).

Fig. 8. Base image for the mascot, generated by the DALL-E 2 artificial intelligence system (OpenAI 2022).

5   Final Considerations

This work presents and describes the different stages in the development of a digital game for training social cognition in adolescents with ASD. The development team comprised seven individuals from the areas of computing and psychology, giving the project an interdisciplinary character. So far, one of seven scenarios has been developed. As the project was based on prototyping, the other scenarios should be developed more quickly.

When developing software or games in the health and education area it is particularly important to take into account the target audience. Moreover, specialists in the area in question should be involved throughout the development process.

This project has some limitations that should be noted. First, the lack of extensive testing of the game with groups of individuals with autism. Second, the rate of voice recognition may vary due to diction problems in these patients. And finally, whether the screens created will be considered attractive by the target audience.

In respect of future work, we intend to use this game with adolescents with autism to evaluate the effectiveness of the game. It is envisaged that the game will be used systematically in a clinical setting and be part of a longitudinal doctoral research study.

In this way, we hope to move the project forward so that the application becomes a therapeutic tool that can be used by professionals in the field of psychology, providing them with an effective way to work with their autistic patients and monitor their progress. Overall, the project represents a significant effort to assist autistic adolescents to develop social skills and overcome the challenges they encounter in their daily lives. The successful application of the game as a therapeutic mediator in a clinical setting would show that technology can be applied in innovative ways to support people with ASD.

Acknowledgements. This work was carried out with the support of the Coordination for the Improvement of Higher Education Personnel - Brazil (CAPES) - Excellence Program - Proex 1133/2019.

References

American Psychiatric Association (APA): Manual diagnóstico e estatístico de transtornos mentais: DSM-5. 5.ed. Artmed, Porto Alegre (2014)

American Psychiatric Association (APA): Manual diagnóstico e estatístico de transtornos mentais: DSM-5-TR. 1.ed. Artmed, Porto Alegre (2023)

Arenales-Loli, M.S., Ferreira Abrão, J.L., Ravelli Parré, R., de La Plata Cury Tardivo, L.S.: O Jogo como mediador na entrevista–um novo lugar no processo psicoterápico com adolescentes. Boletim Academia Paulista de Psicologia **33**(85), 405–426 (2013)

Carmo, T.R., Martins, T.E.M., Melo, Á.J., da Silva Barros, R.: Intervenção analítico-comportamental em adolescentes e adultos diagnosticados com Transtorno do Espectro Autista: uma revisão sistemática. Perspectivas em Análise do Comportamento **12**(2), 487–501 (2021)

da Rocha, R.V., Bittencourt, I.I., Isotani, S.: Análise, Projeto, Desenvolvimento e Avaliação de Jogos Sérios e Afins: uma revisão de desafios e oportunidades. In: Brazilian Symposium on Computers in Education (Simpósio Brasileiro de Informática na Educação-SBIE), vol. 26, no. 1, pp. 692–702 (2015)

Gikovate, C.G., Figueiredo, T.: Transtorno do Espectro Autista. Tratado de Cognição Social, 1st edn., vol. 2, pp. 23–38. Editora Ampla, Rio De Janeiro (2022)

Figueiredo, T. (org.): Tratado de cognição social: uma abordagem multidimensional, vol. 1. Editora Ampla, Belo Horizonte (2022)

Grossard, C., Grynspan, O., Serret, S., Jouen, A.L., Bailly, K., Cohen, D.: Serious games to teach social interactions and emotions to individuals with autism spectrum disorders (ASD). Comput. Educ. **113**, 195–211 (2017). https://doi.org/10.1016/j.compedu.2017.05.002

Jonsson, U., et al.: Long-term social skills group training for children and adolescents with autism spectrum disorder: a randomized controlled trial. Eur. Child Adolesc. Psychiatry **28**, 189–201 (2019). https://doi.org/10.1007/s00787-018-1161-9

Kandalaft, M.R., Didehbani, N., Krawczyk, D.C., Allen, T.T., Chapman, S.B.: Virtual reality social cognition training for young adults with high-functioning autism. J. Autism Dev. Disord. **43**, 34–44 (2013). https://doi.org/10.1007/s10803-012-1544-6

Mecca, T.P., Dias, N.M., Berberia, A.A.: Cognição Social: Teoria, Pesquisa e Aplicação. Mennon Edições Científicas, São Paulo (2016)

OpenAI DALL-E 2 (2022). https://openai.com/product/dall-e-2. Accessed 13 Apr 2023

Orsmond, G.I., Kuo, H.Y.: The daily lives of adolescents with an autism spectrum disorder: discretionary time use and activity partners. Autism **15**(5), 579–599 (2011). https://doi.org/10.1177/1362361310386503

Olsson, N.C., et al.: Social skills training for children and adolescents with autism spectrum disorder: a randomized controlled trial. J. Am. Acad. Child Adolesc. Psychiatry **56**(7), 585–592 (2017). https://doi.org/10.1016/j.jaac.2017.05.001

Sommerville, I. (ed.): Software Engineering. Pearson Education Inc. (2011)

Virues-Ortega, J., Julio, F.M., Pastor-Barriuso, R.: The TEACCH program for children and adults with autism: a meta-analysis of intervention studies. Clin. Psychol. Rev. **33**(8), 940–953 (2013). https://doi.org/10.1016/j.cpr.2013.07.005

Zakari, H.M., Ma, M., Simmons, D.: A review of serious games for children with autism spectrum disorders (ASD). In: Ma, M., Oliveira, M.F., Baalsrud Hauge, J. (eds.) SGDA 2014. LNCS, vol. 8778, pp. 93–106. Springer, Cham (2014). https://doi.org/10.1007/978-3-319-11623-5_9

Zmudzinski, P.: Mobile speech recognizer (2016). https://assetstore.unity.com/packages/tools/audio/mobile-speech-recognizer-73036. Accessed 21 Oct 10

A Study on the Interaction of the Elderly with Digital Games Under the User Experience Approach

Meuriam Silva de Assis⬤, Thiago Siqueira Garbuio⬤, Valéria Farinazzo Martins⬤, and Maria Amelia Eliseo(✉)⬤

Laboratório de Tecnologias Interativas (TecInt), Universidade Presbiteriana Mackenzie, São Paulo, SP 01239-001, Brazil
{valeria.farinazzo,mariaamelia.eliseo}@mackenzie.br

Abstract. The world is currently experiencing a significant demographic shift with a rapidly growing older population. This rise indicates a potential use of technological products that need to adapt to the characteristics of this population. Thus, this work focuses on understanding the interaction between the elderly and digital games based on UX (User Experience) strategies, considering, cognitive and motor limitations. In this article, a UX assessment was carried out to verify whether the three games selected by the research authors meet the needs of the target audience's limitations during their interaction. Tests were conducted with elderly individuals aged between 67 and 82 years old. From the applied tests, it was noticed that the users' feelings in relation to the analysed games were positive, even with difficulties throughout the game process, such as reports of effort, feeling of pressure, difficulty in managing time and pressing the necessary buttons and the frustration with the result of a portion of users.

Keywords: Elderly · Digital Games · User Experience · UX · Methodologies · UX Evaluation

1 Introduction

According to the World Population Prospects report, by 2050, one-sixth of the global population will be over 65 years old [1]. Currently, the world is undergoing an unprecedented demographic shift [2]. In Brazil, the Brazilian Institute of Geography and Statistics (IBGE) confirmed the same prediction. Currently, individuals aged 60 and above represent 14% of the population. Population growth will increase as the global population ages, reaching over 1.55 billion people by 2050. Almost 10 million people develop dementia each year, with 6 million in low and middle-income countries in developing nations [3].

Aging is an irreversible social and emotional process that affects biological aspects. The biological dimension is expressed through structural changes and the minimization of functional capacity, not caused by diseases, but by changes that occur gradually throughout life. Aging, in turn, is a series of changes in disease conditions that can

P. H. Ruiz et al. (Eds.): HCI-COLLAB 2023, CCIS 1877, pp. 29–39, 2024.
https://doi.org/10.1007/978-3-031-57982-0_3

accompany an individual throughout the aging process, affecting physical losses such as vision, hearing, motor coordination, and sensory perception. The most accurate translation of the aging brain process is dementia. Dementia is directly related to cognitive problems [4].

Types of dementia can be divided into two categories: reversible and degenerative. The most common dementias include Alzheimer's disease, Lewy body dementia, vascular dementia, and frontotemporal dementia. In the field of dementia prevention, research suggests recommended habits such as quality physical activity, dietary reeducation, adequate sleep, and brain stimulation [5].

According to reference [6], there was an increase in internet usage by the elderly in Brazil in 2021. According to the research, 48% of the elderly access the internet. Even with the increase, among the elderly who do not use the internet, 72% state that the reason is a lack of skill with the equipment. Considering the increasing elderly population and their interest in using technology, there is a potential use of digital games for this age group.

Digital games can contribute to the life cycle of an elderly person by promoting training in cognitive, physical, and social skills. However, there are few accessible and inclusive games for everyone to have a pleasant experience. User Experience (UX) is the area that concerns the experience of using a product, for example, the user's experience when navigating a website with a specific goal, which can have a positive or negative impact on this access [7].

The objective of this research is to understand how the elderly interact with digital games based on User Experience (UX) strategies, considering that the focus is on bringing what is most important to the center of solutions in a development track, always focusing on who will interact with the product, in this case, only through the use of computers, considering that the selected games used in this research were developed for desktop. From this, the practices of the elderly are identified, considering vulnerability due to natural losses. These characteristics should not be obstacles to interaction with technology but should emphasize the need for them to have special configurations. Adaptations are not specific only to the elderly but for any group, aiming to provide a more inclusive and comprehensive experience.

To achieve the goal, cognitive limitations due to aging were studied; concepts from the User Experience area for the elaboration of data collection instruments; understanding of the digital barriers that the elderly face in interacting with digital games. For the collection of study materials, three digital games from the ProBrain game collection, a developer of interactive and educational games for the stimulation of communicative, memory, and attention skills, were selected. These games were subjected to tests with users from the target audience, and then a questionnaire was provided, where the data were analyzed. With the collected data.

The work is being divided as follows: Sect. 2 contains the theoretical framework that underpins this research, in addition to related works; Sect. 3 presents the methodology; Sect. 4 discusses the analysis of the results obtained after the tests; and finally, Sect. 5 addresses the final considerations and future work.

2 Theoretical Framework

This theoretical framework presents some characteristics acquired throughout life to understand the interaction needs of the elderly. It introduces the concepts of User Experience with a focus on the elderly and their interactions with digital games. Finally, it presents related works.

2.1 Elderly - Cognitive and Physical Losses Throughout Life

Aging is a complex process involving multiple endogenous and exogenous factors. According to reference [8], endogenous factors determine individual receptivity, such as genetics, anatomy, and physiology of the human organism. This process does not initiate in individuals over 60 years old but rather represents a persistent and variably graded degenerative process that affects everyone's life [9]. Such changes are characterized by the gradual decline of functional reserve. In other words, under normal circumstances, older individuals will be able to survive adequately; however, they may experience difficulties due to physical, emotional stress, etc. [10].

Cognitive function is linked to functions such as perception, learning, memory, attention, and reasoning. Additionally, psychomotor function (reaction time, movement, performance speed) is often included in this concept. During the natural aging process, some changes occur in individuals' bodies, and some of these cognitive abilities begin to exhibit decline, primarily in slow processing, reduced attention, and memory [11].

However, these losses can be compensated for by gains in wisdom, knowledge, and experience. Fortunately, most of the time, cognitive decline is due to disuse (lack of practice), illness (such as depression), behavioral factors (such as alcohol and drug consumption), psychological factors like lack of motivation, lack of confidence, and low expectations, and social factors (such as loneliness and isolation) more than aging itself [12]. The speed at which information is processed represents another cognitive change. In the elderly, cognitive delay affecting other functions is evident and may be responsible for deficits in understanding texts, the need for a richer and broader explanation, and more time to perform calculations [13].

2.2 UX Applied to Elderly in Games

UX is defined as: the perceptions and responses that result from the use and/or anticipated use of a product, system, or service [14]. A complement to this definition is that user experience explores how a person feels when using a product. That is, the experiential stage, affective, meaningful, and valuable aspects of product use [15].

The primary goal and focus for designing accessible products are to ensure their universality, making the product more flexible and comprehensive. The application of UX aims to make interfaces more perceptible and understandable for users in various circumstances, environments, and conditions. Concern at this level will benefit all individuals with some form of cognitive or motor limitation, which is related to the circumstances and the device used [16].

Elderly individuals represent potential users for the use of digital games. This is directly attributed to the benefits of certain features available in games. However, some games have not been developed or structured with the elderly in mind. Therefore, often games are not accessible to them.

Older individuals need more time and follow a slower pace. Learning to manipulate and understand the workings of these artifacts is slow, whether for personal and daily use or in professional activities. Games do not always have a user-friendly interface to adapt to the characteristics of older individuals. For example, considering the font size and type, icon size, color contrast, and interaction design, as well as using sounds with lower frequency [17].

Elderly individuals do not enjoy playing complex games, with many rules to follow during the stages [3]. Various works have emerged with the goal of making digital games a form of recreation and leisure. With researchers' interest in revealing cognitive potential, especially quality of life, studies on the elderly stand out, some of which address memory loss, hearing, vision, and motor coordination, which are more prominent in the age group above 60 years.

It is asserted that elderly individuals do not use gaming technologies in general because there is no incentive, preparation, and accessibility targeting this audience. Moreover, these characteristics are not always taken into account in gaming culture. Technology developed for the elderly must meet their essential expectations for them to accept and adopt it in their daily lives [18].

To mitigate such a problem, it is necessary to use methodologies that can include such characteristics of the elderly audience, such as UX, which, by understanding users' feelings and emotions in using a product, offers more appropriate solutions. This involves focusing the development process on the target audience, from the necessary requirements for interaction design to the analysis of user experience, in addition to a study regarding the game's objective. This focus allows the construction of a standard design that is easy to understand, interpret, and use according to the interaction between the user and the product.

2.3 Related Works

Several works related to this research were found in the literature. Reference [19] analyzed gamers' feelings during game practice, considering the needs of the developers' industry, assessing the overall user experience. The authors also address interaction techniques as evaluative methods for an enhanced user experience, such as gestures, eye tracking, and input and bio-physiological feedback. Subsequently, reference [20] approached, based on specific games, the evaluation of user experience with terms of real analysis, including data collection, which is like the present study.

Reference [21] discusses the challenge of adaptive digital educational games and their challenges in user experience. The authors focus the research on experiments, whether in game learning or usability, in a user-centered design approach.

Reference [22] presents the development of a serious game based on the Corsi test that trains and assesses the visuospatial memory of the elderly audience. They rely on guidelines for game development for this audience, with testing involving elderly participants. Meanwhile, reference [23] presents the usability evaluation of this same game, involving usability experts.

This work stands out for evaluating the interaction of the elderly audience with digital games under the User Experience approach. The mentioned articles played an important role during the elaboration of this study, providing a more in-depth understanding of the subject.

3 Methodology

A literature review was conducted to search for studies, research, applied methodologies, and obtained results that served as the foundation for the development of this research. A study was conducted on the elderly audience and their characteristics, addressing issues related to the concept of User Experience and evaluation metrics.

After the theoretical research, three games available on the ProBrain platform were chosen. This platform provides gamified solutions to stimulate brain skills related to communication, hearing, and learning for both adults and children. The chosen games were: "Achei" (I Found It), "Achei o chapéu" (Find the Hat), and "Supermercado" (Supermarket). These games target motor coordination skills, auditory perception, and memory stimulation. Figure 1 shows the interface of each game.

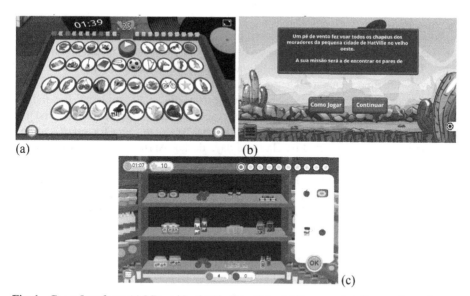

Fig. 1. Game Interfaces (a) I Found It, (b) Find the Hat e (c) Supermarket. Source: https://www. probrain.com.br/

After defining the assessment method and data collection instrument, 12 elderly participants, aged between 67 and 82 years, were selected to undergo the test, where information about their use of the games was collected. All had some experience with technology but had never used a computer for gaming purposes. Of these respondents, 33% were male, and 67% were female. During the test application, users were given predefined instructions, and the administrators were available in case of any doubts. Users engaged in the practice of three memory stimulation games, and some had questions during the experience. The majority achieved the game objectives without assistance from the test administrators.

After the game practice, "The Game Experience Questionnaire" (GEQ) was administered. This questionnaire, created by Eindhoven University of Technology, allows mapping users' sensations throughout the game exercises, capturing what was felt and evaluating the interfaces [24].

Considering that an evaluation of the first usage experience involves the responses and perceptions of an individual resulting from the use of a product, system, or service, the questionnaire was applied to participants with their first usage experience, observing their responses and perceptions [14]. The objective of this application was to individually assess the user's perspective for each game based on the GEQ criteria.

The questionnaire has a structure consisting of three modules: the Main questionnaire, the Social Presence module, and the post-game module. These modules were administered immediately at the end of the game test session in the mentioned order. The first part analyzes the gaming experience, the second part examines the psychological and behavioral involvement of the player, and the third and final part evaluates how players felt after completing the game session.

3.1 Test Planning

The objective was to assess the experience of each elderly user while interacting with the games. Test planning took into consideration these objectives, the equipment to be used, the browser, the time spent on each test step, the tasks to be performed by the testers, the tasks to be carried out by the test observer, and the data collection instrument. To validate this plan, two researchers performed the tasks, responded to the questionnaire, timed the duration of each activity, and considered an additional 10% of this time for test execution. Thus, the tests were conducted on alternate days during April 2022, with twelve (12) elderly users aged between 67 and 82. Two researchers were responsible for conducting tests with six (6) individuals each. Before starting the test session, users were informed about the research objectives by the facilitators. Collection procedures were communicated in advance to the testers, including the anticipated time for the entire test session. It was made clear to the testers that the evaluation focused on interaction rather than user expertise. Testers were also informed that the collected data would be anonymized and used for the purposes of this research, ensuring privacy and confidentiality.

The study was conducted at the testers' homes, with two notebooks provided by the researchers, equipped with internet access. The game pages were pre-opened by the researchers in the Chrome browser for users to initiate the gameplay experience in the following sequence: "I Found It," "Find the Hat," and "Supermarket." After trying out the three games, the GEQ questionnaire was administered.

Each user was individually assessed, with the opportunity to ask questions related to technology or the game with the facilitators, which occurred with four users who sought some form of assistance or had doubts regarding the game.

In total, the experience lasted for 40 min, as planned and validated in the pilot test, divided into: 5 min for contextualizing the research and providing instructions on the objectives of each game, 5 min for preparing the tool and opening the games in the Chrome browser, 15 min for users to play one level of each game ("I Found It," "Find the Hat," and "Supermarket"). During this phase, researchers observed and recorded the behavior of each user. At the end of the test, 15 min were allocated for each tester to respond to the GEQ questionnaire, translated into Portuguese to identify the testers' feelings during the game experience. The 33 questions were used to evaluate the user's experience after playing. The scale used ranged from 0 to 4, where: 0 represents "Not at all"; 1 represents "Slightly"; 2 would be "Moderately"; 3 represents "Considerably"; and 4 would be "Extremely."

4   Results

This section presents and discusses the data collected from users during the tests conducted by the authors of this study.

4.1   Interviewees Profile

Tests were conducted with 12 users ranging in age from 67 to 82 years; 33% were male, while 67% were female. All had previous experience with technology use, although none had ever used a computer for gaming purposes.

Analyzing Fig. 2, it is possible to perceive that 98% of users enjoyed the experience, with 94% feeling challenged by the game. Meanwhile, 94% found the game aesthetically pleasing, which aligns with the 96% who assessed the experience as rich.

Analyzing Fig. 3, it is possible to conclude that 67% of users had to exert effort to play. However, only 23% felt pressured, considering the 48% of users who reported difficulty; only 19% felt frustrated. One user expressed frustration for not having a reward at the end of the game, with only the achieved score being displayed.

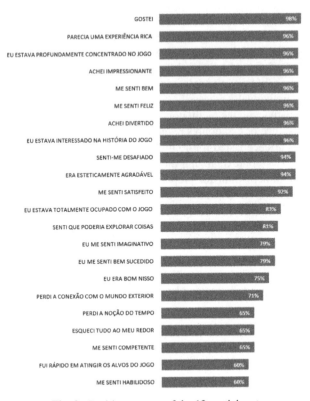

Fig. 2. Positive aspects of the 12 participants

From the collected data on positive aspects, it can be concluded that despite the challenges faced by users, there was a good experience considering that 96% of respondents felt good while playing. Regarding the negative points, it is evident that despite the user's effort to achieve their goals and experiencing some difficulties during the experience, this was not a determining factor for them to feel irritated or in a bad mood, considering the 6% for each sentiment. Effort and difficulty could be mitigated if players were informed about the objectives of tasks in the game in clear and simple language, as indicated in reference [19].

Additionally, based on the observations of facilitators during the tests, it was noticed that 16.7% of users understood that the color red indicated a button with a connotation of something that could not be clicked, and green had a clickable connotation, indicating that interface design should consider users' cultural considerations. Another situation observed was that a user with mild hearing impairment, upon successfully completing a game stage, received a sound notification for the stage passage, but no visual or textual alternative was presented on the screen, leading to the tester's uncertainty about achieving the goal. Moreover, if the sound had low frequency, it might have been audible as mentioned in reference [17]. It was also observed that the size of buttons, icons, clickable areas, and fonts sometimes need to be enlarged, a recommendation already pointed out in reference [17].

Fig. 3. Negative aspects pointed out by respondents

As points of observation, some highlighted by users who underwent the experience include: less information on the screen facilitates understanding; button size should be considered; it should be clear to the user what is volume and sound; synchronization of sounds characteristic of the respective actions of the games with the corresponding information and images on the screen; be cautious with font size and careful with the use of colors, for example: red may have the connotation of danger and alert, indicating something that cannot be clicked, and green may have a positive connotation and should be clicked, which is not necessarily true.

5   Final Considerations and Future Work

This study aimed to evaluate the interaction and feelings of the elderly audience towards digital games. It was conducted based on studies involving individuals aged between 67 and 82 years, considering the physical and cognitive limitations associated with aging. The three games were selected by the article's authors and provided by ProBrain. These games were designed to stimulate motor coordination, auditory perception, and memorization skills. Twelve (12) elderly users tested the games to collect information and identify their feelings through interaction with digital games.

While the research achieved its objectives, some limitations were noted, such as the low number of testers and the use of a single data collection instrument, the GEQ questionnaire.

As for future work, there is a plan to expand the data collection instruments for game tests using thinking aloud and interviews about the experience immediately after task execution, enhancing result fidelity. The intention is to develop a guide of best practices for the development and adaptation of accessible and inclusive games for the elderly, considering different forms of interaction and stimuli.

Acknowledgments. This research had the support of Probrain Soluções Neurotecnológicas para Saúde e Educação LTDA, the intellectual property owner of the games used in this study.

Disclosure of Interests. The authors have no competing interests to declare that are relevant to the content of this article.

References

1. United Nations, Department of Economic and Social Affairs: World Population Ageing 2019, New York (2020). https://www.un.org/development/desa/pd/sites/www.un.org.dev elopment.desa.pd/files/files/documents/2023/Jun/world_population_ageing_2019_report_ 3aug.2021_1.pdf
2. de Ávila, R.T.: Efeito das funções executivas no desempenho cognitivo de idosos com envelhecimento normal e patológico. Dissertação para obtenção do título de Mestre junto ao Programa de Pós-Graduação em Medicina Molecular da Universidade Federal de Minas Gerais, Belo Horizonte (2014). http://hdl.handle.net/1843/BUBD-9ZKFDP
3. De Oliveira Cardoso, N., Landenberger, T., de Lima Argimon, I.I.: Jogos Eletrônicos como Instrumentos de Intervenção no Declínio Cognitivo – Uma Revisão Sistemática. Revista De Psicologia Da Imed (2017). https://dialnet.unirioja.es/servlet/articulo?codigo=6504037
4. Duque, E.M., Ishitani, L.: Uma análise da adequação de desafios em jogos móveis considerando o público idoso. In: Proceedings of SBGames 2016, São Paulo. Anais eletrônicos..., pp. 346–355. Universidade de São Paulo, São Paulo (2016). https://www.sbgames. org/sbgames2016/downloads/anais/157090.pdf
5. Farias, A.A., Castro, C.A.L., Almeida, W.R.M.: Desenvolvimento de Jogos Digitais como estratégia na melhoria de cognição e motricidade de idosos utilizando técnicas de memorização e movimentação. Anais do Comput. Beach 81-90 (2015). https://doi.org/10.14210/cotb. v0n0.p081%20-%20090
6. Comitê Gestor da Internet no Brasil. TIC Domicílios: Pesquisa Sobre o Uso das Tecnologias de Informação e Comunicação nos Domicílios Brasileiros, São Paulo (2022). https://cetic.br/pt/publicacao/pesquisa-sobre-o-uso-das-tecnologias-de-informacao-e-comunicacao-nos-domicilios-brasileiros-tic-domicilios-2022/
7. Teixeira, F.: Introdução e boas práticas em UX Design. Editora Casa do Código, São Paulo (2014)
8. Ordonez, T.N., Borges, F., Kanashiro, C.S., Santos, C.C.D.N., Hora, S.S., Lima-Silva, T.B.: Actively station: effects on global cognition of mature adults and healthy elderly program using eletronic games. Dement. Neuropsychol. **11**, 186–197 (2017). https://doi.org/10.1590/ 1980-57642016dn11-020011
9. Petry, L.C.: O conceito ontológico de jogo. In: Alves, L., Coutinho, I.J. (eds.) Jogos digitais e aprendizagem: fundamentos para uma prática baseada em evidências, pp. 17–42. Papirus, Campinas (2020)
10. dos Santos, R.P., da Silva Vasconcellos, L.A.: A matemática por trás do sudoku. C.Q.D. - Revista Eletrônica Paulista de Matemática, Bauru **12** (2018). https://sistemas.fc.unesp.br/ojs/ index.php/revistacqd/article/view/158
11. Silva, R.B., Ferreira, R.L.R., Duque, E.M., Dias, A.I., Ishitani, L.: Impacto da Competitividade em Jogos Digitais para Smartphones, com Foco na Terceira Idade: Um Estudo de Caso. Simpósio de Brasileiro de Jogos e Entretenimento Digital, XIV. Anais eletrônicos, Teresina, Teresina, pp. 1059–1066 (2015). https://www.sbgames.org/sbgames2015/anaispdf/cultura-full/147704.pdf

12. Vasconcelos, A., Silva, P.A., Caseiro, J., Nunes, F., Teixeira, L.F.: Designing tablet-based games for seniors: the example of CogniPlay, a cognitive gaming platform. In: Proceedings of the 4th International Conference on Fun and Games (FnG 2012), pp. 1–10. Association for Computing Machinery, New York (2012). https://doi.org/10.1145/2367616.2367617

13. Veloso, A.I., Costa, L., Ribeiro, T.: Jogos Digitais Na Promoção Da Saúde: Desafios e Tendências. Revista da FAEEBA - Educação e Contemporaneidade **25**(46), 159–186 (2016). https://doi.org/10.21879/faeeba2358-0194.2016.v25.n46.p159-186

14. ISO 9241-110:2020(en) Ergonomics of human-system interaction—Part 110: Interaction principles (2020). https://www.iso.org/obp/ui/#iso:std:iso:9241:-110:ed-2:v1:en

15. Vermeeren, A.P., Law, E.L.C., Roto, V., Obrist, M., Hoonhout, J., Väänänen, K.: User experience evaluation methods: current state and development needs. In: Proceedings of the 6th Nordic Conference on Human-Computer Interaction: Extending Boundaries (NordiCHI 2010), pp. 521–530. Association for Computing Machinery, New York (2010). https://doi.org/10.1145/1868914.1868973

16. Rodrigues, B.: Guia de boas práticas para acessibilidade de interfaces digitais para usuários daltônicos. PCC (graduação), Universidade Federal de Santa Catarina, Centro de Comunicação e Expressão (2017). https://repositorio.ufsc.br/xmlui/handle/123456789/181985

17. Ijsselsteijn, W., Nap, H.H., de Kort, Y., Poels, K.: Digital game design for elderly users. In: Proceedings of the 2007 Conference on Future Play (Future Play 2007), pp. 17–22. Association for Computing Machinery, New York (2007). https://doi.org/10.1145/1328202.1328206

18. Bolaños, M., Collazos, C., Gutiérrez, F.: Reference framework for measuring the level of technological acceptance by the elderly: a virtual assistants case study. In: Agredo-Delgado, V., Ruiz, P.H., Villalba-Condori, K.O. (eds.) HCI-COLLAB 2020. CCIS, vol. 1334, pp. 203–212. Springer, Cham (2020). https://doi.org/10.1007/978-3-030-66919-5_21

19. Bernhaupt, R., Ijsselsteijn, W., Mueller, F.F., Tscheligi, M., Wixon, D.: Evaluating user experiences in games. In: CHI 2008 Extended Abstracts on Human Factors in Computing Systems (CHI EA 2008), pp. 3905–3908. Association for Computing Machinery, New York (2008). https://doi.org/10.1145/1358628.1358953

20. Bernhaupt, R. (ed.): Evaluating User Experience in Games: Concepts and Methods. Springer, Cham (2010). https://doi.org/10.1007/978-1-84882-963-3

21. Law, E.L.C., Sun, X.: Evaluating user experience of adaptive digital educational games with Activity Theory. Int. J. Hum.-Comput. Stud. **70**(7), 478–497 (2012). https://doi.org/10.1016/j.ijhcs.2012.01.007

22. Kawamoto, A.L.S., Martins, V.F.: Application designed for the elderly using gestural interface. Revista Brasileira de Computação Aplicada **5**(2), 96–109 (2013). https://doi.org/10.5335/rbca.2013.3269

23. Kawamoto, A.L.S., Martins, V.F., Silva, F.S.C.: Usability evaluation of an application designed for the older adults. In: Anacleto, J.C., Clua, E.W.G., Correa, F.S., Silva, S.F., Yang, H.S. (eds.) ICEC 2013. LNCS, vol. 8215, pp. 189–192. Springer, Heidelberg (2013). https://doi.org/10.1007/978-3-642-41106-9_28

24. Ijsselsteijn, W.A., de Kort, Y.A.W., Poels, K.: The game experience questionnaire. Technische Universiteit Eindhoven (2013). https://pure.tue.nl/ws/files/21666907/Game_Experience_Questionnaire_English.pdf

Adaptative Videogames for Education: An Initial Study

Rosanna Costaguta[1](✉) ⓘ, Silvana Aciar[2] ⓘ, Patricia Paderewski[3] ⓘ,
and Francisco Gutierrez-Vela[3] ⓘ

[1] Universidad Nacional de Santiago del Estero, Santiago del Estero, Argentina
rosanna@unse.edu.ar
[2] Universidad Nacional de San Juan, San Juan, Argentina
silvana.aciar@conicet.gov.ar
[3] Universidad de Granada, Granada, Spain
{patricia,fgutierr}@ugr.es

Abstract. The videogames are frequently used in educational contexts because improve in the students their motivational levels and learning performances. There is a belief that to develop adaptive videogames according to individual characteristics of each student could generate positive effects on the learning and gaming experience. The goal of this paper is to elaborate an initial study of the literature about the adaptive educative videogames. Three digital libraries were queried (ACM Digital Library, IEEE Xplore Digital Library, and Science Direct), 40 studies were collected, and 13 studies were described and analyzed. Four research questions were elaborated and answered. The results show that there are several concrete initiatives of adaptive video games developed to improve different students´ competences or skills, such as attention, memory, reasoning, etc. In addition, most of the videogames involve some kind of experimentation with real students. Based on this study, an adaptive and collaborative educational videogame is being designed to be used by students of environmental careers.

Keywords: Educative Videogame · Adaptation · Personalization

1 Introduction

The use of videogames is often a more successful means of education than traditional classroom-style teaching. According to Kickmeier *et al.* [10] one of the crucial factors for successful educative games can be the game's ability to maintain student's motivation and interest by adapting the individual learning and gaming experiencing. Obviously, another crucial factor for the success of educational videogames can be to develop a suitable and creative learning game design. But sheer design cannot cover individual differences, having mechanisms to assess what learners need and what they want, and then adjusting the learning game.

In general, the adaptability concept in learning environment context, is related to three kinds: adaptive presentation (adjusting colors, audios, sounds, etc. according to individual preferences or needs), adaptive curriculum sequencing (adjusting content according to individual preferences, goals, learning styles, or prior knowledge), and adaptive

P. H. Ruiz et al. (Eds.): HCI-COLLAB 2023, CCIS 1877, pp. 40–49, 2024.
https://doi.org/10.1007/978-3-031-57982-0_4

problem-solving support (providing the student with feedback, hints, recommendations, etc., during the problem-solving process).

The objective of this paper is to present an initial study of the literature about the developing and using of educative videogames that considering or include adaptability. This initial study will provide us with some of the knowledge necessary to design an educational videogame that includes both adaptive and collaborative features.

The paper is organized as follows: Sect. 2 describes the method applied for conducting the literature review, Sect. 3 presents the results obtained with this study, and finally, Sect. 4 presents some conclusions and future lines of research in the area.

2 Systematic Mapping

For conducting the literature review the method described for Petersen, Feldt, Mujtaba & Mattsson [12] were used. These authors focus on the mapping process and propose a method consisting of five steps: definition of research questions, search for primary studies, screening of papers for inclusion and exclusion, keywording of abstracts, and finally, data extraction and mapping of studies. The main steps, applied on this study, will be described in the following subsections.

2.1 Definition of Research Questions

The research questions defined in this work aims to gather information about how to create adaptative educative videogames. Based in this objective four research questions were elaborated:

RQ1 – What aspects of the educative videogames are adapted or personalized?
RQ2 – What students characteristics are used to personalize or adapt the educative videogames?
RQ3 – What method or intelligent techniques are used to reach the adaptive goals?
RQ4 – Are there empirical results of the use of adaptive or personalized educative videogames?

2.2 Search for Primary Studies

The search included scientific journal articles and conference papers. To collect high-quality contributions, we queried the following databases: ACM Digital Library, IEEE Xplore Digital Library, and Science Direct. In this initial study, these sources were chosen as the most representative in the area. However, we intend to incorporate other sources in the future to conduct a comprehensive systematic literature review.

The search phrase contains synonyms and was applied to abstract: ("serious game" OR videogame OR "video game") AND (adaptive OR personalized) AND (educational OR educative). After the search string execution, formatted according to the rules of each digital library, 40 candidate primary papers were collected from the period 2010–2023. Considering the total number of papers, 12 were returned by ACM Digital Library, 10 by IEEE Xplore Digital Library, and 18 by Science Direct.

2.3 Screening of Papers for Inclusion or Exclusion

The criteria of exclusion and inclusion for the selection of relevant studies were:

a) For exclusion: papers were not in the educative context, duplicated papers, papers published as poster, papers belonging to the same study that do not add relevant information, papers that do not explain how the adaptation was included.
b) For inclusion: modeling of students' characteristics in videogames, adaptation, or personalization the different aspects in videogames as interfaces, contents, etc.

When this step finished, the 40 primary collected studies were reduced at 13.

2.4 Data Extraction

To answer the research questions defined in Systematic Mapping section, we conducted a deeper analysis of the 13 selected papers that are briefly presented below.

Antonova, Dankov & Bontchev [1] present the APOGEE *(smArt adaPtive video GamEs for Education)* software platform and the smart services, designed to facilitate the construction of rich maze videogames for education by non-technologist specialists such as teachers and education experts. The authors explore the architecture and services of the APOGEE for managing the design and development of adaptive educational videogames. APOGEE offer a personalized and adaptive videogame tailoring to the user profile, which combines both a player and a student preference model. The learning content is personalized upon the player/student model attributes such as demographic characteristics, demonstrated outcomes, learning/playing style, and emotional status. Particularly, to achieve the personalization of learning content and adaptation of game mechanics and difficulty of learning tasks, APOGEE is able to: recommend a selection of mini-games for the maze halls and propose the types of the mini-games that are most suitable to be included into a given hall, depending on both the learner and the player models; recommend the appropriate learning elements and allowing personalization of the didactic content (text, images, and audio) depending on the student's model characteristics such as age, gender, and learning style; select the game content for the maze and the embedded mini-games; adapt the game's difficulty depending on the player model. Using the APOGEE platform, the teachers can adapt videogames to their specific educational context by selection of learning scenario, recommendation of mini-games, adaptation of learning elements, and adaptation of game content. The APOGEE platform can personalize automatically specific game elements and game dynamics considering: the individual students' preferences and needs, the player profile and the student profile, the feedback of the analytics services, and the student performance. With the participation of Bulgarian teachers and students, the authors tested a prototype by constructing a maze game for traditional carpet handicraft.

Demediuk *et al.* [2] present a method to measure the skill level of the player by investigating the performance of the player against an adaptive artificial opponent. The authors developed the *Dynamic Difficulty Adjustment* agent that using Monte Carlo Tree Search to closely match the skill level of the current opponent. The strength of the actions that the artificial opponent choses to employ against the player are recorded and a mean strength of the artificial opponent is calculated. The difficulty level of artificial opponent is based on the skill level of the player, the player skill level can be inferred from the strength of the opponent. The authors used a real-time fighting game to validate their approach. Two different experiments were conducted. First, bots playing against the agent. Second, few human players playing against the agent. This method for measuring player skill does not require players to compete directly with each other, and for this reason it is suitable for use in educational and training environments where direct competition may not be feasible.

Demmel *et al.* [3] present the collaborative and adaptive videogame, called *weMake-Words,* to train social and reading skills. In this game, children collaborate in playing motivating stories like saving animals that escaped from the zoo into a dangerous city. The kids combine alphabetical words or Chinese ideographs out of individual letters or symbol components and are thus familiarized with German, English or Chinese. In addition, they gain social competencies as the game only continues with the next round if all teammates fully built up their words. To help each other they can send letters to teammates and ask for support when having difficulties. This behavior of the game also reduces frustration and encourages the collaboration. The game automatically adapts to the playing children in three ways. First, the word or symbol is selected to become increasingly difficult with each correct answer. Second, different letters or strokes dependent on the current performance of the child. Third, providing different amounts of scaffolding through a watermark. The authors tested their game with children aged between 4 and 8 years.

Feldman, Monteserin & Amandi [4] present an approach to recommend videogames. With this objective the authors analyze which features exhibit by educative videogames are related to students' behaviors described by learning styles. The authors quantified the features exhibit by 13 educational video games that match student's learning styles. They used a Support Vector Machine classifier to determine whether an educative videogame matches the student's learning styles. Based on experimental results with undergraduate Computer Science students the authors infer that educative videogames features are related to students' behaviors. Furthermore, considering the students' behaviors (according to their learning styles), the authors state that most of the students prefer to play educative videogames that match their learning styles. So, the authors demonstrated that it is possible to recommend educative videogames by analyzing the game features and the students' learning styles.

Frommel, Schrader & Weber [5] propose to detect the players' current emotional state using input parameters in combination with in-game performance to adapt the videogames features. The authors extracted 46 features, trained machine learning models, and evaluated their performance to predict emotion levels. So, using the trained models and corresponding emotion labels, they to predict unobtrusively the players' current emotional. To evaluate their machine learning models, the authors developed *Hiramon*, a single player videogame. In the game, the players learn how to write hiragana characters by writing them on a graphics tablet. The authors affirm that to detect undesired emotion levels can be used to provide adaptive content generation.

Hamdaoui, Khalidi & Bennani [6] propose an adaptive mechanism with two components. The first one adapts the gameplay based on the player style, decisions, and performance in the game. The second one adapts the learning content depending on the learner's knowledge and learning style. Different algorithms and approaches of Artificial Intelligence used to adapt the gameplay are described. The authors present the architecture of their adaptive mechanism and explain a simple case. The authors don't include experimentation results.

Hooshyar *et al.* [7] present an adaptive computer game, called *AutoThinking*, for teaching computational thinking skills and conceptual. The game was developed for primary and secondary school students that uses icons rather than text, code, or programming commands. *AutoThinking* requires players to develop strategies for moving a mouse through a maze while eating cheese, escaping cats, and collecting points. Gameplay ends when all the cheese is consumed, or time expires. The player (mouse) must avoid randomly and/or intelligently moving cats to eat the cheeses. Benefiting from a non-invasive assessment which builds and updates a cognitive model of each player, provided by a probabilistic models presented as a Bayesian networks, *AutoThinking* seeks to engage players through personalized and fun game while offering timely cognitive pedagogical support, as hints, feedbacks, and tutorials. Adaptability in learning is provided by the game in two different phases, before or after running the solution. When the player "run" the solution without using the debug button, receives adaptive feedback or hints about the shortcomings and mistakes. When the player utilizes the "debug" button, receives the estimation of the suitability of their solution, so, if necessary, can change and improve their solution. The game was tested by 70 students.

Hwang *et al.* [8] propose a personalized game-based learning approach based on the students' learning style. To evaluate the effectiveness of the proposed approach, a role-playing game has been implemented based on the approach, and an experiment was conducted on an elementary school natural science course. In the game there is an ancient kingdom in which the people are infected by poisoned water in a river. After referring to an ancient medical book, the king decides to look for the plants that can cure his people. To complete the learning missions, the students play the role of the king to find the target plants. They should pass several tests during the play. The videogame has two different interfaces according to the cognitive features of the two learning styles. The authors evaluated their propose by real students of a natural science course (with knowledge of the plants) divided in two groups: control group (no personalized game) and experimental group (personalized game). The learning achievements of experimental group were significantly better that those of the students in the control group.

Hussaan, Sehaba & Mille [9] present a system that generates learning scenarios considering the student profiles and their learning objectives. The student profile is used to represent the cognitive skills and the domain competences of each student. The system records all activities of students during the interaction with the game and can generate learning scenarios considering their competencies and deficiencies. So, these learning scenarios are composed of a suite of activities selected and parameterized by the system according to the student profile and learning objectives. The scenarios are presented to the student via a videogame. The authors don't include experimentation results.

Kickmeier *et al.* [10] present a non-invasive approach to continuously assess learning and gaming processes and the oscillations of motivation and immersion within a game. The authors develop a fusion of the micro adaptivity concept with techniques of interactive digital storytelling to create a personalized sequencing of learning situations and units. These elements and the personalized adjustments of the game are elaborated considering individual needs and preferences using an ontology-driven learner (and player) model. The approach proposes macro and micro adaptations. Macro adaptation refers to adjust presentation and navigation on the level of learning objects. Micro level interventions may be personalized hints, suggestions, warnings, or feedback. The authors tested their approach with French, Austrian and British students. The results showed that providing the student with appropriate and personalized interventions improve motivational level and learning performance.

Ku, Hou & Chen [11] present a customized game-based learning system and a personalized game-based learning system. The authors conducted two empirical studies to examine how learning styles affected learner's reactions to these two game-based learning systems. In the customized system students can select game elements based on their needs. The authors examined how the students with different learning styles reacted to the customized system and applied these results to develop a personalized system. The experimental results demonstrated that customization and personalization were useful to enhance learners' learning performance, regardless of their cognitive styles.

Sampayo-Vargas *et al.* [13] present two versions of the same game to analyze the impact of the difficulty adjustment game element on motivation and learning. The objective of playing the game for students is to translate English words into Spanish words. The first game version was developed with adaptive difficulty adjustment and the second version considering non-adaptive incremental difficulty adjustment. During experimentation, 234 students were randomly sub-divided to either play the adaptive or the incremental version of the game. Finally, a written activity was designed to study the effectiveness of both game versions. The results showed significantly higher learning outcomes in students who played the adaptive game. Besides, the analysis of game log indicated that the adaptive difficulty adjustment game version provided a scaffolding structure to enhance student learning.

Vandewaetere *et al.* [14] present a theoretical framework to define the level of player-centered adaptivity in educative videogames. The authors propose different player and game characteristics that can be integrated in the framework. The authors propose to create videogame states using a probability model where the student, player and game characteristics are integrated. Besides, they propose creating a player model separated in three layers to include all characteristics. The authors don't include experimentation results.

3   Results

Considering the four research questions defined in a previous section, in this section their answers are presented.

RQ1 – What aspects of the educative videogames are adapted or personalized?

Several educative videogames adapted their contents [1, 3–7, 9–11, 13]. The difficult level was adapted in [1, 2, 11]. The adapted recommendations or adapted feedback were included in [1, 3, 7, 10]. The interfaces were adapted only in [1] y [8].

RQ2 – What students characteristics are used to personalize or adapt the educative videogames?

The analyzed papers consider different student characteristics to adapt the videogame. In [1, 7, 9, 14] the authors create a student profile but do not describe the included variables. In [1] y [14] the authors propose a player profile, but do not describe the variables included in this profile. In [2] the student characteristic considered to adapt the videogame are the player skills. The videogame used by authors is a real-time fighting game, where two players face off in a 2-dimensional arena with the objective of to reduce the opposing player's health points to zero, using a combination of attacks and movement actions (e.g., punches, kicks and jumping). The player skills are demonstrated by players during the fighting game. In [3, 5, 9, 13] the authors used the student performance. Particularly, in [3], the authors considered the Chinese symbols and their meanings remembered by players after playing the game. In [5], the authors considered the performance as a measure of how well players' competence matches a game's challenges to write Japanese characters. In [9], the authors measured the student performance in the videogame considering intellectual disabilities related to the following cognitive domains: perception, attention, memory, oral language, written language, logical reasoning, visual-spatial and transverse competencies, and in [13] the authors measured the students´ success to translate English words into Spanish words. In [4, 8, 11] was the student learning style the characteristic selected. Particularly, in [4], the authors recommended certain videogames whose features were related to students' learning styles. In [8], two versions of videogame interface were provided based on students´ learning style, and in [11], the authors adapted three elements of the game based on students' learning styles: the narrative, the music, and the hints.

RQ3 – What method or intelligent techniques are used to reach the adaptive goals?

Only in [4–7, 10, 14] intelligent adaptability methods or techniques were proposed. While in [4] and [7] the authors proposed a Bayesian Networks and Support Vector Machine to implement the recommendation strategies, in [10] an ontology that contains information about motivational aspects, learning progress, and game progress of each user was applied. In [5, 6, 14] affirm the use of machine learning methods, probabilistic model, etc. but they do not present more details of the implementation.

RQ4 – Are there empirical results of the use of adaptive or personalized educative videogames?

Only in [1–4, 7, 8, 10, 11, 13] there are information about the experimentation results with real students. In these papers, the authors defined variables to measure the success achieved through the implemented adaptations. In general, such variables were related to the performance demonstrated by the student using each videogame. The experiences involved students of different genders and ages.

The contribution of each paper to the research questions is showed in Table 1.

Table 1. Research questions, papers, and contributions

RQ	[1]	[2]	[3]	[4]	[5]	[6]	[7]	[8]	[9]	[10]	[11]	[13]	[14]
RQ1	X	X	X	X	X	X	X	X	X	X	X	X	
RQ2	X	X	X	X	X	X	X	X	X	X	X	X	X
RQ3				X	X	X	X			X			X
RQ4	X	X	X	X			X	X		X	X	X	

4 Conclusions and Future Work

This paper has addressed a systematic mapping for investigating how the student and player characteristics are considered in educative videogames. To develop this study three digital libraries were consulted, and 40 papers were collected. During review process, considering defined criteria, 27 papers were excluded and 13 were included. With a careful reading and analyzing of the resultant papers, to answer four research questions was possible.

The results show that there are several concrete initiatives of adaptive video games and that their authors sought to improve the cognitive level or skills achieved by students using these videogames (attention, memory, reasoning, solving mathematical exercises, language learning, etc.). It is noteworthy that there is a coinciding opinion among authors regarding the benefits that educational videogames bring to the learning process by increasing students' motivation and commitment.

On the other hand, the obtained results seem indicate research challenges and directions to be addressed by the scientific community, for example, what aspects to adapt to reach certain learning objectives, or what is the impact that adaptive educative videogames have on different learning variables in real students. Finally, the methods or intelligent techniques that can be applied to develop adaptive videogames require most research.

Based on these conclusions, an educational video game is being designed. This videogame will have environmental content, and adaptive and collaborative features. The adaptation will be done on the narrative and interfaces of the videogame considering the learning styles of the students. The students will be distributed in learning groups. These groups will have between 2 and 3 members. The videogame will be validated through experiences with university students in the field of ecology.

Acknowledgments. This study was funded by the Asociación Universitaria Iberoamericana de Postgrado (AUIP), the Universidad Nacional de Santiago del Estero (UNSE) by the Research Project 23/C176-A-2022, the Universidad Nacional de San Juan (UNSJ), and the Universidad de Granada (UGR) by the Research Project FEDER/Junta de Andalucía-Consejería Transformación Económica, Industria, Conocimiento Universidades/Proyecto B-TIC-720-UGR20.

References

1. Antonova, A., Dankov, Y., Bontchev, B.: Smart services for managing the design of personalized educational video games. In: 9th Balkan Conference on Informatics Proceedings, article 20, pp. 1–8. Association for Computing Machinery (2019). https://doi.org/10.1145/3351556.3351574

2. Demediuk, S., Tamassia, M., Raffe, W., Zambetta, F., Mueller, F., Li, X.: Measuring player skill using dynamic difficulty adjustment. In: Australasian Computer Science Week Multiconference Proceedings, article 41, pp. 1–7. Association for Computing Machinery (2018). https://doi.org/10.1145/3167918.3167939

3. Demmel, R., Köhler, B., Krusche, S., Schubert, L.: The serious game: weMakeWords. In: 10th SIGPLAN Symposium on New Ideas, New Paradigms, and Reflections on Programming and Software PROCEEDINGS, pp. 109–110. Association for Computing Machinery (2011). https://doi.org/10.1145/2048237.2048253

4. Feldman, J., Monteserin. A., Amandi, A.: Recommending educational video games based on game features and student's Learning Styles. In: IEEE Biennial Congress of Argentina Proceedings, pp. 1–6. Institute of Electrical Electronics Engineers (2016). https://doi.org/10.1109/ARGENCON.2016.7585274

5. Frommel, J., Schrader, C., Weber, M.: Towards emotion-based adaptive games: emotion recognition via input and performance features. In: Annual Symposium on Computer-Human Interaction in Play Proceedings, pp. 173–185. Association for Computing Machinery (2018). https://doi.org/10.1145/3242671.3242672

6. Hamdaoui, N., Khalidi, M., Bennani, S.: AMEG: Adaptive mechanism for educational games based on IMSLD and artificial intelligence. In: 10th International Conference on Intelligent Systems: Theories and Applications Proceedings, pp. 1–6. SITA, Morocco (2015). https://doi.org/10.1109/SITA.2015.7358424

7. Hooshyar, D., Malva, L., Yang, Y., Pedaste, M., Wang, M., Lim, H.: An adaptive educational computer game: Effects on students' knowledge and learning attitude in computational thinking. J. Educ. Comput. Res. **59**(3), 383–409 (2021). https://doi.org/10.1177/0735633120965919

8. Hwang, G., Sung, H., Hung, C., Huang, I.: Development of a personalized educational computer game based on students' learning styles. Educ. Tech. Res. Dev. **60**, 623–638 (2012). https://doi.org/10.1007/s11423-012-9241-x

9. Hussaan, A., Sehaba, K., Mille, A.: Helping children with cognitive disabilities through serious games: project CLES. 13th International ACM SIGACCESS Conference on Computers and Accessibility PROCEEDINGS, pp. 251–252. Association for Computing Machinery (2011). https://doi.org/10.1145/2049536.2049592

10. Kickmeier, M., Mattheiss, E., Steiner, C., Dietrich, A.: A psycho-pedagogical framework for multi-adaptive educational games. Int. J. Game-Based **1**, 45–58 (2011). https://doi.org/10.4018/ijgbl.2011010104

11. Ku, O., Hou, C., Chen, S.: Incorporating customization and personalization into game-based learning: a cognitive style perspective. Comput. Hum. Behav. **65**, 359–368 (2016). https://doi.org/10.1016/j.chb.2016.08.040

12. Petersen, K., Feldt, R., Mujtaba, S., Mattsson, M.: Systematic mapping studies in software engineering. In: 12th International Conference on Evaluation and Assessment in Software Engineering Proceedings, pp. 68–77. Association for Computing Machinery (2018). https://doi.org/10.14236/ewic/EASE2008.8

13. Sampayo-Vargas, S., Cope, C., He, Z., Byrne, G.: The effectiveness of adaptive difficulty adjustments on students' motivation and learning in an educational computer game. Comput. Educ. **69**, 452–462 (2013). https://doi.org/10.1016/j.compedu.2013.07.004
14. Vandewaetere, M., Cornillie, F., Clarebout, G., Desmet, P.: Adaptivity in educational games: including player and gameplay characteristics. Int. J. High. Educ. **2**, 106–114 (2013). https://doi.org/10.5430/ijhe.v2n2p106

An Approach to Cluster Scenarios According to Their Similarity Using Natural Language Processing

Juliana Delle Ville[✉] , Diego Torres , Alejandro Fernández ,
and Leandro Antonelli

Lifia, Fac. de Informática, UNLP, La Plata, Bs As, Argentina
{juliana.delleville,diego.torres,alejandro.fernandez,
leandro.antonelli}@lifia.info.unlp.edu.ar

Abstract. Scenarios are ideal to capture knowledge in human computer interface software engineering. Requirements engineering is a fundamental part of software development. If errors appear in this stage, it will be expensive to correct them in further stages. The domain experts and the developer team belong to different worlds. This generates a gap in communication between them. Because of it, it is important to use artifacts in natural language to communicate both sides. One simpler approach to specify requirements is Scenarios. They are widely used artifacts that generally describe the dynamics (tasks, activities) to be carried out in some specific situation. Generally, scenarios promote communication and participation from both sides. This can cause some problems. One of these problems is redundancy, that occurs when two stakeholders describe the same situation in different artifacts. This paper proposes an approach to analyze a set of scenarios by grouping them according to their similarity. The similarity is calculated through a series of comparisons of the different attributes of the scenario. This paper also describes a prototype implementing this method. Finally, the paper shows the result of a preliminary evaluation with results about the applicability of the approach.

Keywords: Scenarios · Natural language processing · Similarity

1 Introduction

The scenarios are ideal to capture knowledge from the experts in Software Engineering in general, and they are even more necessary in human computer interface software engineering (HCI-SE) [1]. Requirements engineering is a critical stage of software development. Errors made at this stage can cost up to 200 times to repair when the software is delivered to the client [2].

Experts and development teams belong to different worlds and use different languages [3]. The experts use the language of the domain, while development teams use a computer science language. To cope with this communication gap, it is important to use artifacts in natural language that are readable by both parties [4].

P. H. Ruiz et al. (Eds.): HCI-COLLAB 2023, CCIS 1877, pp. 50–62, 2024.
https://doi.org/10.1007/978-3-031-57982-0_5

Scenarios are widely used artifacts. Although scenarios have many conceptions, they generally describe the dynamics (activities, tasks) to be carried out in some specific situation, which should be different from the situation and dynamics described in other scenarios. Nevertheless, multiple scenarios might still depict the same objective. This definition applies for scenarios in software engineering as well as in finance, catastrophic events, etc. [5].

Scenarios are suitable to capture knowledge because they simply tell a story, and people know how to tell stories (funny anecdotes, stories for children, etc.). This story telling approach is effective because it is a way to incorporate details that are essential to provide a rich consolidation of knowledge. Because scenarios use natural language, experts can use them without the need to learn complex formalisms. Moreover, scenarios also promote communication and cooperation when there is a wide variety of experts [6], as many of them can describe different scenarios, improve them (if necessary), while learning from each other.

This collaborative writing of scenarios also introduces some challenges. For example, two stakeholders can describe the same situation in different artifacts (scenarios) with different levels of detail. Thus, redundancy appears. It is very important to provide tools to identify similar artifacts to avoid redundancy. Similar scenarios can be merged if they describe the same situation. If they are similar but describe different tasks to obtain the same result, they need to be enriched to express the details that make them different.

If we consider texts as sets of words, we can compare them using Jaccard's similarity index [7]. Jaccard's similarity is defined as the size of intersection of the sets divided by the size of the union of the sets. The higher the value, the more similar they are.

Nevertheless, comparing two scenarios is not as easy as directly computing Jaccard's similarity index on their texts. The scenario has a structure, and this structure can be used to assess similarity with better results than simply applying Jaccard's similarity (or any other method) directly to the whole description of the scenario.

This paper proposes a method to assess similarity among a group of scenarios. Particularly, the method consists in comparing scenarios by pairs, and according to their similarities, the groups of scenarios are ranked. Thus, this method can be seen as a way of ranking pairs of scenarios by similarity so an expert can deal with them and finally decide whether scenarios are similar or not.

The rest of the paper is organized in the following way. Section 2 presents background concepts about scenarios. Section 3 details our contribution, that is, the proposed approach. Section 4 describes the tool to support the proposal. Section 5 discusses related work. Finally, Sect. 6 discusses some conclusions.

2   Scenarios

A scenario is an artifact that describes situations in a specific domain using natural Language [6]. It describes a situation that occurs in a specific context to reach a certain goal. There is a sequence of steps to achieve that goal: the scenario's episodes. These episodes describe actions that are performed by actors using resources.

Scenarios can be seen as descriptions of real-world situations, captured in a set of small stories [8, 9]. Then, these scenarios can be used in more complex artifacts to model software requirements. For example, one Use Case can include several Scenarios: a scenario describing the happy path, another scenario that describes the alternative path, and another scenario that describes the exceptional path [10, 11].

There are many proposals to represent scenarios. Leite [12] proposes a structure with the following attributes: a title, a goal, a context, the actors, the resources, and a list of episodes. The goal of a scenario is the objective to be attained by executing the scenario. The actor is the subject who performs the actions described in the episodes. The context is defined by the place, time, and conditions that allow the scenario to start. The resources are the tools, materials, and data necessary to perform the scenario. And finally, the episodes are a collection of tasks described using an actor, an action, and a resource.

Let's consider the agricultural domain where a farmer sow's tomatoes. In that domain, the irrigation can be done manually (with a watering can), or it can be done with some infrastructure such as pipes and a pump. The scenario "Irrigate by hand" (Table 1) and "irrigate manually" (Table 2) describe through different scenarios the same activity performed using a watering can. Then, the scenario "irrigate with pump" (Table 3) describes the irrigation using a complex infrastructure of pipes and valves. Finally, the scenario "sow tomato seeds" (Table 4) describes how to put the seed into the soil.

Table 1. Description of the scenario "Irrigate by hand".

Attributes	Description
Scenario	Irrigate by hand
Goal	Provide H2O to the tomato
Context	The tomato plant is in any state of grow
Resources	Water, watering can
Actors	Farmer
Episodes	The farmer fills the watering can with water The farmer pours the water to the base of the plant

Table 2. Description of the scenario "Irrigate manually".

Attribute	Description
Scenario	Irrigate manually
Goal	Supply water to the tomato plant
Context	Have the tomato plant in any state of grow, but mainly in the fruit formation stage
Resources	Water, watering can, worm leachate
Actors	Farmer
Episodes	The farmer fills the watering can with water The farmer adds worm leachate to the watering can The farmer approaches the tomato plant The farmer visually assesses the humidity of the soil The farmer approaches the watering can to the plant's base The farmer pours the water

Table 3. Description of the scenario "Irrigate with pump".

Attribute	Description
Scenario	Irrigate with pump
Goal	Provide water for the seeds and the tomato plants
Context	Tomato plant in any state of grow. Deployed an infrastructure of pipes, valves, pumps
Resources	Cistern with enough water
Actors	Farmer, technician
Episodes	The farmer determines the sector to irrigate The technician opens the valves of the sector to irrigate The farmer decides the intensity of the irrigation The technician sets the pump to the intensity of the irrigation The technician starts the pump

Table 4. Description of the scenario "Sow tomato seeds".

Attribute	Description
Scenario	Sow Tomato Seeds
Goal	Place the Tomato Seeds in the seedbed

(*continued*)

Table 4. (*continued*)

Attribute	Description
Context	The seedbeds are already prepared
Resources	Seed, substrate, water
Actors	Farmer
Episodes	The farmer digs a hole in the seedbed The Farmer places the seeds in the seedbed The Farmer covers the seeds with substrate The farmer sprays the seedbed with water

3 The Proposed Approach

3.1 Our Approach in a Nutshell

The proposed approach aims to analyze a group of scenarios, comparing them pairwise and sorting the pairs based on their similarity. Then, an expert can analyze the pairs of scenarios (from the most to the least similar) to confirm whether the scenarios are the same (in this case, they should be merged) or not (in this case their differences should be emphasized). The similarity of the scenarios is calculated by comparing their attributes: title, goal, context, actors, resources, and episodes. The approach is summarized in the algorithm depicted in Table 5.

The approach consists of comparing attributes by attributes to obtain a general assessment of similarity. Concepts and verbs are extracted from every attribute and a relation between number of equal elements (the intersection) divided the total number of elements (the union) is obtained (this is Jaccard's method). Then, the similarity between two scenarios is calculated. To do so, some attributes are grouped (goal with context, and actors with resources).

It is important to mention that the comparison is merely syntactical, that is, synonyms are considered as different words. For example, provide and supply, H2O and water, tomato plant and plant, base of the plant and plant's base are different concepts for the approach.

The steps to compare the expressions are the following. First, every word is converted to its root form (lemma). And then, the words with semantic meaning are filtered (that is, the stop words are removed).

Table 5. Algorithm of the approach.

Line	Code
1	Similarity (Si.attribute, Sj.attribute)-> si.attribute
2	Convert to lemma (Si.attribute) -> si.attribute
3	remove stop words (Sj.attribute)-> sj.attribute
4	Convert to lemma (Sj.attribute) -> sj.attribute
8	return Jaccard_Similarity (Si.attribute, Sj.attribute)
9	Jaccard_Similarity (Si.attribute, Sj.attribute)
10	Local intersection
11	Local union
12	calculate intersectionof(Si.attribute,Sj.attribute) ->intersection
13	calculate union of (Si.attribute, Sj.attribute)-> union
14	Return size(intersection) / size(union)
15	rank (scenarios)
16	for each scenario Si, Sj in scenarios
17	Similarity (Si.title, Sj.title)-> title.similarity
18	Similarity (Si.goal, Sj.goal)-> goal.similarity
19	Similarity (Si.context, Sj.context)-> context.similarity
20	Similarity (Si.resources, Sj.resources) -> resources.similarity
21	Similarity (Si.actors, Sj.actors) -> actors.similarity
22	Similarity (Si.episodes, Sj.episodes) -> episodes.similarity
23	Title.similarity + ((goal.similarity + context.similarity)/2) + ((actors.similarity + resources.similarity)/2) + episodes.similarity)/4->rank
24	Answer add Pair (Si, Sj) with rank rank
25	Return answer order by rank descending.

3.2 Example

Let's consider the four scenarios that describe situations in the agricultural domain depicted in Tables 1, 2, 3, and 4. Two scenarios are quite similar and describe how to irrigate manually (let's identify them as Scenario A, the one described in Table 1, and Scenario B, the one described in Table 2). Then, another scenario describes how to irrigate with pipes and pumps (Table 3, identify it as Scenario C), so it resembles the previous scenario, but it is not so similar. Then, the fourth scenario describes how to sow seeds (Table 4, let's identify it as Scenario D). This scenario is quite different from the previous ones.

Scenario A and B are quite similar since both describe how to irrigate manually. The differences between the scenarios are two. Firstly, scenario A is shorter than scenario B, since scenario A only describes how to supply water while scenario B also considers worm leachate. Scenario B also describes in detail how to pour the water. Secondly, scenarios A and B use synonyms or different expressions to refer to the same elements or actions. The following Table 6 and 7 summarizes the comparison and its final rank which is 0.635.

Table 6. Comparison between scenario A and B (attribute by attribute).

	Scenario A	Scenario B	Intersection/Union
Title	Irrigate	Irrigate	1/1 = 1
Actors	Farmer	Farmer	1/1 = 1
Resources	Water, watering can	Water, watering can, worm leachate	2/3 = 0.66
Goal	Provide, h2o, tomato	Supply, water, tomato plant	0/6 = 0
Context	Tomato plant, state of grow	Tomato plant, state of grow, fruit formation stage	2/3 = 0.66
Episodes	Farmer, fill, watering can, water, pour, base of the plant	Farmer, fill, watering can, water, add, worm leachate, approach, tomato plant, assess, humidity of the soil, plant's base, pour	5/13 = 0.38

Table 7. Comparison between scenario A and B final rank.

Attributes	Similarity
Title	1
Actors and resources	(1 + 0.66)/2 = 0.83
Goal and context	(0 + 0.66)/2 = 0.33
Episodes	0.38
Final rank (average)	2.54/4 = 0.635

Scenario A and C describe the same activity (irrigation), but it is done in different ways. Scenario A describes how to irrigate manually, while scenario C describes how to irrigate with a pump (a complex infrastructure of pipes, valves and pumps). The following Table 8 and 9 summarizes the comparison. The final rank is 0.305.

Scenario A and D describe completely different activities: irrigation and sowing. The following Table 10 and 11 summarizes the comparison. The final rank is 0.191.

Table 12 summarizes the comparison among all the scenarios.

Table 8. Comparison between scenario A and C (attribute by attribute).

	Scenario A	Scenario C	Intersection/Union
Title	Irrigate	Irrigate, pump	1/2 = 0.5
Actors	Gardener	Farmer, technician	1/2 = 0.5
Resources	Water, watering can	Cistern, water	1/3 = 0.33
Goal	Provide, h2o, tomato	Provide, water, seed, tomato plant	1/6 = 0.16
Context	Tomato plant, state of grow	Tomato plant, state of grow, deploy, pipe, valve, pump	2/6 = 0.33
Episodes	Farmer, fill, watering can, water, pour, base of the plant	Farmer, determine, sector to irrigate, technician, open, valve, decides, intensity of the irrigation, set, pump, start	1/15 = 0.06

Table 9. Comparison between scenario A and C final rank.

Attributes	Similarity
Title	0.5
Actors and resources	(0.5 + 0.33)/2 = 0.415
Goal and context	(0.16 + 0.33)/2 = 0.245
Episodes	0.06
Final rank (average)	1.22/4 = 0.305

Table 10. Comparison between scenario A and D (attribute by attribute).

Scenario		Scenario D	Intersection/Union
Title	Irrigate	Sow, tomato seed	0/3 = 0
Actors	Farmer	Farmer	1/1 = 1
Resources	Water, watering can	Seed, substrate, water	1/4 = 0.25
Goal	Provide, h2o, tomato	Place, tomato seeds, seedbed,	0/6 = 0
Context	Tomato plant, state of grow	Seedbed, prepared	0/4 = 0
Episodes	Farmer, fill, watering can, water, pour, base of the plant	Farmer, dig, hole, seedbed, places, seeds, covers, substrate, spray, water	2/14 = 0.14

Table 11. Comparison between scenario A and D final rank.

Attributes	Similarity
Title	0
Actors and resources	$(1 + 0.25)/2 = 0.625$
Goal and context	$(0 + 0)/2 = 0$
Episodes	0.14
Final rank (average)	$0.765/4 = 0.191$

Table 12. Final rank of the scenarios

Scenario i	Scenario j	Rank
Scenario A	Scenario B	0.635
Scenario A	Scenario C	0.305
Scenario B	Scenario C	0.230
Scenario A	Scenario D	0.191
Scenario B	Scenario D	0.155
Scenario C	Scenario D	0.010

4 Tool Support

A software tool was prototyped to assist the application of the proposed method. The prototype is a web application written in Python [13] using Spacy [14] and NLTK [15] libraries to deal with natural language processing.

As input, the prototype receives a set of scenarios and as output it produces a set of tuples with the following information ('rank', 'scenario_i', 'scenario_j'). The application processes every possible pair of scenarios and calculates the rank of similarity for every pair.... 1. Describes a snapshot of the application (Fig. 1).

The process to calculate the similarity has different steps. The first step consists in tokenizing the scenarios. It can be done in two different ways. If the attribute is a list of words (actors and resources), it is processed by lowering them and removing stop words. If the attribute is a sentence or a group of sentences (title, goal, context, episodes), stopwords are removed and they are lemmatized and lowered. Then, nouns and verbs are collected. Then, Jaccard's method receives the data from the two scenarios from the previous step and calculates the jaccard similarity. This result and the scenarios are stored in a tuple as ('rank', 'scenario_i', 'scenario_j'). Figure 2 summarizes this process.

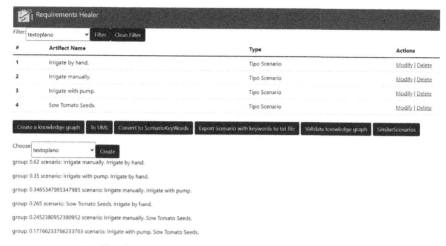

Fig. 1. Prototype with the scenarios used as example.

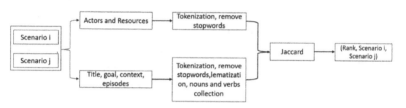

Fig. 2. Summary of the implementation.

5 Related Works

There are many works that use Jaccard to determine similarity in natural language artifacts. Some of them analyze requirements specification [16], some other are used in information retrieval [17], while some others are used for bugs reports [18–20]. Instead of Jaccard's similarity, other works [21, 22] rely on cosine similarity. And some other defines their own method [19, 23–25].

Regarding requirements specification, some papers analyze User Stories [24] to search duplicated or to compare similarity with the use case descriptions [26], some others analyze UML diagrams [23] to measure similarity between use case description and sequence diagram in a requirement specification, and some others uses documents without an specific template to evaluate the benefits of automatic similarity analysis [16]. There is one approach [23] that analyzes UML (Uses Cases) and documents at the same time. Another approach is by using similarity in queries [17] to obtain better results in the search. And another approach is by using a discriminating model [27] detect duplicated requirements.

Many methods rely on syntactic similarity [28, 29], although some of them also relies on semantic similarity [21, 24, 25].

Priyadi et al. [26] propose a method to assess the similarity of User Stories but they do not focus simply on the artifact, they also deal with the elicitation process to determine the suitability between the requirements elicitation and requirement modeling. Barbosa et al. [24] propose a method to assess the similarity of User Stories in the scrum process based on Jaccard and cosine similarity for syntactic similarity. The method proposed in this paper only focuses on the requirement artifact scenario and can be used in any elicitation technique.

Yanis et al. [23] deal with UML, particularly with Use Cases and Sequence diagrams studying the similarity between them and the section object of a software development document to determine the suitability of these two. In this paper, the method proposed only focuses on text similarity. Sari et al. [28] propose a study of semantic similarity via Wu Palmer method through functional requirements with use case diagrams. al. [22] propose a method to obtain a linkage between software reusability and similarity text, to find similarity between projects and reuse components. The method proposed in this paper uses the Jaccard similarity method to cluster scenarios by syntactic similarity through its field. Dag et al. [16] analyzed the benefits of automated similarity analysis of textual requirements focused on market-driven development. This paper is not focused on any development method, is an approach with a general application of scenarios to help to determine duplicated scenarios. Rao et al. [30] propose a method to detect duplicate requests in the requirements analysis stage using similarity techniques. The approach proposed in this paper focuses on the written scenarios not on the requests. Rago et al. [25] propose a tool, reqAligner, that combines text processing techniques and creates an abstract representation to identify duplicated functionality with semantic similarity. This paper only focuses on syntactic similarity.

6   Conclusions and Future Work

This paper described a method to rank a set of scenarios according to their similarity. This method compares every pair of scenarios to scenarios to determine the level of similarity between them, and then it sorts them in order from the most to the least similar. This paper also presents a software prototype implementing the proposed method. The results are promising, even though there is still much work to be done. The work of different people in the same project obtaining scenarios can generate a duplication of different scenarios with different levels of details. The contribution of the proposed approach can help detecting similar scenarios. Nevertheless, this approach relies on syntactic similarity. This analysis can be more complex with semantic similarity. Because different people can describe the same activity or object in different words. For example, watering the plant is the same as irrigating the plant. This can be even more complex with hypernyms. Thus, we plan to continue with the proposal adding some semantic similarities. Moreover, it is necessary to perform a detailed validation of the proposed approach. That is, we plan to perform a case study in order to assess the usability and applicability of the proposed approach. And we also plan to perform an experiment in order to assess the effectiveness of the proposed approach in comparison with some other approaches. Finally, we plan to improve the prototype with some usability functionality. Particularly, we believe that awareness is an important feature that should be included to foster practitioners to use the tool (hence the approach).

References

1. Benyon, D., Macaulay, C.: Scenarios and the HCI-SE design problem. Interact. Comput. **14**(4), 397–405 (2002). https://doi.org/10.1016/s0953-5438(02)00007-3
2. Boehm, B.W.: Software Engineering, Computer society Press, IEEE, (1997)
3. Potts, C.: Using schematic scenarios to understand user needs. In: Proceedings of the 1st Conference on Designing Interactive Systems: Processes, Practices, Methods, & Techniques, pp. 247–256 (1995)
4. Lim, S.L., Finkelstein, A.: StakeRare: using social networks and collaborative filtering for large-scale requirements elicitation. IEEE Trans. Softw. Eng. **38**(3), 707–735 (2012). https://doi.org/10.1109/TSE.2011.36
5. Cockburn, A.: Writing Effective Use Cases. Addison-Wesley, Boston (2001)
6. Carrol, J. M.: Five reasons for scenario-based design. In: Proceedings of the 32nd Annual Hawaii International Conference on Systems Sciences pp. 2–5 (1999)
7. vor der Brück, T., Pouly, M.: Text similarity estimation based on word embeddings and matrix norms for targeted marketing. In: Proceedings of the 2019 Conference of the North American Chapter of the Association for Computational Linguistics: Human Language Technologies, vol. 1. pp. 1827–1836. (2019)
8. Gough, P.A., Fodemski, F.T., Higgins, S.A., Ray, S.J.: Scenarios: an industrial case study and hypermedia enhancements. In: Proceedings of IEEE International Symposium on Requirements Engineering (RE 1995), pp. 10–17. IEEE Computer Society Press, Los Alamitos (1995)
9. Carroll, J.M.: Making Use: Scenario-Based Design of Human-Computer Interactions. MIT Press, Cambridge (2000)
10. Alexander, I., Maiden, N.: Scenarios, Stories, Use Cases, Through the System Development Life Cycle. John Wiley & Sons, Hobokens (2004)
11. Sutcliffe, A.G., Maiden, N.A., Minocha, S., Manuel, D.: Supporting scenario-based requirements engineering. IEEE Trans. Softw. Eng. **24**, 1072–1088 (1998)
12. Leite, J.C.S.D.P., Rossi, G., Balaguer, F., Maiorana, V., Kaplan, G., Hadad, G., Oliveros, A.: Enhancing a requirements baseline with scenarios. Requir. Eng. **2**, 184–198 (1997)
13. Python. https://www.python.org/. Accessed 17 May 2023
14. spaCy · Industrial-strength Natural Language Processing in Python. https://spacy.io/. Accessed 17 May 2023
15. NLTK Natural Language Toolkit, https://www.nltk.org/, accessed 17/5/2023
16. Nattoch Dag, J., Regnell, B., Carlshamre, P., Andersson, M., Karlsson, J.: A feasibility study of automated natural language requirements analysis in market-driven development. Requir. Eng. J. **7**, 20–33 (2002)
17. Rinartha, K., Suryasa, W.: Comparative study for better result on query suggestion of article searching with MySQL pattern matching and Jaccard similarity. In: Proceedings 5th International Conference on Cyber and IT Service Management (CITSM), pp. 1–4. IEEE (2017)
18. Runeson, P., Alexandersson, M., Nyholm, O.: Detection of duplicate defect reports using natural language processing. In: Proceedings of 29th International Conference on Software Engineering (ICSE 2007) , pp. 499–510. IEEE (2007)
19. Khtira, A., Benlarabi, A., El Asri, B.: Detecting feature duplication in natural language specifications when evolving software product lines. In: Proceedings of International Conference on Evaluation of Novel Approaches to Software Engineering (ENASE), pp. 257–262. IEEE (2015)
20. Sureka, A., Jalote, P.: Detecting duplicate bug report using character n-gram-based features. In: Proceedings of Asia Pacific Software Engineering Conference, pp. 366–374. IEEE (2010)

21. Qurashi, A. W., Holmes, V., Johnson, A.P.: Document processing: methods for semantic text similarity analysis. In: Proceedings of International Conference on INnovations in Intelligent SysTems and Applications (INISTA), pp. 1–6. IEEE (2020)

22. Mihany, F.A., Moussa, H., Kamel, A., Ezzat, E., Ilyas, M.: An automated system for measuring similarity between software requirements. In: Proceedings of the 2nd Africa and Middle East Conference on Software Engineering (2016)

23. Yanis, R.Z.I., Priyadi, Y., Puspitasari, S.Y.: Measurement of similarity between use case description and sequence diagram in software requirement specification using text analysis for dtrain application. In: Proceedings of 2nd International Conference on Electronic and Electrical Engineering and Intelligent System (ICE3IS), pp. 328–333. IEEE (2022)

24. Barbosa, R., Silva, A.E.A., Moraes R.: Use of similarity measure to suggest the existence of duplicate user stories in the scrum process. In: Proceedings of 46th Annual IEEE/IFIP International Conference on Dependable Systems and Networks Workshop. IEEE (2016)

25. Rago, A., Marcos, C., Diaz-Pace, J.A.: Identifying duplicate functionality in textual use cases by aligning semantic actions. Softw. Syst. Model. **15**(2), 579–603 (2016)

26. Priyadi, Y., Putra, A.M., Lyanda, P.S.: The similarity of elicitation software requirements specification in student learning applications of SMKN7 Baleendah based on use case diagrams using text mining. In: Proceedings of 5th International Conference on Information Technology, Information Systems and Electrical Engineering (ICITISEE), pp. 115–120. IEEE (2021)

27. Sun, C., Lo, D., Wang, X., Jiang, J., Khoo, S.C.: A discriminative model approach for accurate duplicate bug report retrieval. In: Proceedings of the 32nd ACM/IEEE International Conference on Software Engineering, vol. 1. pp. 45–54 (2010)

28. Sari, E. J., Priyadi, Y., Riskiana, R. R.: Implementation of semantic textual similarity between requirement specification and use case description using WUP method (case study: sipjabs application). In: Proceedings of IEEE World AI IoT Congress (AIIoT), pp. 681–687. IEEE (2022)

29. Lerch, J., Mira M.: Finding duplicates of your yet unwritten bug report. In: 17th European Conference on Software Maintenance and Reengineering, pp. 69–78. IEEE (2013)

30. Rao, D., Bian, L., Zhao, H.: Research of duplicate requirement detection method. In: Proceedings of 7th International Conference, Smart Computing and Communication, SmartCom 2022, New York City, NY, USA, 18–20 November 2023, pp. 213–225. Springer, Switzerland (2023). https://doi.org/10.1007/978-3-031-28124-2_20

Applying Design Thinking with Virtual Reality Applications as a Support for Bachelor Students with Disabilities

Alejandro Moreno-Cruz[1]([⊠]) (ID), Jaime Muñoz-Arteaga[1] (ID),
Julio C. Ponce-Gallegos[1] (ID), and Héctor Cardona-Reyes[2] (ID)

[1] Universidad Autónoma de Aguascalientes, Avenida Universidad #940, Ciudad Universitaria,
20100 Aguascalientes, Ags, México
alejandro_moreno_cruz@outlook.com, {jaime.munoz,
julio.ponce}@edu.uaa.mx
[2] CONAHCYT-CIMAT, Calle Lasec y Andador Galileo Galilei, Manzana 3, Lote 7 Quantum
Ciudad del Conocimiento, 98160 Zacatecas, Zac, México
hector.cardona@cimat.mx

Abstract. When a student has a disability, this is usually considered a huge barrier to learning, especially for students in high school or higher. In the present work, an approach based on the Design Thinking methodology has been implemented to develop a virtual reality application prototype that supports the learning of students with disabilities in Student Care Center with disabilities. Disabilities. Working in close collaboration with teachers who instruct a group of 18 students between the ages of 15 and 27, the critical stages in the application development process are defined to overcome some barriers. That these students face every day in their education. The methodology used has allowed constant improvement in the creation of the prototype through the development of several iterations of each of the stages of this approach. This study highlights the importance of constant communication with users, in this case, students with disabilities and the teachers who instruct them, to ensure the application's design is optimally adapted to individual needs. As a result, the distinct phases of the prototype creation are presented using the Design Thinking methodology, illustrating the joint work of teachers, students, and researchers both in the definition and in the development of virtual reality applications focused on improving inclusive education.

Keywords: Inclusive education · Virtual reality · Design thinking methodology · Educational applications · Bachelor students

1 Introduction

Inclusive education poses a relevant challenge for high school institutions, which strive to adopt new teaching strategies daily. Although there is already significant progress in adapting the institutions in terms of infrastructure and trained administrative departments [1], there are still areas where there is an opportunity for improvement, especially

P. H. Ruiz et al. (Eds.): HCI-COLLAB 2023, CCIS 1877, pp. 63–76, 2024.
https://doi.org/10.1007/978-3-031-57982-0_6

speaking of learning and motivation to participate in academic activities. Emerging technologies such as virtual reality, learning objects, and serious games can be implemented to support teaching methods.

Virtual reality has evolved from basic environmental sounds and three-dimensional simulations using image visualization to immersive experiences that engage multiple senses through full-body haptic equipment.

The main objective of this project is to develop a virtual reality application prototype using a methodology that provides academic support in specific areas for individuals with disabilities. The aim is to address individual challenges, including decreasing motivation and reinforcing knowledge from previous grades, enabling students to overcome past doubts; ideally, the work can support all students with any disability, students with cognitive and psychosocial disabilities will benefit the most.

The project will serve as didactic support for students in the open high school modality of the Attention Center for Students with Disabilities (CAED in its acronym in Spanish). By engaging in interactive virtual activities, students can improve their motivation, attention, and academic performance. Enhances their prospects for success, whether entering the job market or pursuing higher education.

The chapter is structured as follows: a summary provides an overview of the chapter's content, followed by an introduction that contextualizes the topic. It includes the project's objectives and expected outcomes based on the applied methodology. After that, there are some related works about using emerging technologies. The fundamentals section defines vital concepts related to design thinking and outlines the adapted procedures. The chapter concludes with partial results, conclusions, future work suggestions, and acknowledgments to the institutions supporting this research.

2   Related Work

Next table describes several works related to the application of virtual reality technologies have been developed to support students with certain specific disabilities, two that focused on people with Attention-Deficit/Hyperactivity Disorder (ADHD) will be mentioned below and 1 using augmented reality as rehabilitation activities.

The articles mentioned in Table 1 were found through a review of various academic repositories, looking for which ones were most similar to what we wanted to do; these works served as an inspiration to identify some ways in which it is possible to focus educational strategies so that students interact with current and relevant technologies such as virtual reality, the projects focus on people with ADHD, which is one of the disabilities present in CAED students and, therefore, it is appropriate to take the approaches of the works as a guide.

Table 1. Some related works to support learning for students with ADHD.

Work	Applied technology	Advantages
A Lean UX Process Model for Virtual Reality Environments Considering ADHD in Pupils at Elementary School in COVID-19 Contingency [2]	project developed to generate an application that implements a virtual reality environment on Android devices that allows primary school students to interact with activities following a series of instructions provided by Non-Player Character (NPC) within the virtual environment	They identified the number of times that each student needed to review the instructions to measure the level of care that they presented, in addition to contributing to pleasant and fun learning in the areas of education, health, and technology
Development of virtual reality rehabilitation games for children with attention-deficit hyperactivity disorder [3]	Development of an application to be used in HTC VIVE headsets that showed interactions that promoted motor coordination in children with ADHD	Improvement of attention, cognitive abilities, and abstract reasoning
Using Augmented Reality and Gamification to Empower Rehabilitation Activities and Elderly Persons. A Study Applying Design Thinking [4]	A combined system of augmented reality and gamification within an application to support the rehabilitation activities of people with disabilities	The data collected with the use of the application can be visualized by the therapists who will identify how effective the support is being and what strategies can be applied to improve the focus

3 Conceptual Background

3.1 Educational Applications

In recent years, innovative technologies have become increasingly significant in the field of education, as well as in the training programs of numerous organizations that actively recruit new members for their teams. These technologies have revolutionized traditional learning materials such as audiovisual aids, CDs, and books, either by replacing them or by serving as valuable complements. Integrating interactive activities, these applications provide students and learners with hands-on experiences that facilitate a deeper understanding of the topic through an innovative way [5].

3.2 Virtual Reality

Within these technologies, there are three types: augmented reality, virtual reality, and mixed reality, which include characteristics of the first two and combine them according to the needs.

The concept of virtual reality is not limited to a single, specific definition. Instead, it encompasses a diverse array of technologies [6]. These technologies span a spectrum, ranging from the simple experience of watching a video on a two-dimensional screen to the immersive interaction with systems that enable users to control actions using various parts of their bodies. Advanced virtual reality setups may involve haptic gloves and vests, which facilitate touch-based interactions and enhance the overall sensory experience, see Fig. 1.

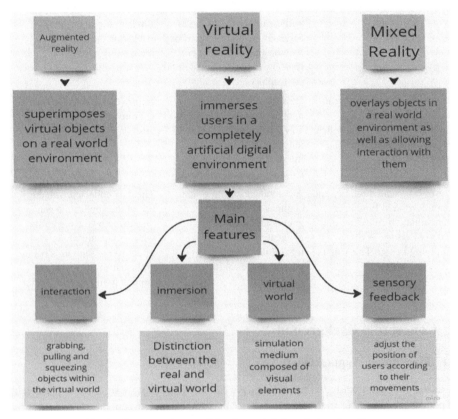

Fig. 1. Conceptual map of the characteristics of virtual reality.

3.3 Care Center for Students with Disabilities

At most basic educational levels, programs are enhanced to support the development and learning of students with disabilities. However, as one progresses to higher levels, the limitations become more visible and complex. For this reason, various strategies have been executed, such as the CAEDs [7]. These centers have adapted classrooms that offer opportunities for students with one or more disabilities studying high school in Mexico, with multiple locations throughout the country. Some of the disabilities usually present in the students of these centers are visual, motor, cognitive, auditory, and psychosocial [8]. Currently, these centers have various teaching resources, such as audiobooks, sign language glossaries, and computers with Braille keyboards. The educational program consists of twenty-two modules (Fig. 2) that belong to 4 disciplinary areas: communication, social sciences and humanities, experimental sciences, and mathematics [9].

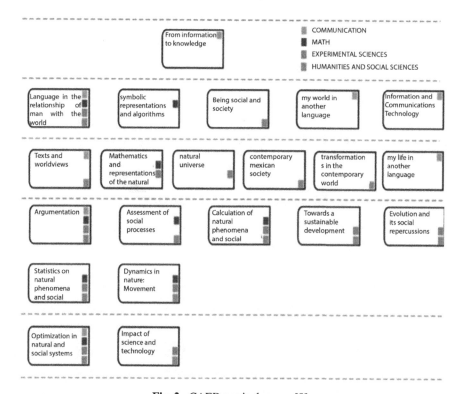

Fig. 2. CAED curricular map [9].

Regarding the topics, this study aims to explore the integration of emerging technologies, particularly virtual reality, to address the challenges faced by students with disabilities during their academic pursuits. By implementing these technologies, strategies can be devised to help these students' overcome barriers and ensure that they receive an education comparable to their non-disabled peers in high school. Can provide them with equal opportunities for further studies at the university level or entry into the work market.

4   Design Thinking Methodology in the Inclusive Education

The approach we will be using is based on the Design Thinking methodology. This iterative process is commonly employed in various domains, particularly software engineering. By adopting this model, the project team gains insights into the target users and their specific needs, enabling them to generate innovative solutions that meet the required functionalities while addressing user requirements.

The methodology comprises five main phases: empathize, define, ideate, prototype, and test [10]. These stages can be performed in a specific order, but it is possible to return to a past step or pass another; they are not performed to obtain a result from the beginning but intending to do them several times to polish each stage, i.e., to improve the product each iteration (Fig. 3). The latter is the main objective of the methodology to be employed.

Fig. 3. Design Thinking Methodology [10].

- Empathize. In this phase we seek to prioritize research, understanding the needs of users and the problems to which we want to find a solution. The key actions to perform this stage correctly are listening and understanding, focusing all attention on what user request, and recommending being truly innovative and meeting the requirements of customers and/or users. [11]
- Define. Gathering all the information obtained in the first stage, we analyze it to organize it in a way that allows us to focus our attention on the strategies that could be conducted to fulfill what was requested. [12]
- Ideate. Brainstorming is generated and those schemes that shape these ideas are made, a creative strategy is established to develop the prototypes and include functionalities according to the user's needs.
- Prototype. Having the ideas, a little clearer, we begin to shape them to have a first development and experiment with this, making various modifications to not get stuck in having the ideas, but a working prototype, although not all the specifications requested by users are covered. [13]
- Test. In this last stage several options are considered, having a working prototype at hand, it is presented to both co-workers and users to whom the product is addressed, thus achieving data collection to improve the current prototype in future developments [11].

Developing interactive applications with virtual reality is considered a non-trivial task, even if this grows to be an educational application, adding another extra considering that our primary users to whom it is directed are students who suffer from one or more disabilities, so it is crucial to be visiting who will be the primary users to understand more how they interact with their environment, how they are given better study and retention of acquired knowledge, for this reason, it was decided to adopt this model to be able to improve as progress is made to the product.

- For the first stage (empathizing), the focus is on data collection, surveys, and first-hand observations of the CAEDs' ways of working with the students who belong to them.
- With the data obtained, the needs are established and defined from highest to lowest priority, which will help to contemplate which actions will be the next to be carried out in the development of our application.
- Subsequently, brainstorming, or other maps focused on the needs established in the previous stage are made to translate them into more concrete functionalities.
- What has been defined and designed in the previous stages is captured to have advances in the functionalities within the application and to be able to work on new advances while the current ones are tested and continue in constant improvements; for this reason, Design Thinking is an innovation methodology focused on the needs of the users.

In the last stage, the code is tested, reviewing the terms used in the code, structure, syntax, and the usability of the application itself, if possible, in conjunction with some real users to identify any faults or opportunities for improvement. Finally, the next iteration starts again from the first stage (empathize) to advance the application requirements.

5   Applying Design Thinking with Augmented Reality Applications

In the following section, we outline the Design Thinking stages employed in developing the application discussed in this study. Development team identify how technologies can enhance the educational activities designed by teachers working with students with disabilities. Subsequently, we delineate the imminent requirements that must be addressed. Technologist then devise strategies for achieving considerable progress and generate functional prototypes aligned with the established objectives. Rigorous testing is conducted on these prototypes. Furthermore, this iterative process enables us to refine and enhance existing developments while making new strides.

5.1   First Iteration

Empathize. During a visit made by the technologists to the Attention Center for Students with Disabilities (CAED) at CBTis 168 in Aguascalientes, a collaboration was established with 2 teachers and 18 students, primarily with intellectual disabilities. The objective was to explore the use of virtual reality as a means of supporting regular activities. A collaboration network was formed, with CAED teachers providing requirements and researchers ensuring their fulfillment.

Define. The team determined strategies to adapt activities to students' needs, emphasizing the inclusion of instructions and motivational stages to encourage continuous learning.

Ideate. Extensive research was conducted to identify tools compatible with virtual reality and available equipment. After careful analysis, Unity was selected as the development engine. To gather specific requirements, a simple activity was created to highlight the possibilities and gather valuable insights from users.

Prototype. Using Unity, a program was developed to classify objects within a virtual environment visually. The activity involved users interacting with colored figures and placing them on corresponding tables. This initial prototype did not incorporate audio or text instructions, see Fig. 4.

Fig. 4. Virtual environment, first prototype.

Test. The CAED teachers were given a demonstration to highlight the potential applications of these technologies in their strategies. It was evident that certain study modules aligned well with these activities. The intuitive controls required minimal instructions and were easily managed by the teachers.

5.2 Second Iteration

Empathize. In the CAED, the teachers identified two modules, Mathematics and Representations of the natural system (module 8) and Calculus in natural phenomena and social processes (module 15) (Fig. 2), as areas where students face significant challenges. A visit was made to these modules, introducing the project, and seeking student participation. Surveys were conducted to assess the teachers' and students' proficiency with information and communication technologies, and an empathy map was created to understand the students' needs and perspectives, see Fig. 5.

Define. Modules 8 and 15 of the CAED curricula (Fig. 2) were addressed together to provide immediate support and improvements. Blender software was chosen for 3D

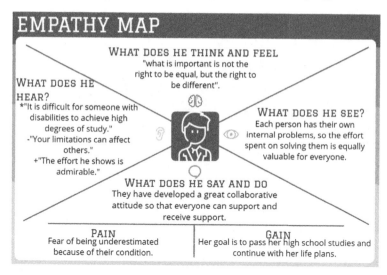

Fig. 5. Empathy map to know students' feelings.

modeling due to its versatility and availability. Drawings created by the students were selected to be integrated as characters within the application, providing instructions for the activities. Some ideas were discarded to avoid copyright issues.

Ideate. Some of the drawings made by the students are selected to be part of the characters within the application; these will give the students indications on what activities should be performed next.

Some ideas were discarded due to their similarity with existing characters and implementing them would incur certain copyright infringements.

Prototype. The first character was developed using Blender to test its ability to perform human-like movements and exhibit natural behavior. However, specific movements caused the model to deform beyond realistic limits. It was decided that these movements must be restricted, and the final model will be exported to Unity, see Fig. 6.

Test. After conducting the initial movement tests, it was determined that the character performed as expected. However, to ensure optimal performance, adjustments are necessary to prevent excessive deformation. The upcoming phase will focus on finalizing and exporting the model to Unity for further evaluation and advancement.

5.3 Third Iteration

Empathize. Frustration is a common experience for students in CAED, especially those with physical and mental limitations. Addressing their challenges and finding effective solutions to enhance their learning experience is crucial.

Define. To overcome the barriers of frustration, strategies incorporating modern technologies should be implemented to increase attention and motivation among learners in CAED.

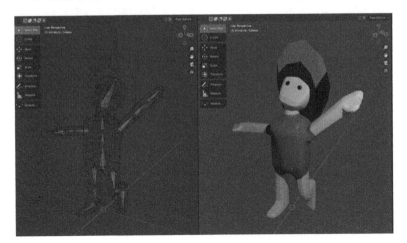

Fig. 6. Creation and structuring of the first character in Blender.

Ideate. One potential solution is to integrate pop-up windows within the application, displaying motivational messages to help students remain calm and perform activities more effectively. These messages should also facilitate long-term learning beyond task completion, see Fig. 7.

Prototype. The designed pop-up windows were successfully integrated into the application in the development phase.

Fig. 7. Implementation of motivational messages within the application.

Test. The functionality of the pop-up windows was tested with a group of students, revealing challenges faced by students with vision problems who struggled to identify the texts within the windows.

5.4 Fourth Iteration

Empathize. It was investigated whether the students suffered from hearing problems that prevented them from following the instructions.

Define. As there were no hearing problems, the possibility of implementing audio systems within the application was added to cover more needs and barriers for those students with vision problems.

Ideate. With the Audacity audio recording and editing tool, a track of each instruction present in the application was made to provide the possibility for each student to carry out the activities within the virtual environment in a way that was accessible to them.

Prototype. Icons with the button function were added so that dictation of the text is played when pressed; said text is usually the one that is immediately next to each corresponding button, see Fig. 8.

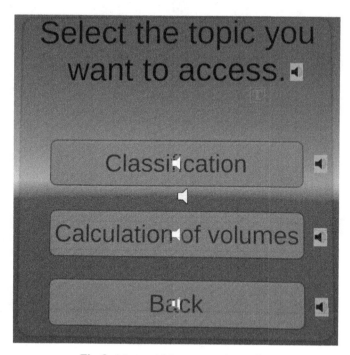

Fig. 8. Menu with buttons to play audio.

Test. Sixteen students were able to follow the directions, which brings us closer to the goal; however, the two students with severe visual problems could not even make out the audio playback icons.

5.5 Fifth Iteration

Empathize. Another subject of great difficulty within the modules in progress is volume calculation, so the activity that can be applied next is sought in conjunction with the teachers.

Define. Questions were selected to remember the formulas to calculate the volume of the most familiar figures (sphere, cube, cylinder, cone, prism).

Ideate. A small quiz with three-dimensional models is applied next to the questions so that they can be guided both by their memory and by a small visual aid that users can analyze in real-time.

Prototype. A scene different from that of the other activity was generated with the colored figures to be able to separate each environment with its own activity, and these do not interrupt each other, see Fig. 9.

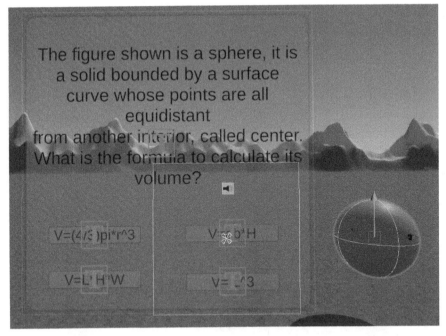

Fig. 9. Question and 3D model for calculating the volume of a sphere.

Test. The students were able to remember through trial and error, also competing among themselves to identify who could solve the questions with fewer errors and in the shortest possible time.

6 Results

The results of this study highlight the positive impact of the virtual reality application developed through the Design Thinking approach in the field of inclusive education. Throughout the different stages of development, the application was continuously improved thanks to the constant feedback from the students and teachers involved in the process.

The implementation of the prototype of the application in the Attention Center for Students with Disabilities (CAED) showed encouraging results. Increased student motivation and participation during learning activities were observed, reflected in a higher level of commitment and better academic performance.

Additionally, students and teachers reported greater ease in accessing educational resources and overcoming specific barriers due to their disabilities. The app provided a more immersive and personalized learning experience tailored to the individual needs of each student.

In summary, the results of this study support the effectiveness of the virtual reality application developed with the Design Thinking approach in improving inclusive education. These findings highlight the importance of involving end users in designing and developing educational technologies, thus ensuring their relevance and adaptation to the real needs of students with disabilities.

7 Conclusions and Future Work

The development of a prototype using virtual reality technology and the application of the design thinking methodology has proved to be crucial in this study. The prototype is an interactive tool for students, supporting their learning process. The iterative design thinking approach allowed for continuous improvements and the incorporation of user feedback, particularly from students with disabilities, ensuring that the prototype meets their specific needs.

The implementation of virtual reality technology was successful in engaging students and enhancing their learning experiences. Most students quickly grasped the controls and navigated the virtual environment with ease. However, it was observed that students with severe visual impairments faced challenges in selecting buttons and following on-screen instructions, impacting their ability to complete the activities fully.

The work presented shows compliance with the proposed main objective, which is to correctly use the selected methodology (Design Thinking) in the planning and creating of a Virtual Reality application; however, the application still has excellent opportunities for improvement.

In conclusion, developing a prototype by integrating virtual reality and design thinking methodology has demonstrated its significance in addressing the unique learning needs of students with disabilities. The iterative design process allows for constant refinement and adaptation, ensuring that the prototype aligns with the requirements and capabilities of the students. By continuing to apply this approach, the aim is to create a more inclusive and effective educational environment for students with disabilities.

Future work will continue to employ the design thinking model and iterate on the prototype to develop activities tailored to the student's abilities. Specifically, the focus will be on adapting activities related to Mathematics and representations of the natural system (module 8) and calculus in natural phenomena and social processes (module 15) in the CAED curricular map.

Acknowledgments. This work is possible thanks to the support provided by the "Consejo Nacional de Humanidades, Ciencia y Tecnología" (CONAHCYT) with CVU number 1198948, in addition to the collaborative work carried out jointly with the CAED CBTis168 and the Universidad Autónoma de Aguascalientes.

References

1. Pérez-Castro, J.: La inclusión de las personas con discapacidad en la educación superior en México. Sinéctica **46** (2016)
2. Cardona-Reyes, H., Muñoz-Arteaga, J., Villalba-Condori, K., Barba-González, M.: A lean UX process model for virtual reality environments considering ADHD in pupils at elementary school in COVID-19 contingency (2021)
3. Ou, Y.K., Wang, Y.L., Chang, H.C., Yen, S.Y., Zheng, Y.H., Lee, B.O.: Development of virtual reality rehabilitation games for children with attention-deficit hyperactivity disorder. J. Ambient Intell. Human. Comput. **11**, 5713–5720 (2020)
4. Korn, O., Buchweitz, L., Rees, A., Bieber, G., Werner, C., Hauer, K.: Using augmented reality and gamification to empower rehabilitation activities and elderly persons. a study applying design thinking. In: Ahram, T.Z. (ed.) AHFE 2018. AISC, vol. 787, pp. 219–229. Springer, Cham (2019). https://doi.org/10.1007/978-3-319-94229-2_21
5. Jiménez, Y.M.: Herramientas web interactivas en el proceso de enseñanza y aprendizaje en educación media (2018)
6. Sherman, W.R., Craig, A.B.: Understanding virtual reality: Interface, application, and design. Morgan Kaufmann Publishers (2018)
7. De la Cruz Orozco, I.: Educación inclusiva en el nivel medio-superior: análisis desde la perspectiva de directores. Sinéctica, Revista Electrónica de Educación (2020). ISSN 2007-7033. https://doi.org/10.31391/S2007-7033(2020)0054-008
8. Medina, B.A.: Formación integral, inclusión educativa y responsabilidad social. DOCERE Maga. 33–36 (2019)
9. CBTIS 225. Centro de Atención para Estudiantes con Discapacidad (CAED) (2023). https://www.cbtis225.edu.mx/servicios/programas/caed
10. Interaction Design Foundation. What is Design Thinking? (2022). https://www.interaction-design.org/literature/topics/design-thinking
11. Latorre-Cosculluela, C., Vázquez-Toledo, S., Rodríguez-Martínez, A., Liesa-Orús, M.: Design Thinking: creatividad y pensamiento crítico en la universidad. Revista Electrónica de Investigación Educativa (REDIE) **22** (2020). https://doi.org/10.24320/redie.2020.22.e28.2917
12. Frade, N.D.: Las 5 fases del Design thinking, o cómo idear la solución genial. Geniallyblog (2021). https://blog.genial.ly/fases-design-thinking/
13. Márquez, B.L.V., Hanampa, L.A.I., Portilla, M.G.M.: Design Thinking aplicado al diseño de experiencia de usuario. Innovación y software **2**(1), 6–19 (2021). https://doi.org/10.48168/innosoft.s5.a35

Approach for Feature Models Definition in Software Product Lines Based on Collaborative Work

Jazmín Gómez[1] 📷, Pablo H. Ruiz[3] 📷, Vanessa Agredo Delgado[1]([⊠]) 📷,
and Marta Cecilia Camacho[2] 📷

[1] Corporación Universitaria Comfacauca - Unicomfacauca, Popayán, Colombia
{jgomez,vagredo}@unicomfacauca.edu.co
[2] Institución Universitaria Colegio Mayor del Cauca, Popayán, Colombia
cecamacho@unimayor.edu.co
[3] Universidad Nacional Abierta y a Distancia - UNAD, Popayán Cauca, Colombia
pablo.ruiz@unad.edu.co

Abstract. A Software Product Line (SPL) consists of a set of software products that share common features and also have some differences. Feature models are a key tool for managing variability and customization of this set of products. The feature model definition is a complex task that involves the collaboration of people with diverse knowledge, perspectives and experiences, to achieve a successful definition, it is crucial to follow communication and teamwork guidelines Otherwise, there is a risk of obtaining a poor definition of this vital artifact for the SPL's. This paper presents an approach for defining feature models based on Collaborative Work called CINDIRELLA, which defines execution elements such as: workflows, tasks, collaborative patterns associated with Thinklets or Gamestorming, roles, and input and output artifacts. As main results we can say that CINDERELLA is an easy to use approach, however, it is necessary to improve the description of its instructions and guidelines in order to achieve a better understanding. In addition, it is a useful approach because its elements are coherent and described in an organized way. Finally, it is a complete approach because it has sufficient and necessary elements for the features models definition.

Keywords: Software Product Lines · Collaborative Work · Features Model

1 Introduction

Software Product Lines (SPL) provide an approach to software production that is based on planned reuse, which seeks to improve productivity, development time, time-to-market and increase the quality of the software products [1, 2]. An indispensable and necessary element for the definition of an SPL are the Features Model, where the characteristics of the software products of the product line are identified and materialized. In its simplest form, a features model comprises a list of features and an enumeration of all combinations of valid features [3]. However, defining feature models is a complex, time-consuming activity, due to the involvement of several people with different ideas and expertise. In addition, it is necessary to understand and properly interpret various opinions about the model needs that should emerge from the modeling team. In the

P. H. Ruiz et al. (Eds.): HCI-COLLAB 2023, CCIS 1877, pp. 77–92, 2024.
https://doi.org/10.1007/978-3-031-57982-0_7

feature identification is necessary to abstract and understand the domain knowledge of various experts, as well as to search for information in different sources such as: books, user manuals, design documents, and source code [4]. All of the above aspects must be combined for the feature models definition, which makes the definition activity complex, since it mainly involves an adequate collaboration between people who use techniques to manage and elicit information sources, which, if not well related, can lead to a poor definition of the model and therefore make it not very useful [4]. In the Collaborative work requires that participants performing an activity share the knowledge creation process [5, 6], which implies providing spaces for interaction between people to achieve an objective based on the use of different collaboration elements (roles, tasks, strategies, tools, metrics, etc.) that allow the incorporation of the participants' perspectives and their teamwork [7]. According to the general problem and taking into account that the adoption of collaborative work elements can support the definition of SPL's features models, this paper presents CINDIRELLA, spanish acronym for DefiniCIóN de moDElos de caRactErísticas en SPL basado en trabajo coLAborativo), an approach for features models definition based on collaborative work, to achieve the strengthening of the SPL's definition. The main results about CINDERELLA are that it is an easy to use approach, however, it is necessary to improve its description in order to achieve a better understanding. In addition, it is a useful and complete approach because it has sufficient and necessary elements for the feature models definition.

This paper is organized as follows: Sect. 2 presents a brief conceptual framework and related work. Section 3 briefly describes the methodology used for the execution of the research. Section 4 describes part of the CINDIRELLA approach. Section 5 shows the validation of CINDERELLA and finally Sect. 6 shows the conclusions.

2   Conceptual Framework and Related Work

Collaborative Engineering
Collaborative Engineering (CI) is an approach to the design and implementation of collaborative processes that includes collaborative work practices in recurring activities where teamwork is a relevant success factor [8, 9]. The term collaboration comes from the Latin word collaborare which means "to work with". Therefore, collaborative efforts are joint, rather than individual. Collaborative efforts should be directed toward a group goal. This means that collaboration involves multiple people combining their knowledge and efforts to achieve a common desired and proposed goal. Therefore, collaboration is defined as joint effort toward a group goal [8].

Collaboration Patterns
Patterns of collaboration in CI are used to classify group activities in terms of the changes they produce. Collaboration patterns characterize the ways in which group activities direct or move a group towards one or more common goals. Five general patterns of collaboration were identified for a working group to achieve its objectives: generate, reduce, clarify, organize, evaluate, create consensus, and create a common goal or goals [8].

ThinkLets
Building blocks or design units called thinkLets are used to propose a collaborative process. A thinkLets is a predictable pattern of interactions between people working

together to achieve a goal [10]. A thinkLets is a written and named procedure that reliably creates predictable variations in the collaborative patterns by which a group moves through its activities [11].

Gamestorming

Gamestorming is a comprehensive, game-based approach to collaboration that enables everyone in a group to participate through creative, learning-oriented activities. Gamestorming brings together a set of strategies and practices that have been called games, specific games aimed at exploring and examining business challenges, improving collaboration among team members, and generating new approaches and possibilities for situations or products. Dave, Sunni and James explain that serious games help organizations solve complex problems through collaborative play [12].

2.1 Feature Models

The Feature Model was first presented as part of the feature-oriented domain analysis (FODA) [13]. The main focus of this method is the identification of salient or distinguishing features of software systems that are produced from the analysis of the domain. In [4] explains the concept of features and the objectives of feature modeling, provides guidelines for domain analysis that emerge from the execution of several industrial cases, and provides a set of guidelines for domain analysis. On the other hand in [14] FODA is integrated with the processes and work products of the reuse-driven software engineering business RSEB (Reuse-Driven Software Engineering Business). RSEB is a systematic reuse process based on use cases. In [15] a semi-automated approach to build feature models based on requirements clustering is proposed. This approach tries to automate the activities of feature identification, organization and variability modeling. Alternatively, in [16] presents an algorithmic and customizable approach to compute a logical and appropriate hierarchy of features that includes feature groups, written feature attributes, domain values and relationships between these attributes. In [17], the application of automated analysis of feature models (AAFM), which consists of computer-aided extraction of information from feature models, is proposed. On the other hand, in [18] a method is proposed, which employs a two-layer feature model: application and infrastructure. This method helps the interested parties to have a complete knowledge about the application and infrastructure levels of the desired products in a visual way.

2.2 Collaborative Work in SPL's

In [19], a support approach for coordinating teamwork decision making in the context of product configuration is proposed. The approach is based on the configuration of feature models; from which it is shown that misconfiguration can cause the production of invalid product specifications. On the other hand [20] proposes a collaborative process for scope definition in SPLs. Furthermore, he explains how to design a process for collaborative scoping, which is consistent with collaborative engineering guidelines, based on thinkLets as building blocks. With respect to collaborative work in the scope definition of in SPL's, in [21] an exploratory study is shown to identify some problems related to collaborative work in scoping from a practical perspective. In addition, a collaborative approach to scoping is presented that seeks to combine scoping practices with collaboration patterns and thinkLets, with this combination seeking the effective participation of the required roles in the scoping activity [22]. Practical experiences of adopting agile principles and collaborative practices in the SPL planning activity are presented in [23]. This approach tries to balance agility and the intrinsic needs of this activity within the SPL approach. An alternative approach is presented in [24], which seeks to create a Collaborative Software Product Line Engineering Lab. This lab aims to be available to all communities interested in SPL's in a way that allows collaborations to support their maturation. In addition, it aims to encourage the use of SPL's both in industry and academia.

The above works show different perspectives related to feature models and some approaches using collaborative work in the SPL's framework. These papers have different views and strategies on how to create, manipulate and manage feature models and how to use collaborative engineering in the context of SPL's, but none involve or are based on collaborative work to build feature models. Therefore, none use elements of collaborative engineering that specifically support the creation of feature models, which is the major contribution of this paper.

3   Methodology

This work was developed following the multi-cycle action research methodology with bifurcation which defines three cycles: conceptual, methodological and evaluation [25]. The execution of the cycles is briefly described below:

- *Conceptual cycle:* in this cycle, the planning and execution of the systematic mapping was carried out to identify the characteristics of the different approaches in the creation of SPL's feature models. A characterization of the available approaches that supported the definition of CINDIRELLA was obtained.
- *Methodological cycle:* in this cycle, the basic structure of elements that are part of CINDIRELLA was defined and incorporated incrementally. In this cycle, through expert evaluation, the collaborative work patterns that were most appropriate for the SPL's context were also classified and incorporated.
- *Evaluation cycle:* in this cycle an experiment was conducted as an evaluation mechanism of CINDIRELLA, the objective was to evaluate the usefulness, ease of use and completeness of the approach to define feature models, from the point of view or perspective of the participants, as well as the level of collaboration achieved by the working group.

4   CINDERELLA

This section presents a part of CINDERELLA, an approach for the definition of feature models in SPL's, which is based on collaborative work. CINDERELLA uses collaborative patterns in most of its tasks in order to improve the input or contribution of the participating roles and thus make the definition of feature models more appropriate. The goal of CINDERELLA is to systematically guide the definition of feature models using a coherently organized flow of tasks, roles and artifacts.

CINDERELLA was defined using the extension of the HAMSTERS notation, which consists of providing elements to describe collaborative tasks. This notation allows graphically defining relationships and representing information between tasks and their participants (roles). HAMSTERS offers a series of elements that complement the representation of the tasks that make up a collaborative process, elements such as: relationships between tasks/activities, input/output information, detailed collaborative tasks, among others [26]. Tasks consist of the following elements: task, description, collaborative pattern, ThinkLets, input/output artifacts, steps and rules.

4.1 CINDERELLA's Task Flow

To support the definition of feature models, CINDERELLA defines a task flow that graphically supports their execution, see Fig. 1. The flow is made up of 11 tasks: Contextualize Concepts, Identify the SPL Domain, Disclose Existing Products, Explore

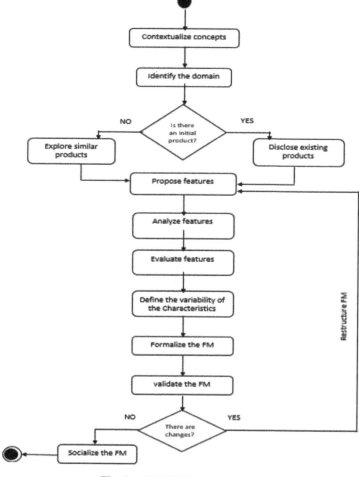

Fig. 1. CINDERELLA's task flow

Similar Products, Propose Features, Analyze Features, Evaluate Features, Define the variability of the characteristics, Formalize the FM, Validate the FM, Socialize the FM.

To develop each of the CINDERELLA tasks, collaboration patterns, thinkLets and gamestorming were used; Table 1 shows the associations between these elements and each of the tasks.

Table 1. Relationships between tasks, collaborative patterns, thinkLets, gamestorming.

Task	Collaborative pattern	ThinkLets/Gamestorming
Contextualize Concepts	Clarify	Visual Glossary
Identify the SPL Domain	Reduce	Dot Voting
Disclose Existing Products	Not Applicable	Not Applicable
Explore Similar Products	Not Applicable	Not Applicable
Propose Features	Generate	FreeBrainstorm
Analyze Features	Reduce	GarlicSqueezer
Evaluate Features	Reduce	StrawPoll
Define the variability of the characteristics	Reduce	Dot Voting
Formalize the FM	Not Applicable	Not Applicable
Validate the FM	Reduce	Dot Voting
Socialize el FM	Not Applicable	Not Applicable

4.2   Collaborative Description of CINDERELLA Tasks

The description of each task is represented by a model, a table and some examples of work products, see Fig. 2. The model is represented by a figure or graphic, where the task is symbolized by a rectangle composed of five fields, in the upper left field the task identifier is placed, the upper right field is intended for the name of the associated thinkLets or gamestorming, the left field describes the main collaboration pattern to be used in each task, the largest field is used to place the task name and finally the lower right triangle contains the acronym of the participants or mandatory roles, this acronym is composed of the first letters of the name of the role.

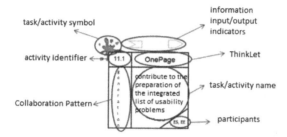

Fig.2. Collaborative task description used in CINDERELLA.

Below is an example of the collaborative notation of the first task of the flow defined in CINDERELLA.

4.2.1   Task: Contextualize feature model

The task contextualize feature models is collaborative and can be evidenced because in the upper part of the rectangle the thinkLets is indicated and in the lower left part a collaborative pattern is shown, see Fig. 3. In the right section of the model the steps are presented, and it specifies the step that is performed by the whole group of participants, in addition to the contribution of each of the roles. The specification of this task is completed with the textual description in Table 2.

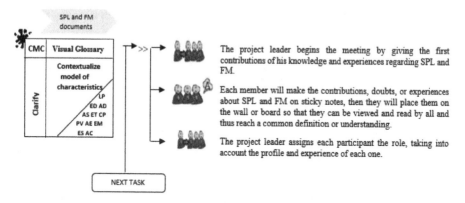

Fig. 3. Task: Contextualize Feature Model

It is important to clarify that CINDERELLA has 11 tasks which are described similarly to the task described in Fig. 3 and Table 2 and which for space reasons will not be detailed here.

Table 2. Contextualize feature Model

Task	Contextualize feature Model
Description	The focus of this meeting is to clarify, define and inform the interests and knowledge involved in the definition of a Software Product Line (SPL) and the importance of the creation of the Feature Model (FM), in addition to assigning to each participant the roles required for the creation of the model
Mandatory Roles	Project Leader Domain Expert Software Architect Business Administrator Marketing Expert SPL Expert Collaborative Work Consultant Potential Customer Sales personnel
Optional Roles	Not Applicable
Collaborative Pattern	Clarify
ThinkLet/ Gamestorming	Visual Glossary
Input artifacts	SPL and FM documentation
Output artifacts	Minutes of attendance
Steps	The project leader starts the meeting by giving the first contributions of his knowledge and experiences regarding SPL and FM Each member will write on sticky notes the contributions, doubts, or experiences about SPL and FM, then place them on the wall or board so that they can be visualized and read by all and thus reach a common definition or understanding The project leader assigns a role to each participant, taking into account the profile and experience of each one

5 Validation

To validate CINDERELLA this approach was applied in an educational context, where the usefulness, ease of use and completeness in the definition of feature models in SPL's was evaluated from the perspective of the experiment participants.

5.1 Experiment Context

The experiment was carried out with 15 students of the software engineering II course of the VI semester of the Systems Engineering program at the Corporación Universitaria Comfacauca (UNICOMFACUCA), located in the city of Popayán (Colombia). Specifically, the students participated in the development of the experiment, which was a controlled execution environment of CINDERELLA.

5.2   Experiment Design

Table 3 shows a summary of the activities planned for the development of the experiment, where the estimated time for its execution and the support instruments for its development have been defined.

Table 3. Summary of experiment activities

Experimentation Activities	Duration	Support instruments
1. Socialize and contextualize the academic experiment	20 min	Power Point presentation of the Introduction to the academic experiment and conceptual elements
2. Present the CINDERELLA approach: task flow to create or define SPL Feature Model, based on Collaborative work	30 min	Power Point presentation and document with the description of the approach
3. Apply the proposed approach	2 h and 30 min	Guidance document, online spreadsheets, diagram of tasks to execute the approach,
4. Resolve questionnaire	15 min	Survey
Total time: 3 h 45 min		

5.3   Hypotheses

To evaluate the ease of use, usefulness and completeness of CINDERELLA, from the perspective of the group of UNICOMFACAUCA students, the following hypotheses were evaluated:

Table 4. Hypotheses of the experiment

Hypotheses	Variables	
H.1.1 Users understand the instructions and guidelines of the approach	*Ease of understanding:* the degree of ease with which a person can understand and use the approach. This variable represents a perceptual judgment of the effort required to understand the approach	Ease of use
H.1.2 Users understand the supporting examples provided by the approach		
H.2.1 Users perceive that the approach has the necessary information to guide its application	*Ease of application:* the degree of ease with which a person can apply the approach. This variable represents a perceptual judgment of the effort required to apply the approach	
H.3.1 Users perceive that the approach is useful in the process of defining SPL Feature Models	*Perceived Usefulness:* The degree of usefulness perceived by a person about the in-focus for the definition of the SPL Feature Model. This variable represents a useful perceptual judgment of the approach	Utility
H.3.2 Users perceive the approach to be organized and consistent		
H.4.1 Users perceive that the elements of the approach are necessary and sufficient for the definition of an feature model	*Completeness:* The degree to which a person can perceive that the elements of CINDERELLA are sufficient and necessary for the definition of a Feature Model. This variable represents a perceptual judgment of the completeness of CINDERELLA	Completeness

5.4 Execution

The following is a general description of how the tasks performed for the validation of CINDIRELLA were carried out.

Activity 1: In this first part, a socialization and contextualization of the experiment was made. Also, it was shown and explained how the execution of the activities to be developed during the whole experiment would be carried out.

Activity 2: A general presentation on CINDERELLA was made in order to explain its structure and guide its application with the support material used, as well as to explain and clarify some concepts used in its description.

Activity 3: In this activity, the participants of the experiment applied CINDERELLA using the guide for the definition of SPL's Characteristics Models. As a result, the participants filled in the artifacts defined by CINDERELLA in each of their tasks.

Activity 4: In this last activity, students answered a survey with questions about the ease of use, usefulness and completeness of the approach.

5.5 Qualitative Analysis and Results

The qualitative analysis was done by studying the survey responses, which were based on the Linkert scale, which is a form of measurement that allows us to evaluate attitudes and determine the degree of agreement with a set of statements.

The scale for measuring survey responses is as follows:

- Value 1 for option: strongly disagree.
- Value 2 for option: disagree.
- Value 3 for option: neither agree nor disagree.
- Value 4 for option: agree.
- Value 5 for option: strongly agree.

From the hypotheses initially defined in Table 4, the following null hypotheses were proposed:

- H.1.1, $\pi 1 <= 60\%$, where $\pi 1$ is the percentage of perception that evaluates the ease of understanding of CINDERELLA instructions and guidelines.
- H.1.2, $\pi 2 <= 60\%$, where $\pi 2$ is the perceptual percentage assessing the ease of understanding of CINDERELLA examples.
- H.2.1, $\pi 3 <= 60\%$, where $\pi 3$ is the percentage of perception that evaluates that CINDERELLA has the necessary information for its application.
- H.3.1, $\pi 4 <= 60\%$, where $\pi 4$ is the measure that evaluates the perception of the usefulness of CINDERELLA, to define an SPL Feature Model.
- H.3.2 $\pi 5 <= 60\%$, where $\pi 5$ is the measure assessing the perception that CINDERELLA is organized and consistent.
- H.4.1, $\pi 7 <= 60\%$, where $\pi 7$ is the percentage of perception that assesses the completeness of CINDERELLA elements.

The following alternative hypotheses were obtained from the null hypotheses:

- H.1.1, $\pi 1 > 60\%$, where $\pi 1$ is the percentage of perception that evaluates the ease of understanding of CINDERELLA instructions and guidelines.
- H.1.2, $\pi 2 > 60\%$, where $\pi 2$ is the percentage of perception that evaluates the ease of understanding of the CINDERELLA examples.
- H.2.1, $\pi 3 > 60\%$, where $\pi 3$ is the percentage of perception that evaluates that CINDERELLA has the necessary information for its application.
- H.3.1 $\pi 4 > 60\%$, where $\pi 4$ is the measure that evaluates the perception of the usefulness of CINDERELLA to define an SPL Feature Model.
- H.3.2. $\pi 5 > 60\%$, where $\pi 5$ is the measure assessing the perception that CINDERELLA is organized and consistent.
- H.4.1, $\pi 7 > = 60\%$, where $\pi 7$ is the percentage of perception that assesses the completeness of the CINDERELLA elements.

To validate the hypotheses, the results of the survey conducted by the participants of the experiment were used. The results are presented below in Tables 5, 6 and 7.

Table 5. Results on perceived ease of use

Ease of use							
Hypothesis	Questions	Strongly agree	Agree	Neither agree nor disagree	Strongly disagree	Disagree	Validation
H1.1	Question 1	16,7%	66,7%	8,3%		8,3%	**Rejected**
	Question 3	8,3%	41,7%	33,3%		16,7%	
H1.2	Question 2	25%	66,7%			8,3%	**Accepted**
	Question 5	8,3%	58,3%	33,3%			
H2.1	Question 4	16,7%	58,3%	16,7%		8,3%	**Accepted**
	Question 6	8,3%	58,3%	16,7%		16,7%	

For the ease of use variable, the percentage of students' perception in relation to the sum of the percentages "agree and strongly agree", according to questions 1, 2, 3, 4, 5 and 6 is 83.4%, 91.7%, 50%, 75%, 66.6% and 66.6% respectively, it was determined that:

- H1.1 can be rejected, thus it can be said that the CINDERELLA instructions and guidelines are not fully understood.
- H1.2 can be accepted, thus it can be said that the CINDERELLA examples are easy to understand.
- H2.1 can be accepted, thus it can be said that the supporting information of CINDERELLA is sufficient for its application

Table 6. Results on perceived utility

Utility							
Hypothesis	Questions	Strongly agree	Agree	Neither agree nor disagree	Strongly disagree	Disagree	Validation
H3.1	Question 1	25%	75%				**Accepted**
	Question 4	16,7%	83,3%				
H3.2	Question 2	8,3%	91,7%				**Accepted**
	Question 3	16,7%	75%	8,3%			

For the Utility variable, the percentage of students' perception in relation to the sum of the percentages "agree and strongly agree", according to questions 1, 2, 3 and 4 is 100%, 100%, 100%, 91.7% and 100% respectively, it was determined that:

- H3.1 can be accepted, therefore, it can be said that CINDERELLA tasks, are useful for the definition of SPL feature models.

- H3.2 can be accepted, thus, it can be said that CINDERELLA is an organized and coherent approach.

Table 7. Results on Perceived Completeness

Completeness

Hypothesis	Questions	Strongly agree	Agree	Neither agree nor disagree	Strongly disagree	Disagree	Validation
H4.1	Question 1		75%	25%			**Accepted**
	Question 2	8,3%	66,7%	25%			
	Question 3		66,7%	33,3%			
	Question 4	8,3%	66,7%	25%			
	Question 5		50%	50%			
	Question 6	8,3%	66,7%	16,7%	8,3%		
	Question 7	8,3%	66,7%	25%			
	Question 8	8,3%	33,3%	33,3%		16,7%	

For the Completeness variable, the percentage of students' perception, in relation to the sum of the percentages "agree and strongly agree", according to questions 1, 2, 3, 4, 5, 6, 7 and 8 is 75%, 75%, 66.7%, 75%, 50%, 75%, 75%, 75% and 41.6% respectively, it was determined that:

- H4.1 can be accepted, considering that 6 of the 8 questions obtained a value higher than 60%, therefore, it can be said that all elements (artifacts, tasks, examples) of CINDERELLA are complete.

According to the results of the experiment and the validation of each of the hypotheses, the following can be said: H1.1 was not accepted, however, it can be deduced that the students perceived that CINDERELLA has the necessary information to describe its guidelines and instructions, only that a complete understanding of its description was not achieved, the above taking into account that one of the questions assigned to this hypothesis reached 50%. H1.2 was accepted, so it can be said that the students were able to easily and clearly understand the examples of CINDERELLA and thus comply with the development of their tasks. H2.1 was accepted, so it can be inferred that the students perceived that CINDERELLA has sufficient information to guide its application; after the results of the previous hypotheses, it is concluded that CINDERELLA is an approach with ease of use, since, of the three hypotheses assigned to this variable, two were fulfilled, that is, they were accepted; however, it should be emphasized that the description of the instructions and guidelines should be improved to achieve an adequate understanding. Regarding H3.1 and H3.2, it can be deduced that the students perceived that the elements, tasks and artifacts of CINDERELLA are coherent and are elaborated and described in an organized manner, and that it is a useful approach for the definition of

SPL feature models. Finally, with H4.1 it can be affirmed that the participants concluded that the elements of CINDERELLA are sufficient and necessary for its development, i.e. it is an approach that is perceived as complete.

6 Conclusions

This paper shows CINDERELLA as a collaborative approach for building feature models in SPL's, defines a workflow based on detailed defined collaborative tasks. CINDERELLA uses the notation of an extension of the HAMSTERS notation, which consists of providing elements for describing collaborative tasks that allow to graphically define relationships and represent information between tasks and their participants. The tasks consist of a description, collaborative pattern, ThinkLets, input/output artifacts, steps and rules in order to encourage the diverse and productive participation of each participant.

According to the results of the experiment it can be concluded that CINDERELLA is an approach that is easy to use, due to the fact that, of the three hypotheses of this variable, two were fulfilled; however, it should be emphasized that the description of the instructions and guidelines should be improved in order to achieve a better understanding of its definition. Regarding usefulness, it can be concluded that the elements that make up CINDERELLA are coherent and are described in an organized manner, in such a way that it is perceived as a useful approach for the definition of feature models in SPL's. Finally, with respect to completeness it can be said that the elements that define CINDERELLA are sufficient and necessary, i.e. the approach is perceived as complete.

Finally, it can be concluded that CINDIRELLA contributes to the definition of feature models in SPL's through collaborative work, this is reflected in the fact that the participants were able to work together, sharing knowledge and experiences, since they were able to provide information, classify it and evaluate it through collaborative tasks, as well as collaborate in the presentation and proposal of features and feature models. CINDERELLA being a collaboratively designed approach can increase the possibility of obtaining more complete and useful feature models.

References

1. Garcia Peñalvo F.: Capítulo 7. Ingeniería del software de ciencia de la computación e ingeniería artificial en proyecto docente e investigador. catedrático de universidad. perfil docente: ingeniería del software y gobierno de tecnologías de la información. perfil investigador: tecnologías del aprendizaje. Área de ciencia de la computación e inteligencia artificial, pp. 277–388. Salamanca, España (2018)
2. Northrop, L.M., et al.: A framework for software product line practice 5.0. Software Engineering Institute (2012)
3. Apel S., Batory D., Kästner C., Saake G.: Feature-Oriented Software Product Line. Springer, New York (2013). https://doi.org/10.1007/978-3-642-37521-7
4. Lee, K., Kang, K.C., Lee, J.: Concepts and guidelines of feature modeling for product line software engineering. In: Gacek, C. (ed.) ICSR 2002. LNCS, vol. 2319, pp. 62–77. Springer, Heidelberg (2002). https://doi.org/10.1007/3-540-46020-9_5

5. Dillenbourg, P., Baker, M., Blaye, A., O'Malley, C.: The evolution of research on collaborative learning. In: Spada, E., Reiman, P. (eds.) Learning in humans and machine: Towards an interdisciplinary learning science, pp. 189–211. Elsevier, Oxford (1996). https://doi.org/10.1007/978-1-4020-9827-7_1

6. Roschelle, J., Teasley, S.D.: The construction of shared knowledge in collaborative problem solving. In: Computer Supported Collaborative Learning, pp. 69–97. Springer, Heidelberg (1995). https://doi.org/10.1007/978-3-642-85098-1_5

7. Kozar, O.: Towards better group work: seeing the difference between cooperation and collaboration. Engl. Teach. Forum **48**(2), 16–23 (2010)

8. Briggs, R., Kolfschoten, G., Vreede, G.-J.D.: Defiining key concepts for collaboration engineering. In: AMCIS 2006 Proceedings, vol. 17, pp. 121–128 (2006)

9. De Vreede, G., Briggs, R., Massey, A.: Collaboration engineering: foundations and opportunities: editorial to the special issue on the journal of the association of information systems. J. Assoc. Inf. Syst. **10**, 121–137 (2009). https://doi.org/10.17705/1jais.00191

10. Briggs, R., de Vreede, G., Nunamaker, J., Tobey, D.: ThinkLets: achieving predictable, repeatable patterns of groupinteraction with group support systems (GSS). In: Proceedings of the 34th Hawaii International Conference on System Sciences. IEEE Xplore (2001). https://doi.org/10.1109/HICSS.2001.926238

11. de Vreede, G., Kolfschoten, G., Briggs, R.: ThinkLets: a collaboration engineering pattern language. Int. J. Comput. Appl. Technol. **25**(2/3), 140–154 (2006). https://doi.org/10.1504/IJCAT.2006.009064

12. Gray, D., Brown, S., Macanufo, J.: Gamestorming: A playbook for innovators, rulebreakers, and changemakers, 0'REILLY (2010)

13. Kan, K.C., Cohen, S., Hess, J., Peterson, A.: Feature oriented domain analisys (FODA). Technical Report. Software Engineering Institute. Pittsburgh, Pennsylvania (1990)

14. Griss, M., Favaro, J., d'Alessandro, M.: Integrating feature modeling with the RSEB. In: Proceedings. Fifth International Conference on Software Reuse, pp. 76–85. IEEE (1998). https://doi.org/10.1109/ICSR.1998.685732

15. Chen, K., Zhang, W., Zhao, H., Mei, H.: An approach to constructing feature models based on requirements clustering. In: 13th IEEE International Conference on Requirements Engineering. IEEE (2005). https://doi.org/10.1109/RE.2005.9

16. Bécan G., Behjati R., Gotlieb A., Acher M.: Synthesis of attributed feature models from product descriptions: foundations. In: Proceedings of the 19th International Conference on Software Product Line – SPLC 2015, pp.1–10 (2015). https://doi.org/10.1145/2791060.2791068

17. Galindo, J., Benavides, D., Trinidad, P., Gutiérrez, A., Ruiz, A.: Automated analysis of featuremodels: quo vadis? Computing **101**, 387–433 (2018). https://doi.org/10.1007/s00607-018-0646-1

18. Farahani, D., Habibi, J.: Feature model configuration based on two-layer modeling in Software Product Lines. Int. J. Electr. Comput. Eng. (IJECE) **9**(4), 2648–2658 (2019). https://doi.org/10.11591/ijece.v9i4.pp2648-2658

19. Mendonca, M., Bartolomei, T., Cowan, D.: Decision-making coordination in collaborative product configuration. In: Proceedings of the 2008 ACM Symposium on Applied Computing - SAC 2008, pp. 108–113 (2008). https://doi.org/10.1145/1363686.1363715

20. Noor, M., Grünbacher, P., Briggs, R.: A collaborative approach for product line scoping: a case study in collaboration engineering. In: IASTED International Multi-Conference Software Engineering, pp. 216–223 (2007)

21. Camacho, M., Álvarez, F., Collazos, C.: Identifying collaborative aspects during software product lines scoping. In: Proceedings of 23rd International Systems and Software Product Line Conference SPLC 2019, vol. B, pp.98–105 (2019). https://doi.org/10.1145/3307630.3342420

22. Camacho, M., Álvarez, F., Collazos, C., Leger, P., Hurtado, J., Bermúdez, J.: A collaborative method for scoping software product lines: a case study in a small software company. Appl. Sci. **11**(15), 6820 (2021). https://doi.org/10.3390/app11156820

23. Noor, M., Rabiser, R., Grünbacher, P.: Agile product line planning: a collaborative approach and a case study. J. Syst. Softw. **81**(6), 868–882 (2008). https://doi.org/10.1016/j.jss.2007.10.028

24. Weiss, D., Li, D., Workshop on collaborative software product line engineering. In. 25th IEEE Conference on Software Engineering Education and Training, pp. 77–78 (2012). https://doi.org/10.1109/CSEET.2012.28

25. Pino, F., Piattini, M., Horta, G.: Managing and developing distributed research projects in software engineering by means of action engineering by means of action-research. Revista Facultad de Ingeniería Universidad de Antioquia **68**, 61–74 (2013). https://doi.org/10.17533/udea.redin.17161

26. Solano, A., Granollers, T., Collazos, C.: Modelado de Procesos Colaborativos Extendiendo Elementos de la Notación HAMSTERS. Revista Colombiana de Computación **16**(2), 144–161 (2016). https://doi.org/10.29375/25392115.2555

Automation of Granollers Heuristic Evaluation Method Using a Developed Support System: A Case Study

Adrian Lecaros$^{(\boxtimes)}$ ⓘ, Arturo Moquillaza ⓘ, Fiorella Falconi ⓘ, Joel Aguirre ⓘ, Carlos Ramos ⓘ, and Freddy Paz ⓘ

Pontificia Universidad Católica del Perú, Av. Universitaria 1801, San Miguel, Lima 32, Lima, Peru
{adrian.lecaros,ffalconit,aguirre.joel, carlos.ramosp}@pucp.edu.pe, {amoquillaza,fpaz}@pucp.pe

Abstract. Heuristic evaluation is one of the most popular usability methods since a group of usability evaluation experts can find approximately 75% of all usability problems in the reviewed interfaces. Due to its benefits, there are various proposals on how to carry out a heuristic evaluation. One of them is the proposal by Granollers. Although this evaluation method is practical, direct, and valuable to obtain a quantitative result of the percentage of usability this continues to be carried out manually by using a template. As part of this research, it was proposed to develop a system that supports the heuristic evaluation method of T. Granollers. Likewise, to measure the perception of the usability evaluators who used this new system in comparison with the template, it was proposed to carry out a case study in which two groups of evaluators could perform a heuristic evaluation using the method of Granollers to a transactional e-commerce website. Team A used the template to carry out the evaluation, while Team B used the proposed support system. The results allowed us to demonstrate that the team that used the support tool for the heuristic evaluation method of Granollers had a better perception of the evaluated TAM criteria. For this reason, the system is easy to use, it is perceived as useful for conducting evaluations, and evaluators have a great interest in using it in their heuristic evaluations, which highlights the importance of promoting the use of heuristic evaluation methods through automated tools available to usability experts.

Keywords: Human-computer Interaction · Usability · Heuristic Evaluation · Software Engineering · TAM · Case Study

1 Introduction

Due to the importance of usability, a fundamental aspect of users' use, acceptance, and interaction with software products [1], some methods have been proposed to ensure that new software projects have the essential usability characteristics [2]. One of these methods is the heuristic evaluation, which is one of the most popular since it is proposed that a group of usability evaluation experts (between three and five) can find approximately 75% of all usability problems in the reviewed interfaces [3].

© The Author(s), under exclusive license to Springer Nature Switzerland AG 2024
P. H. Ruiz et al. (Eds.): HCI-COLLAB 2023, CCIS 1877, pp. 93–108, 2024.
https://doi.org/10.1007/978-3-031-57982-0_8

For this reason, due to its benefits, there are various proposals for a heuristic evaluation. One of them is the proposal by T. Granollers, which defines a single list of heuristics based on the ten heuristic principles proposed by J. Nielsen, which allows the evaluation of any type of software [4].

This methodology is composed through the evaluation of fifteen (15) heuristic principles, where evaluation questions are included for each one. In addition, it is proposed to use a rating scale where the evaluator could define if the question associated with the heuristic principle is met, if it is not met, if it is partially met, or if it does not apply to the reviewed interfaces. Once the questions have been qualified, the evaluation method provides a usability percentage considering the sum of the score obtained by answering all the questions divided by the number of questions that apply for the usability inspection.

Although this evaluation method is practical, direct, and valuable to obtain a quantitative result of the percentage of usability of the evaluated interfaces, the process continues to be carried out manually by using a template in MS Excel format. For this reason, as part of this research, it was proposed to develop a system that allows the support of the heuristic evaluation method of T. Granollers, where the usability results obtained by all the evaluators involved can be compiled to show a general usability report.

Likewise, to measure the perception of the usability evaluators who used this new system in comparison with the traditional template, it was proposed, as the main reason for this research, to carry out a case study in which two groups of three evaluators each could perform a heuristic evaluation using the method of T. Granollers to a transactional e-commerce website called "Juntoz". The difference between the two teams is that the first, Team A, used the template to carry out the evaluation, while the second one, Team B, used the proposed support system.

Then, when both teams carried out the evaluation, they answered a questionnaire that was made as a part of this research. This allowed the comparison of the perception that the evaluators had where TAM criteria proposed and validated by F. Davis were applied [5]. The results allowed us to demonstrate that the team that used the support tool for the heuristic evaluation method of T. Granollers, Team B, had a better perception of the three evaluated criteria.

For this reason, the system is considered to be easy to use, it is perceived as helpful in conducting evaluations, and evaluators have a great interest in using it in their heuristic evaluations, which highlights the importance of promoting the use of heuristic evaluation methods through automated tools available to usability experts.

This paper is structured as follows: Sect. 2, describes the main concepts belonging to the Human-Computer Interaction area used in the study. In Sect. 3, we present the key points of developing the support system to automate T. Granoller's heuristic evaluation method. In Sect. 4, we present the construction of the case study that allowed us to compare the execution of the heuristic evaluation using the traditional template versus the developed support system. In Sect. 5, we present the execution of the case study and its results for the usability percentage of the website and the perception of the tools used by the evaluators with TAM criteria. Finally, in Sect. 6, we present the conclusions of the research and the future works to be done.

2 Background

In this section, we present the main concepts related to this work.

2.1 Usability

As defined by ISO 9241-210-2019 [6], Usability refers to the degree to which a specified group of users can effectively, efficiently, and satisfactorily accomplish specific goals when using a system, product, or service within a given context of use.

Furthermore, Jacob Nielsen [3] outlines five essential attributes that a system's user interface should possess for optimal usability. These attributes include:

- Learnability: The system should be easy to grasp, allowing users to quickly acquire the necessary knowledge and skills to perform tasks efficiently.
- Efficiency: The system should facilitate efficient usage, enabling users to achieve a high level of productivity during their interactions with it.
- Memorability: The system should be easily remembered, ensuring that users, even after a period of not using it, can return to it without the need to relearn its operation.
- Errors: The system should minimize errors, aiming for a low error rate to help users avoid mistakes and swiftly recover from any errors that do occur. Critical or catastrophic errors must be prevented.
- Satisfaction: The system should provide a pleasurable user experience, ensuring users feel subjectively satisfied while using it.

2.2 Heuristic Evaluation

As stated by Andreas Holzinger [2], Heuristic Evaluation (HE) is a usability inspection method and is widely used as an informal approach. This method requires the expertise of usability professionals who can assess whether the elements of dialogue or other interactive software components adhere to established usability principles.

According to Jacob Nielsen [3], heuristic evaluation enables examining both positive and negative aspects of a system's interface. This evaluation can be conducted based on individual opinions or, ideally, by utilizing well-defined guidelines. Nielsen emphasizes that the main objective of this evaluation is to identify usability issues in the interface design. A group of evaluators assesses and judges the interface based on usability principles known as heuristics.

It is worth noting that a single evaluator can only identify approximately 35% of the usability problems present in an interface. However, different evaluators tend to encounter diverse types of problems. To achieve the best cost-benefit ratio, Nielsen recommends involving 3 to 5 evaluators in the process. These evaluations are conducted individually, and their results are then compared to perform an overall usability analysis.

2.3 Granollers Heuristic Evaluation Method

According to Toni Granollers [4], the traditional way of performing a heuristic evaluation needs to be improved, and for that reason, it also needs to be updated. For this reason, he proposes a new list of fifteen heuristic evaluation principles based on the revision, comparison, and integration of Jacob Nielsen's ten general principles for interaction design and Tognazzini's first principles of interaction design. Also, he proposes a set of precise questions for each principle (60 questions in total) as a result of proposing "something more specific" for the evaluators to perform UI evaluations effectively. These questions need to be answered by each evaluator by using an easy 4-option rating scale ("Yes", "Neither", "No", "Not applicable") for each of the questions to determine the usability of the evaluated interfaces. Finally, he proposes a method to score the rating results of each question ("Yes" – 1 point, "Neither" – 0.5 points, "No" – 0 points, "Not applicable" – Not considered in the total score) to obtain a quantitative result called usability percentage, which presents a quantifiable way to determine the usability of the user interface.

2.4 TAM Criteria

According to Fred Davis [5], the measurement scales to predict the user's acceptance of the proposal of new systems were scarce at the time. For this reason, the practices used to conduct an evaluation were very subjective and needed a valid basis. In addition, their relationship with the use of the system was unknown. For this reason, the author developed and validated criteria to be able to measure the perceived usefulness and ease of use of the systems where, through the definition of those variables, he presented a list of elements for each criterion that could be rated through quantifiable scales. These results provided a quantitative study of the perceived usefulness and ease of use of the participants who used the systems, thus being able to make comparisons between results.

3 Developing a Software Product that Supports and Automates the Heuristic Evaluation Method Proposed by T. Granollers

As part of a previous research project [7], a process was proposed that can support the execution of Heuristic Evaluation and Tree Testing methods through an integrated process from the UX perspective that contemplated from the planning phase of the evaluation project through the selection of the type of evaluation to be carried out, as well as the planning, execution, and analysis of the selected evaluation. Within this investigation, the unified modeling of both processes was considered, which was validated by usability experts through the presentation of the BPMN diagrams models of the proposed process. Figure 1 shows the proposal of the formal process for the User Experience evaluation.

Then, two methods to perform the heuristic evaluation were considered within the usability evaluations. The first, through the formal process proposed by Freddy Paz [8], which was selected as the most complete heuristic evaluation process in previous research [9], and the second, through the evaluation method proposed by Toni Granollers [4]. Figure 2 shows the phases of (1) planning, (2) execution, and (3) analysis to be able to carry out these evaluations.

Finally, after having raised what the user experience evaluation support process would be like, a system was developed that allowed the selected evaluations to be carried out through a system.

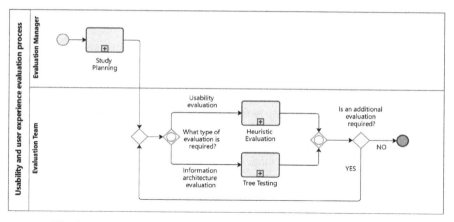

Fig. 1. Formal process for User Experience evaluation (obtained from [7])

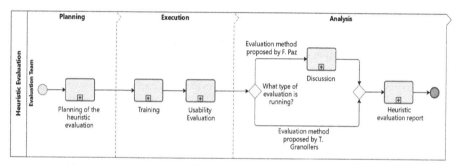

Fig. 2. Heuristic evaluation method within the process (obtained from [7])

As a scope of this study, we focused on the automation of the evaluation method of T. Granollers by the development of a web system module that allowed the completion of every step that is necessary to perform the evaluation, where the user interested in developing the heuristic evaluation (evaluation manager) first completed the general information of the project to be carried out, such as the objective of the evaluation, the website to be evaluated, the team that will perform the evaluation, as well as the heuristics, sub-heuristics and rating scale to be used. Then, the evaluation manager could send the evaluation to the selected team so that they can carry out the evaluation and thus obtain the percentage of usability of the evaluated interfaces by the evaluator, and in total, through customizable automated reports.

However, after having completed the development of the system, it was necessary to validate whether the proposed system effectively contributed to a better perception in the execution of the heuristic evaluation of T. Granollers compared to the traditional template in MS Excel that was used to be able to carry it out. For this reason, a case study was developed for this research that allowed us to make this comparison and will be explained in detail in the next section.

4 Elaboration of the Case Study

Juntoz.com is an e-commerce website where various products from areas such as technology, sports, clothing, and supermarkets, among others, are distributed under the shop-in-shop format, where stores make available to customers the catalog of products that can be purchased on the page.

Said page was used as a case study for the execution of a heuristic evaluation using the heuristic evaluation method of T. Granollers, which consists of carrying out the evaluation using a questionnaire of questions divided by the heuristics proposed by the author to obtain the usability percentage of the website. Table 1 shows the questions for each heuristic [4].

In addition, to qualify the problems, a Likert 3 scale was used, in which the answers could be the following: "Yes" – 1 point, "Neither" – 0.5 points, "No" – 0 points, "Not applicable" – Not considered in the total score.

For the design of the comparative case study, there were two scenarios: (1) a group that performs the heuristic evaluation using the heuristic evaluation method of T. Granollers using a template in MS Excel format, and (2) another group that performs the evaluation using the developed web application. The evaluators that made up the teams are usability experts since they already have considerable experience performing heuristic usability evaluations of software products.

To carry out the case study, two teams of 3 evaluators each were convened to carry out the heuristic evaluation of the website using the traditional evaluation template and the developed system. The first team, team A, was composed of 3 testers, who were usability experts, to use the template in MS Excel format, while team B, also three usability expert testers, used the support system.

Then, the following steps were followed for the execution of the case study:

- Each member of both teams was trained in the heuristic evaluation method by T. Granollers to show them the questionnaire they had to use to conduct the evaluation.
- Both teams carried out the evaluation: Team A used the template, and Team B used the proposed evaluation support system by T. Granollers.
- Each team member completed a questionnaire that allowed knowing the perception of the execution of the heuristic evaluation.
- A comparative analysis of the perception of both teams was carried out.

Figure 3 shows the case study execution flow:

After carrying out the heuristic evaluation following the proposed flow, a comparison was made between the perception of the execution of the evaluation. The TAM criteria, validated by F. Davis, were used and adapted for this. For the present case study, 3 of these criteria have been selected: (1) ease of use, (2) perceived usefulness, and (3) intent of use. Figure 4 shows the relationship between each of these criteria.

Each criterion was measured based on a scale from 1 to 5: 1 - Highly negative perception, 2 - Negative perception, 3 - Neutral perception, 4 - Positive perception, and 5 - Highly positive perception.

Table 2 shows the questions asked for each of these criteria, adapted to the present case study.

Table 1. T. Granoller's heuristics and questions

Code	Heuristic	Questions
HG01	Visibility and system state	• Does the application include a visible title page, section, or site? • Does the user always know where it is located? • Does the user always know what the system or application is doing? • Are the links clearly defined? • Can all actions be visualized directly? (No other actions are required)
HG02	Connection between the system and the real world, metaphor usage and human objects	• Does information appear in a logical order for the user? • Does the design of the icons correspond to everyday objects? • Does every icon do the action that you expect? • Does the system use phrases and concepts familiar to the user?
HG03	User control and freedom	• Is there a link to come back to the initial state or homepage? • Are the functions "undo" and "re-do" implemented? • Is it easy to come back to an earlier state of the application? • Do link labels have the same names as their destinations? • Do the same actions always have the same results? • Do the icons have the same meaning everywhere? • Is the information displayed consistently on every page? • Are the colors of the links standard? If not, are they suitable for its use? • Do navigation elements follow the standards? (Buttons, check box,...)

(*continued*)

Table 1. (*continued*)

Code	Heuristic	Questions
HG04	Consistency and standards	• Do link labels have the same names as their destinations? • Do the same actions always have the same results? • Do the icons have the same meaning everywhere? • Is the information displayed consistently on every page? • Are the colors of the links standard? If not, are they suitable for its use? • Do navigation elements follow the standards? (Buttons, check box,…)
HG05	Recognition rather than memory, learning and anticipation	• Is it easy to use the system for the first time? • Is it easy to locate information that has already been searched for before? • Can you use the system at all times without remembering previous screens? • Is all content needed for navigation or tasks found in the "current screen"? • Is the information organized according to logic familiar to the end user?
HG06	Flexibility and efficiency of use	• Are there keyboard shortcuts for common actions? • If there are, is it clear how to use them? • Is it possible to easily perform an action done earlier? • Does the design adapt to the changes of screen resolution? • Is the use of accelerators visible to the normal user? • Does it always keep the user busy? (Without unnecessary delays)
HG07	Help users recognize, diagnose, and recover from errors	• Does it display a message before taking irreversible actions? • Are errors shown in real time? • Is the error message that appears easily interpretable? • Is some code also used to reference the error?

(continued)

Table 1. (*continued*)

Code	Heuristic	Questions
HG08	Preventing errors	• Does a confirmation message appear before taking the action? • Is it clear what information needs to be entered in each box on a form? • Does the search engine tolerate typos and spelling errors?
HG09	Aesthetic and minimalist design	• Is used a design without redundancy of information? • Is the information short, concise and accurate? • Is each item of information different from the rest and not confused? • Is the text well organized, with short sentences and quick to interpret?
HG10	Help and documentation	• Is there the "help" option? • If so, is it visible and easy to access? • Is the help section aimed at solving problems? • Is there a section of frequently asked questions (FAQ)? • Is the help documentation clear, with examples?
HG11	Save the state and protect the work	• Can users continue from a previous state (where they had previously been or from another device)? • Is "Autosave" implemented? • Does the system have a good response to external failures? (Power cut, internet not working,…)
HG12	Color and readability	• Do the fonts have an adequate size? • Do the fonts use colors with sufficient contrast with the background? • Do background images or patterns allow the content to be read? • Does it consider people with reduced vision?
HG13	Autonomy	• Does it keep the user informed of system status? • Moreover, is the system status visible and updated? • Can the user take their own decisions? (Personalization)

(*continued*)

Table 1. (*continued*)

Code	Heuristic	Questions
HG14	Defaults	• Does the system or device give the option to return to factory settings? • If so, does it clearly indicate the consequences of the action? • Is the term "Default" used?
HG15	Latency reduction	• Is the execution of heavy work transparent to the user? • While running heavy tasks, is remaining time or some animation shown?

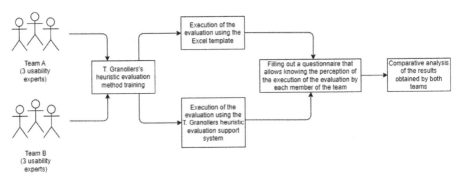

Fig. 3. Case study execution flow

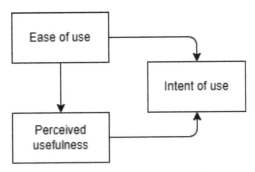

Fig. 4. Relationship between TAM criteria

Finally, to make the comparison between the results obtained by each evaluator, a Shapiro-Wilk test was carried out to determine if the samples belonged to a normal population, whose hypotheses will be the following:

- H0: The evaluated data belong to a normal population.
- H1: The data evaluated does not belong to a normal population.

Table 2. TAM criteria questionnaire

Ease of use
• Using the T. Granollers heuristic evaluation method support tool in my heuristic inspections would allow me to complete the evaluations more quickly
• Using the tool to support the heuristic evaluation method of T. Granollers would improve my performance in heuristic inspections
• Using the tool to support the heuristic evaluation method of T. Granollers in my heuristic inspections would increase my productivity
• Using the tool to support the heuristic evaluation method of T. Granollers would improve the effectiveness of my heuristic inspections
• I would find T. Granollers' heuristic evaluation method support tool useful in my heuristic inspections
Perceived usefulness
• Learning to use the tool to support the heuristic evaluation method of T. Granollers would be easy for me
• I would find it easy to make the T. Granollers heuristic evaluation method support tool does what I want it to do
• My interaction with the T. Granollers heuristic evaluation method support tool could be clear and understandable
• I would consider that the support tool for the heuristic evaluation method of T. Granollers is flexible to interact with
• It would be easy for me to become an expert in using T. Granollers' heuristic evaluation method support tool
• I would consider that the support tool for the heuristic evaluation method of T. Granollers is easy to use
Intent of use
• I would intend to use the tool to support the heuristic evaluation method of T. Granollers in my heuristic inspections
• Promote the use of the tool to support the heuristic evaluation method of T. Granollers to carry out heuristic inspections
• Using the tool to support the heuristic evaluation method of T. Granollers would increase interest in performing heuristic inspections
• I would love to use T. Granollers' heuristic evaluation method support tool in my heuristic inspections
• I would use the tool to support the heuristic evaluation method of T. Granollers as an alternative to carry out heuristic inspections

Depending on the results for each criterion, at a significance level of 0.05, the T-Student or U Mann-Whitney test was used to determine which tool is the best.

5 Execution of the Case Study and Its Results

To carry out the case study, six usability experts were contacted, who were trained in how to carry out the heuristic evaluation of T. Granollers and were told which would be the website to be evaluated (Juntoz.com) and what would be the tool they were going to use to carry out the evaluation. These evaluators were divided into groups of three: the first, Team A, carried out the evaluation using the MS Excel template, while the second, Team B, carried out the evaluation using the proposed support system.

The results of the usability percentage obtained by team A were the following:

- The three heuristics with the best score were: (1) "User control and freedom" with 3 out of 3 points, (2) "Help and documentation" with 4 out of 5 points, and (3) "Flexibility and efficiency of use" with 2.83 out of 3.67 points.
- The three heuristics with the worst score were: (1) "Help users to recognize, diagnose, and recover from errors" with 1 out of 3 points, (2) "Preventing errors" with 1.33 out of 2.67 points, and (3) "Consistency and standards" with 3.5 out of 6 points.
- The usability percentage obtained was 68.09%, which can be considered a good result for the website's usability. Figure 5 shows the results obtained by Team A for the usability percentage from the report generated by the MS Excel template.

RESULTADOS / RESULTS	
	Valores/Values
1- Visibilidad y estado del sistema / Visibility and system state	3.33
2 - Connexión entre el sistema y el mundo real, uso de metáforas y objetos humanos / Connection between the system and the real world, metaphor usage and human objects	3.00
3 - Control y libertad del usuario / User control and freedom	3.00
4 - Consistencia y estándares / Consistency and standards	3.50
5 - Reconocimiento en lugar de memoria, aprendizaje y anticipación / Recognition rather than memory, learning and anticipation	3.50
6 - Flexibilidad y eficiéncia de uso / Flexibility and efficiency of use	2.83
7 - Ayuda a los usuarios a reconocer, diagnosticar y rehacer-se de los errors / Help users recognize, diagnose and recover from errors	1.00
8 - Prevención de errores / Preventing errors	1.33
9 - Diseño estético y minimalista / Aesthetic and minimalist design	2.17
10 - Ayuda y documentación / Help and documentation	4.00
11 - Guardar el estado y proteger el trabajo / Save the state and protect the work	1.17
12 - Color y legibilidad / Color and readability	2.50
13 - Autonomía / Autonomy	2.00
14 - Valores per defecto / Defaults	0.00
15 - Reducción de la latencia / Latency reduction	1.17
0	34.50
% de preguntas contestadas	100.0%
Número de preguntas NO contestadas (deben contestarse TODAS)	0
Número de preguntas contestadas que computan (sin las No aplica)	51
Porcentaje de usabilidad *"Usability" percentage*	**68.09%**

Fig. 5. Usability percentage results – Team A

In the same way, the results of the usability percentage obtained by Team B were the following:

- The three heuristics with the best score were: (1) "Consistency and standards" with 5.5 out of 6 points, (2) "Connection between the system and the real world, metaphor usage, and human objects" with 3.5 out of 4 points and a tie between (3) "Visibility and system state" and (4) "Recognition rather than memory, learning and anticipation" with 4.33 out of 5 points.
- The three heuristics with the worst score were: (1) "Flexibility and efficiency of use" with 2 out of 5.33 points, (2) "Defaults" with 0.67 out of 1.67 points, and (3) "Help users recognize, diagnose and recover from errors" with 1.67 of 4 points.
- The usability percentage obtained was 59.82%, which can be considered a mixed result for the website's usability. Figure 6 shows the results obtained by Team B for the usability percentage from the report automatically generated by the support system.

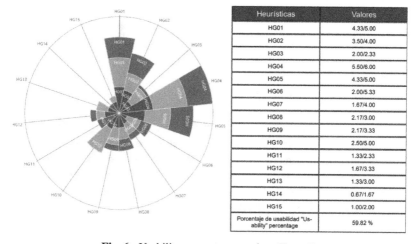

Heurísticas	Valores
HG01	4.33/5.00
HG02	3.50/4.00
HG03	2.00/2.33
HG04	5.50/6.00
HG05	4.33/5.00
HG06	2.00/5.33
HG07	1.67/4.00
HG08	2.17/3.00
HG09	2.17/3.33
HG10	2.50/5.00
HG11	1.33/2.33
HG12	1.67/3.33
HG13	1.33/3.00
HG14	0.67/1.67
HG15	1.00/2.00
Porcentaje de usabilidad "Usability" percentage	59.82 %

Fig. 6. Usability percentage results – Team B

After carrying out the evaluation, each evaluator was asked to complete a questionnaire that was prepared considering the TAM criteria defined in the case study approach (ease of use, perceived usefulness, and intent of use). After that, the results were quantified to obtain the average of each criterion of Group A and Group B. To compare the results and determine if it was a normal population, the Shapiro-Wilk test was used. Table 3 shows the results obtained from the test.

Since the p-value of each criterion was greater than 0.05, then it could be concluded that the sample belonged to a normal distribution, so the T-Student test could be used to determine if the results were statistically significant. Table 4 shows the test results.

After performing the T-Student test, it was obtained that although the results of Team B were superior to those obtained by Team A, they were not statistically significant since every p-value was above 0.05, so it will be necessary to carry out an additional study as a

Table 3. Shapiro-Wilk test results

Team	Criterion	Mean	Standard deviation	Significance level	p-value
Team A	Ease of use	4.40	0.60	0.05	**1.00**
	Perceived usefulness	4.22	0.54	0.05	**0.53**
	Intent of use	4.20	0.87	0.05	**0.38**
Team B	Ease of use	**4.60**	0.53	0.05	**0.64**
	Perceived usefulness	**4.44**	0.96	0.05	**0.13**
	Intent of use	**4.60**	0.69	0.05	**0.13**

Table 4. T-Student test results

Criterion	Team	Mean	Standard deviation	Significance level	p-value
Ease of use	Team A	4.44	0.60	0.05	0.74
	Team B	**4.60**	0.53	0.05	0.74
Perceived usefulness	Team A	4.22	0.54	0.05	0.75
	Team B	**4.44**	0.96	0.05	0.75
Intent of use	Team A	4.20	0.87	0.05	0.57
	Team B	**4.60**	0.69	0.05	0.57

future work where a more significant number of teams of evaluators need to be involved in validating if indeed the general perception of the evaluators when using the system is better. These results give us the basis for concluding that perception will most likely be better since with the tested sample we obtained a better perception result in each of the criteria by the team that used the system.

6 Conclusions and Future Works

The results obtained in this research were (1) a quantitative analysis of the usability percentage of the Juntoz.com website and (2) the perception that usability evaluators had when carrying out the heuristic evaluation of the website using the method of T. Granollers divided into a group that used the traditional template in MS Excel format (Team A) and another that used a heuristic evaluation support system as a result of a previous investigation (Team B).

Regarding the usability percentage, a usability percentage of 68.09% was obtained for the evaluation of Team A. In comparison, the usability percentage of Team B was 59.82%, which shows that the usability of the website is between regular and good, being the heuristic "Help users recognize, diagnose and recover from errors" the one that obtained the worst result average, so it should be the principle that should be given priority to improve the usability of the site.

Regarding the perception obtained, it was noted that for the three TAM criteria (ease of use, perceived usefulness, and intent of use), a better result was obtained for Team B, which was the team that used the proposed support system, which allows us to conclude that the perception of the system has been better than the traditional template, which demonstrates a significant contribution to the execution of usability tests using support systems. Although the results were not statistically significant after performing the T-Student test, the fact that the system has had a better perception gives us the basis for concluding that with a greater number of teams of evaluators to apply the case study, we could obtain a similar perceptual result that reassures that evaluators will prefer to use a support system to perform the heuristic evaluation method rather than performing it through a template.

In future work, the possibility of carrying out the case study with a more significant number of teams of evaluators with vast experience in HCI is considered in order to perform new numerical experimentation of the perception results to confirm that the results obtained are statistically significant and allow us to ensure the positive impact of automating usability tests through support systems. In the same way, it could be considered to include new versions of the Toni Granollers method as part of future evaluations and new versions of TAM, such as TAM 2, for the comparative analysis of a future case study.

Acknowledgments. This work is part of the research project "Virtualización del proceso de evaluación de experiencia de usuario de productos de software para escenarios de no presencialidad" (virtualization of the user experience evaluation process of software products for non-presential scenarios), developed by HCI-DUXAIT research group. HCI-DUXAIT is a research group that belongs to the PUCP (Pontificia Universidad Católica del Perú).

This work was funded by the Dirección de Fomento a la Investigación at the PUCP through grant 2021-C-0023.

References

1. Huang, Z.: Usability of tourism websites: a case study of heuristic evaluation. New Rev. Hypermedia Multimed. **26**, 55–91 (2020). https://doi.org/10.1080/13614568.2020.1771436
2. Holzinger, A.: Usability engineering methods for software developers. Commun. ACM. ACM **48**, 71–74 (2005). https://doi.org/10.1145/1039539.1039541
3. Nielsen, J.: Usability inspection methods. In: Conference Companion on Human Factors in Computing Systems, pp. 413–414 (1994)
4. Granollers, T.: Usability evaluation with heuristics, beyond Nielsen's list. In: ACHI 2018 Eleventh International Conference on Advanced Computing Interactions, pp. 60–65 (2018)
5. Davis, F.D.: Perceived usefulness, perceived ease of use, and user acceptance of information technology. MIS Q. Manag. Inf. Syst. **13**, 319–339 (1989). https://doi.org/10.2307/249008
6. International Organization for Standardization: ISO 9241-210-2019 (2019)
7. Paz, F., Lecaros, A., Falconi, F., Tapia, A., Aguirre, J., Moquillaza, A.: A process to support heuristic evaluation and tree testing from a UX integrated perspective. In: Latifi, S. (ed.) ITNG 2023, pp. 369–377. Springer, Cham (2023). https://doi.org/10.1007/978-3-031-28332-1_42
8. Paz, F., Paz, F.A., Pow-Sang, J.A., Collazos, C.: A formal protocol to conduct usability heuristic evaluations in the context of the software development process. Int. J. Eng. Technol. **7**, 10–19 (2018). https://doi.org/10.14419/ijet.v7i2.28.12874

9. Lecaros, A., Moquillaza, A., Falconi, F., Aguirre, J., Tapia, A., Paz, F.: Selection and modeling of a formal heuristic evaluation process through comparative analysis. In: Soares, M.M., Rosenzweig, E., Marcus, A. (eds.) Design, User Experience, and Usability: UX Research, Design, and Assessment, pp. 28–46. Springer, Cham (2022). https://doi.org/10.1007/978-3-031-05897-4_3

Computational Playful Strategy to Measure the Level of Technological Acceptance by Older Adults

Manuel Bolaños[1]([✉]) [iD], Carlos Guzmán[1] [iD], César A. Collazos[2] [iD],
and Francisco L. Gutiérrez[3] [iD]

[1] University of Nariño, San Juan de Pasto, Colombia
mbolanos@udenar.edu.co
[2] University of Cauca, Popayán, Colombia
ccollazo@unicauca.edu.co
[3] University of Granada, Granada, Spain
fgutirr@ugr.es

Abstract. This article presents the results of a study developed to find out the intention of a group of older adults to use an intelligent virtual assistant, and to evaluate the ease of use of a memory game implemented in this type of device. The collection of information was conducted through direct observation and the application of a structured survey to the older adults participating in the workshops that were conducted following a defined protocol of activities, focused on explaining to the group of older adults, the functioning of the virtual assistant and the game. The information collected made it possible to show that virtual assistants are especially useful to improve interaction with older adults thanks to their friendly interface and low complexity. It was also possible to determine that recreational activities facilitate learning from a recent activity, evidencing that the stress of the participants and the anxiety generated by it are reduced when learning by playing and even more so when group activities are conducted.

Keywords: Older Adult · Virtual Assistant · Memory Game · Technology Acceptance

1 Introduction

The evolution of information and communication technologies (ICT), make people use different electronic devices daily, either as work items, entertainment media, media or for activities as important as health; and with this, the need for training in this area is evident to generate the necessary skills for a correct management of these [1]. For this type of task, virtual assistants have become an immensely helpful element to facilitate the use of new technologies and integrate their functionalities into people's daily lives, thus generating greater activity with technological means [2].

In the case of older adults, they can live pleasant experiences when interacting with virtual assistants, since they will reduce certain problems that these users have in terms

P. H. Ruiz et al. (Eds.): HCI-COLLAB 2023, CCIS 1877, pp. 109–120, 2024.
https://doi.org/10.1007/978-3-031-57982-0_9

of low levels of acceptance of technology; Virtual assistants are systems based on the voice interaction paradigm, they generate a friendly and natural interaction, they do not require as much learning, they are easy to use and they integrate well with the person's social environment, which facilitates their acceptance [3].

Older adults according to the Colombian Ministry of Health are people aged sixty or over [4], and it is a population that globally is increasing faster than the rest of the population segments [5], which is very important if one takes into account that from this age there is an advanced degree of aging which is a biological process that affects all living beings [6]. This process is characterized by structural and functional changes, which are not the cause of any disease and accidents, which occur over time. The World Health Organization defines it as "aging is the consequence of the accumulation of a wide variety of molecular and cellular damage over time, which leads to a gradual decline in physical and mental capacities" [6], and this is where the initiative to create a computational ludic strategy to keep the mental capacities of older adults active was born.

The developed experience is a playful strategy based on the game, this is done to make it more attractive to the end user and easy to learn, since learning requires creativity and motivation, and through the game can stimulate those capacities. In adults, creativity is highly dependent on good mental health; but a stimulus for creativity is the game, since it generates a sensation of pleasure through compensation by obtaining progress and positive results, and that motivates the search for new and better ways to achieve the objectives set [7].

Virtual assistants can be especially useful for older adults, as they can provide support and facilitate various tasks in their daily lives. For this reason, this study was conducted, which allowed direct interaction with a group of older adults, to teach them to interact with the functionalities of a virtual assistant and a memory game with a natural language interface, and to know their appreciations about the use of this type of devices.

2 Background

2.1 Virtual Assistants

Virtual assistants are applications that run across different devices and respond to natural language, understanding and processing sentences, to complete tasks requested by the end user. These types of applications may be available on different devices such as smartphones, computers, and independent and specific devices such as Amazon Echo or Google Home [8].

The most important characteristics of an application to be considered a virtual assistant are that it understands commands issued in natural language, whether written or voiced, and that it can complete the requested task; but with the evolution of technology the spectrum of compliances is increasing. Currently it is important that an application, to be recognized as a virtual assistant, is hosted in the cloud and has a platform based on artificial intelligence (AI) in order to have high availability of the application and that it can apply techniques such as machine learning and in this way to be able to improve the prediction of the needs of the end user and train frequently in the different ways in which the data will enter [9].

A virtual voice assistant meets all the characteristics of a conventional virtual assistant, but its particularity is the way you interact with it. These virtual assistants manage an oral interface that must be executed and interpreted by a smart speaker. These devices have an internet connection, integrated high-precision microphones, speakers, among other components; in addition to having integrated the virtual assistant or artificial intelligence (AI) [10]. It should be noted that these devices are compatible with different components, expanding the range of tasks that can be performed from a smart speaker (home automation sensors and actuators, interactive screens, among others).

Among the most prominent virtual assistants are Alexa, Google Assistant and Siri.

2.2 Older Adults

Older adults are people who, due to their age, are associated with two characteristics: old age, defined as a social construction that shows the person in a process of degenerative changes, increasing their limitations and decreasing their opportunities and strengths that appear in the last course of life [11], and the second characteristic is aging, which we could define as a natural and deadly process that varies according to each individual's genetics and environment. Aging is part of the whole life of the living being, but old age belongs to the last stage of aging [12].

As aging progresses, the human being loses roles that he played during his most active stages. In the progression of aging, mental health and physical health are the most affected.

2.3 Playful Activities

The concept of ludic comes from the Latin ludo, whose meaning translates into "I play" or if we want to find a more detailed definition, we can say it as "an action that produces fun, joy and pleasure" [13].

These types of activities are found in each of the stages of people's lives and are fundamental because they allow us to learn and relate to the environment that surrounds us in a more enjoyable, motivating and even active way [14]. These activities are important for both children and adults, as they help develop cognitive, physical, emotional, and social skills. The game and playful recreation allow to explore, experiment, solve problems, make decisions, and learn more effectively. In addition, playful activities can also be a way to relieve stress, release tension, and strengthen social bonds by engaging in shared activities with others [14]. In general, the main objective of recreational activities is to provide entertainment, stimulate creativity, encourage social interaction, promote learning, and improve emotional well-being.

A good application of playful activities generates correct work and social interaction atmospheres, therefore, each one of the participants acquires confidence and they are ideal alternatives for traditional learning methods, and it is at this point where the game is found as a functional strategy for the correct development of these recreational actions [15].

Memory Games. They are characterized by generating in their participants an increase in their cognitive abilities, this is acquired in the player through perception and attention. To be able to conduct these types of activities, concentration and perseverance are particularly important, since they are games that train the brain, and its development improves the more the activity is repeated. This improvement is not something that is obtained immediately, so the participant must be patient and constant if he hopes to achieve satisfactory results and thus improve his cognitive abilities; proficiency in these activities is directly proportional to the constancy of their practice. Among the most outstanding games is the famous memo or concentrate [16].

3   Playful Experience Developed

The study was conducted to find out the intention of a group of older adults to use an intelligent virtual assistant, and to evaluate the ease of use of a memory game implemented as a Skill for the Amazon Alexa virtual assistant.

Considering that it would work with older adults, a memory game was chosen, which is a playful activity that can improve cognitive ability through stimulation [17]. Memory games are especially useful to activate the brain and to activate its own characteristics such as concentration and retention in the medium, short, and long term. In addition, it is important to highlight that the brain is an organ that never stops developing and it is at an early age where most of this development occurs, but when you are at an advanced age it is important to keep it in constant exercise [17].

It was decided to implement the game in the Amazon Alexa virtual assistant for the following reasons:

- There is a community of developers who are supporting the production of Alexa-based software thanks to the Open-Source philosophy of their Development Kit.
- There are many libraries and application programming interfaces.
- Easy integration with the cloud and with Amazon services, which helps in the tasks that you want to schedule.

The game is available as a Skill for Amazon Alexa with the name in Spanish "*Hagamos un cuento*", its purpose is to stimulate memory and help the social skills of older adults, since it should always be played in a group. "*Hagamos un cuento*" contains a sequential and guided oral interface, which, in a descriptive way, guides the user through the different sections of the menu and the necessary commands to be able to use each of the implemented functions.

This application allows you to listen to the rules and an explanation of the game, register the number of players, register each player with a name and play sequentially in turns. When the game starts, the first registered participant will begin by saying a word and the second must repeat the mentioned word and add another word to the story, and so on. At the end of each round (every time a player is wrong), the game removes the losing player and continues with the other players, until a winner remains; the game can start again with the registered players or start by registering new players. This application is available in Spanish, it has a wide spectrum of phonetic structures and validations to consider the command given when playing the game correct or incorrect.

To conduct the evaluation, fifteen older adults participated, eight women and seven men between the ages of 60 and 82, who have no problems listening and communicating orally, with whom discussion sessions were conducted. I work in groups of three older adults, developing the following protocol:

Device training: (10–20) minutes.

- Presentation of the Alexa Virtual Assistant.
- Explain some basic features of the Virtual Assistant (alarm programming, Internet queries, and playing music, among others).
- Use the functionalities explained with the participants.

Training with the game: (20–30) minutes.

- Explain how the game starts.
- Explain each of the functions, moments, and gameplay.
- Play a few rounds with the participants and the organizer.

Gameplay: (20–30) minutes.

- Allow participants to play without the organizer being part of the game.
- Feedback on the fly.

Feedback: (10) minutes.

- Application of surveys.
- Space for questions and suggestions.

To collect information in addition to observing the behaviors of the participants, a survey was used with seventeen closed questions that are rated in ranges from 1 to 5, where 1 is the lowest rating and five the highest, they were also parameterized in three categories, device handling, game experience and subjective perception. In Fig. 1 you can see the groups of older adults interacting with the device.

Fig. 1. Working groups during the developed experience.

4 Results

The information collected with the observation of the participants and that registered in the surveys, allow to demonstrate the aptitudes and the perception of the participants towards the acceptance of the virtual assistant, and the game *"Hagamos un cuento"*.

4.1 Participants Observation Stage

Through the observation of the participants, different patterns of behavior and learning were identified regarding the activity conducted in an objective manner, giving priority to cognitive processes when learning to use the device and when playing. Based on the above, ten evaluation points were defined, classified into three categories (Acceptance of the device, Mastery of the game and Personal skills), with the aim of quantifying the data and being able to better interpret the results obtained, as can be seen in the Table 1.

Table 1. Observation process data.

Evaluation point	Average	Category	Average by category
Device usage learning process	4.73	Device acceptance	4.44
Acceptance of the oral interface	4.87		
Appropriation when using the device	3.73		
Game Understanding	4.47	Game proficiency	4.04
Game menu management	4		
Understanding the rules	4.07		
Retentive capacity	4.07	Personal skills	4.69
Social ability during the game	4.93		
Level of attention	4.87		
Ability to improvise and create	4.27		

In each of the evaluation points or sublevels, it is decided to address the evolution of different skills in the participants, taking as a starting point the knowledge that they presented in the presentation stage of the device and when they made the first interactions with it. From that point forward, cognitive, and relational progress with the device and the Skill could be measured during the workshop.

From the data collected through observation, it is recognized that the participants were very receptive to the device and the position that the players took in the activity was a very influential factor, since they were extremely interested in learning how to use the assistant virtual.

Implementing a playful strategy allowed a significant social environment, where people who were having a superior domain oversaw teaching and guiding their peers who had difficulties when learning. In most cases, the retention capacity was improving at a great level, because the repetition of the actions allowed to increase the levels of attention, and along with this the game improved its fluidity by not interrupting the story; Although some cases were evidenced in which it was not very easy to remember, this is due to external factors but incidents facing the investigation, such as cognitive deterioration due to aging, but the condition of the participant was taken into account to make the qualification.

Regarding the gameplay, most of the participants understood the dynamics and helped each other, it was easy to understand the game and the concept that manages the playful activity, although repetitive errors were made when playing when short words were used, the concept that a connector is a word was very difficult to understand and in these cases the error was always due to the union of two short words, which is why the qualification of the subcategory "understanding the rules" does not present the expected score, because the understanding of the regulation is of vital importance for a correct development of the activity.

Table 1 shows the average by category in the data collected through observation, most of the participants had good skills during the development of the activity, such as teamwork, in addition, progress was evidenced in retention as the game progressed.

After completing the workshop, several of the participants demonstrated that they could use the device autonomously, which motivated interest in continuing to use it. In each group, one of the participants who took the lead helped the others to make effective use of the device or to generate strategies to facilitate the learning process. These same participants showed a greater proficiency in the device at the end of the workshop, performing activities for their own interest and without any guidance.

The score in the game proficiency category is the lowest, due to the difficulty of some participants in understanding the rules and the menu. The concept of the game was truly clear, but it was not easy to adapt to the gameplay. Having little time to answer and not being able to use two short words to answer, caused difficulty to carry a good gameplay. When talking about a brief time to respond, it is not considered as a rule of the game, since it is an imposition of the device that limits some functions when developing a Skill.

The menu was the other low but understandable point, given the complexity of interacting without a visual guide, although the menu was correctly guided, the participants did not understand the indications very well, but as the game progressed, they improved their attention levels, analytical skills, and understanding of the menu.

4.2 Survey Process

Table 2 shows the results corresponding to the information recorded by the fifteen participants, and which allows knowledge of relevant data for the investigation.

When analyzing the data obtained in the surveys, the first piece of information that stands out is that **familiarity** with virtual assistants in this population group obtains the lowest average compared to the other categories, this is an expected value, since adults The elderly are not people who are very involved with new technologies and the approach they have towards this type of instrument is due to a social context such as children, grandchildren and even great-grandchildren.

When focusing the analysis of the **"game experience"** category, the game was very pleasant for each player, in addition, by using a natural language it was very explanatory and easy to understand the game in its conceptual way. The participants felt a great gaming experience and a good learning curve in the face of a process unknown to them. Facing the game experience in the workshops. It is evident that the game allowed to generate a familiar environment for each one of the participants, this can be observed that it was allowed by the natural language and the detailed instructions that guide the process during the execution of the Skill, which improves the technological acceptance of the software. Implemented.

Table 2. Result of the survey.

Ask	Category	Average	Average by category
Does the device used for the activity seem easy to use?	Device handling	4.93	4.48
Was it easy for you to recognize the voice commands used in the activity?	Device handling	4.73	
Before the activity, were you familiar with this type of technology?	Device handling	3.2	
Does the type of communication with the device seem to you to use a natural language?	Device handling	4.8	
Was the absence of a visual interface easy for you to understand or did it cause you any kind of anxiety or insecurity?	Device handling	4.73	
Do you think that the main menu of the game is quite informative?	Game experience	4.87	4.84
Were the rules of the game clear?	Game experience	4.87	
Are the in-game voice commands easy to use?	Game experience	4.93	
Do you think that the game gives a correct orientation as you use each of the modules?	Game experience	4.8	
Was it easy for you to play?	Game experience	4.53	
Was the game to your liking?	Game experience	4.93	
Do you think the game uses a natural language?	Game experience	4.93	
Was I able to play without presenting any type of anxiety or fear?	Subjective perception	4.8	4.47
Didn't I have comprehension or development problems when playing?	Subjective perception	4.33	
Didn't I have problems when using the device?	Subjective perception	4.47	
Do you think you could teach your family or friends how to play?	Subjective perception	4.13	
Do you think you could teach your family or friends how to use the device?	Subjective perception	4.6	

When analyzing the category of "**management of the device**", although this type of device is not so well known, it was easy to learn and, in some cases, it became a very favorable environment for the participants, because the Skill and the device allowed to manage a natural language to interact. The adaptation to an oral interface was something quite easy for the different users, thus giving a better game environment since it allowed wide social interaction between the participants.

In the **subjective perception** it is recognized that the participants felt very comfortable in their work teams, in addition, being a playful activity, it generated greater familiarity among the participants showing a very high level of camaraderie and social interaction, many of the participants think that They could not teach much about the development of the activity, but it can be concluded from this that it may be more due to shyness than due to lack of knowledge or skills. A very remarkable point of this category is that the level of acceptance of the device was high, thus giving better results to the workshops.

4.3 Analysis of Results

To analyze the data, the first thing that must be taken into account is that the personal perception of each participant is going to be confronted, against the observation of the researchers who generate a judgment based on the expertise; These two positions allow evaluating technological acceptance, through the TAM model (Technology Acceptance Model) and using data collection instruments adapted to work with older adults [18], which allow determining whether users accept or reject the software. For this, two positions suggested by the model were used, which are: the perceived usefulness and the perceived ease of use [19, 20].

To obtain the **perceived usefulness**, it starts with the observation of the participants, where they highlight the usefulness of implementing a playful activity for learning new technologies. Observing that the interaction of the participants with this type of technology is not high, we can compare that at the end of the workshops conducted, the participants highlighted that the device is **easy to use**, a comfortable language is used for interaction and when clear instructions are given for the management of the software, they saw themselves in the ability to teach how to use these devices. This is achieved when the activity they conduct is to their liking and arouses the interest of each of the participants.

With the above, it can be determined that the development of a playful activity allows a better performance when conducting teaching activities, generating a **positive sensation** in the participants. This sensation was measured with the parameters collected in this study, which are shown in Table 3.

With the data recorded in Table 3, it can be determined that the use of a recreational activity is reflected in the participants as a positive activity to improve adaptation and learning when using new technologies. In the case of the game, it is observed that it is very useful when it comes to maintaining the **attention** of the participants and, along with it, improving adaptability. The retention capacity allows them to recognize and appropriate the use of voice commands to conduct activities in an assistant virtual and their acquired knowledge, gives them the **confidence** to give a high rating from their perception when they want to teach the use of new technologies to other people.

Table 3. Perceived utility.

Parameters	Average
Device usage learning process	4.73
The game was to your liking	4.93
I did not present comprehension or development problems at the time of playing	4.33
Do you think you could teach your family or friends how to play	4.33
Do you think you could teach your family or friends how to use the device?	4.6
Social ability during the game	4.93
Appropriation when using the device	3.73
Level of attention	4.87
Retentive capacity	4.07
Total average	4.50

The lowest point when analyzing this position is the **appropriation** when using the device, and through observation it can be said that this is due to the incidence of soft skills, since it was a group workshop, there was always a person who He took the lead and stood out from his peers, but they all ended up with the ability to interact with the device.

When analyzing the **perceived ease of use**, the perception of the participants and some points of observation that are relevant are highlighted. For this, the data referring to the adaptation to the technological environment and the Skill implemented are highlighted. Table 4 shows the parameters and their rating.

Table 4. Ease of use.

Parameters	Average
Believe that the game uses a natural language	4.93
It was easy for him to recognize the voice commands used in the activity	4.73
Do you think that the main menu of the game is quite informative?	4.87
The rules of the game were clear	4.87
Game voice commands are easy to use	4.93
He believes that the game gives a correct orientation as he uses each of the modules	4.8
It was easy for him to play	4.53
Game Understanding	4.47
Game menu management	4
Understanding the rules	4.07

(*continued*)

Table 4. (*continued*)

Parameters	Average
Acceptance of the oral interface	4.87
Total average	4.64

In the data of table 4, it can be observed that the participants saw in the Skill and in the device an easy-to-use technological option, where the oral interface and simple voice commands for carrying out activities are highlighted, this allowed that the game was easy to play regardless of the complexity of the rules, although the participants perceived that the rules were clear.

Finally, it should be noted that the oral interface was not an impediment for the elderly, on the contrary, it was possible to appreciate that the **fluency** of the workshop improved, since there was no fear in the interaction as caused by a screen.

5 Conclusions

Virtual assistants are very useful to improve interaction with older adults due to their friendly interface and low complexity, it is true that it does not allow multitasking actions due to device limitations, but this was good for the research, due to because it allowed all the attention of the participants to be focused on a single activity at a time, avoiding the dispersion of attention.

The workshops conducted demonstrated that playful activities facilitate learning in the face of a new activity, evidencing that the stress of the participants and the anxiety generated by it is reduced when learning by playing and even more so when group activities are conducted.

The sessions with small groups of participants allowed for greater control when attending and instructing on the use of the virtual assistant and the game that was implemented.

As future work to take advantage of the characteristics of the Skill developed, it is proposed to conduct a study, which allows to verify if this memory game generates in the participants an increase in their cognitive abilities and helps to reduce the degenerative speed in the memory of adults greater.

Create different models of memory stimulation adaptable to the memory game created, to give a variation to the difficulty.

References

1. Zuluaga Serna, D.A.: Procesos de alfabetización digital en el adulto mayor Elaborado Univ. Nac. Abierta Y a Distancia - Unad Esc. Ciencias La Educ. - Ecedu, pp. 1–69 (2021)
2. Guijarro Marco, P.: Asistente virtual para un sistema de información (2020). https://rua.ua.es/dspace/bitstream/10045/101934/1/Asistente_virtual_para_un_sistema_de_informacion_G UIJARRO_MARCO_PABLO.pdf

3. Palacios, J., Bosquez, V., Palacios, Á.: Integración De Un Asistente Virtual En Ambientes De Vida Asistida Por Computador Para Personas Con Discapacidad Fisica Rev. Investig. Talent. **7**, 48–61 (2020). https://doi.org/10.33789/talentos.7.1.122

4. Cubillos, A., Matamorros, M.P.S.: Boletines Poblacionales: Personas Adultas Mayores de 60 años Minsalud - Gob. Colomb., p. 10 (2020)

5. United Nations: Perspectivas de la Población Mundial 2019, New York, NY, USA (2019)

6. OMS: Envejecimiento y salud. https://www.who.int/es/news-room/fact-sheets/detail/ageing-and-health

7. Díaz, J.: El juego como estrategia educativa en la formación de adultos. https://javierdisan.com/2011/09/01/el-juego-como-estrategia-educativa-en-la-formacion-de-adultos/

8. McLaughlin, M.: What Is a Virtual Assistant and How Does It Work? https://www.lifewire.com/virtual-assistants-4138533

9. Pathak, S., Islam, S.A., Jiang, H., Xu, L., Tomai, E.: A survey on security analysis of Amazon echo devices High-Confidence Comput. 2 (2022)

10. DOMOTICADA: Asistentes de voz.☎ Alexa, Google Assistant, Siri y más. https://www.domoticada.com/alexa-google-assistant-siri-asistentes-de-voz/

11. Ministerio de Salud y Protección Social: Envejecimiento y Vejez. https://www.minsalud.gov.co/proteccionsocial/promocion-social/Paginas/envejecimiento-vejez.aspx

12. Sanhueza, C.: Programa de entrenamiento cerebral en adultos mayores sin deterioro cognitivo, atención, memoria y funciones ejecutivas. Madrid, Madrid, España. (2014). https://www.academia.edu/16300422/UNIVERSIDAD_COMPLUTENSE_DE_MADRID?auto=download

13. Paredes, J.: CAPÍTULO PRIMERO Del juego, pp. 12–124 (2013)

14. Candela Borja, J.M., Benavides Bailón, J.: Actividades lúdicas en el proceso de enseñanza-aprendizaje de los estudiantes de la básica superior ReHuSo Rev. Ciencias Humanísticas y Soc. **5**, 78–86 (2020)

15. Posligua, J., Chenche, W., Vallejo, B.: Incidence of recreational activities in the development of the creative thinking in students of Basic General Education Dominio las. Ciencias **3**, 1020–1052 (2017)

16. Prior, O.: La importancia de los juegos educativos y didácticos infantiles – Afrikable. https://www.afrikable.org/la-importancia-de-los-juegos-educativos-y-didacticos-infantiles/

17. Vitae Health Innovation: JUEGOS para mejorar la MEMORIA - ¡Entrena tu mente! https://www.psicologia-online.com/juegos-para-mejorar-la-memoria-4453.html

18. Bolaños, M., Collazos, C., Gutiérrez, F.: Adaptation of technological acceptance models to work with older adults Rev. Colomb. Tecnol. Av. **1**, 37–42 (2021) https://doi.org/10.24054/rcta.v1i37.1267

19. Mazmela, M., Lasa, G., Aranburu, E., Gonzalez, I., Reguera, D.: TAMUX model for industrial HMI evaluation from UX and task performance perspective. In: ACM International Conference Proceeding Series, pp. 10–14 (2018). https://doi.org/10.1145/3233824.3233837

20. Davis, F.D.: Perceived usefulness, perceived ease of use, and user acceptance of information technology MIS Q. Manag. Inf. Syst. **13**, 319–339 (1989). https://doi.org/10.2307/249008

Design Thinking: Empowering Innovation and Transformation in Industry 4.0 - Lessons Learned from Early Adoption in SMEs

Juan Manuel González-Calleros[1]([⊠]) [iD], Josefina Guerrero-García[1],
and Claudia González Calleros[2]

[1] Benemérita Universidad Autónoma de Puebla, 72592 Puebla, Puebla, Mexico
{juanmanuel.gonzalez,josefina.guerrero}@correo.buap.mx
[2] Universidad Veracruzana, 91020 Xalapa-Enríquez, Veracruz, Mexico
claudia.gonzalez@uv.mx

Abstract. Small and Medium Enterprises [SMEs] have the potential to benefit from Industry 4.0 technologies, but their adoption has been limited, hindering their ability to fully leverage digitalization. Design Thinking has emerged as a promising approach to address the challenges faced by SMEs in adopting Industry 4.0. This paper explores the role of Design Thinking in facilitating innovation and transformation in SMEs within the context of Industry 4.0. Through literature review and case studies, key findings and lessons learned from early adopters of Design Thinking are uncovered. The study reveals a lack of interest among SMEs in embracing digital transformation in the Latin American context. The paper provides an overview of the state of the art, describes the methodology employed, presents the study's results, and discusses the implications. It concludes by highlighting the pivotal role of Design Thinking in Industry 4.0 adoption and offering recommendations for practitioners and researchers.

Keywords: Small and Medium Enterprises [SMEs] · Industry 4.0 · Design Thinking · digital transformation · innovation · case studies

1 Introduction

Small and Medium Enterprises [SMEs] play a crucial role in the economy, contributing to employment, innovation, and economic growth. However, the adoption of Industry 4.0 technologies in SMEs has been relatively low, hindering their ability to fully leverage the benefits of digitalization [1]. Industry 4.0, characterized by the integration of digital technologies into various aspects of business operations, holds great potential for SMEs to enhance their sustainability and productivity through data capture and analysis [1].

Despite the transformative potential of Industry 4.0, its adoption in SMEs faces some challenges, including data security, interoperability, and skills development [2]. These challenges further contribute to the low level of adoption among SMEs and highlight the need for effective strategies to overcome them. Design Thinking has emerged as a

P. H. Ruiz et al. (Eds.): HCI-COLLAB 2023, CCIS 1877, pp. 121–129, 2024.
https://doi.org/10.1007/978-3-031-57982-0_10

promising approach to address these challenges by identifying unmet needs, generating innovative ideas, and rapidly prototyping and testing solutions [3].

One such case study by [1] highlights the influence of design thinking on the digitalization approach of a MedTech SME. The study emphasizes the transformative potential of design thinking and emphasizes the importance of skill development, usability, and practical guidance for SMEs in effectively utilizing Industry 4.0 technologies. Similarly, [4] present a case study demonstrating how Design Thinking can modernize production machinery in a steel plant, improving economic feasibility and worker experience [4].

This paper aims to explore the role of Design Thinking in facilitating innovation and transformation in the context of Industry 4.0, with a specific focus on SMEs. By relying on existing literature and case studies, this study aims to uncover key findings and lessons learned from early adopters of Design Thinking in the digitalization journey of SMEs. Our findings revealed that despite the growing demand for digital transformation in the Latin American context [5], SMEs showed a lack of interest in embracing these changes.

The remainder of this paper is structured as follows. Section two provides an overview of the related work in the field, incorporating a comprehensive literature review. Section three outlines the methodology employed in this study. It describes the research design, data collection methods, and analysis techniques used to investigate the low level of adoption of Industry 4.0 among SMEs and the impact on their organizations. In section four, the results of the study are presented and discussed in detail. The findings related to the lack of interest shown by SMEs in embracing digital transformation in the Latin American context are analyzed. Finally, section five concludes the paper by summarizing the key findings, implications, and contributions of the study.

2   Related Work

Findings revealing the low level of adoption and its impact on the organization Industry 4.0 [I4.0] encompasses the changes brought about using digital technologies in companies [1]. Digitization plays a crucial role in enabling manufacturers to become more sustainable and productive by capturing and analyzing data [1]. The integration of physical and virtual systems, the Internet of Things and Services, and the emergence of cyber-physical systems are defining characteristics of Industry 4.0 [3]. However, the adoption of Industry 4.0 is still in its early stages and faces challenges such as data security, interoperability, and skills development [2]. To address these challenges, Design Thinking has been proposed as an effective approach that allows for the identification of unmet needs, generation of new ideas, and rapid prototyping and testing of solutions [3].

A case study presented by Mesa [1] illustrates the role of designers and design thinking in the context of digitalization. The study examines the influence of design thinking on a MedTech SME's digitalization approach, highlighting the transformative potential of design. The case study analyzes the decision-making process through documentation review, reports, prototypes, and autoethnography. It emphasizes the importance of skill development, usability, and providing practical guidance for SMEs in effectively utilizing Industry 4.0 technologies. While the study acknowledges its limitations as a single-case analysis, it underscores the value of design thinking frameworks in addressing digitalization challenges.

A case study demonstrating how Design Thinking can be applied to modernize production machinery in a steel plant is presented in [4]. The study emphasizes the economic feasibility and positive impact on worker experience and plant efficiency. Technologies such as Big Data, Sensor Networks, Embedded Computing, and Machine Learning are highlighted as catalysts for industry transformation. The study introduces the concepts of "Operator 4.0" and "Manager 4.0," emphasizing the collaboration between humans and automation in Industry 4.0. The authors highlight the importance of integrating human and machine systems to improve efficiency and safety in the industry [4].

In the context of education and graduate preparation, the 4th Industrial Revolution poses challenges due to job replacements and eliminations. [6] argue that future education should prioritize soft skills development and innovative learning approaches to address these challenges. Design thinking is identified as a valuable tool for graduates to understand their roles, excel in organizations, and enhance employability. However, implementing these approaches in engineering curricula faces obstacles related to skills alignment and mentor-student thinking shifts [6].

The adoption of emerging technologies, such as Industry 4.0 and non-destructive evaluation [NDE] 4.0, requires a managed innovation approach, conscious skill development, and a new type of leadership [7]. Design Thinking has been proposed as an effective methodology for facilitating the adoption of these technologies by understanding users, challenging assumptions, and identifying alternative solutions [3, 7]. Nested applications of Design Thinking have been shown to aid in designing management approaches for NDE 4.0 [7]. A number of case studies have utilized Design Thinking to identify unmet needs, generate ideas, and prototype solutions iteratively [7].

A pragmatic approach based on Design Thinking to help companies develop Industry 4.0 use cases is discussed in [8]. The approach focuses on the human role in the design process, aligning with the principles of Design Thinking. It provides a methodological framework and emphasizes the importance of considering human needs and interests when integrating Industry 4.0 technologies into production systems [8].

Finally, [9] offer a comprehensive guide based on existing literature for managing continuous business transformation [9]. The guide highlights smart innovation, connected innovation, and data analytics as key elements. It emphasizes the importance of defining a digitization strategy, optimizing technology mix, and setting priorities in the production area. Connected innovation involves opening the innovation process to external partners and customers, while data analytics facilitates informed decision-making and continuous improvement. The guide draws on insights from previous works by [8–11] to support its recommendations [10–12].

In this review, numerous key findings have been identified regarding the role of design thinking and the adoption of Industry 4.0. Firstly, it is highlighted that the adoption of Industry 4.0 is still in its early stages and faces significant challenges such as data security, interoperability, and skills development. Design thinking has emerged as an effective methodology to address these challenges by identifying unmet needs, generating new ideas, and rapidly prototyping and testing solutions.

The transformative impact of design thinking on digitalization is evident in the presented case studies. These cases demonstrate how a design-focused approach influenced digitalization strategies and provided practical guidance to overcome specific challenges of Industry 4.0, such as skill development and usability. However, further research is needed to validate the utility of design thinking frameworks in broader Industry 4.0 projects and to provide more robust guidelines for SMEs in their digitalization process.

Another important finding is the need to address the challenges in education and graduate preparation within the context of the fourth industrial revolution. The review emphasizes the importance of developing soft skills and innovative learning approaches to effectively prepare graduates. Design thinking is presented as a valuable tool to help graduates understand their roles, excel in organizations, and improve their employability. However, more effort is required to implement these practices in engineering curricula and align skills with industry requirements.

Regarding areas of opportunity and research gaps, several future directions are identified. Further research is needed to validate and evaluate the effectiveness of design thinking approaches in Industry 4.0 projects, especially in different contexts and industrial sectors. Additionally, there is a need for deeper exploration of how to effectively integrate human and machine systems in the industry to enhance efficiency and safety.

In the educational realm, more research is needed to develop solid strategies and approaches that facilitate the effective integration of soft skills and innovative learning in engineering curricula. This requires close collaboration between educational institutions and industry to ensure that graduates are prepared for the challenges and opportunities of Industry 4.0.

In conclusion, this review highlights the pivotal role of design thinking in the adoption of Industry 4.0 and provides a comprehensive overview of findings and areas of opportunity in this field. Design thinking offers an effective approach to tackle the challenges of the industry 4.0 revolution and provides valuable insights for practitioners and researchers alike.

3 Methodology

The methodology followed in this study employed a combination of design thinking and traditional data collection and analysis methods. Design thinking was utilized for the understanding and proposal of solutions, while data collection and analysis were carried out using observation, interviews, and surveys. Design thinking, as an iterative and human-centered approach, was applied to gain a deep understanding of the challenges faced by SMEs in adopting Industry 4.0 and to generate potential solutions. This involved empathizing with the SMEs, defining the problem, ideating possible solutions, prototyping, and testing them. The design thinking process allowed for the identification of unmet needs, the generation of innovative ideas, and the rapid development and testing of solutions.

In addition to design thinking, traditional data collection methods were employed to gather empirical data and insights. Observation, through the careful observation and documentation of SMEs' practices and behaviors, provided valuable qualitative data. Interviews were conducted with key stakeholders, such as SME owners, managers, and employees, to obtain in-depth perspectives on their experiences, challenges, and attitudes towards digital transformation. Surveys were also administered to a larger sample of SMEs to collect quantitative data on their adoption patterns, motivations, and barriers.

The collected data from observations, interviews, and surveys were then analyzed using various techniques, such as thematic analysis, qualitative coding, and statistical analysis. This allowed for the identification of common themes, patterns, and trends within the data, enabling a comprehensive understanding of the low level of adoption of Industry 4.0 among SMEs and its impact on their organizations.

By combining design thinking with traditional data collection and analysis methods, this study aimed to provide a holistic and multidimensional perspective on the challenges and potential solutions for the digital transformation of SMEs.

3.1 Description of the Experiment

The experiment involved 20 participants who were divided into four teams, with each team tasked with adopting a design thinking strategy to propose solutions for small and medium-sized enterprises [SMEs]. The teams were created randomly to ensure unbiased distribution. Each team had the freedom to choose an SME to work with, allowing for diverse project focuses.

The design thinking process was followed by each team, which typically includes various iterative stages such as empathizing with the SME's needs, defining the problem, ideating potential solutions, prototyping, and testing. The teams collaborated, brainstormed, and iterated on their proposed solutions to address the challenges faced by their chosen SMEs.

Once the design thinking process was completed, the evaluation of the proposed solutions took place. This evaluation involved conducting interviews and surveys with the SMEs to gather their feedback and assess the effectiveness and practicality of the solutions presented. The interviews and surveys aimed to capture the SMEs' perspectives on the proposed solutions, their potential benefits, and any reservations or concerns they might have had.

The findings of the evaluation revealed that while the SMEs found the proposed solutions beneficial, none of them had adopted the solutions. Despite recognizing the potential value of the ideas presented, the SMEs may have faced challenges in implementing the solutions, such as resource constraints, operational limitations, or competing priorities. The experiment highlighted the gap between conceptualizing solutions and their practical implementation in real-world SME environments.

These results emphasize the importance of considering not only the viability and desirability of proposed solutions but also the feasibility of their implementation within the specific contexts of SMEs. Further research and exploration could be conducted to better understand the barriers preventing the adoption of the proposed solutions and to develop strategies to bridge this implementation gap.

3.2 Empathy Design Process

To initiate the solution, each team conducted a collaborative brainstorming session to explore innovative ways to incorporate industry 4.0 to SMEs. A diagnosis was carried out by using the test presented in [13] which was a preliminary perspective an key step to get a depth perspective of the current states of SMEs. They focused on identifying key areas for improvement, potential additions, and assessing the complexity of implementing these enhancements. With a clearer vision of how to enhance existing platforms, they employed various techniques to foster empathy with both employees and owners. These techniques included:

1. Safari method: By immersing ourselves in the users' perspective, we gained insights into their most common needs and challenges.
2. Storyboards: Through the creation of visual narratives, we gained a deeper understanding of how our platform would be utilized for specific tasks.
3. Participatory observation: We observed students engaging in online classes to observe their interactions and identify the current issues they face with existing platforms.
4. Empathy maps: Utilizing this tool, we explored the emotions, desires, and needs experienced by users, allowing us to design a more user-centered platform.
5. Personas: By creating representative user profiles, we captured the diverse user types that may engage with our platform.
6. User stories: These stories helped us understand how the software's functionalities would fulfill the users' needs.

Armed with a comprehensive understanding of the challenges and requirements of SMEs using current technology, each team proceeded to prototype their solution.

4 Generated Solutions and Evaluation

The proposed solutions in this project revolve around the development of a comprehensive dashboard for controlling and obtaining information from various IoT devices in an SME setting. The aim is to enhance operational efficiency, security, and decision-making through the integration of smart devices and data analysis (See Table 1).

As we can see in Table 2, projects are often evaluated based on their effectiveness and usefulness. One commonly used method for assessing usability is the System Usability Scale [SUS] [13], which measures user satisfaction with a product or solution. However, it is important to recognize that the perception of usefulness can differ from the SUS evaluation. This opinion piece aims to shed light on a scenario where a project received positive SUS scores but was not perceived as useful by its intended users, particularly due to a lack of evident cost-benefit advantages.

Table 1. Projects generated for SMEs.

ID	Description
01	This project focuses on the creation of a dashboard to control devices proposed such as Smart CCTV Camera with facial and object recognition, aimed at improving security by monitoring exchanges with suppliers. Another proposed device is an attendance module using NFC cards and a fingerprint sensor for employee check-ins
02	The project aims to develop a dashboard for controlling and obtaining information from IoT devices in an SME, including tracking devices using GPS locations, the flow of client's section collects data on client flow during opening hours, allowing analysis of high-traffic hours, client count, and busy days. Monitoring room temperature and humidity of temperature and humidity in zones of the building
03	The Dashboard view provides a summary of various data collected by the system, such as employee attendance, selected products, warehouse temperature, customer count, and security system configuration. An Intelligent Thermostat System potentially beneficial for refrigerators without temperature sensors. An RFID Attendance System and a motion detection system was acknowledged as helpful but with a desire for wider installation beyond just the branches
04	The dashboard where users can visualize and interpret the data collected by the sensors for better understanding and decision-making. Weight checker/alarm for inventory: A weight sensor that monitors inventory levels and emits an alert when a product reaches a minimum weight. The alert includes a buzzer and an LED indicator. IoT Network sensor: An IoT network with sensors to collect data on crop conditions, pest and disease management, humidity, temperature. A sensor placed in the fermentation zones to detect high levels of carbon dioxide. It emits an alarm and sends alerts to ensure worker safety and prompt maintenance response. Rotation per bottle: An IoT device that assists in the riddling process by accurately calculating rotation angles for each wine bottle. It uses a gyroscope sensor and communicates with the user through wireless notifications

While the SUS evaluation is a valuable tool for assessing usability, it should not be considered the sole determinant of a project's perceived usefulness. It is essential to recognize that user perceptions are shaped by a range of factors, including the perceived cost-benefit proposition of a solution. By taking a user-centric approach and incorporating cost-benefit analysis into project planning and design, organizations can bridge the gap between usability and perceived usefulness, resulting in more successful and impactful projects.

Table 2. Evaluation of proposed projects.

ID	Description
01	The sensors are properly placed in various areas of the company; however, the quality of their implementation needs improvement as poor quality is perceived. One of the main conclusions is that while the company identifies areas for improvement and potential new prototypes, it is evident that the devices could greatly enhance the company. The SUS evaluation unequivocally indicates an excellent solution proposal
02	The client expressed interest in the devices, highlighting benefits such as clear data visualization, improved control, cost reduction, and better decision-making. They showed enthusiasm for testing and deploying the devices. The project evaluation included a System Usability Scale [SUS] evaluation by the owner of the company, indicating overall satisfaction with the dashboard's usability. The owner found the system easy to use, except for one potentially erroneous response
03	After presenting the prototype application to the SME, additional comments were gathered. The Storage section was seen as information-workload, but the records area and thermometer section were deemed useful. The Dashboard view received positive feedback for providing valuable information for branch managers' daily work. The Security view was well-received, particularly the attendance and security tools. During the evaluation, participants performed tasks within the application to assess usability. The tasks were completed without difficulty, and a System Usability Scale [SUS] evaluation was conducted. The average score indicated a "Good" rating for the user interface, with room for improvement highlighted by the participants. The report acknowledges the challenges faced during the project, including integrating different devices into a unified platform and creating meaningful and user-friendly interfaces. Feedback from the PYME members emphasized the need to avoid information workload, improve clarity of the active view, and refine the user interface. Despite the areas for improvement, the project was successful in delivering a functional prototype that received positive feedback from the SME
04	There was interest in the cost-effectiveness and accuracy of the proposed system. However, the company currently relies on their existing working system and did not express immediate interest in the prototypes. Overall, the project demonstrates the potential for enhancing the making process through automation and data analysis. The prototypes offer cost-effective solutions and improved monitoring capabilities, leading to better quality control and decision-making

5   Conclusion

This study highlights the pivotal role of design thinking in facilitating innovation and transformation in the context of Industry 4.0, particularly for SMEs. The findings underscore the need for effective strategies to overcome the challenges faced by SMEs in adopting Industry 4.0 technologies. Design thinking offers a promising approach to address these challenges by identifying unmet needs, generating innovative ideas, and rapidly prototyping and testing solutions. The study emphasizes the importance of skill development, usability, and practical guidance for SMEs in effectively utilizing Industry 4.0 technologies. Further research is needed to validate the utility of design thinking frameworks in broader Industry 4.0 projects and to provide more comprehensive guidelines for SMEs in their digitalization journey.

References

1. Mesa, D., Renda, G., Gorkin, R., Kuys, B., Cook, S.M.: Implementing a design thinking approach to de-risk the digitalisation of manufacturing SMEs. Sustainability **14**(21), 14358 (2022). https://doi.org/10.3390/su142114358
2. Lee, J., Bagheri, B., Kao, H.A.: A cyber-physical systems architecture for industry 4.0-based manufacturing systems. Manuf. Lett. **3**, 18–23 (2015). https://doi.org/10.1016/j.mfglet.2014.12.001
3. Liedtka, J., Ogilvie, T.: The Why and How of Design Thinking in Designing for Growth: A Design Thinking Tool Kit for Managers, 1st edn. Columbia Business School Publishing, New York (2011)
4. Burresi, G., et al.: Smart retrofitting by design thinking applied to an industry 4.0 migration process in a steel mill plant. In: 2020 9th Mediterranean Conference on Embedded Computing, MECO 2020, pp. 1–6. IEEE (2020). https://doi.org/10.1109/MECO49872.2020.9134210
5. Mon, A., Del Giorgio, H.R., Collazos, C., Calleros, J.M.G.: Analysis of companies in industry 4.0 to characterize their users: the cases of Argentina and Mexico. In: Agredo-Delgado, V., Ruiz, P.H., Correa-Madrigal, O. (eds.) Communications in Computer and Information Science, pp. 28–40. Springer, Cham (2022). https://doi.org/10.1007/978-3-031-24709-5_3
6. Satpathy, S., Dash, K.K., Mohapatra, M.: A study on the new design thinking for industrial revolution 4.0, requirements and graduate readiness. Rupkatha J. Interdiscip. Stud. Humanit. **12**(4) (2020). https://doi.org/10.21659/rupkatha.v12n4.09
7. Vrana, J., Singh, R.: NDE 4.0—a design thinking perspective. J. Nondestruct. Eval. **40**(1), 8 (2021). https://doi.org/10.1007/s10921-020-00735-9
8. Bauer, W., Pokorni, B., Findeisen, S.: Production assessment 4.0 – methods for the development and evaluation of industry 4.0 use cases. In: Karwowski, W., Trzcielinski, S., Mrugalska, B., Di Nicolantonio, M., Rossi, E. (eds.) Advances in Intelligent Systems and Computing, pp. 501–510. Springer, Cham (2019). https://doi.org/10.1007/978-3-319-94196-7_46
9. Ochs, T., Riemann, U.: Industry 4.0: how to manage transformation as the new normal. In: The Palgrave Handbook of Managing Continuous Business Transformation, Palgrave Macmillan UK, London (2016). https://doi.org/10.1057/978-1-137-60228-2_11
10. Brown, J.S.: Innovation's golden goose Report of the Industrie 4.0 working group. Munich: Herbert Utz Verlag. Harvard Bus. Rev. **87**(5), 22–23 (2009)
11. Henning, K., Wolfgang, W., Johannes, H.: Recommendations for implementing the strategic initiative INDUSTRIE 4.0 April 2013 Securing the future of German manufacturing industry Final report of the Industrie 4.0 Working Group Forschungsunion. Forschungsunion, acatech, no. April, pp. 1–84 (2013). https://en.acatech.de/publication/recommendations-for-implementing-the-strategic-initiative-industrie-4-0-final-report-of-the-industrie-4-0-working-group/
12. Armbrust, M., et al.: A view of cloud computing. Commun. ACM **53**(4), 50–58 (2010). https://doi.org/10.1145/1721654.1721672
13. Lewis, J.R.: IBM computer usability satisfaction questionnaires: psychometric evaluation and instructions for use. Int. J. Hum. Comput. Interact. **7**(1), 57–78 (1995). https://doi.org/10.1080/10447319509526110

Development and Evaluation
of a Non-conventional Interaction Wearable
Device

Matheus Mendes Giorgini[1] ⓘ, Mario Guizerian[1] ⓘ,
Valeria Farinazzo Martins[1,2(✉)] ⓘ, and Bruno da Silva Rodrigues[1] ⓘ

[1] Computing and Informatics Department, Mackenzie Presbyterian University, São Paulo, Brazil
{valeria.farinazzo,bruno.rodrigues}@mackenzie.br
[2] Applied Computing Department, Mackenzie Presbyterian University, São Paulo, Brazil

Abstract. Consisting of accessories with embedded electronics aimed at capturing real-time user information, wearable technologies have attracted the interest of both industry and researchers. With applications in various sectors, developing reliable, comfortable, and clothing-integrated wearable devices is a challenge. In this regard, this work presents the development of a wearable technology prototype integrated with an IMU (Inertial Measurement Unit) that aims to detect wrist/elbow supination and pronation movements, as well as wrist extension and flexion. Additionally, the work includes the development of a motion-controlled electronic game utilizing detected movements from the wearable device. Following the system development, an evaluation was conducted using heuristics specifically designed for wearable devices, and the main results of that verification are reported in this paper. In general lines, is possible to present the system was well evaluated, showing that the pattern of glove use is constant, with low latency between the command and the game's response, and the autonomy heuristic obtained a good classification.

Keywords: Non-conventional Interaction · Wearable Device · Manual Function · Usability Evaluation and Digital Games

1 Introduction

Wearable technologies have been around us for a long time [1], but they have greatly advanced in the last two decades. This technology is widely used as an accessory containing embedded electronics, allowing capturing real-time user information.

Among the main applications in which wearable technologies are being used, it is possible to mention the so-called fitness trackers for the analysis of sports activities [2], as well as for monitoring the physical and mental health of individuals [3, 4].

When health care is addressed, the use of wearable devices has shown to be a promising technology to monitor and evaluate motor performance during rehabilitation sessions [5], as well as to serve as a human-computer interface (HCI) integrating

P. H. Ruiz et al. (Eds.): HCI-COLLAB 2023, CCIS 1877, pp. 130–142, 2024.
https://doi.org/10.1007/978-3-031-57982-0_11

wearables to computational systems and digital games to keep patients engaged during motor rehabilitation sessions [6].

Despite the diversity of wearable devices available on the market and their ability to integrate computational elements into clothing being discussed since the first works of science fiction, developing wearable devices has not proven to be an easy task [7]; wearable interfaces are integrated with the user, whether it is a piece of clothing or an accessory [8]. So, it is necessary to develop comfortable products that merge the appearance of these devices with those of individuals with idealized functionalities.

When analyzing the usability of these devices, unlike a desktop environment, wearable technologies allow a very new interaction for the user [9, 10], as they transcend the evaluation of the visual elements of a web page through voice communication, touch, and facial recognition, among others.

As the market exploration by wearable technologies is still very recent, several companies and their developers have been trying to apply new ideas to consolidate their products [11]. However, developing new products without going through usability evaluations can lead to non-full acceptance by consumers [12].

Given this, this work aims to present the development of a system composed of a wearable device and a desktop application (game) controlled by this device, where the purpose of the system is to support therapists during upper limb rehabilitation sessions. This paper provides an overview of the ideation phase, the choice of materials, and the usability evaluation with experts.

This work is structured as follows: Sect. 1, Introduction. Section 2, Theoretical Foundation, topics related to research are addressed: Wearable Technologies and related works. Section 3, Development Methodology, brings the necessary steps to achieve the objective of this study. Section 4 presents the results obtained. Finally, Sect. 5 presents the findings of this research and future work.

2 Theoretical Foundation

2.1 Wearable Technologies

In the evolution of interfaces between users and computational systems, it is possible to highlight three main paradigms chronologically: first, Command Line Interfaces (CLI), then Graphical User Interfaces (GUI) and, more recently, Natural User Interfaces (NUI) [13].

In recent years, a series of devices began appearing on the market as new modes of interaction: touch screens, voice commands and gesture recognition. NUIs are classified into haptic, organic, wearable, gestural, and voice interfaces. NUI is an acronym that designates Human-Computer Interaction (HCI) using unconventional devices based on natural elements. In this case, the term "natural" is used in opposition to most computer interfaces that use devices whose operation must be learned. In this interface type, it can be assumed that the interaction is based on the user's previous experience. Therefore, learning and becoming an expert is easy [14].

Wearable technologies are directly or indirectly integrated into a person, which can be an independent and interconnectable device or a way to collect data [15]. Developed as watches, clothes, hats, glasses and others, these interfaces integrate into the user's silhouette to provide computational functionalities while adding to the wearer's look [16].

Regarding social issues, [8] they explore the relationship between the emergence of new types of wearable technology and the demands of the population. In this case, innovative products that offer much functionality are desired. These products are sought to meet everyday needs (utility) and satisfy user desires (pleasure, fun and satisfaction).

However, as much as consolidated products act in the market, innovations in wearable technologies have a little difficulty integrating into our daily lives, given the interference they cause in the user's profile. As seen in [7], appearance is one of the central points in the acceptance process of these products, and even though the size of these devices has decreased considerably, examples such as Google Glass show that there is still room for improvement.

Godfrey [15] states that although wearable technologies have great potential for common trends, there are still barriers to further development (e.g., difficulty reaching audiences of all age groups, low variety, limitations in design and technology dependencies still on the rise).

2.2 Related Works

Several works related to the theme of this research were found in the literature. Regarding the development of wearable technologies, Jing [17] presented a wearable device where the capture of user movements was based on fiber optic tension sensors. With a main focus on characterizing the sensors used in the project, the presented device proved promising in detecting wrist flexion-extension and abduction-adduction movements.

Flexion-extension movements were also addressed in the works proposed by [18] and Xiao [19]. In both works, they developed wearable exoskeletons composed of surface electromyography (sEMG) sensors capable of detecting the intention of wrist movement through the electrical activity produced by the contractions of the muscle fibers responsible for the movement. In addition to detecting movement, in both projects, actuators into the devices were integrated to assist in the execution of movements.

In the study proposed by Narejo [20], a low-cost wearable device was developed using inertial movement unit (IMU) sensors to assess the elbow's range of flexion and extension. With success in detecting the amplitude of the movements, the paper also mentions the possibility of integrating the device into a virtual reality system to help the patient in the execution of movements during physiotherapy sessions.

Like Narejo [20], Alexandre [21] also proposed integrating wearable devices into electronic games to assist in upper limb rehabilitation sessions. Focusing on developing the manual function, the proposed project used IMUs to obtain linear acceleration and rotational hand movements readings and piezoresistive sensors to detect finger flexion movements. Integrating the wearable device with the game allowed the physiotherapist to extract information about the patient's motor skills playfully and motivate and engage the patient in the rehabilitation sessions.

Regarding evaluating the device's usability, the work proposed by [22] discussed the problems related to wearable technologies and presented a set of heuristics formulated to meet this type of product. A group of usability experts validated these heuristics.

Subsequently, the heuristics were applied in a real scenario with a commercial device and evaluated by another set of usability experts. This set of heuristics was used to validate the prototype presented in this work.

3 Development Methodology

Concerning the methodology used in this project, the work had as its starting point the bibliographic review of the topics involved in the research. This review aimed to understand ways to create devices sensitive to hand and forearm movement, how games can help in rehabilitation, and how wearable devices can be integrated into these games. After the idealization, development and conclusion of the wearable device project and the game into which the device was integrated, an inspection phase was conducted by experts in the Computing area, where a heuristic evaluation of the integration of the wearable device into the game happened. The following steps were taken to achieve the objectives proposed in this work:

1. Literature review of the topics involved (Wearable devices, sensors, serious games and heuristic evaluation of wearable devices).
2. Meetings with technology, hardware and development experts.
3. Research of sensors for use in the wearable device.
4. Study on forms of integration between wearable devices and electronic games.
5. Development of electronic games for future application in rehabilitation.
6. Evaluation of system usability by experts.
7. Analysis of post-test results.

In subsequent topics, aspects related to the development of the wearable device and the game will be addressed.

3.1 Description of the Wearable Device Idea

For this project, it was proposed to develop a wearable device that allows mapping and collecting information on the user's upper limb movement (wrist and forearm) and integrating this device into a digital game. The first definitions of the project were based on the guidelines proposed in the framework for developing serious games controlled by wearable technologies [23]. In this approach, the authors mapped the relationship among electronic sensors, sensory-motor skills and electronic games. They presented how to integrate these technologies to meet requirements that fulfill the needs of health professionals involved in rehabilitation. Based on this understanding and the discussion with a multidisciplinary team of engineers, computer scientists and physiotherapists, a wearable device was designed using a micro-controlled system composed of an IMU responsible for identifying the user's hand movement. Figure 1 presents a conceptual diagram of the prototype designed for the project.

As the diagram in Fig. 1 shows, the data collected by the IMU will be sent to a desktop where the digital game will receive information regarding the movement of the user's hand, providing this user with an unconventional, intuitive interaction with a high degree of control over game elements. After defining the project, the development of the

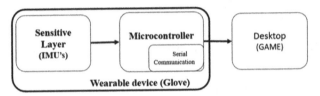

Fig. 1. Conceptual diagram of the prototype to be developed.

prototype was divided into two stages: the development of the wearable device and the development of the desktop application (game), which will be discussed in topics 3.2 and 3.3.

3.2 Wearable Devices

Due to the importance of the elbow-wrist complex in the development of daily activities and the impact on the life quality that a disorder in this complex can cause for individuals [24], the development of the wearable device proposed in this work aimed to detect the movements of wrist/elbow supination and pronation (forearm rotation), as well as detecting wrist extension and flexion movements (Fig. 2). After defining the movements that the wearable device should measure, a study was performed to identify the wearable that best adapted to the needs of the project, and also the possible sensors that could be integrated into this device. Finally, besides the ability to detect user interaction accurately, for the design of the device, the use of low-cost commercial sensors has been established as a requirement, which ensures the system's reproducibility, as well as the use of sensors capable of detecting movements with little amplitude, guaranteeing the use of the system by people with reduced mobility or undergoing rehabilitation treatment.

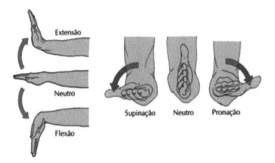

Fig. 2. Flexion, Extension, Supination and Pronation Movements [25].

3.3   System Software

As the project proposed by this study involves the integration of the Arduino platform with a game created for the desktop, to describe the development of the software used in the project, this section will be divided into firmware development, which refers to the code created for the Arduino platform and game development referring to the game created to be used with the interaction device.

According to the requirements imposed by the project, it was decided to use a glove where a three-axis accelerometer ADXL335 model responsible for detecting the movements of the user's hand was attached to his back. This accelerometer is integrated into an Arduino UNO open-source electronic prototyping board responsible for acquiring analog information from the IMU and converting analog signals into digital signals through an internal 10-bit AD (Analog-Digital) converter. After converting the IMU information into digital signals, the Arduino will pre-process the information and transmit the data to a microcomputer through a UART (Universal Asynchronous Receiver/Transmitte) serial connection/communication.

Firmware Development

The Arduino firmware was developed using the C/C++ language and performs the task of processing information from the accelerometer to identify the movement of the user's hand in real-time. A communication protocol was designed and implemented at the application level, synchronizing and standardizing the sending of information on the spatial coordinates of hand movement to the game, aiming at performing the integration between the device and the game running on the desktop. Data transmission occurred at 9600 bps (bit per second).

Game Development

For the game development, it was defined that the game should be simple, fun, and the interaction between the glove and the game control should be intuitive. Based on these requirements, it was decided to develop a game similar to Arcade Pac-Man. This 80's classic consists of a game where the player controls a character inside a maze whose objective is to eat the most points while avoiding being found by the ghosts that patrol the place. Besides being fun, the game has a simple dynamic that enables fluid gameplay and can be understood by players of different ages.

Another important feature of Pac-Man that enabled/influenced its use in this project is the intuitive relationship between the user's hand movements and Pac-Man's movements. Thus, the extension and flexion movements will move Pac-Man up and down, respectively, and the supination and pronation movements will be responsible for moving the character to the left and right. All game development was done on the Unity platform, using the C# language. The game/glove integration was performed using the SerialPort library available for development in Unity. Figure 3 presents the game screen of the Pac-Man game developed for this work.

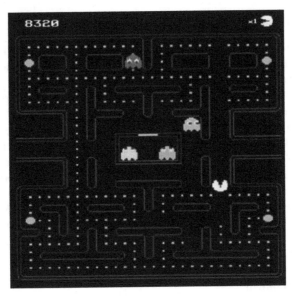

Fig. 3. Game screen of the Pac-Man game developed on the Unity platform for this project.

3.4 Usability Evaluation

Some paths can be used concerning the involvement or not of potential end users to evaluate the usability of a system. In the first, involving users, their experiences are collected to assess the quality of the system's elements and the interactions that occur in it. Second, they rely on the help of experts to conduct an inspection process, following the knowhow [12].

According to Nielsen [12], the heuristic evaluation is based on inspecting an interface using an already established list of heuristics. It usually involves a group of evaluators to improve the quality of the analysis. Individually and after compiling the data of all evaluators, problems found in the interface that violate such heuristics are pointed out, along with their degrees of severity.

Given the unconventional nature of these interfaces, consolidated heuristics often fail to cover intrinsic peculiarities in new technologies during the evaluation process. Considering this framework and, since the quality of products is directly related to the application of usability evaluations, [22] a set of heuristics that allow the evaluation of wearable interfaces was established, based on Nielsen's proposal [12, 26] and on the specificities of the wearable technology itself. Some of them have been adapted, excluded or added. The heuristics used in this project are:

- Visibility of the system status; Connection between the system and the real world; User control and freedom; Consistency and patterns; Flexibility and efficiency of use; Help users recognize, diagnose and recover from errors; Errors prevention; Aesthetics and minimalist design; Help and documentation are heuristics addressed by Nielsen [12] and that were interpreted for the glove scenario. Some guiding questions were added to each heuristic to facilitate its understanding. For example, in the case of the

"Error Prevention" heuristic, one of the guiding questions was: In the case of gestural interactions, does the system tolerate certain variations of the same gesture? (Or is a precise action expected?).

- Save status and work protection: refers, in this case, to the user being able to stop the game and continue where he left off.
- Colors and readability: use appropriate colors, contrast and button font sizes.
- Autonomy: refers to the user always keeping in mind their location in the interface and what they can do.
- Initial settings: refers to a question, such as: Does the system come with factory settings? If not, does it allow you to configure it during the first use?
- Latency Reduction: gets from guiding questions like: Is there a synchronization between actions and feedback (visual or audible) in the system?
- Environmental Conditions: obtained from guiding questions such as: Does the interface (sensors) depend on the surrounding environment?
- Privacy: relates to the user's data collection and awareness that data is being collected.
- User acceptance: refers to the comfort and acceptance of that technology on the user's body.

In all, there were nineteen wearable device usability heuristics that were evaluated through sixty guiding questions, where each question could be classified using a scale from 1 ("Totally disagree") to 10 ("Totally agree"). As the questionnaire used for this research was developed to evaluate different types of interfaces, the evaluator was instructed to mark "Not Applicable" if any question was unrelated to the evaluated device. Ultimately, the product and the questionnaire could be evaluated in free text fields.

4   Results

To ascertain the user experience during the use of the system and evaluate the quality of the system elements and the interactions that occur in it, five experts in the Computing area were invited to perform the tests, two specialists in HCI. An observer who took notes on the test and any comments made by the experts and a moderator who provided the first guidelines could answer questions from the participants and apply the evaluation questionnaire also participated in the tests.

To proceed with the test, the moderator instructed the experts on the procedures for conducting the test to provide all participants with an overview of the system's main functionalities. Then the participants put on the glove (without the moderator's help), and the moderator performed a calibration routine of the glove sensors. After the calibration of the sensors, the game was started, and the expert no longer received instructions on how to interact with the game. Figure 4 shows a picture of the expert performing the test with the system.

After playing Pac-Man by interacting with the game through the glove, all experts received two links containing evaluation forms for the device. The forms contained the heuristics presented in Sect. 3.5. The evaluation occurred in November 2022 at the university where the study was held. Table 1 presents the results of the heuristics

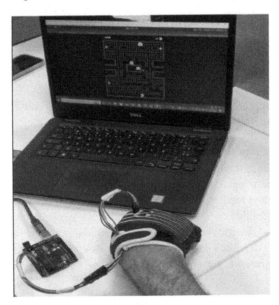

Fig. 4. Glove Controlled Pac-Man

compiled in each class to which it belongs. Heuristics classified as "Not Applicable" are represented by "-" in the Table.

The individual percentages of usability, presented in Table 1, were obtained through the average of the fields (questions) that were not marked as "Not Applicable", resulting at the end in the general usability given by the evaluator.

The values represent the individual experience of each expert and therefore have no meaning beyond their personal opinions, which explains the choice of certain fields as "Not applicable". However, when observing the individual percentages of each evaluator, even with the disagreements by opinion, it is seen that the values are consistent. Thus, when removing the outlier (evaluator E in Table 1), there is a 13% margin of discrepancy among the analyzes.

Some heuristics are worth further discussion, as they initially caused strangeness to the researchers, as shown below:

- "Flexibility and Efficiency" refer to the user being able to use the system in multiple ways and with different speeds of use. In this case, the system was designed to be used only by the glove, given the development focus on rehabilitation. Thus, it is understood that it has been classified as bad or not applicable.
- "Help and documentation" was classified as low usability because there was no complete explanation, via the system, of how to use all the functionalities. It also did not allow to help the user in running the game.
- "Save Status and Work Protection" refers to the users being able to return to the status where they stopped playing. This functionality was not contemplated in the game because it was not the game's objective. One of the evaluators may not have fully understood the meaning of the heuristic, classifying it as 50% and another as

Table 1. Results of Heuristic Evaluation by five experts.

Heuristic	Evaluators				
	A	B	C	D	E
Visibility of the system status	73,30%	82%	57,50%	93,30%	94%
Connection between the system and the real world	67,50%	100%	47,50%	72%	90%
Connection between the system and the real world	67,50%	100%	47,50%	72%	90%
User control and freedom	-	53&	90%	80%	10%
Consistency and patterns	97,50%	100%	94%	94%	100%
Recognition rather than memory, learning and anticipation	95%	100%	50%	80%	100%
Flexibility and efficiency of use	-	70%	2,50%	55%	-
Help users recognize, diagnose and recover from errors	100%	100%	2%	-	100%
Errors prevention	55%	86%	53%	100%	100%
Aesthetics and minimalist design	96,60%	90%	45%	100%	100%
Help and documentation	-	66%	-	53,30%	7,50%
Save status and work protection	-	50%	-	10%	-
Colors and readability	90%	93%	66%	76,60%	60%
Autonomy	100%	100%	30%	100%	100%
Initial settings	100%	82%	33%	78%	46%
Latency Reduction	-	100%	100%	100%	60%
Environmental Conditions	100%	53%	45%	100%	27,50%
Privacy	-	10%	-	40%	26,60%
User Acceptance	20%	80%	-	80%	90%
Grade given to the questionnaire	7	9	6	8	10
Medium	**Usability Percentage**				
71,86%	82,91%	79%	51,11%	77,19%	69%

10%, so it is concluded that it may be necessary to exclude this heuristic from the evaluation in future investigations.

- "Privacy" can refer to notifying the user about data collection. In this case, the software, in its initial version, had no implementation that notifies the user about any information collection, so this functionality will be implemented a posteriori, considering the need discussed through the result of the application of this heuristic.

The set of heuristics proposed by [22] was developed generically to be suitable for any wearable interface. Although it was possible to evaluate the prototype using such heuristics, it can be noticed that some of them did not completely serve to evaluate this interface. A subset of these heuristics could have presented a better result in less time for the evaluation, facilitating this process by experts.

It can also be seen from Table 1 that there was a diversity of understanding of the questionnaire by the evaluators. This is clear, for example, in the heuristics "Flexibility and Efficiency", "User Acceptance," and "Save Status and Work Protection". In the "Latency Reduction" case, it seems evident that the first evaluator did not understand the heuristic, assigning "Not applicable".

Another issue worth discussing is the grade the evaluators assign to the questionnaire. When asked about the grade, several pointed out the excess guiding questions they had to evaluate, which made the usability assessment quite tiring, even reflecting on the lack of attention when reading some questions.

5   Conclusions

This paper presented the development of a prototype of a wearable technology integrated into an IMU that aimed to detect the movements of supination and pronation of the wrist/elbow and extension and flexion of the wrist, as well as presenting the development of a digital game controlled through the movements detected by the wearable device. Among the many challenges that involve the development of systems that integrate wearable devices and computational systems, the development of comfortable wearable devices that integrate with clothing and meet the needs of users should be the first requirement to be evaluated.

A usability evaluation was performed using heuristics based on Nielsen's proposal and adapted to the specificities of wearable technology to evaluate the system presented in this project,

The evaluators did not understand some heuristic issues in this evaluation process, which may have partially compromised the results. Thus, we conclude that we should have utilized only a subset of the heuristics used in this work, focusing the evaluation only on questions applicable to this prototype.

In general, the system was well evaluated, showing that the pattern of glove use is constant, with low latency between the command and the game's response, and the autonomy heuristic obtained a good classification. In observing the test, it became clear that the use of the glove was very intuitive and that a possible product originating from this research has a good chance of being accepted by consumers.

On the other hand, some heuristics were essential to discuss functionalities that should be modified or included in the system. In addition, in future work, we consider conducting tests with more users who could test the prototype and verify the acceptance rate of this technology, using, for example, the Technology Acceptance Model 3 (TAM 3) [27]. Finally, shortly, we hope to test the system under the supervision of health professionals with typical users and during upper limb rehabilitation sessions, thus obtaining feedback on using the system.

Acknowledgments. The work was supported by the MackPesquisa (project: 231657) from Universidade Presbiteriana Mackenzie.

References

1. Ometov, A., et al.: A survey on wearable technology: history, state-of-the-art and current challenges. Computer Networks **193**, 108074 (2021). https://doi.org/10.1016/j.comnet.2021.108074
2. Anzaldo, D.: Wearable sports technology-Market landscape and compute SoC trends. In: 2015 International SoC Design Conference (ISOCC), pp. 217–218 (2015)
3. Vidal, M., Turner, J., Bulling, A., Gellersen, H.: Wearable eye tracking for mental health monitoring. Comput. Commun. **35**(11), 1306–1311 (2012). https://doi.org/10.1016/j.comcom.2011.11.002
4. Bhattacharyya, A., Mazumder, O., Chakravarty, K., Chatterjee, D., Sinha, A., Gavas, R.: Development of an interactive gaming solution using MYO sensor for rehabilitation. In: 2018 International Conference on Advances in Computing, Communications and Informatics (ICACCI) 2127–2130 (2018). https://doi.org/10.1109/ICACCI.2018.8554686
5. Daneault, J.F., et al.: Accelerometer data collected with a minimum set of wearable sensors from subjects with Parkinson's disease. Sci. Data, **8**(1), 48(2021). https://doi.org/10.6084/m9.figshare.13342055
6. Ferreira, D.R., Baptista, C.K., da Silva Rodrigues, B., Siqueira, B.C., Blascovi-Assis, S.M., Corrêa, A.G.: Development and test of a serious game for dorsiflexion and plantarflexion exercises of the feet. J. Interact. Syst. **12**(1), 58–68 (2021). https://doi.org/10.5753/jis.2021.1916
7. Dunne, L.E., et. al.: The social comfort of wearable technology and gestural interaction. In: 36th Annual International Conference of the IEEE Engineering in Medicine and Biology Society, pp. 4159–5162 (2014). https://doi.org/10.1109/EMBC.2014.6944540
8. Cantanhede, L.R.C., et. al.: Comportamento do consumidor de tecnologia vestível: características que influenciam na intenção de consumo. In: Revista Eletrônica de Administração (Porto Alegre), pp. 244–268 (2018). https://doi.org/10.1590/1413-2311.225.85428
9. Krombholz, K., Dabrowski, A., Smith, M., Weippl, E.: Ok glass, leave me alone: towards a systematization of privacy enhancing technologies for wearable computing. In: Brenner, M., Christin, N., Johnson, B., Rohloff, K. (eds.) FC 2015. LNCS, vol. 8976, pp. 274–280. Springer, Heidelberg (2015). https://doi.org/10.1007/978-3-662-48051-9_20
10. Gemperle, F., Ota, N., Siewiorek, D.: Design of a wearable tactile display. In: Proceedings Fifth International Symposium on Wearable Computers, pp. 5–12 (2001). https://doi.org/10.1109/ISWC.2001.962082
11. Kawamoto, A.L.S., Marques, D., Martins, V.F.: Revisão Sobre Usabilidade em Sistemas de Interação Não-Convencional. Revista Ibérica de Sistemas e Tecnologias de Informação **E26**, 624–636 (2020)
12. Nielsen, J.: Introduction to Usability. Nielsen Norman Group (2012). https://www.nngroup.com/articles/usability-101-introduction-to-usability
13. Fernandez, R.A.S., Sanchez-Lopez, J.L., Sampedro, C., Bavle, H., Molina, M., Campoy, P.: Natural user interfaces for human-drone multi-modal interaction. In: 2016 International Conference on Unmanned Aircraft Systems (ICUAS). (2016). https://doi.org/10.1109/ICUAS.2016.7502665
14. Blake, J.: Natural User Interfaces in. Manning Publications Company, Net. Manning Pubs Co Series (2013)
15. Godfrey, A., Hetherington, V., Shum, H., Bonato, P., Lovell, N.H., Stuart, S.: From A to Z: wearable technology explained. Maturitas **113**, 40–47 (2018). https://doi.org/10.1016/j.maturitas.2018.04.012
16. Wright, R., Keith, L.: Wearable tecnology: if the tech fits, wear it. J. Electron. Resour. Med. Libr. **11**(4), 204–216 (2014). https://doi.org/10.1080/15424065.2014.969051

17. Li, J., Liu, J., Li, C., Zhang, H., Li, Y.: Wearable wrist movement monitoring using dual surface-treated plastic optical fibers. Materials **13**(15), 3291 (2020). https://doi.org/10.3390/ma13153291

18. Lambelet, C., Lyu, M., Woolley, D., Gassert, R., Wenderoth, N.: The eWrist - A wearable wrist exoskeleton with sEMG-based force control for stroke rehabilitation. In: 2017 International Conference on Rehabilitation Robotics (ICORR), pp. 726–733 (2017). https://doi.org/10.1109/ICORR.2017.8009334

19. Xiao, F., Gu, L., Ma, W., Zhu, Y., Zhang, Z., Wang, Y.: Real time motion intention recognition method with limited number of surface electromyography sensors for A 7-DOF hand/wrist rehabilitation exoskeleton. Mechatronics **79**, 102642 (2021). https://doi.org/10.1016/j.mechatronics.2021.102642

20. Narejo, A., Baqai, A., Sikandar, N., Absar, A., Narejo, S.: Physiotherapy: Design and implementation of a wearable sleeve using IMU sensor and VR to measure elbow range of motion. Int. J. Adv. Comput. Sci. Appl. **11**(9) (2020). https://doi.org/10.14569/ijacsa.2020.0110953

21. Alexandre, R., Postolache, O., Girão, P. S.: Physical rehabilitation based on smart wearable and virtual reality serious game. In: 2019 IEEE International Instrumentation and Measurement Technology Conference (I2MTC), pp. 1–6 (2019). https://doi.org/10.1109/I2MTC.2019.8826947

22. Guizerian, M.K. Martins, V.F.: Proposal of a set of heuristics for evaluation of wearable interfaces usability. In: XXIII International Conference on Human Computer Interaction, pp. 1–8. Leida, Spain, 2023 (2024). https://doi.org/10.1145/3612783.3612791

23. Ferreira, D.R.D.M.J., de Lima, T.F.M., de Assis, G.A., Ruivo, E.L.P., da Silva Rodrigues, B., Corrêa, A.G.D.: Design of exergames controlled by wearable devices for sensorimotor skills: a framework proposal. In: 2022 IEEE 10th International Conference on Serious Games and Applications for Health (SeGAH), pp. 1–8. IEEE (2022). https://doi.org/10.1109/SEGAH54908.2022.9978550

24. Moser, N., O'Malley, M.K., Erwin, A.: Importance of wrist movement direction in performing activities of daily living efficiently. In: 2020 42nd Annual International Conference of the IEEE Engineering in Medicine & Biology Society (EMBC), pp. 3174–3177 (2020). https://doi.org/10.1109/EMBC44109.2020.9175381

25. Paschoarelli, L.C., Menezes, M.S.: Design e ergonomia: aspectos tecnológicos [online]. São Paulo: Editora UNESP; São Paulo: Cultura Acadêmica, vol. 279, p. ISBN 978–85- 7983–001–3 (2009). https://doi.org/10.7476/9788579830013

26. Granollers, T.: Usability evaluation with heuristics, beyond Nilsen's list. In: Proceedings of Eleventh International Conference on Advances in Computer-Human Interactions, pp. 60–65 (2018)

27. Venkatesh, V., Bala, H.: Technology acceptance model 3 and a research agenda on interventions. Decis. Sci. **39**(2), 273–315 (2008). https://doi.org/10.1111/j.1540-5915.2008.00192.x

DUXAIT NG: A Software for the Planning and Execution of User Experience Evaluations and Experiments

Joel Aguirre$^{(\boxtimes)}$ [ID], Adrian Lecaros [ID], Carlos Ramos [ID], Fiorella Falconi [ID], Arturo Moquillaza [ID], and Freddy Paz [ID]

Pontificia Universidad Católica del Perú, Av. Universitaria 1801, San Miguel, Lima 32, Lima, Perú

{aguirre.joel,adrian.lecaros,carlos.ramosp, ffalconit}@pucp.edu.pe, {amoquillaz,fpaz}@pucp.pe

Abstract. During the COVID-19 pandemic, conducting UX evaluations was difficult, increasing the pressure to develop usable software. For this objective, different methods and tools for the evaluation of usability were delivered, but no clear process or method to use in a determinate context was found in the literature. In that sense, previous studies showed interest in a formal process to conduct Usability evaluations. First, a formal process to conduct Heuristic Evaluation was proposed by Lecaros, A. followed by the process to conduct Tree Testing, proposed by Tapia A., both proposals were integrated into a process to conduct generic UX evaluations. In this study, we developed a software tool that supports the integrated process previously proposed by the authors, DUXAIT-NG, which is an academic software for usability and User Experience Evaluation. This tool is intended to support the evaluation process, from gathering the participants to performing the evaluation and interpreting the results.

DUXAIT NG is capable of handling different types of UX Evaluation and Testing methods. This software allows us to perform complete usability testing, not only the stage of design or planning, which was the problem evidenced in the literature with other software used in the Usability area. The first approach was software that supported a formal process for the Heuristic Evaluation, continued by another software for Tree Testing. As a team, we decided to develop a more general software to create a standard and support a unified process that allows the researchers to conduct any usability evaluation focused in a collaborative and remote environment. The first version is available on www.duxait-ng.net.

Keywords: Heuristic Evaluation · Usability Evaluation · Development · User Experience · Software Engineering · Human-Computer Interaction · Tree Testing · Sub heuristics

1 Introduction

For the final user of a system, the whole association with it and the impression of the system is considered User Experience (UX) [1]. Evaluating UX encompasses all the interactions between the final user and the company itself and the technology and services

P. H. Ruiz et al. (Eds.): HCI-COLLAB 2023, CCIS 1877, pp. 143–155, 2024.
https://doi.org/10.1007/978-3-031-57982-0_12

they offer [1]. UX encloses many aspects, including Usability [2], which nowadays has a crucial role in the interaction between humans and software products. In that sense, there is interest in evaluating usability and many existing methods for assessing a usability level, some of them made by UX practitioners with vast knowledge, such as Heuristic Evaluation, and others made with the help of the final user, such as Tree Testing [3].

During the COVID-19 pandemic, conducting a User Experience Evaluation in a usability laboratory was not possible. This context increased the pressure on developing usable systems and many methods and tools to support User-Centered Design (UCD) [4] projects and usability experiments. The evidenced difficulty was that we needed to find formal processes for the different methods, so the existing tools were heterogeneous despite supporting the same stage of the UCD process. There is no agreement on which method or tool is appropriate in which circumstance [4].

We focused on the Evaluation Phase due to the lack of tools that support conducting the methods in an integrated perspective. As a first approach, in the studies of Lecaros, A. [5] and Tapia, A. [6], The authors proposed two processes to conduct standard Heuristic Evaluation and tree testing, respectively, two of the most used evaluation usability methods. However, the processes only support one test each, the specific one for which they were designed. In a previous study, we proposed an integrated perspective that supports the two Tests from the beginning and is capable of adding more.

This study aims to present DUXAIT-NG, a software that supports an integrated usability evaluation process. This software supports UX practitioners to get more reliable results using standardized processes and methods.

This paper is presented as follows, the second section explains the background and related studies that motivated the creation of this software, the third section describes the prototyping, development, and final deployment, the fourth section explains the architecture of the software, and in the last section, we talk about the conclusions and future works.

2   Background and Related Works

This section presents and describes the main concepts and technologies that have been worked on within the context of the implemented software.

2.1   Evaluation Methods

As part of one of the methods which the developed tool supports, the heuristic evaluation, according to Paz [7], is a method proposed by Jakob Nielsen, where experts evaluate a software product in depth to confront them with a set of principles called heuristics to identify usability problems. This method has as output a set of problems ordered by severity, which serves as input for redesign processes and design proposal iterations, among others. However, despite the benefits provided by this method for improving user interfaces, a limited amount of information detailing the execution of the heuristic method is found, which generates different interpretations and roles for the execution of the method, which affects the complexity of the method's execution and the final result. For this reason, Freddy Paz established a framework based on an analysis of the selected studies that will allow the execution of heuristic inspections in a structured, organized, and detailed manner [7]. This framework establishes five main phases: preparation, training, execution, and discussion. These phases enable the identification of usability criteria, training of the involved evaluators, inspection of interfaces, discussion of usability issues found, and generating a report consolidating the previously discussed information [7].

Furthermore, to carry out a heuristic evaluation is necessary to define a set of heuristics to be evaluated. In this regard, it is required to adapt these heuristics to the specific needs of the evaluated system, which leads evaluators to combine different expert recommendations in these evaluations. As a result, it creates an extra effort, leads to the repetition of heuristics, and obtains an imprecise degree of interface usability [8]. In this sense, a method is established to execute the heuristic evaluation by standardizing intuitively formulated questions, allowing for the quantification of interface usability based on the fulfillment of a checklist associated with different heuristics [9]. With this method, each specialist is responsible for conducting the heuristic evaluation and assigns a score to an evaluation item, ultimately generating a degree of compliance with the proposed heuristics [9].

On the other hand, the second type of evaluation that the tool supports is Tree testing, defined as a usability evaluation technique focused on assessing the software architecture of a web page [6, 11]. This evaluation is performed by having a user search for items in a menu, which allows for evaluating the hierarchy among the defined items [10].

2.2 Tools and Related Works

Based on the proposal from the paper developed by Paz et al. [6], a process is established to support heuristic evaluation and tree testing from an integrated UX perspective. It means that tests are considered with HCI specialists and end users of the analyzed interfaces. In order to integrate both evaluation methods, we took as a reference the work done by Lecaros [13], who defined a BPMN (Business Process Model and Notation) diagram for conducting a heuristic evaluation. Similarly, for conducting the Tree Testing evaluation, Tapia established a remote Tree Testing evaluation process based on a systematic review and literature analysis.

By considering both previous works in detail using a BPMN diagram, the development of this new process focuses purely on integrating both methods. We validate this integration through experts' opinions in this type of evaluation and the fulfillment of minimum process requirements. Therefore, Fig. 1 details the activities of the integrated usability evaluation process. Additionally, the authors highlight the possibility of developing a web platform for the automation and standardization of this process, presented in this paper.

Moreover, software tools have been developed to support these activities to prevent new researchers from conducting subjective and ad hoc usability evaluations without a defined process or heuristics to evaluate an interface [14, 15].

Usability evaluation tools are defined as those capable of collecting and providing test data to stakeholders such as developers or experts [15]. For this reason, systematic reviews of these tools were carried out, highlighting the works of Castro and Lecaros. The first article addresses three questions related to the state of the art regarding the tools

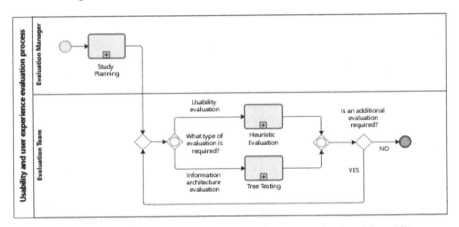

Fig. 1. Usability and User Experience Evaluation Process (retrieved from [6]).

currently used for usability evaluations and the techniques that benefit from them. The second article focuses on determining which usability tools currently enable heuristic evaluations.

The results showed that fourteen out of fifteen studies obtained by Castro were software applications, with only one focusing on heuristic evaluations. The mentioned tool is OwlEye, which performs a heuristic evaluation using a neural network on different screens of an application [16]. However, despite its potential for detecting interface problems, it has limitations in terms of compatibility with additional tools used. In other words, it is not capable of evaluating all presented interfaces.

On the other hand, Lecaros focused his study on heuristic evaluations, where he obtained four software tools. One of them supports the execution of Heuristic Evaluations through data collection and reporting via a web platform. The other tools support the heuristic evaluation tasks performed by an expert, focusing on specific heuristics such as system visibility or navigability.

From the presented tools, we could identify that there needed to be an integrated support tool that encompasses the entire process of a heuristic evaluation, which fails to automate and facilitate the tasks that an evaluator faces when conducting a heuristic evaluation, from planning to resulting discussion. Furthermore, this characteristic in the presented tools needs to be improved to ensure evaluators conduct inspections in various manners, which could result in imprecise findings regarding usability issues.

For this reason, in 2022, a thesis project was presented focusing on developing a web application to automate the heuristic evaluation process, addressing difficulties related to heuristic selection, execution, and data processing due to the lack of an integrated tool [14]. Ultimately, this application presented positive results as it demonstrated its usefulness through a case study, where it was perceived as an easy-to-use tool of interest for future evaluations by experts [14].

3   Software Development Process and Deployment

To develop DUXAIT NG, we started with the design of interfaces. Initially, for the design phase, the software was thought of as a Module for the UX evaluation in remote contexts that would reduce the manual tasks, the complexity of documenting the process, and reduce costs and time in general. As the first step, only the planning phase was prototyped as part of a design workshop. As an example of the final prototypes, Fig. 2 shows the 'My Projects' section, where the user would search for all the projects they are participating in and create a new one. Figure 3 shows the process for creating a new project.

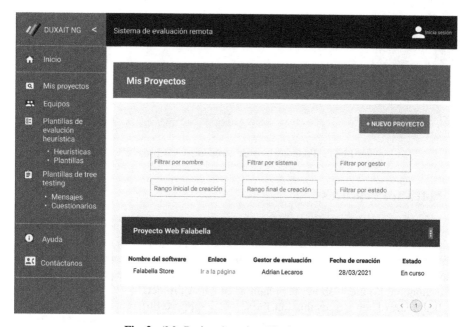

Fig. 2. 'My Projects' section. Final prototypes.

For the development phase, we created two teams within the group; the front-end team would develop using React JS, a framework widely used in web development, and the back-end team would develop using Python with Flask Restful for a serverless solution. In this way, deployment would be easier using lambda functions in AWS.

We followed a development framework that allowed us to deliver iterable MVPs, which permit testing and continuous development of the software tool. Finally, when the software was ready, we deployed it using Amazon Web Services and gave it the domain of www.duxait-ng.net.

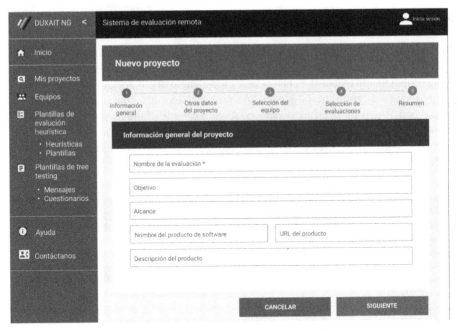

Fig. 3. Four-step process to create a new project.

4 Software Features

In the latest version, the users can select different evaluations for a new project, starting with Heuristic Evaluation and Tree Testing, based on previous works of Lecaros A. and Tapia A., respectively. Once finished the planning of the new project, the evaluation manager is asked to complete the evaluation details and notify the participants to start the evaluation. Figure 4, shows the planning of a new project.

In the case of heuristic evaluation, the software supports different types of conducting them. First, it offers two formal Heuristic Evaluations, the process proposed by Paz, F. and the Sub Heuristic Approach by Granollers, T. Fig. 5 shows the details of a heuristic evaluation, where the manager could choose between available methods to conduct the evaluation.

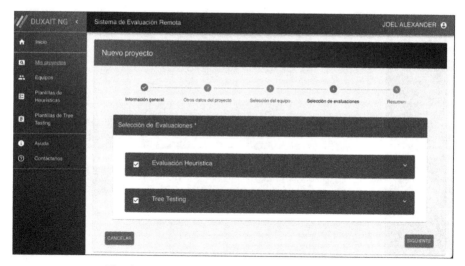

Fig. 4. Final four-step process to create a new project.

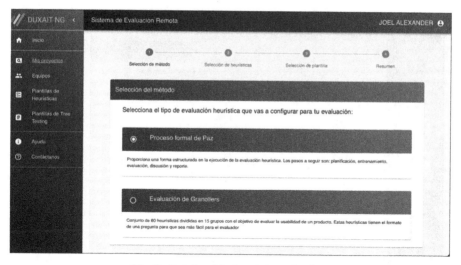

Fig. 5. Details of the heuristic evaluation.

The software offers the evaluators an intuitive view based on the manual tools proposed by the method selected authors. For example, Fig. 6 shows the Granollers sub-heuristic approach in a web-style view, similar to a form where the participants could input the scale and commentaries.

Finally, for the evaluator manager, the software facilitates the analysis of results by automating reports. For example, in the sub-heuristic method of conducting heuristic evaluations, the final results could be filtered by participants, and a graphic with the usability scale is shown in the interface. Figure 7 shows the results of a sub-heuristic evaluation approach.

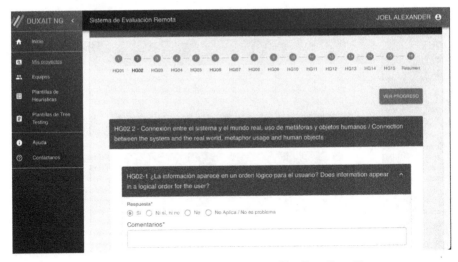

Fig. 6. Fifteen sub-heuristics proposed by Granollers, T.

Fig. 7. Results processed for a Heuristic Evaluation.

5 Software Architecture

The software architecture design had three main expected results, the logic view, the functional view, and the deployment view. The three are explained in this section.

5.1 Logical View

In this view, we designed the ER Diagram with the objects that would be used to develop DUXAIT-NG. This diagram was supposed to be iterated during the development process and serve as a base for the official database. The diagram was made using a collaborative tool during the pandemic carrying virtual sessions.

As explained, Fig. 8 shows the logic view, an entity-relationship diagram with the finally implemented objects.

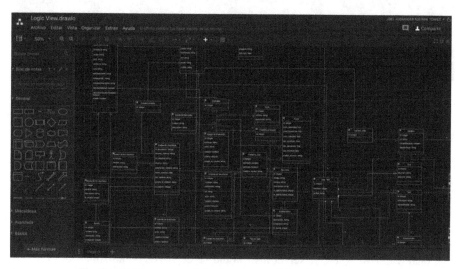

Fig. 8. ER Diagram made in draw.io, a collaborative design tool.

5.2 Functional View

In this view, we designed the Use Case Diagram with the different use cases the software would support. We defined the users; for example, Evaluator, Moderator, and Evaluation Manager. These users interact with a total of thirty use cases, grouped into five modules to be implemented.

As explained, Fig. 9 shows the functional view, a use-case diagram with the use cases to be implemented and supported by DUXAIT-NG.

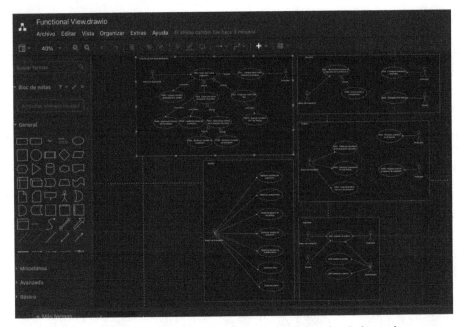

Fig. 9. Use Case Diagram made in draw.io, a collaborative design tool.

5.3 Deployment View

In this view, we described how we deployed the components. The deployment diagram shows the distribution that followed a Client-Server design. Focused on the Server side, we chose AWS as the platform that would host the software.

The front end would be deployed on a website-enabled Amazon S3 bucket service. The back end would be deployed using an AWS Lambda function connected to an Amazon RDS for a relational MySQL Database and Amazon DynamoDB for a non-relational database. The File server also would be deployed on an Amazon S3 bucket service. Finally, the login and authorization process would be handled by the Google API service.

As explained, Fig. 10 shows the Deployment Diagram with the components and deployment distribution.

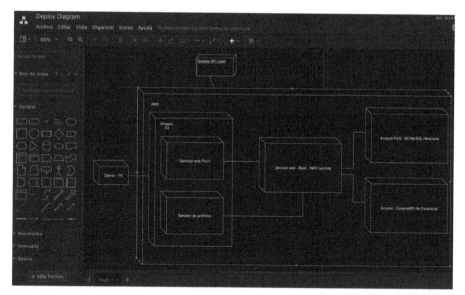

Fig. 10. Deployment Diagram made in draw.io, a collaborative design tool.

6 Conclusions and Future Works

Based on a detailed process of supporting heuristic evaluation and tree testing, an integrated web application tool, DUXAIT-NG, was developed, which automates a usability evaluation process. Building upon the implemented modules, evaluators with varying levels of experience have the opportunity to visualize the evaluation process and its associated tasks. This is achieved by selecting the heuristics that best suit the software under evaluation in the case of heuristic evaluation or by conducting information architecture analysis when planning and executing the Tree testing method. Additionally, the definition of profiles for each project member facilitates the execution of evaluations, whether they are conducted in person or remotely. Furthermore, it enables the visualization of evaluations completed by each evaluator to facilitate discussions regarding the evaluated software.

In this regard, the software has been released, its design and development process have been presented, and its main characteristics have been described in this paper.

As part of future work, it is expected that the tool will be able to perform other types of usability evaluations, such as communicability evaluation, remote usability testing, and semiotic inspection methods. Likewise, conducting various case studies in domains, including mobile, web, and desktop applications, will enhance the tool and its functionalities. These case studies also serve as validation of the software; we plan to organize focus groups or conferences where people would interact with it.

Acknowledgments. This work is part of the research project "Virtualización del proceso de evaluación de experiencia de usuario de productos de software para escenarios de no presencialidad" (virtualization of the user experience evaluation process of software products for non-presential scenarios), developed by HCI-DUXAIT research group. HCI-DUXAIT is a research group that belongs to the PUCP (Pontificia Universidad Católica del Perú). This work was funded by the Dirección de Fomento a la Investigación at the PUCP through grant 2021-C-0023.

References

1. Munim, K.M., Islam, I., Khatun, M., Karim, M.M., Islam, M.N.: Towards developing a tool for UX evaluation using facial expression. In: 2017 3rd International Conference on Electrical Information and Communication Technology (EICT), pp. 1–6. Khulna, Bangladesh (2017). https://doi.org/10.1109/EICT.2017.8275227
2. Pinto Corredor, J.D., Agredo Delgado, V., Collazos, C.A.: Construyendo una guía para la evaluación de la usabilidad en EVAs. Campus Virtuales, 7(2), 93–104 (2018). https://dialnet.unirioja.es/servlet/articulo?codigo=6681861
3. Paz, F., Lecaros, A., Falconi, F., Tapia, A., Aguirre, J., Moquillaza, A.: A process to support heuristic evaluation and tree testing from a UX integrated perspective. In: Latifi, S. (eds) ITNG 2023. AISC, vol. 1445, pp. 369–377. Springer, Cham (2023). https://doi.org/10.1007/978-3-031-28332-1_42
4. Ferre, X., Bevan, N.: Usability planner: a tool to support the process of selecting usability methods. In: Campos, P., Graham, N., Jorge, J., Nunes, N., Palanque, P., Winckler, M. (eds.) INTERACT 2011. LNCS, vol. 6949, pp. 652–655. Springer, Heidelberg (2011). https://doi.org/10.1007/978-3-642-23768-3_105
5. Lecaros, A., Moquillaza, A., Falconi, F., Aguirre, J., Tapia, A., Paz, F.: Selection and modeling of a formal heuristic evaluation process through comparative analysis. In: Soares, M.M., Rosenzweig, E., Marcus, A. (eds.) Design, User Experience, and Usability: UX Research, Design, and Assessment. HCII 2022 LNCS, vol. 13321, pp. 28–46. Springer, Cham (2022). https://doi.org/10.1007/978-3-031-05897-4_3
6. Tapia, A., Moquillaza, A., Aguirre, J., Falconi, F., Lecaros, A., Paz, F.: A process to support the remote tree testing technique for evaluating the information architecture of user interfaces in software projects. In: Soares, M.M., Rosenzweig, E., Marcus, A. (eds.) Design, User Experience, and Usability: UX Research, Design, and Assessment. HCII 2022. LNCS, vol. 13321, pp. 75–92. Springer, Cham (2022). https://doi.org/10.1007/978-3-031-05897-4_6
7. Paz, F., Paz, F.A., Pow-Sang, J.A., Collazos, C.: A formal protocol to conduct usability heuristic evaluations in the context of the software development process. Int. J. Eng. Technol. 7, 10–19 (2018). https://doi.org/10.14419/IJET.V7I2.28.12874
8. Bonastre, L., Granollers, T.: A set of heuristics for user experience evaluation in e-commerce websites. In: International Conference on Advances in Computer-Human Interaction (2014). https://www.thinkmind.org/articles/achi_2014_2_10_20126.pdf
9. Granollers, T.: Experimental validation of a set of heuristics for user experience evaluations in e-commerce websites. 2016 IEEE 11th Colombian Computing Conference, CCC 2016 - Conference Proceedings. 27–34 (2016). https://doi.org/10.1109/COLUMBIANCC.2016.7750783
10. Laubheimer, P.: Tree testing: fast, iterative evaluation of menu labels and categories (2023). https://www.nngroup.com/articles/tree-testing/
11. Borisova, L.: How startups should evaluate their websites' UX? Comparison of UX evaluation methods through evaluation of UX of the prototype of a matching platform for the rental housing market in Finland – Sopia. Master's thesis, Aalto University School of Business. International Design Business Management (2019). https://aaltodoc.aalto.fi/handle/123456789/42377?locale-attribute=en

12. Castro, J.W., Garnica, I., Rojas, L.A.: Automated tools for usability evaluation: a systematic mapping study. In: Meiselwitz, G. (ed.) Social Computing and Social Media: Design, User Experience and Impact. HCII 2022. LNCS, vol. 13315, pp. 28–46. Springer, Cham (2022). https://doi.org/10.1007/978-3-031-05061-9_3

13. Liu, Z., Chen, C., Wang, J., Huang, Y., Hu, J., Wang, Q.: Owl eyes: spotting UI display issues via visual understanding. In: Proceedings - 2020 35th IEEE/ACM International Conference on Automated Software Engineering, ASE 2020, pp. 398–409 (2020). https://doi.org/10.1145/3324884.3416547

14. Lecaros, A.: Implementación de una aplicación web de soporte al proceso formal de evaluaciones heurísticas. Pontificia Universidad Católica del Perú. Departamento de Ingeniería (2022). https://tesis.pucp.edu.pe/repositorio/handle/20.500.12404/22388

Eye Tracking-Based Platform for Programming Teaching

Guillermo A. Guerrero$^{(\boxtimes)}$ ⬤, Jorge P. Rodríguez⬤, and Laura A. Cecchi⬤

Grupo de Investigación en Lenguajes e Inteligencia Artificial, Facultad de Informática,
Universidad Nacional del Comahue, Neuquén, Argentina
`{guillermo.guerrero,j.rodrig,lcecchi}@fi.uncoma.edu.ar`

Abstract. Currently, the benefits of learning about Computer Science in general, and algorithms and programming in particular, are widely recognised. There is a vulnerable student population with motor disabilities that could benefit from programming learning environments featuring interaction methods beyond conventional ones, such as a keyboard and mouse.

In this work, we present the definition and design of a platform dedicated to programming education that utilises eye tracking as the primary mechanism for human-computer interaction. This techno-pedagogical device supports the creation of simple software components, serving as a tool to reinforce the learning of concepts in the field of algorithms and programming. Additionally, an open-source prototype is introduced, implementing key aspects of the designed platform. This prototype allows users who are unable to interact through conventional means to develop, modify, and execute programs using their gaze as the primary means of human-computer interaction. The purpose is to contribute to narrowing the gaps created by conventional input methods when aiming to include students with motor disabilities in environments designed to learn programming practices and concepts.

Keywords: Eye Tracking · Programming Teaching · Computer Science Education

1 Introduction

Currently, the benefits of learning Computer Science in general, and specifically about Algorithms and Programming, are widely recognised. These benefits are primarily oriented towards developing Computational Thinking skills, which are crucial for improving problem-solving abilities. Consequently, the teaching of computer science is encouraged from the early stages of compulsory education [1, 2], aiming to enhance opportunities for understanding and engaging in today's society. As a result, there is a global trend to incorporate subjects directly related to programming into curriculum designs [3–8].

Eye tracking is a set of techniques, methods, and devices that allows the recording, measurement, analysis, and interpretation of data regarding the position and movement of

P. H. Ruiz et al. (Eds.): HCI-COLLAB 2023, CCIS 1877, pp. 156–168, 2024.
https://doi.org/10.1007/978-3-031-57982-0_13

the eyeball [9]. Eye tracking is widely used as a human-computer interaction mechanism for individuals with motor disabilities [10].

The primary tools through which a student interacts with a computer and, consequently, with a programming language, are the keyboard and mouse. These physical means pose obstacles for students with full motor capacity, in terms of coordination and fine motor control, often leading to repetitive strain injuries in hands and wrists [11]. For individuals with reduced motor capacity or movement impairments in their limbs, interacting with a computer becomes even more challenging.

There is a student population with motor disabilities that could benefit from programming learning environments utilising eye tracking as an interaction method, facilitating coding and program execution. The target population consists of individuals with multiple disabilities who are users of assistive technology. These individuals have difficulties due to insufficient motor skills to establish seamless interaction with a conventional programming environment, and although they are able to understand language, they have trouble expressing themselves verbally. These devices could potentially broaden and enhance employment opportunities for these vulnerable individuals.

In this paper, we introduce a definition for platforms designed for teaching programming that use eye tracking as the primary mechanism for human-computer interaction. Additionally, we present a design that models the proposed definition. It is a techno-pedagogical device that supports the construction of simple software components, positioning itself as a didactic resource to support learning concepts in the field of Algorithms and Programming. In this context, an open-source prototype is presented, implementing core aspects of the designed platform and utilising conventional and low-cost hardware devices. Thus, a user who lacks the ability to interact via keyboard and mouse can develop, modify, and execute programs using their eyes as the primary means of computer interaction. The aim is to contribute to narrowing the gaps caused by conventional input methods, such as the mouse and keyboard, when integrating students from the target population into environments designed for learning programming practices and concepts.

Developing platforms that use affordable hardware and offer alternative input methods, taking into account these challenges and providing an initial approach to computational knowledge, is of great interest. In this regard, the platform and prototype presented in this work expand didactic possibilities and the target population.

The rest of this paper is organised as follows. Section 2 provides an analysis of related works. Section 3 introduces the definition and design of the platform, specifying its components and the programming language. Details of the prototype implementation based on the presented platform are described in Sect. 4. Additionally, the user's performance in that environment is analysed. Finally, in Sect. 5, conclusions and future work are presented.

2 Related Work

At present, there are several general-purpose tools and platforms, such as HIRU by IRISBOND and Tobii Eye Tracker by Tobii Technology, that integrate eye tracking techniques into a wide variety of domains, including video games, user-customised vehicles, and healthcare, among others [12, 13]. The utilisation of this technology is particularly notable for improving communication possibilities for individuals with motor disabilities. Typically, these tools utilise specialised hardware and provide proprietary licenses for the software, hardware, or both.

In the field of education, some eye movement-based systems have been developed to observe and assess the level of attention and concentration maintained by students during educational activities. These techniques allow the collection of information that is not consciously controlled by students and is generally more challenging to obtain through traditional methods [14–16]. Other applications have been developed to address observation and evaluation of the activity and the attitudes displayed by students during online exams [17]. Moreover, eye tracking has been used during the coding process to assess the cognitive effort required when using different programming tools [18].

Furthermore, in the context of software testing and maintenance, there are numerous open-source development proposals that offer alternative input methods aimed at facilitating and streamlining code navigation. These tools enable simple code edits, such as selecting and moving small text fragments, with the intention of providing a smoother interaction, primarily based on keyboard shortcuts and user eye tracking through cameras. Javardeye [11] is a prototype text code editor for Java that integrates eye tracking technology. Similarly, EyeNav [19], an extension for the text editor Brackets.io[1], uses external hardware for eye tracking. This technique is employed in these works to facilitate program navigation by positioning the editing cursor over code lines with the gaze, eliminating the need to move hands from the keyboard to control the mouse. Therefore, they relegate eye tracking to a supporting role for programming rather than a primary input method for programming. These products are not designed as eye tracking-based development environments; instead, they focus on the code review and maintenance process. Consequently, unlike the platform presented in this work, these tools are intended for individuals who already know how to program. They are not proposed for learning but are oriented towards improving the interaction for developers without disabilities, offering an alternative means of interaction to the familiar ones.

3 Definition and Characteristics of the Platform

With the primary motivation of contributing to the reduction of gaps caused by conventional input methods in programming education, this work proposes its own definition for the concept of a platform based on Eye Tracking techniques formulated to address this type of educational challenge. In this environment, an individual within the target population of this work can connect with the fundamental principles of programming by constructing their own programs, where the necessary interaction to produce code is supported by eye-tracking techniques.

The platform development process considers the early involvement of education specialists for students with disabilities. This approach allows for a deeper understanding of the educational needs of the target population and the development of a platform more tailored to specific issues at hand. In this direction, there is an effort to concretely construct

---

[1] https://brackets.io/.

a definition for the term *"Eye Tracking-based Platform for Programming Teaching"* that describes its constituent components and their relationships. The *Eye Tracking-based Platform for Programming Teaching* consists of a programming language that enables the visual development of programs, an integrated development environment that allows for the selection of language elements to generate code through eye tracking, and a runtime environment that provides the space to visualise the behaviour of the produced program. Figure 1 presents the diagram describing a design based on the proposed definition of the platform.

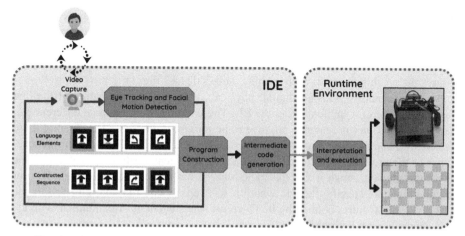

Fig. 1. Diagram of the Platform for Programming Education based on Eye Tracking.

The programming language was defined by specifying its syntax through four basic instructions and an associated grammar. The instructions, symbolised by pictograms designed to be intuitive for students, dictate four possible movements for an agent on a grid-represented arena. The language design is based on the work presented in [20].

The instructions include *Move Forward* and *Move Backward*, corresponding to translational movements that modify the agent's current position, and *Turn Left* and *Turn Right*, rotational movements that change its current orientation. In Fig. 2, the set of pictograms representing the instructions that constitute the language is depicted. A sequence of these instructions determines a program and, consequently, a sequence of movements for the agent within a runtime environment.

A program developed in this language is interpreted from left to right, with its instructions arranged sequentially. Thus, the program has a single linear reading direction, making it easy to follow and interpret at a glance.

The Integrated Development Environment (IDE) records user eye movements and some facial expressions using Eye Tracking techniques and resources provided by Facial Landmark Detection. This information is employed by the IDE to select and sequence language elements during the program construction and editing stage. This process is cyclically repeated until the intended program is achieved (see Fig. 1). Once this stage is completed, the code created with pictograms is processed to produce a textual version of

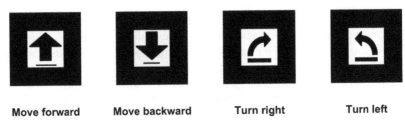

Move forward   Move backward   Turn right   Turn left

Fig. 2. Pictograms representing the language instructions.

the program expressed in an Intermediate Language. This generated code serves as input for execution in a Runtime Environment. Additionally, the platform provides a Runtime Environment (RE) for a program coded in the intermediate language, encompassing the interpretation and execution of the code. It also serves as the space where students can observe the result generated when running their code (see Fig. 1).

Various scenarios, whether digital, physical, or mixed (a combination of the first two), can be used for implementing the RE. These scenarios incorporate different elements, which do not necessarily all have to be present in the same RE. Among these elements we can mention: the area, referred to as the arena (sandbox), where the execution of the program takes place, which allows the agent's path to be delimited, the agents that move through it and the static objects that may appear. Although the user program does not specify the area where it will run, its construction must follow the constraints and features defined by it. Therefore, the student must be familiar with the RE's characteristics beforehand.

With the assistance of the *Eye Tracking-based Platform for Programming Teaching*, a student can construct their own program using eye movement and some facial expressions as interaction devices. Once the code generation process is finished, the student can execute it in various environments depending on the platform's implementation.

4 Platform Development Aspects

The development of the interactive platform was carried out in the Python programming language, utilising a set of purpose-specific libraries that extend the language's functionalities. The cross-platform framework MediaPipe and the library OpenCV, both of which are open source, were employed for the detection of the face structure and the eye and facial movements.

The MediaPipe[2] framework [21] allows obtaining digitised data from the human face in real-time, based on video capture. MediaPipe Face Mesh uses machine learning (ML) to infer the 3D facial surface, requiring only a single camera input without the need for a dedicated depth sensor, offering suitable performance for live experiences.

In the detection of 3D facial landmarks, MediaPipe Face Mesh employs the transfer learning technique in ML. To train the network, it uses rendered synthetic data to predict the coordinates of 3D landmarks and labelled real data for predicting semantic contours in

---

[2] https://developers.google.com/mediapipe.

2D. The resulting network makes reasonable predictions of 3D landmarks on real-world data.

The OpenCV library is used to access the video camera and retrieve a frame that is sent to MediaPipe Face Mesh. To generate the network of 3D landmarks, the framework receives this cropped video frame without additional depth input. From the frame, once the presence of a face is detected with sufficient confidence, the model generates the positions of the 3D points. Thus, a real-time visual representation of the prediction model's result is obtained. In Fig. 3, we can observe an example of how OpenCV visually represents the landmark network resulting from applying MediaPipe Face Mesh.

The MediaPipe Face Mesh model can locate a maximum of 468 landmarks. For this development, we are primarily interested in those that can provide information related to gaze. In this regard, for the platform's operation, we analyse the identifiers assigned by the model to each landmark, isolating 40 indicators associated with the external structure of the eyes. Out of these, 32 form the contour of the orbital regions, and 8 delineate the horizontal and vertical borders of the pupils.

While the model generates landmark positions in a three-dimensional space, it should be considered that the intention when using the platform is to face the camera. In this scenario, the usefulness of the Z-axis or depth provided by each landmark is not relevant. We can consider this exception as the projection of these indicators from the three-dimensional space onto a two-dimensional space.

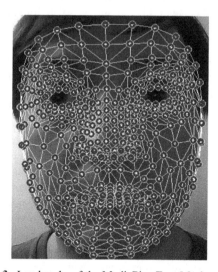

Fig. 3. Landmarks of the MediaPipe Face Mesh model

From these data, we calculate two types of averages. On one hand, for each eye, the 2D Euclidean distance between its outermost indicators horizontally is calculated, and then these two distances are averaged. On the other hand, depending on whether we are analysing movements to the right or left of the eyes, the averages are calculated according to (1).

$$
\begin{aligned}
Avg\_EyeMov\_Right &= [EuclideanDist\_2D(LeftEye\_MedialCommissure,\ LeftEye\_Pupil)+ \\
&\quad EuclideanDist\_2D(RightEye\_LateralCommissure,\ RightEye\_Pupil)]/2 \\
Avg\_EyeMov\_Left &= [EuclideanDist\_2D(LeftEye\_LateralCommissure,\ LeftEye\_Pupil)+ \\
&\quad EuclideanDist\_2D(RightEye\_MedialCommissure,\ RightEye\_Pupil)]/2
\end{aligned}
\tag{1}
$$

In these calculations, we consider as external indicators those located at the lateral corners (see Fig. 4a, yellow circle) and the mid-corners of the eyes (see Fig. 4a, green circle). Finally, we estimate eye movement by measuring two ratios that relate to the mentioned averages: one between the first average and Avg_EyeMov_Right, and its counterpart, between the first average and Avg_EyeMov_Left.

To measure the gaze direction, a threshold was estimated based on experimental tests, whose value indicates how much the eye should move for the platform to consider it a gaze event in a particular direction. Thus, when the obtained ratio exceeds the established threshold value, a gaze event towards one of the directions is detected. The reason for using a ratio between distances, rather than just the distance between external indicators and pupils, is that these distances can increase or decrease based on the user's proximity to the camera, rendering the use of this measure obsolete for gaze event detection.

From the landmarks estimated by MediaPipe that border the pupils, and using the `minEnclosingCircle` function from the OpenCV library, the minimum-radius circumference containing these landmarks is obtained (see Fig. 4b, magenta circle on the face). The centre of the pupil is obtained through the properties of this circumference: its radius and the coordinates of its centre (see Fig. 4b).

The described features are associated with the design and implementation considerations taken into account in the development of a *gaze detection event*. This event indicates to the platform whether there has been a pupil movement that exceeded the threshold and in which direction it occurred.

It is important to note that a gaze detection event can occur many times per second. Therefore, if an action is to be associated with such an event, the user will not have precise control over the number of times that action will occur. On the other hand, there is the possibility of a gaze detection event that is not intentional on the part of the user. For example, a user may inadvertently focus their gaze on some part of the screen far enough in a certain direction, surpassing the established threshold, triggering a gaze detection event. In this sense, two events were developed to provide the user with more control by associating an action with an event. Initially, the user indicates the intention for their gaze detection event to be considered from that moment on. This milestone is called an *activation event* and is triggered by analysing mouth movements. When the user slightly opens their mouth, the activation event is triggered, and from that moment on, the *gaze detection event* is activated. The behaviour of the activation event attempts to address the aforementioned issues in the following way:

- A gaze detection event cannot occur without a preceding activation event.

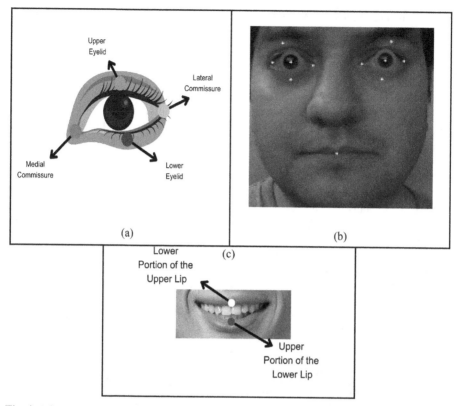

Fig. 4. Visual depiction of the landmarks registered by the platform. **(a)** Eye structure (left). **(b)** Eye and pupil estimate (magenta), landmarks used for interaction (white). **(c)** Mouth structure.

- *An activation event cannot occur more than once every 5 s.*

To verify the mouth opening, two new landmarks provided by the MediaFace Mesh model are required: one is the position of the bottom of the upper lip, and the other is the top of the lower lip (see Fig. 4c). When the 2D Euclidean distance between these two indicators exceeds a certain threshold, the mouth is considered open, and the *activation event* is detected. Finally, a *selection event* was developed that indicates to the platform that once the user has navigated their gaze through the list of language pictograms and stopped, they want to confirm the selection of a language element, implying the inclusion of that element in the user's program construction. This event is detected when both eyelids are closed for 3 s. The indicators used for detection include the upper eyelid, lower eyelid, and the 2D Euclidean distance between them. When this distance is sufficiently small, the event is detected, and the selection is confirmed.

After addressing the software aspects necessary for the operation of the platform, it remains to highlight that, from the hardware point of view, a conventional computer and an additional low-cost external device are required. To capture the frames used by the MediaPipe framework, which are employed in detecting facial structure and eye and facial movements, a webcam with a minimum resolution of 720p is sufficient to meet the platform's requirements. MediaPipe does not require any dedicated video graphics card or special features for image processing.

4.1 The User in the Environment

The implemented prototype provides an environment that allows the user to quickly familiarise themselves with the elements that contribute to the tool's functionality. To achieve this, each component of the user interface has a clear visual delineation of its elements, maintaining a clean, intuitive, and simple interface. The goal is to offer an interaction strongly tailored to individuals with motor disabilities. In this direction, and in order to achieve good usability of the tool, there was early involvement of special education experts, who provided guidance regarding the definition and arrangement of interface elements to better suit the user's needs. These components correspond to: Settings Area, Video Capture Area, Selection Area, Code Editing Area, Controls Area, and Output Area. Figure 5 and Fig. 6 present screenshots of the platform where the mentioned areas are distinguished. We want to highlight that the prototype user interface is written in Spanish. For that reason, in the figures describing a screenshot, many words are in Spanish.

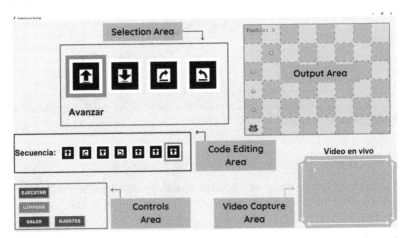

Fig. 5. Selection Area (outlined in red), Code Editing Area (outlined in blue), Controls Area (outlined in magenta), Video Capture Area (outlined in orange), and Output Area (outlined in green).

In the Settings Area, sensitivity and duration parameters for gaze detection and selection events are configured, adaptable to user needs. This area is enabled by pressing the Settings Button (*Ajustes* in Spanish) located in the Controls Area (see Fig. 5). The platform has default values, which were determined experimentally. These values can be adjusted by the user to control, for example, how much they need to close their eyes to trigger a selection event, as well as the time they need to keep them closed. Another possible adjustment is to reduce or increase the magnitude of the ratio used to determine a gaze event. Thus, one can regulate how much gaze in a direction should be detected as a gaze detection event. Figure 6 shows a screenshot of the Settings Area with various parameters that can be configured.

Fig. 6. Settings Area screenshot.

The Video Capture Area (Fig. 5) displays the video streaming obtained from the camera. Moreover, the user can also visualise the landmarks at key points on the face, generated by MediaPipe Face Mesh, which are used for detecting the mentioned events (see Fig. 4b). Thus, in real-time, the user can see how the tool records its movements, providing feedback about the effectiveness of tracking and the ability to test and adjust the sensitivity of detecting different events. Furthermore, this feedback enables the user to verify if the device is functioning properly.

The Selection Area exhibits the elements that constitute the language. These elements are pictograms that depict the action corresponding to each instruction (see Fig. 2). A green box over one of the language elements serves as a visual indicator of the instruction currently being focused (see Fig. 5). The user can focus on different instructions through *gaze detection events*. These events allow moving the selector in the direction of the gaze and subsequently confirming the selection of a language element through the *selection event*.

Every time the user confirms the selection of one of the pictograms, it becomes part of the user's program under construction. That is, the sequential set of instructions the user chose to solve a given problem. This construction is displayed in the Code Editing Area, in the form of reduced versions of the visual representations of the language instructions, and in the order they were selected by the user (see Fig. 5).

In the Controls Area, there are a series of buttons that allow performing a set of actions within the environment. The Execute Button (*Ejecutar* in Spanish) is used to run the program created by the user, causing an agent to move within an arena, following the sequence of instructions. The Clear Button (*Limpiar* in Spanish) removes the sequence built within the Code Editing Area. The Settings Button (*Ajustes* in Spanish) opens the Settings Area. The environment can be closed by using the Exit Button (Salir in Spanish). In the current version of the platform, assistance from a person is required to help the user interact with the Control Area through conventional means.

Pressing the Execute Button activates the Output Area, which in the current version consists of a grid-board and a character, shown as a frog-shaped animated sprite, on the starting square [20] (see Fig. 7).

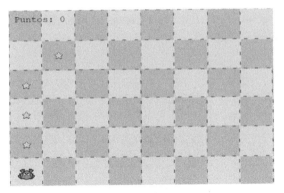

Fig. 7. Output Area.

Some of these squares have objects that can be collected by the character when it is positioned on the grids containing them. When the user presses the Execute Button, the environment takes the solution created in the Code Editing Area and moves the character following the order of the instructions of the given user program.

With the set of elements arranged in the Output Area (starts, the frog and the grid) it is possible to present different challenges: obtaining a solution that collects all the objects on the board, collecting all objects on the board using the fewest instructions, obtaining a solution that avoids collecting objects, among others.

5 Conclusions and Future Work

The integration of eye tracking as a human-computer interaction mechanism into programming environments for education opens up didactic possibilities for a student population with motor disabilities. *The Eye Tracking-based Platform for Programming Teaching* and the prototype presented in this work represent a step forward in this regard.

The use of eye tracking technology for computer science education is a relatively unexplored field; however, we believe it has significant potential to make this type of learning accessible to a broader group of people. As far as we know, this techno-pedagogical device supporting the construction of simple programs is innovative, and there are no similar tools developed for this purpose. These digital resources that support the teaching and learning processes of programming and that require only a low-cost hardware device as an additional component expand the possibilities to understand and intervene in the world for a particularly vulnerable population. Understanding computing is a key element for exercising citizenship and broadens opportunities for labour integration.

From the development of the prototype presented in this work, future lines of work emerge that provide continuity and contribute elements to strengthen the consistency of this research. In this sense, two dimensions of work are identified: on the one hand, those oriented towards defining methodological approaches to guide the integration of such resources into real teaching and learning scenarios; and on the other hand, those aimed at expanding aspects related to the development of the technological platform to enhance its didactic possibilities. In this context, fieldworks of an experimental nature are planned based on participatory design and participatory research approaches. In regard to the evaluation of the platform usability, a series of meetings are planned with students who are part of the platform target population. Specialists in motor disability will participate in the meetings, with the objective of, on one hand, initiating the evaluation of the tool in a real-use scenario. And on the other, assessing the possibility of expanding the range of characteristic cases that were not initially considered but fall within the spectrum of motor disabilities covered. Information is expected to be gathered to involve stakeholders in defining specific methodological approaches to the domain, improving aspects related to the usability of the prototype, evaluating the relevance of alternative execution areas to the one adopted in the current version, and adding features that allow personalising the environment according to gender, maturation age, and personal preferences.

References

1. Papert, S.: Mindstorms: Children, Computers, and Powerful Ideas. Basic Books Inc, USA (1980)
2. Wing, J.: Computational thinking. Commun. ACM **49**, 33–35 (2006). https://doi.org/10.1145/1118178.1118215
3. The K–12 Computer Science Framework. The Computer Science Teachers Association, New York (2016)
4. Bonello, M., Czemerinski, H.: Program.ar: una propuesta para incorporar ciencias de la computación a la escuela Argentina (2015)
5. Smith, M.: Computer science for all. The White House (2016)
6. Falkner, K., et al.: An international comparison of k-12 computer science education intended and enacted curricula, pp. 1–10 (2019). https://doi.org/10.1145/3364510.3364517
7. Society, R.: After the reboot: Computing education in UK schools. Policy Report (2017)
8. Consejo Provincial de Educación de la Provincia de Neuquén: Diseño Curricular Jurisdiccional de los tres primeros años de la Escuela Secundaria Neuquina. Resolución Nº1463/18 (2018)
9. Bialowas, S., Szyszka, A.: Eye-tracking research, pp. 40–60 (2021). kd3g
10. Maboe, M., Eloff, M., Schoeman, M.: The role of accessibility and usability in bridging the digital divide for students with disabilities in an e-learning environment, pp. 222–228 (2018). https://doi.org/10.1145/3278681.3278708
11. Santos, A.L.: Javardeye: gaze input for cursor control in a structured editor, p. 31–35. Programming 2021, Association for Computing Machinery, New York, NY, USA (2021). https://doi.org/10.1145/3464432.3464435
12. Jara Guillén, B.C., Barzallo Vallejo, B.P.: Desarrollo de un software para realizar evaluaciones educativas a niños con parálisis cerebral entre 5 a 7 años de edad con el uso de sistemas eye-tracking. B.S. thesis, Universidad del Azuay (2018)
13. Rotariu, C., Costin, H., Bozomitu, R.G., Petroiu-Andruseac, G., Ursache, T.I., Doina Cojocaru, C.: New assistive technology for communicating with disabled people based on gaze interaction. In: 2019 E-Health and Bioengineering Conference (EHB), pp. 1–4 (2019). https://doi.org/10.1109/EHB47216.2019.8969981
14. Molina, A.I., Navarro, Ó., Ortega, M., Lacruz, M.: Evaluating multimedia learning materials in primary education using eye tracking. Comput. Stand. Interfaces, **59**, 45–60 (2018). https://doi.org/10.1016/j.csi.2018.02.004
15. Jamet, E.: An eye-tracking study of cueing effects in multimedia learning. Comput. Hum. Behav. **32**, 47–53 (2014). https://doi.org/10.1016/j.chb.2013.11.013

16. Hyönä, J.: The use of eye movements in the study of multimedia learning. Learn. Instruction **20**(2), 172–176 (2010). https://doi.org/10.1016/j.learninstruc.2009.02.013

17. Dilini, N., Senaratne, A., Yasarathna, T., Warnajith, N., Seneviratne, L.: Cheating detection in browser-based online exams through eye gaze tracking. pp. 1–8 (2021). https://doi.org/10.1109/ICITR54349.2021.9657277

18. Katona, J.: Measuring cognition load using eye-tracking parameters based on algorithm description tools. Sensors **22**(3) (2022). https://doi.org/10.1109/ICITR54349.2021.965727

19. Radevski, S., Hata, H., Matsumoto, K.: Eyenav: gaze-based code navigation, pp. 1–4 (2016). https://doi.org/10.1145/2971485.2996724

20. Ramos, M.C.: Una plataforma para la Programación Tangible. Tesis de Licenciatura en Ciencias de la Computación, Facultad de Informática. Universidad Nacional del Comahue (2021)

21. Lugaresi, C., et al.: Mediapipe: a framework for building perception pipelines (2019). https://doi.org/10.48550/arXiv.1906.08172

Facial Emotion Recognition with AI

Jesús A. Ballesteros[1], Gabriel M. Ramírez V.[2(✉)] (iD), Fernando Moreira[3] (iD),
Andrés Solano[4] (iD), and Carlos Alberto Pelaez[4] (iD)

[1] Universidad de la Rioja, Logroño, Spain
[2] Facultad de Ingeniería, Universidad de Medellín, Medellín, Colombia
gramirez@udemedellin.edu.co
[3] REMIT, Universidade Portucalense and IEETA, Universidade de Aveiro, Aveiro, Portugal
fmoreira@upt.pt
[4] Universidad Autónoma de Occidente, Kmt.2 Vía Cali-Jamundí, Cali, Colombia
{afsolano,capa}@uao.edu.co

Abstract. The paper presents a work with AI on using computer vision algorithms to detect human emotions in the context of the video when the user looks at different video images. This work aims to present the development of software that detects emotions by recognizing users' facial expressions using AI algorithms and image process pipelines. The process of seeing emotions is done by evaluating users with images, which has allowed the application of computer vision algorithms that detect images according to the authors of the discipline of psychology, who propose the emotions and how they can be recognized. In this work, it has been demonstrated that it is possible to recognize emotions with the algorithms used and the development and training of the software performed from facial expressions. However, for a correct interpretation of emotions, the system must be trained in a context with more images and other complementary algorithms that allow differentiating emotions represented by facial expressions with very similar patterns to improve certainty and accuracy.

Keywords: Facial emotion · Recognition · AI

1 Introduction

Affective computing is an interdisciplinary field that involves studying and developing systems capable of understanding and interpreting human emotions [1]. One of the primary motivations for research in this field is the simulation of empathy: endowing machines with the ability to detect and interpret users' emotional states and thus generate adaptive behaviour based on the recognized information.

Facial expressions are crucial in communication, conveying complex mental states during an interaction. In nonverbal communication, the face transmits emotions [2]. Using machine learning techniques such as face recognition, information obtained from facial expressions can be processed to infer their emotional state.

P. H. Ruiz et al. (Eds.): HCI-COLLAB 2023, CCIS 1877, pp. 169–184, 2024.
https://doi.org/10.1007/978-3-031-57982-0_14

Affective computing, recognizing users' emotional states, proposes to enrich the form of user-machine interaction. A system with this capability could generate more appropriate responses considering users' emotional states [1].

The application of affective computing offers a wide range of possibilities. In marketing, analyzing emotions is essential to determine the impact of a given advertisement or product on the public. More and more companies are betting on projects related to affective computing, such as the detection and prevention of stress in workers or the development of video games capable of adapting to players.

This work presents the development of software capable of detecting the emotions of a user through computer vision techniques using AI algorithms, specifically neuronal convolutional networks; face recognition is performed using the MTCNN framework or Multitask Cascade Convolutional Networks, considering the theories of emotions and how to evaluate emotions with different algorithms and thus determine the emotions of people. The paper is structured as follows, Sect. 1 Introduction, Sect. 2 Background, Sect. 3 software development, Sect. 4 Evaluation, results and Discussions, and Sect. 5 Conclusions and future work.

2 Background

Psychology of Emotion

Emotions play a vital role in humans, providing essential information for survival and environmental adaptation. *Emotion perception* can be defined as the ability to take actions or direct thoughts appropriately and identify emotions in oneself or other individuals [2]. Emotions arise unconsciously briefly without requiring explicit mental processing. Primarily, emotions are physical responses, which are represented by a characteristic's physiological activation pattern. Sometimes, two or more emotions may share specific physiological responses [1].

In 1994 the psychologist and anthropologist Paul Ekman proposed six emotions, joy, anger, fear, disgust, sadness and disgust, not determined by sociocultural factors [3]. These emotions were called fundamental or universal because they are closely related to survival behaviours and evolutionary patterns in the human species [4]. Subsequently, this initial set of universal emotions would be expanded with contempt [3].

The set of universal emotions has given rise to different models that try to explain by combining two or more basic emotions the great variety of emotions that exist. Attempts to classify emotions have given rise to circumplex models based on fuzzy categories and factorial models [5]. These models propose using the opposite extremes of the emotional categories to respond to humans' emotional states [6].

Plutchik's circumplex model consists of eight basic emotions: joy, trust, surprise, aversion, sadness, anticipation, and anger. Plutchik argues that the emotional states described in his model, see Fig. 1, are similar. For Plutchik, this similarity facilitated combining one or more of these emotional states to obtain a more complex emotion [7].

The relationship between emotion categories has a representation in the model. The vertical dimensions of the cone represent the intensity of the emotion. In contrast, the cone sections describe the degree of similarity in the intensity of the emotions. In the displayed model, the blanks represent the secondary emotions resulting from combining two primary ones.

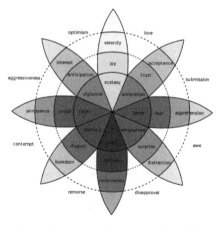

Fig. 1. Plutchik's Circumplex Model [8].

Russell [5] argues that affective states result from two independent neurophysiological systems: one is in charge of establishing the valence of the emotion, and the other is related to the state of activation of the individual. Therefore, emotions can be interpreted as the linear combination of these two dimensions [8]. This theory describes the organization of emotional states based on two orthogonal axes. The horizontal axis represents the valence dimension, unpleasant and pleasant, while the vertical axis represents the activation and deactivation dimensions (See Fig. 2.).

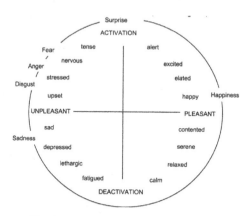

Fig. 2. Russell's Circumplex Model [7].

Facial Recognition

Face recognition originated in the 1960s when a research team led by W. Bledsoe conducted experiments to determine whether a computer could recognize human faces. Bledsoe's team sought to establish relationships between the minutiae of the human face so that the computer could find a set of matches that would allow recognition of those faces [9, 10].

Bledsoe's experiments could have been more successful, but they were vital in laying the groundwork for using biometric information in face recognition [11].. For many years, the techniques used in face recognition did not develop significantly until 2001, when Paul Viola and Jones published a method for object detection that offered previously unheard-of hit rates.

The Viola-Jones method is one of the most widely used techniques for face recognition tasks today. This algorithm comprises two phases: a first phase of training an AdaBoost classifier [12] and a second stage of detection using the classifier with unknown images [13]. This method uses Haar features of the image instead of pixel level, see Fig. 3. The Haar features of an image represent the difference in intensity in adjacent areas, which allows for detecting intensity changes in different orientations. They are calculated as the difference of the sum of the pixels of two or more contiguous rectangular areas based on the light intensity of the pixels [14].

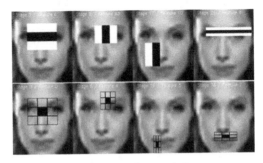

Fig. 3. Haar characteristics.

The Viola-Jones method proposes using an intermediate, Integral Image to reduce complexity when dealing with images. As seen in Fig. 4, the Intermediate Image represents the original image, where each point corresponds to the sum of the pixels located to its left and above it [15]. This type of transformation on the image reduces the algorithm's complexity from $O(N^2)$ to $O(1)$.

						0	0	0	0	0	0	
1	2	2	4	1		0	1	3	5	9	10	
3	4	1	5	2		0	4	10	13	22	25	
2	3	3	2	4		0	6	15	21	32	39	
4	1	5	4	6		0	10	20	31	46	59	
6	3	2	1	3		0	16	29	42	58	74	

input image   integral image

Fig. 4. Integral Image Calculation [11].

Nowadays, the high availability of labelled data and the continuous improvement of GPUs have played a crucial role in developing new face recognition algorithms based on Deep Convolutional Neural Networks. The widespread use of these neural networks was motivated by the 2012 ImageNet championship [13]. CNNs are formed by several layers of neurons, with the convolutional layer being the most important one. As shown in Fig. 5, the input of this layer is a vector of pixel values. Its operation is based on applying a series of filters that move through the image to obtain the layer outputs [14].

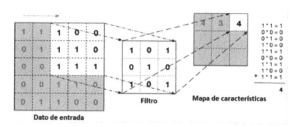

Fig. 5. Convolution algorithm operation by applying a 3 × 3 filter [15].

In addition to the filter size used in the convolutional layers, two fundamental parameters modify its behaviour: stride and padding. The stride controls how the filter moves through the image. When the size of the stride is increased, the convolutional layer is fixed in more distant areas of the image, which implies a dimensionality reduction. Dimensionality reduction is the prevalent use of the Zero-Padding technique, filling with zeros the edges of the output obtained by applying filters [16].

Other layers are intermixed with the convolutional layers, the intermediate layers. The purpose of these layers is to eliminate the nonlinearities while maintaining the dimensions to improve the robustness and avoid overtraining of the neural network. These layers employ RELU activation units, which are computationally more efficient than traditional Sigmoid or Tangh [17]. As one goes deeper into the neural network and traverses more convolutional layers, one obtains activation maps that represent more complex features of more significant regions in the image: the first layers recognize more basic image structures in a small region. In comparison, deeper layers obtain higher-level representations from the elements identified in the first layers [14].

Figure 6 corresponds to the architecture of the AlexNet convolutional neural network [13], the winner of the 2012 ImageNet championship. AlexNet was a turning point in the field of computer vision.

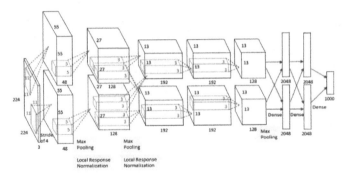

Fig. 6. Convolutional Neural Network. AlexNet architecture [13].

3 Development

Problem Statement

Facial expressions play a fundamental role in communication, conveying complex mental states during interaction. The human face is the main component for transmitting emotions during nonverbal communication [2].

There are six basic emotions with their associated facial expressions, considered universal and innate [3]. Studies by Ekman and Friesen [16] present that subjects can recognize these emotions adequately but without achieving perfect levels of identification.

According to [6], the set of universal emotions is composed of: disgust, fear, joy, anger, surprise and sadness. Expressing an emotion involves a complex muscular configuration, giving rise to a pattern that makes an emotion recognizable. The pairs of forehead-eyebrows, eyes-eye-lids, and the lower part of the face (the area around the mouth) are the main ones responsible for the manifestation of these emotions [9].

Emotions are a fundamental aspect of the human being and are vital when making decisions. New technologies based on artificial intelligence are increasingly integrated into society: they can recommend movies and series according to user preferences, select personalized advertising based on search and purchase history, and learn from daily routines and how users interact with applications.

Affective computing recognizes users' emotional states and proposes to enrich the form of user-machine interaction. A system with this capability can generate the most appropriate responses considering users' emotional states [1].

Research Question

How to develop emotion recognition software using computer vision techniques through the recognition of facial expressions?

Objectives

The objectives for the development of the project and the solution to the problem are the following:

- **General objective:**

To develop an emotion recognition software using computer vision techniques that allows the detection of users' emotions through the recognition of facial expressions.

- **Specific objectives:**

1. Design the software architecture that defines the end-to-end of an application that allows the detection of users' emotions through a capture device.
2. To implement a graphical interface that supports the application and allows real-time visualization of the images provided by the capture device. In addition, this graphical interface must be able to display the results obtained by processing the input images.
3. Implement a software component to perform facial recognition of users, employing an input image from the capture device. This component must be sufficiently computationally efficient to ensure the correct operation of the application in real time.
4. Implement a software component to classify emotions from a user's facial expressions. This component must be sufficiently computationally efficient to ensure the correct functioning of the application in real time.
5. Validate the obtained application. Evaluating the system's performance will provide the necessary information to determine the feasibility of emotion detection by recognizing users' facial expressions.

Methodology and Research Approach

The nature of the objectives set in this work requires using a descriptive applied research methodology. The research approach used throughout this work will be a mixed approach. Data will be taken from videos that will be made with users to detect emotions, and this data will be classified and converted with a neural network and a classification model to identify the emotion according to the concepts of emotions; here are mixed quantitative and qualitative data.

Mixed research is characterized by collecting and analyzing qualitative and quantitative data in the same study, thus responding to the approach [18].

The SCRUM methodology will guide the software development process. This AGILE methodology allows adapting the work organization to the project's current needs to obtain the best possible result.

SCRUM is based on short iterations known as Sprints, which have a fixed duration. At the end of these iterations, an intermediate product containing part of the required functionality will be obtained [19].

The development of the proposed application for the recognition of emotions using computer vision techniques has been implemented according to the architecture shown in Fig. 7. As can be seen, this architecture is composed of three differentiated parts: Image Capture Process, Processing Pipeline and Result Visualization Process. The design of the solution follows a producer-consumer model using synchronized queues.

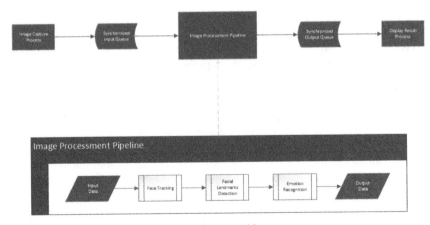

Fig. 7. Software architecture

Graphical Interface

The graphical interface is the main module of the application. In addition to the representation of the elements to be displayed by the users, this module is responsible for the initialization of components and the orchestration of the application.

During the initialization phase, all the components involved in the application are instantiated and configured, the capture device is initialized, and the asynchronous tasks executed during the application life cycle are planned.

Figure 8 shows the logic for developing the solution using the execution flowchart. The orchestration of the application has been based on the event-driven design pattern by generating a timeout event every 20 ms. This event generates a constant flow of images from the capture device. The input images are deposited in an asynchronous queue to be consumed by the processing pipeline.

The data generated by the pipeline are deposited by the pipeline in another asynchronous queue to be consumed by the main application thread. From the data deposited in this queue, the interface's graphical components will be updated, for example, the visualization of the input images obtained by the capture device or the update of the emotion recognition results.

The orchestration of the application takes place in the main loop of the GUI. This main loop is used to orchestrate the application components and the event handling of the GUI.

Image Processing Pipeline

The image processing pipeline defines the steps necessary for emotion recognition from the input data. This pipeline is executed by an asynchronous task that consumes the data deposited in an input queue. The results are deposited in the output queue for the update of graphic components. Figure 9 shows the steps this processing pipeline executes to recognize user emotions [20]. Emotion recognition is performed through the execution of three steps defined in this processing pipeline: Face Tracking, Facial Landmarks Detection and Emotion Recognition.

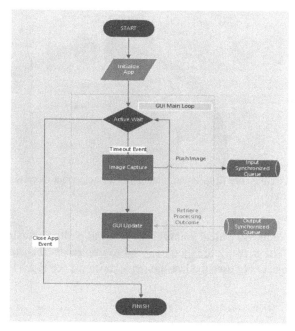

Fig. 8. Application flowchart.

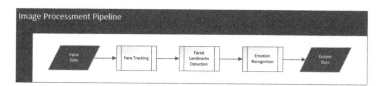

Fig. 9. Image Processing Pipeline.

In the Face Tracking step, the facial recognition of the users is performed. In this step, the coordinates or bounding boxes that delimit the faces detected in the input image are obtained. The results obtained are propagated to the following stages of the pipeline for further use.

Face recognition is performed using the MTCNN framework or Multitask Cascade Convolutional Networks [21]. As shown in Fig. 10, this architecture is composed using three convolutional networks connected in a cascade.

During the Facial Landmarks Detection step, the 64 characteristic points of the face are detected. This pipeline component receives the image from the capture device and the results obtained in the Face Tracking phase as input. This phase aims to determine if the face is being captured correctly. The information obtained from this phase will be beneficial when positioning the capture device.

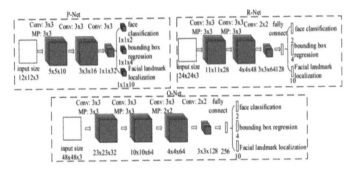

Fig. 10. MTCNN Architecture [21]. Its architecture is a component of convolutional networks P-Net, Q-Net, y O-Net.

The detection of the 64 critical points of the face was performed using convolutional neural networks. The network architecture used to implement this step was Xception Net [22]. This project only uses the last-named algorithms; see Fig. 11.

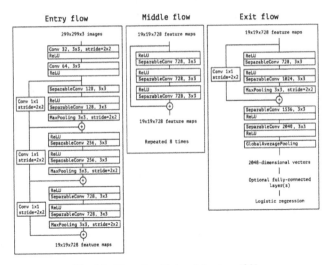

Fig. 11. Xception Net architecture [22].

This architecture is characterized by being constructed as a linear stack of depth-separable convolution layers with residual connections, and this design makes it very simple to define and modify.

The last step of the image processing pipeline is Emotion Recognition. In this final step, emotion recognition is performed from the facial expression of the face obtained after the execution of the Face Tracking step [24].

The classification of facial expressions takes place through convolutional neural networks. The network architecture designed to implement this classifier corresponds to an adaptation of the ResNet architecture; see Fig. 12; we modified the adapt to ResNet to classify the emotions according to the project's requirements.

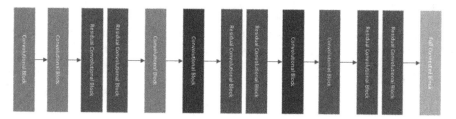

Fig. 12. Adaptation of the ResNet architecture for emotion classification.

The model used to classify facial expressions has been trained using the public dataset FER-2013. This dataset is characterized by being composed of 48x48 pixel grayscale images. FER-2013 contains 28,000 labelled images for the training dataset and 3,500 for the validation dataset [25]; see Table 1. Table 2 shows the hyperparameters used during model training. Metrics were obtained using the set of images to validate the trained model.

Table 1. Classification model evaluation metrics

Category	Precision	Recall	F1-Score	Support
Angry	0.49	0.43	0.46	958
Disgust	0.49	0.55	0.52	111
Fear	0.42	0.25	0.32	1024
Happy	0.87	0.70	0.77	1774
Neutral	0.39	0.78	0.52	1233
Sad	0.54	0.18	0.27	1247
Surprise	0.53	0.84	0.65	831

Table 2. Training hyperparameters

Training parameters	Value
Epoch number	50
Batch size	32
Learning rate	1e-1
Optimization	Stochastic Gradient Descent
Loss function	Cross Entry Loss

4   Evaluation, Results and Discussions

The developed emotion classification and detection software was initially tested with images to obtain results with sad, fearful, angry, surprised, disgusted and happy emotions. Then the classification and emotion detection tests were performed with images and multimedia content of users in real-time to have a control group with which to compare the results obtained and define the accuracy of the detection of emotions.

Tests with Images
This test consists of 19 representative images for each emotional category, except for the "Neutral" category, which will not be evaluated in this test. This test aims to assess the classifier's performance through the previous classification of these images made by the author.

Table 3 presents the results obtained from the test in the form of a confusion matrix. This matrix has been extended with the row: "Neutral/No Clear" to collect the results for the images that have not generated a conclusive result.

Table 3. Test results with images

Category	Sad	Fear	Angry	Surprise	Disgust	Happy
Sad	9	1	1	-	6	-
Fear	-	8	-	1	-	-
Angry	1	1	12	-	2	-
Surprise	-	2	-	14	-	-
Disgust	1	-	-	-	8	-
Happy	-	1	-	2	2	18
Neutral / No Clear	8	1	6	2	1	-
Precision	0.47	0.44	0.63	0.73	0.42	1
Accuracy	0.83	0.93	0.90	0.93	0.89	0.95

Tests with Users Viewing Multimedia Content
This set of tests has been carried out with the collaboration of three volunteers. Each test consists of two audiovisual contents. During the playback of each video, the developed tool will monitor the participants' facial expressions.

The objective of these tests is to determine the tool's ability to detect the emotions expressed by users when viewing the content. Each video used in these tests is designed to provoke an emotion in the viewer: Video #1 is intended to generate positive emotions. In contrast, video#2 seeks to generate rejection emotions in the viewer. Table 4 presents the results obtained from this test conducted with users.

The results obtained in the tests with users by playing video#1 have been satisfactory for most of the volunteers. Positive emotions could be detected throughout the reproduction of the content.

Table 4. Test results with users

User	Id	Result	Evidence
User#1	1	OK	
	2	KO	
User#2	1	OK	
	2	KO	
User#3	1	N/A	
	2	N/A	

On the contrary, the results obtained with video#2 were negative in all cases. The tool could not recognize any of the participant's emotions directly related to the objective of the content. These results could be explained as follows:

a) The trained model has meagre hit rates for negative emotions, implying a more incredible difficulty in recognizing such emotions.

b) b) Test content. Video#2 has not generated enough impact on the users, and this caused the participants to show a relatively neutral expression throughout the test with video#2. The explanation for this behaviour, which contrasts with that observed in the tests performed with video#1, may be because users know they are being monitored. That may imply a certain degree of conditioning when expressing some negative emotion.

5 Conclusions and Future Work

Based on the results obtained through user testing and the complexity involved in correctly classifying emotions, it is complex to build a system based solely on computer vision techniques capable of accurately classifying the full range of emotions that can occur in a user.

A single image does not provide enough information to determine the emotion expressed correctly. Although there are facial expressions, such as those representing joy or surprise, that can be easily recognized without the need for prior context.

However, developing an emotion recognition system based on computer vision techniques is possible. The strategy should consider other characteristics that could provide more information besides that extracted from the analysis of facial expressions.

Based on the results obtained, the general objective of creating a tool capable of recognizing a user's emotions using computer vision techniques has been achieved.

The work presented in this paper is a small sample of the effort in affective computing to achieve the correct emotional identification of users interacting with a system.

The tool developed in this work has several shortcomings that require more accuracy when recognizing the proposed set of emotions. That does not detract from the results' importance; it simply highlights the difficulty involved in something simple for humans, such as emotion recognition.

Future work should focus on obtaining greater accuracy in classifying a user's facial expressions. Undoubtedly, providing context to the detected facial expressions is a prerequisite for the correct classification of emotions.

Affective computing is a field in which there is still much research to be done, which has enormous potential for society. As has happened with virtual assistants, systems based on affective computing will shortly be fully integrated into society, offering users a fully personalized experience. The work presented in this paper is a small sample of the effort in affective computing to achieve the correct emotional identification of users interacting with a system. It highlights the complexity of the problem involved.

The tool developed throughout this work has several shortcomings that result in the need for more accuracy in recognizing the set of emotions proposed. This fact does not diminish the importance of the results or the conclusions obtained but shows the difficulty involved in something as apparently simple for humans as emotion recognition. Future work should focus on obtaining greater precision when classifying a user's facial expressions. Providing context to the detected facial expressions is necessary for correctly classifying emotions.

Using LSTM networks, a new emotion classifier could be trained from time series of facial expressions [26]. This series would provide some context to the classification since it would not be based on a single facial expression but on a temporal sequence of images that define the expression of an emotion [27].

References

1. Banafa, A.: Qué es la computación afectiva? Obtenido de OpenMind BBVA (2016).https://www.bbvaopenmind.com/tecnologia/mundo-digital/que-es-la-computacion-afectiva/
2. Darwin, C., Prodger, P.: The Expression of the Emotions in Man and Animals. Oxford University Press, Oxford (1996)
3. Ekman, P. Strong evidence for universals in facial expressions: a reply to Russell's mistaken critique (1994)
4. Salovey, P., Mayer, J.: Emotional Intelligence. Imagin. Cogn. Pers. 9(3), 185–211 (1990)
5. García, A.R.: La educación emocional, el autoconcepto, la autoestima y su importancia en la infancia. Estudios y propuestas socioeducativas 44, 241–257 (2013)
6. Russell, J.A.: A circumplex model of effect. J. Pers. Soc. Psychol. 39(6), 1161 (1980)
7. Ekman, P.: Basic Emotions. En In Handbook of cognition and emotion, pp. 45–60 (1999)
8. Rusell, J. A. Reading emotions from and into faces: Resurrecting a dimensional-contextual perspective (1997)
9. Plutchik, R.: The nature of emotions. Am. Sci. 89(4), 334–350 (2001)
10. Plutchik, R.E., Conte, H.R.: Circumplex models of personality and emotions. Am. Psychol. Ass. xi–484 (1997)
11. Bledsoe, W.W.: Man-Machine Facial Recognition: Report on a Large-Scale Experiment. Technical report PRI 22, Panoramic Research, Palo Alto, California (1966)
12. Schapire, R.E.: Explaining Adaboost. Empirical Inference: Festschrift in Honor of Vladimir N. Vapnik (2013)
13. Wang, Y.Q.: An analysis of the Viola-Jones face detection algorithm. Image Process. Line 4, 128–148 (2014). https://doi.org/10.5201/ipol.2014.104
14. Krizhevsky, A., Sutskever, I., Hinton, G.E.: ImageNet classification with deep convolutional neural networks. In: Advances in Neural Information Processing Systems, vol. 25(2) (2017). https://doi.org/10.1145/3065386
15. Simonyan, K., Zisserman, A.: Very deep convolutional neural networks for large-scale image recognition (2014). https://arxiv.org/pdf/1409.1556.pdf%E3%80%82
16. Sotil, D. A. *RPubs*. Obtenido de (2022). https://rpubs.com/
17. Mathworks (2022).https://www.mathworks.com/help/images/integral-image.html
18. Thomas, J.R., Nelson, J.K., Silverman, S.J. Research Methods in Physical. Human Kinetics, 5th ed (2005)
19. Hernández, Sampieri, R., Fernández, C., Baptista, L.C.: Metodología de la Investigación. Chile: McGraw Hill (2003)
20. Albaladejo, X., Díaz, J.R., Quesada, A.X., Iglesias, J.: proyectos agiles.org. Obtenido de (2021).https://proyectosagiles.org/pm-partners
21. Zhang, K., Zhang, Z., Li, Z., Qiao, Y.: Joint face detection and alignment using multitask cascaded convolutional networks. IEEE Signal Process. Lett. 23(10), 1499–1503 (2016)
22. Centeno, I. D. P. MTCNN face detection implementation for TensorFlow, as a pip package (2021). https://github.com/ipazc/mtcnn
23. Chollet, F. Xception: Deep learning with depthwise separable convolutions. Comput. Vis. Pattern Recogn. (2016). https://doi.org/10.1109/CVPR.2017.195
24. M., S. *FER - 2013*. Obtenido de (2019). https://www.kaggle.com/
25. Choi, D., Song, B.: Facial micro-expression recognition using two-dimensional landmark feature maps. IEEE Access 8, 121549–121563 (2020). https://doi.org/10.1109/ACCESS.2020.3006958

26. Park, S., Kim, B., Chilamkurti, N.: A robust facial expression recognition algorithm based on multi-rate feature fusion scheme. Sensors (Basel, Switzerland) **21**, 6954 (2021). https://doi.org/10.3390/s21216954

27. Abdel-Hamid, L.: An efficient machine learning-based emotional valence recognition approach towards wearable EEG. Sensors (Basel, Switzerland) **23**, 1255 (2023). https://doi.org/10.3390/s23031255

Human-Computer Interaction Research in Ibero-America: A Bibliometric Analysis

Andrés Felipe Solis Pino[1,2]([✉]) [ID], Pablo H. Ruiz[2] [ID], Vanessa Agredo-Delgado[2] [ID], Alicia Mon[3] [ID], and Cesar Alberto Collazos[1] [ID]

[1] Universidad del Cauca, Calle 5 N.º 4-70, Popayán 190003, Cauca, Colombia
{afsolis,ccollazo}@unicauca.edu.co

[2] Corporación Universitaria Comfacauca - Unicomfacauca, Cl 4 N° 8-30 Centro Histórico, Popayán 190001, Cauca, Colombia
{asolis,pruiz,vagredo}@unicomfacauca.edu.co

[3] Universidad Nacional de La Matanza, Florencio Varela 1903 (B1754JEC), 1754 San Justo, Buenos Aires, Argentina

Abstract. Human-computer interaction is a globally significant multidisciplinary field to enhance the usability of electronic devices for work, entertainment, and educational activities about human beings. Within the Ibero-American region, a community of researchers specializing in Human-computer interaction and related interdisciplinary domains has been established. Hence, it is crucial to understand this field's current state and evolution to identify critical contributors, institutions, information sources, and knowledge networks. This knowledge enables the contextualization of research, project planning, resource management, and improved dissemination within the domain. This study employed the Science Mapping Workflow methodology and specialized tools like Bibliometrix to conduct a bibliometric analysis of Human-computer interaction in Ibero-America. The findings reveal that the domain is well-established at the Ibero-American level and exhibits a growth rate of 14.65% in publications, indicating consistent progress. Moreover, Spain and Brazil have emerged as leading contributors in this field. Regarding the knowledge structure, it is evident that numerous technological advancements are focused on enhancing the capabilities of individuals with disabilities or limitations. Furthermore, video games, computer-mediated communication, natural interfaces, and artificial intelligence are identified as prominent trends within Human-computer interaction.

Keywords: Human-Computer Interaction · Bibliometric Analysis · Ibero-America

1 Introduction

Human-Computer Interaction (HCI) is a discipline that aims to facilitate effective and efficient communication between individuals and machines, focusing on creating intuitive and natural interfaces for users. By designing computer interfaces that cater to user needs and minimize physical and mental exertion during the interaction, HCI plays a

P. H. Ruiz et al. (Eds.): HCI-COLLAB 2023, CCIS 1877, pp. 185–199, 2024.
https://doi.org/10.1007/978-3-031-57982-0_15

critical role in ensuring the usability of digital devices [1]. This significance is under-scored by the fact that approximately 64.4% of the global population [2], amounting to approximately 5,160 million individuals, are projected to be internet users via digital devices as of January 2023. Additionally, the number of social media users worldwide was estimated to be 4,760 million, and mobile device usage is expected to reach 18.22 billion by 2025 [3]. Consequently, incorporating HCI principles into the design of dig-ital products becomes imperative to avoid detrimental user experiences caused by poor design choices [4].

It is worth noting that HCI has gained substantial prominence within the global sci-entific community, with the United States and China leading research efforts in this field [5]. However, Ibero-American countries have emerged as promising regions actively seeking to advance research in HCI by exploring novel avenues of investigation [6]. The Ibero-American community focuses on comprehending the region's unique needs, pref-erences, and challenges while proposing contextually fitting solutions for their respective countries [7]. This community operates within specific socioeconomic and technical con-texts, encompassing factors such as linguistic and cultural diversity, a digital divide with more industrialized nations, social inequality, prevalent violence, and a rich and diverse cultural heritage influenced by indigenous, European, African, and Asian cultures. Con-sequently, gaining a deeper understanding of Ibero-American communities and their interaction with information technologies becomes crucial to addressing region-specific issues [8]. Examining the current state of HCI research within Ibero-America is piv-otal as it enables researchers to evaluate the field's progress, identify research gaps and opportunities, foster collaboration networks, and identify emerging technologies.

Considering the points above, bibliometrics is vital to the academic community. It employs quantitative, mathematical, and statistical methods to gather data on various aspects of literature [9]. This enables a deeper understanding of the scientific output in the field of HCI within a particular region, the identification of challenges and new research avenues, and the effective direction of this field of study [10]. To this end, several bib-liometric studies have been conducted in the HCI domain, such as the work by Sandnes [11], which utilizes bibliometric methods to investigate HCI in Nordic-Baltic countries. The findings reveal that Finland, Sweden, and Denmark are the leading countries in this regard, with more collaboration observed with foreign researchers than within the region. The study suggests reducing gaps in HCI research by increasing activity in coun-tries with low research output and promoting collaboration with experienced authors. Another noteworthy study [12] presents a bibliometric analysis of HCI research. The dataset comprises 962 publications from 1969 to early 2017, and the analysis identi-fies 46 significant articles focusing on four primary factors: HCI design aspects, data management, user interaction, and psychology and cognition. The study also highlights emerging trends like workplaces, sensors, and wearables.

Furthermore, an article of significance [13] concentrates on analyzing HCI, user experience (UX), and usability in the context of automotive driving. A total of 2,498 articles published between 2000 and 2019, extracted from the Web of Science (WOS), are analyzed using performance analysis tools and co-word networks like BibExcel and CiteSpace. The results provide a comprehensive understanding of the evolution of UX and usability studies in driving over the past decades. Lastly, a study by [14] examines

274 articles published between 2000 and 2021 using bibliometric methods to identify research progress, key topics, and future directions in the HCI field. This study proposes a framework and demonstrates that HCI has significantly contributed to developing new research areas, such as multimodal analysis of physiological data and utilizing Big data-based safety management platforms. Prospects for future research include computer vision, computer simulation, virtual reality, and ergonomics.

Previous studies have conducted bibliometric analyses on HCI in different areas, but there needs to be knowledge of its application in the Ibero-American region using bibliometrics. Therefore, the main objective of this research is to perform a descriptive and inferential analysis of knowledge on HCI at the Ibero-American level, focusing on authors, affiliations, and new research trends.

2 Materials and Methods

This study presents a scientific examination of the field of HCI in the Ibero-American region using bibliometric analysis. The analysis includes descriptive and inferential methods to assess the state of the HCI research and identify current trends, challenges, and opportunities in the region. This study aims to enhance the visibility of HCI research, foster collaboration among researchers, and evaluate the impact and quality of publications. Moreover, the study identifies gaps and future research needs in the HCI domain [15].

To conduct the bibliometric analysis, it followed the guidelines proposed by Donthu [16], which outline the essential steps for performing statistical analysis in a specific domain. Additionally, it employed the Science mapping workflow [17] as the methodological framework, which is widely accepted as a reference for bibliometric analysis. Furthermore, it incorporated the analysis approach presented by Koumaditis [12], which specifically addresses the HCI domain, and utilized the proposal by Wang [18].

The primary data sources for this analysis were Scopus and WOS. The bibliometrix library [19] in the R programming language was utilized for conducting the bibliometric analysis. Finally, RStudio was employed to create graphical representations of the results.

2.1 Information Collection

It employed the search string presented in Table 1 to gather information systematically. Boolean exclusion operators (AND) were intentionally omitted to ensure comprehensive coverage of all contributions, including conference proceedings, articles related to HCI in the Ibero-American context, and synonymous terms. This approach is reflected in the second part of the search string, explicitly targeting countries within the Ibero-American community, including Spain and Portugal. To access a wide range of high-quality works in the engineering field, it utilized the well-regarded scientific databases Scopus and WOS [20]. Subsequently, it executed the search string in both databases and obtained the relevant data, combined using an R algorithm.

Table 1. Search string applied on WOS and Scopus.

(("human-computer interaction" **OR** "computer-mediated communication" **OR** "human-machine interaction" **OR** "human-based computing" **OR** "human-technology interaction")) **AND** (limit-to (affilcountry, "argentina") **OR** limit-to (affilcountry, "bolivia") **OR** limit-to (affilcountry, "brazil") **OR** limit-to (affilcountry, "chile") **OR** limit-to (affilcountry, "colombia") **OR** limit-to (affilcountry, "costa rica") **OR** limit-to (affilcountry, "cuba") **OR** limit-to (affilcountry, "ecuador") **OR** limit-to (affilcountry, "el salvador") **OR** limit-to (affilcountry, "guatemala") **OR** limit-to (affilcountry, "honduras") **OR** limit-to (affilcountry, "mexico") **OR** limit-to (affilcountry, "panama") **OR** limit-to (affilcountry, "paraguay") **OR** limit-to (affilcountry, "peru") **OR** limit-to (affilcountry, "puerto rico") **OR** limit-to (affilcountry, "dominican republic") **OR** limit-to (affilcountry, "uruguay") **OR** limit-to (affilcountry, "venezuela") **OR** limit-to (affilcountry, "spain") **OR** limit-to (affilcountry, "portugal"))

2.2 Search Execution

The search string employed in this study was confined to the titles, abstracts, and keywords of scientific papers sourced from well-established databases. All selected papers underwent a rigorous peer-review process to ensure academic rigor and validity. The search was not limited to a specific period, as the aim was to map the domain from its inception to the present comprehensively. A total of 9817 documents were identified using the search string, with the search conducted in May 2023, encompassing publications from 1990 to 2023.

To facilitate the subsequent analysis, articles lacking the necessary metadata were excluded from the dataset, resulting in 9812 documents. Moreover, duplicate studies were removed, ensuring only one article instance remained in each database. Secondary studies were also considered during the analysis. Finally, the resulting set of documents was exported to bibliometrix and VOSviewer software for descriptive and inferential analysis.

3   Results and Discussion

This section describes and analyzes the main results obtained in the HCI domain research in Ibero-America, emphasizing the relevant authors, the most cited articles, the most used journals, the production by country and affiliations, and the existing relationships in the domain. This makes it possible to determine the research area's current state and find new research guidelines.

3.1   General Information on the Domain

In general terms, an analysis of scientific publications in the field of HCI in Ibero-America is presented (Fig. 1). The data cover the period between 1990 and 2023 and include 2400 sources such as journals and books, resulting in a total of 9812 documents published to date. The average annual growth rate in publications is 14.65%, suggesting a significant increase in publications in this field of research over time. The average age of the papers is 8.16 years, indicating that research in this field is relatively recent and constantly evolving.

Fig. 1. General information on the HCI domain in Ibero-America.

The average number of citations per document is 9,216, suggesting that publications in this domain are highly referenced and valued by the scientific community, as well as an indication that Ibero-America is a reference in this area. The total number of references is 238,158, which implies thematic diversity and broad scientific support for its publications. The 9812 documents have 30,707 keywords plus 17,232 keywords proposed by the authors. The total number of authors is 21,401, not necessarily limited to authors from Ibero-America, as networks with foreign countries have been observed.

In terms of collaboration, each paper has an average of 3.83 authors per paper, and the percentage of international co-authorship is 29.11%, indicating frequent cross-border collaboration in this field of research. The types of papers found are articles, books, book chapters, conference papers, conference reviews, data papers, editorial letters, and literature reviews. In summary, HCI in Ibero-America is a dynamic field in constant evolution, with essential collaboration between national and international authors.

3.2 Annual Scientific Production in the Domain

Regarding scientific production in this field (Fig. 2), there have been continuous publications for almost 33 years, from 1990 to 2023. The number of articles published has increased over the years, and this trend has accelerated in recent years.

In particular, the highest number of articles was published in 2019, with a total of 1012 articles, followed by 2017 and 2016 with 812 and 781, respectively. On the other hand, the lowest number of articles is in 1991, with no papers being published, suggesting that the domain has been gradually growing. As for the distribution of articles by year, the data reveal a positively skewed and unimodal distribution, with a peak in 2019. In addition, it is important to note that the data for 2023 are not representative of the full year.

The increase in scientific publications in the last 30 years in the domain may be due to several factors, such as the availability of research funds in the area and the increase in the number of researchers in Ibero-America and the world [21]. The data also suggest that the publication growth will continue in the coming years as more researchers in

Ibero-America become interested in the field and more funds become available to obtain better results [22].

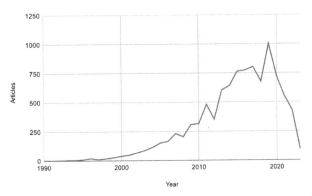

Fig. 2. Publications in the HCI domain in Ibero-America from the 1990s to the present.

3.3 Relevant Sources in the Domain

The field of HCI in Ibero-America has a diverse distribution of sources, as can be seen in Fig. 3, which shows about 2,400 sources in the domain, of which the 14 most relevant are highlighted. It is relevant to note that the source with the most significant number of published articles is "Lecture Notes in Computer Science (including the subseries Lecture Notes in Artificial Intelligence and Lecture Notes in Bioinformatics)", with 2182 documents, which represents more than double the number of articles published by the second most important source, "ACM International Conference Proceeding Series", with 912 articles. These two publications are a series of computer science books that publish research results at different conferences, proceedings, and research monographs.

Notably, of the most published sources in this domain, the first six are book series. As for journals, the two leading publications in this domain are "Computers in Human Behavior" and "IEEE Access".

The most significant number of publications in the domain are in book series and conferences; this could be because there is a solid academic research community in this area; secondly, this field is characterized by an emphasis on applied research, which is commonly presented in congresses. In addition, since this is a constantly evolving field, in which it is essential to present results promptly, publishing in conference proceedings and book series is an efficient way to disseminate new findings, as well as to obtain immediate feedback and interact with other researchers to enrich their work [23].

Overall, there has been a steady and consistent increase in publications. These results suggest that HCI in Ibero-America is constantly developing and receiving more and more attention from the scientific community, consistent with previous studies in this area.

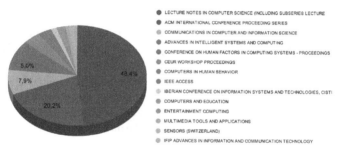

Fig. 3. Distribution of sources of journals and conferences in the HCI domain in Ibero-America.

3.4 Relevant Authors in the Domain

This section analyzes the most prominent authors in Ibero-America concerning HCI. In Fig. 4, the authors are ordered according to the number of published articles. The author with the most publications is Baranauskas from Brazil, with 115 articles, and Collazos from Colombia, with 104. Barbosa, Paiva, and Paz from the list published between 47 and 73 articles in this domain.

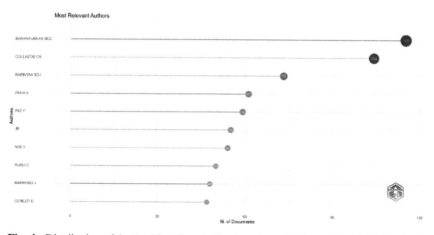

Fig. 4. Distribution of the top 10 authors in the domain and their number of publications.

A relevant aspect of this analysis is that Brazil is in second place as the country that publishes the most in this area, with a notable number of outstanding authors. In contrast, Spain, being the first country in terms of publications in this area, needs authors who have published a large number of articles. This could indicate a greater diversity of authors interested in this area in the Iberian country. In addition, it is essential to note that the diversity of authors in this domain and their respective nationalities suggests that research is concentrated in multiple places, which promotes better opportunities for research and international collaboration.

Regarding the analysis of the production over time (Fig. 5) of the five authors who publish the most, it can be observed that their publications cover the period from 2000 to 2023, with an average of between 4 and 5 articles per year in this domain. In addition, it can be inferred that Baranauskas has a publication cycle spanning from 2000 to 2015, after which he has decreased the number of publications. On the other hand, Paz has increased her number of publications since 2014, reaching its maximum peak with 12 publications in 2021. Also, it can be observed that Baranauskas has been publishing for 23 consecutive years, which speaks of his consistency in this domain, while Barbosa occupies the second place with 19 consecutive years of publication. It is important to note that Collazos is the person who has published the most research articles in a calendar year, with a total of 14 in 2017.

Finally, from Fig. 5, it can be indicated that the top four authors in the domain have decreased their number of publications in recent years, which could indicate a renewal in the research community.

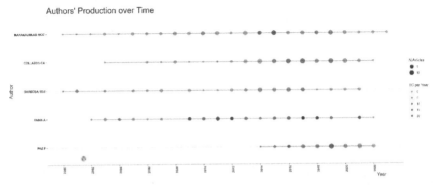

Fig. 5. Distribution of scientific production over time in the HCI domain in Ibero-America.

3.5   Most Productive Countries in the Domain

The analysis of productivity by country in the HCI domain in Ibero-America (Fig. 6) shows that Spain, Brazil, Portugal, and Mexico are the leading countries in this area. Spain is the undisputed leader with 10,769 publications, followed by Brazil with 7,977 publications and Portugal with 5,200 publications. These countries stand out for having the highest GDPs in the region and for making significant investments in science, technology, and innovation through organizations, which could be a determining factor in the improvement of the domain, as mentioned in the literature [24]. Colombia follows these countries with 1,328 publications, Chile with 911 publications, Ecuador with 610 publications, and Argentina with 525 publications. On the other hand, Honduras and Nicaragua have the lowest productivity, with only one publication each.

Ultimately, it is important to note that the productivity in the field in question is conditioned by the productivity of each of the authors, which may result in the assignment of publications to one country or another, giving rise to an overall figure that exceeds the number of records collected in general in that field.

Fig. 6. Contributions to the HCI domain in Ibero-America segmented by countries.

3.6 Relationships Between Countries by Authors

Focusing on analyzing the correspondence authorship of articles in the HCI domain in Ibero-America and their relationships, two categories of publications can be identified: those published in a single country and those published in collaboration with other countries. Single-country publications indicate the number of articles each country publishes within its borders. In contrast, multi-country publications indicate the number of articles each country publishes in collaboration with others [25].

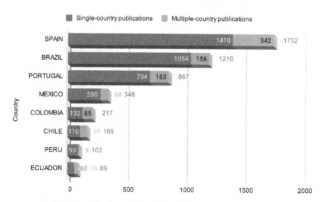

Fig. 7. Single-and multi-author country papers.

Among the most prominent countries in this area is Spain, with the highest number of publications from a single country, with 1410, while multi-country publications account for 342. Regarding collaboration in the top-producing countries, Colombia has the highest percentage of publications in collaboration with other countries, with 39.4% of its total publications. At the same time, Mexico and Spain also have a significant number of publications in collaboration, representing approximately 19% of their total publications in both cases.

Concerning the above, in Fig. 7, the percentages of authorship with authors from multiple countries are generally low compared to those of exclusive national authorship. This contrasts with what has been reported in the literature, which indicates that international collaboration can be beneficial for the exchange of knowledge and resources and for improving the quality and scope of research [26]. Therefore, this aspect could be the subject of further attention in this domain to strengthen this indicator further.

3.7 Collaboration Among Countries - World Map

In the HCI domain in Ibero-America (Fig. 8), the existence of a large number of research networks can be observed. It is important to note that these relationships are not limited exclusively to the Ibero-American region but also extend worldwide, indicating the presence of intercontinental relationships. This phenomenon is mainly due to the participation of various international organizations that finance HCI projects in the region, such as the European Regional Development Fund (ERDF), which has sponsored nearly 300 projects in this area, and other organizations, such as the European Commission.

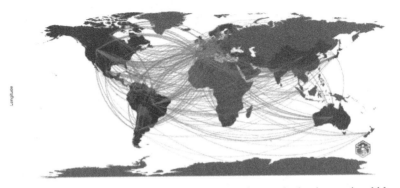

Fig. 8. Relations between countries in the Ibero-American and other international blocs.

As for the most productive countries in the Ibero-American HCI field, Argentina has collaborated mainly with France on a total of 15 occasions and collaborated with Canada and Austria on 4 and 3 occasions, respectively. In addition, Argentina has collaborated with other countries such as Belgium, Slovakia, Luxembourg, the Netherlands, Uruguay, Bulgaria, and China. Brazil has the third largest number of scientific collaborations in the field and has collaborated most frequently with the United States, 122 times, and the United Kingdom 69 times. It has also collaborated with Canada, France, Portugal, Germany, Japan, and Belgium on over ten occasions. Chile, for its part, has published mainly with Peru in the HCI domain. However, countries such as France, Canada, Italy, the United Kingdom, Belgium, and Ecuador have also participated to a lesser extent. Finally, Colombia has collaborated mainly with Chile on a total of 35 occasions and with Saudi Arabia on 17 occasions, as well as with countries such as Canada, Costa Rica, Ecuador, France, and Mexico to a lesser extent.

3.8 Conceptual Structure of the Domain

The conceptual structure of a domain refers to the set of concepts, terms, relationships, and principles that define and describe a specific area of knowledge [27]. In this case, It seeks to define the conceptual structure of the HCI domain in Ibero-America by using keywords of the authors in their respective documents and keywords plus, which are terms used by indexed databases to improve the indexing of documents in different classes.

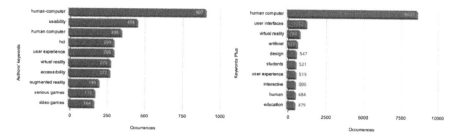

Fig. 9. Keywords proposed by authors used in the HCI domain in Ibero-America.

When reviewing the analyzed documents and the authors' keywords (Fig. 9), it was found that the word "Human Computer" appeared 907 times, while "usability" appeared 456 times. In addition, other relevant words were identified in the domain, such as "user experience", "virtual reality", "accessibility", "serious games" and "video games". This thematic diversity of the domain reflects the number of cross-cutting areas in which HCI can work. Interestingly, technologies such as virtual reality and accessibility, which depend on other fields, contribute significantly to this area. In turn, keywords such as "usability" and "user experience" are also of great importance in this area and are the subject of many studies in HCI [28].

About the terminology used for indexing, it is observed that HCI occupies a predominant place with a total of 8609 occurrences, followed by user interfaces and virtual reality with 1212 and 784, respectively. In terms of keywords plus, two significant elements are students and education and have education as their primary focus, which means that the contributions in the domain are focused on developing tools for students or related to education.

3.9 Thematic Evolution of the Domain

The thematic segmentation of the domain considering its evolution can be analyzed in Fig. 10. Specifically, from the 1990s to 2012, there was a greater focus on topics related to HCI and its foundations, as well as human-robot interaction. Likewise, elements such as evaluating these technologies and affective computing are also observed. From 2013 to 2016, the study of affective computing became more critical, which speaks of trying to make technological devices closer to their users. There was an increased interest in augmented reality. In addition, semiotic engineering gained predominance in the domain, focusing on using children's devices.

Between 2017 and 2019, there is evidence of greater attention toward more specific HCI topics, such as usability. Artificial intelligence gives rise to the emergence of terms such as machine learning and video games. It is important to note that there is a close relationship between augmented reality and natural user interfaces, which are aligned with the evolution of this technology toward eliminating controllers or input devices [29]. On the other hand, video games are starting to play a key role in terms of HCI.

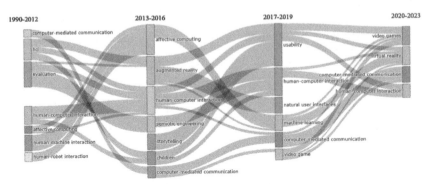

Fig. 10. Thematic evolution of the domain from 1990 to 2023.

Regarding the period from 2020 to 2023, several elements can be identified. First is video games, whose evolution clearly influences machine learning and virtual reality. Particular emphasis is placed on virtual co-communication, which speaks that now the domain is focused on inputs for people with disabilities and being able to improve their possibilities. It was also identified that HCI in Ibero-America is a mature research area with many outstanding researchers. These researchers have established the main bases of HCI and contributed to the advancement of the field in today's world. The many researchers who have contributed to this field and its evolution can refer to the existing thematic diversity. Initially focused on establishing the theoretical foundations of HCI, it has now expanded to specific applications such as video games, virtual reality, and wearables.

Continuing in the years from 2020 to 2023, it is observed to be aligned with the trends of other studies on the evolution of HCI. Voice user interfaces are expected to become increasingly common and natural, allowing people to interact with computers through speech rather than conventional input devices [30]. In addition, virtual and augmented reality seeks to establish virtual, augmented reality to create more immersive and engaging user experiences, merging the physical and digital worlds. Finally, wearable disdevices such as wearables (smart watches, glasses, rings, and wearables) could provide users with more personalized and contextualized information and services [31].

Finally, in the region, the challenges in HCI are similar to those in the rest of the world, starting from the rapid technological evolution towards more interactive and intelligent technologies, such as Artificial Intelligence, Big data, and the Internet of Things [32]. It is critical to address these challenges and emphasize cultural diversity in the design and evaluation of HCI [33]. Establishing a paradigm to explore how to create culturally sensitive and inclusive systems in the Ibero-American context that are accepted and adopted by the community would be a significant step toward the future.

4 Conclusions

In the present study, a bibliometric analysis was carried out in the field of human-computer interaction at the Ibero-American level, without temporal limitations, using the bibliometrix tool. A total of 9,817 documents were examined, from which quantitative information was extracted covering a publication period from 1990 to 2023, emphasizing the main authors, countries of origin, and structure of knowledge. The main result of the research indicates that the Ibero-American HCI community is a scientific leader in the world, addressing problems specific to the current context of the region. It was observed that the field presents an annual growth rate of publications of 14.65%, which suggests that it is in constant evolution. In addition, consolidated research networks between different countries were identified, with Spain and Brazil being the leaders in publications.

In this sense, the HCI field's knowledge structure is mainly based on its derivations, such as usability, user experience, and virtual reality. However, as the domain evolves, there is an emerging trend related to video games, communication-mediated computing, and natural interfaces, which are integrated with the leading global challenges in this area.

References

1. Gupta, N.: An overview on human-computer interaction. Asian J. Multidimens. Res. **10**, 110–116 (2021). https://doi.org/10.5958/2278-4853.2021.01181.2
2. Acharya, C., Thimbleby, H., Oladimeji, P.: Human computer interaction and medical devices. In: Proceedings of HCI 2010, vol. 24, pp. 168–176 (2010)
3. Stanković, M., Karabiyik, U.: Exploratory study on kali NetHunter lite: a digital forensics approach. J. Cybersecur. Priv. **2**, 750–763 (2022). https://doi.org/10.3390/jcp2030038
4. Cockton, G.: Value-centred HCI. In: Proceedings of the third Nordic Conference on Human-Computer Interaction, pp. 149–160 (2004)
5. Gurcan, F., Cagiltay, N.E., Cagiltay, K.: Mapping human-computer interaction research themes and trends from its existence to today: a topic modeling-based review of past 60 years. Int. J. Hum.-Comput. Interact. **37**, 267–280 (2021). https://doi.org/10.1080/10447318.2020.1819668
6. Collazos, C.A., Ortega, M., Granollers, A., Rusu, C., Gutierrez, F.L.: Human-computer interaction in Ibero-America: academic, research, and professional issues. IT Prof. **18**, 8–11 (2016). https://doi.org/10.1109/MITP.2016.38
7. Alvarado Garcia A, et al.: Fostering HCI research in, by, and for Latin America. In: Extended Abstracts of the 2020 CHI Conference on Human Factors in Computing Systems, pp. 1–4. ACM, Honolulu (2020)
8. Castro, L.A., Gaytán-Lugo, L.S., Santana-Mancilla, P.C., Herskovic, V., Valderrama Bahamondez, E.D.C.: Human computer-interaction in Latin America. Pers. Ubiquit. Comput. **25**, 255–257 (2021). https://doi.org/10.1007/s00779-021-01550-3
9. De Carvalho, G.D.G., et al.: Bibliometrics and systematic reviews: a comparison between the Proknow-C and the Methodi Ordinatio. J. Informetr. **14**, 101043 (2020). https://doi.org/10.1016/j.joi.2020.101043
10. Ninkov, A., Frank, J.R., Maggio, L.A.: Bibliometrics: methods for studying academic publishing. Perspect. Med. Educ. **11**, 173–176 (2022). https://doi.org/10.1007/s40037-021-00695-4

11. Sandnes, F.E.: A bibliometric study of human–computer interaction research activity in the nordic-baltic eight countries. Scientometrics **126**, 4733–4767 (2021). https://doi.org/10.1007/s11192-021-03940-z

12. Koumaditis, K., Hussain, T.: Human computer interaction research through the lens of a bibliometric analysis. In: Kurosu, M. (ed.) HCI 2017. LNCS, vol. 10271, pp. 23–37. Springer, Cham (2017). https://doi.org/10.1007/978-3-319-58071-5_2

13. Tan, H., Sun, J., Wenjia, W., Zhu, C.: User experience & usability of driving: a bibliometric analysis of 2000–2019. Int. J. Hum.-Comput. Interact. **37**, 297–307 (2021). https://doi.org/10.1080/10447318.2020.1860516

14. Wang, J., Cheng, R., Liu, M., Liao, P.-C.: Research trends of human-computer interaction studies in construction hazard recognition: a bibliometric review. Sensors **21**, 6172 (2021). https://doi.org/10.3390/s21186172

15. Moral-Muñoz, J.A., Herrera-Viedma, E., Santisteban-Espejo, A., Cobo, M.J.: Software tools for conducting bibliometric analysis in science: an up-to-date review. Prof. Inf. **29** (2020). https://doi.org/10.3145/epi.2020.ene.03

16. Donthu, N., Kumar, S., Mukherjee, D., Pandey, N., Lim, W.M.: How to conduct a bibliometric analysis: an overview and guidelines. J. Bus. Res. **133**, 285–296 (2021). https://doi.org/10.1016/j.jbusres.2021.04.070

17. Aria, M., Cuccurullo, C.: Bibliometrix: an R-tool for comprehensive science mapping analysis. J. Informetr. **11**, 959–975 (2017). https://doi.org/10.1016/j.joi.2017.08.007

18. Wang, L.L., Mack, K., McDonnell, E.J., Jain, D., Findlater, L., Froehlich, J.E.: A bibliometric analysis of citation diversity in accessibility and HCI research. In: Extended Abstracts of the 2021 CHI Conference on Human Factors in Computing Systems, pp. 1–7. ACM, Yokohama (2021)

19. Abbas, A.F., Jusoh, A., Ma'sod, A., Alsharif, A.H., Ali, J.: Bibliometrix analysis of information sharing in social media. Cogent Bus. Manag. **9**, 2016556 (2022). https://doi.org/10.1080/23311975.2021.2016556

20. Singh, V.K., Singh, P., Karmakar, M., Leta, J., Mayr, P.: The journal coverage of Web of Science, Scopus and dimensions: a comparative analysis. Scientometrics **126**, 5113–5142 (2021). https://doi.org/10.1007/s11192-021-03948-5

21. Sarsenbayeva, Z., et al.: Mapping 20 years of accessibility research in HCI: a co-word analysis. Int. J. Hum.-Comput. Stud. **175**, 103018 (2023). https://doi.org/10.1016/j.ijhcs.2023.103018

22. Auranen, O., Nieminen, M.: University research funding and publication performance—an international comparison. Res. Policy **39**, 822–834 (2010). https://doi.org/10.1016/j.respol.2010.03.003

23. Applied research gets starring role in Biden's 2022 budget. In: Science. https://www.science.org/content/article/applied-research-gets-starring-role-biden-s-2022-budget. Accessed 13 May 2023

24. Samimi, A.J.: Scientific Output and GDP: evidence from countries around the world. J. Educ. Vocat. Res. **2**, 38–41 (2011). https://doi.org/10.22610/jevr.v2i2.23

25. Yahya Asiri, F., Kruger, E., Tennant, M.: Global Dental publications in PubMed databases between 2009 and 2019—a bibliometric analysis. Molecules **25**, 4747 (2020). https://doi.org/10.3390/molecules25204747

26. Vahdat, S.: The role of IT-based technologies on the management of human resources in the COVID-19 era. Kybernetes **51**, 2065–2088 (2022). https://doi.org/10.1108/K-04-2021-0333

27. Gómez-Pérez, A., Fernández-López, M., Corcho, O.: Ontological Engineering: with Examples from the Areas of Knowledge Management, e-Commerce and the Semantic Web. Springer, Heidelberg (2006)

28. Razzak, M.A., Islam, M.N.: Exploring and evaluating the usability factors for military application: a road map for HCI in military applications. Hum. Factors Mech. Eng. Def. Saf. **4**, 4 (2020). https://doi.org/10.1007/s41314-019-0032-6

29. Gallo, J.C., Cárdenas, P.F.: Designing an Interface for trajectory programming in industrial robots using augmented reality. In: Martínez, A., Moreno, H.A., Carrera, I.G., Campos, A., Baca, J. (eds.) LACAR 2019. LNNS, pp. 142–148. Springer, Cham (2020). https://doi.org/10.1007/978-3-030-40309-6_14

30. Stigall, B., Waycott, J., Baker, S., Caine, K.: Older adults' perception and use of voice user interfaces: a preliminary review of the computing literature. In: Proceedings of the 31st Australian Conference on Human-Computer-Interaction, pp. 423–427. ACM, Fremantle (2019)

31. Mencarini, E., Rapp, A., Tirabeni, L., Zancanaro, M.: Designing wearable systems for sports: a review of trends and opportunities in human-computer interaction. IEEE Trans. Hum.-Mach. Syst. **49**, 314–325 (2019). https://doi.org/10.1109/THMS.2019.2919702

32. Stephanidis, C., et al.: Seven HCI Grand Challenges. Int. J. Hum.-Comput. Interact. **35**, 1229–1269 (2019). https://doi.org/10.1080/10447318.2019.1619259

33. Salgado, L., Pereira, R., Gasparini, I.: Cultural issues in HCI: challenges and opportunities. In: Kurosu, M. (ed.) HCI 2015. LNCS, vol. 9169, pp. 60–70. Springer, Cham (2015). https://doi.org/10.1007/978-3-319-20901-2_6

Migration of Legacy Java Desktop Applications to Collaborative Web

Antonio Labián[1]([⊠]) [iD], Jesús D. García-Consuegra[1] [iD], and Manuel Ortega[2] [iD]

[1] Computer Systems Department, University of Castilla - La Mancha, Albacete, Spain
{antonio.labian,jesus.gbleda}@uclm.es
[2] Department of Technology and Information Systems, University of Castilla - La Mancha, Ciudad Real, Spain
manuel.ortega@uclm.es

Abstract. The migration of legacy applications to more advanced technology platforms has been a recurring theme in the academic and business sectors. This transformation is driven by the desire to overcome the limitations of traditional desktop applications and integrate advanced remote access and collaboration capabilities. Essential features not only for technology upgrade but also to enable organizations to take advantage of remote collaboration. The COVID-19 pandemic has accelerated this need, forcing many organizations to adopt remote work and online collaboration modalities, forcing them to transform their information systems. There are various methodologies and techniques, such as conversion, redeployment and wrapping, that offer different approaches to facilitate this migration by minimizing the effort required during the process. This paper specifically studies the migration of Java Swing applications to web environments, particularly those that incorporate collaborative functionalities. Several solutions that follow different migration strategies have been evaluated, performing a more detailed analysis of the Vaadin platform as an efficient tool to perform this migration, with limited effort and special attention to the inclusion of new collaborative functionalities. Finally, a migration procedure is defined that has been validated through a case study.

Keywords: CSCW · Migration · Collaborative web application · Vaadin

1 Introduction

The migration of desktop applications to web environments has been the subject of study since the emergence of Web 2.0. Web 2.0 is characterized by active user participation, the use of web-based applications and the exchange of information in real time. These features enable web applications to provide more advanced remote access and collaboration functionalities than are possible with traditional desktop applications [1].

In addition, techniques and approaches have been developed to facilitate the migration of desktop applications to web environments, including software reengineering and refactoring. These approaches make it possible to adapt existing applications to new technologies and software architectures without having to completely rewrite the source

P. H. Ruiz et al. (Eds.): HCI-COLLAB 2023, CCIS 1877, pp. 200–209, 2024.
https://doi.org/10.1007/978-3-031-57982-0_16

code. Some authors have also proposed specific methodologies for migrating legacy applications to web environments, such as ADM (Architecture-Driven Modernization) [2].

The COVID-19 pandemic intensified the need to migrate legacy applications to web environments as many organizations were forced to adopt remote work and online collaboration. After the pandemic, this trend has continued as shown by the data from the study in [3] which presents how the number of managers of large technology companies who expect to have more workers working remotely increases and how they prepare by proposing hybrid work models (*on-site* and remote). In this context, the migration of Swing desktop applications to web environments with collaborative functions is particularly relevant, since beyond the technological update of the application itself, it allows organizations to incorporate the advantages of remote collaboration and access to resources through the web.

This paper reviews the specific solutions to perform this type of migration, analyzing their capabilities with special attention to the inclusion of new collaborative functionalities in the migrated applications. Finally, a migration procedure validated in a case study is proposed.

2 Migration of Java Applications to Web

When addressing the migration of a legacy application, there are three approaches applicable to the process: conversion, reimplementation, and *wrapping* [4].

- The conversion option is based on directly transforming the software from one language to another, manually or automatically. This category includes, for example, transpiler-based solutions.
- Reimplementation involves translating the code into an intermediate language and improving it before producing the new code. This category covers processes that involve software reengineering.
- *Wrapping* proposes to decompose the system into independent components to treat their migration independently and connect them through service interfaces, being able to do the process incrementally.

This section reviews different frameworks and tools available for migrating Java Swing applications to their web version based on their approach to migration. Table 1 presents a comparison of the frameworks based on criteria that can help to make a decision on which one to choose in a migration process. One of the aspects evaluated is the possible collaborative support of the frameworks to incorporate collaborative features. One aspect under evaluation is the potential of frameworks to provide collaborative support, enabling the integration of interactive features in migrated applications. Specifically, the emphasis lies on synchronous text editing and presence control mechanisms, which allow participants to identify who is present in the session and facilitate interaction amongst them.

Swing2Script [5] is a solution for migrating Java Swing applications to Ajax-enabled collaborative web applications. The migration process consists of three phases and is supported by programs that automate it. It allows applications to be migrated without having to rewrite the original source code, improving accessibility and usability. However, in addition to the potential complexity of the process, some advanced features may not be fully migrated due to differences between the Java Swing and Ajax platforms.

FlexMigration [2] is presented as a solution to modernize desktop applications developed in Java Swing to web applications using an ADM approach for automatic reverse engineering of the user interface in web migration. The advantages of the ADM approach include the automation of the migration process [2] by obtaining a web interface similar to the original. However, there may be limitations in terms of the complexity and size of the applications to be migrated.

WebSwing [6] is a solution that allows running Java Swing applications on a remote server and stream the user interface over the web using a remote emulation technique. This technique is based on screen capture and event streaming, allowing users to interact with the application as if it were running locally. One of its advantages is that it does not require code rewriting, since the original application is completely maintained. However, remote emulation consumes high server resources and may introduce latency in the transmission of the user interface. Furthermore, the original application still requires maintenance and the user interface does not improve, so new functionalities such as synchronous collaboration cannot be added.

Vaadin [7] is a platform for the development of web applications with two frameworks and different tools. One of these frameworks is Vaadin Flow, which allows the creation of Progressive Web Applications (PWA) based on web components through Java, following a programming model very similar to that used in Swing. For complex applications, it provides a tool for rendering new views within Swing applications allowing incremental migration. In addition, Vaadin supports real-time collaboration with full awareness management.

Table 1. Comparison between the analyzed frameworks.

	Swing2Script	FlexMigration	WebSwing	Vaadin
Scalability	High	High	Medium	High
Web technology	JavaScript	AJAX	JavaScript	WebComp
Last update	2013	2016	Active	Active
Reusability	High	High	Medium	Medium
Collaborative Support	No	No	No	Yes
Performance	High	Medium	Low	High
Difficulty	Easy	Medium	Easy	Medium

(*continued*)

Table 1. (*continued*)

	Swing2Script	FlexMigration	WebSwing	Vaadin
Migration type	*Wrapping*	Reimplement	*Wrapping*/Reimplement	Reimplement
Process type	Automatic	Semiautomatic	Manual	Manual
Complex applications	No	No	Yes	Yes
Execution	Client	Client	Client/Server	Server

3 Framework Vaadin

In an initial phase, Vaadin has been pre-selected, for its capabilities in application migration and its support for collaborative features, to carry out a migration test of part of a live application developed in Java Swing. At the architecture level, Vaadin Flow runs on the server side, on the Java Virtual Machine (JVM), as part of a Java web application. The application runs on an application server or servlet container, such as Apache Tomcat, Jetty, WildFly, GlassFish, WebLogic or WebSphere, among others. When developing an application with Vaadin Flow, the application logic is written in Java, while the client side, which runs in the user's browser, uses *WebComponents* and JavaScript. Vaadin Flow takes care of the communication between the server and the browser, allowing to focus on the application logic and user interface without worrying about the details of the communication between the client and the server.

3.1 Performance

Server-side execution model environments can be a bottleneck in CPU (Central Processing Unit) or memory consumption. In the case of Vaadin Flow the session size per application instance is quite small, with low CPU consumption. In [8], a study is presented evaluating the resource consumption of a test application and its latency for different volumes of virtual users. Thus, for two thousand virtual users, the CPU consumption was approximately 12.5% with a total memory consumption of 470 MB. In this same study it is recommended to dedicate between 1–1.5 GB of memory for every thousand concurrent users.

3.2 Collaborative Features

Vaadin Collaborative Kit is the platform's solution for including collaborative aspects of data synchronization and awareness support in a Vaadin Flow application. The solution, embodied in a library, is composed of a collaborative engine and an extension on the Flow framework components.

The extension allows implement real-time collaboration functionalities in Web-Components, abstracting from low-level details such as message distribution, event concurrency management or state synchronization between application instances.

At the view or section level, the awareness support [9] provided focuses on the dimensions of presence and identity of users connected to the same topic. At the component level, the dimensions of presence and identity are maintained, also adding that of location dimension. This support is provided by generating notifications of who is interacting in which component, as long as they work within the same topic.

3.3 Topic

A topic is a data structure that enables real-time collaboration between users in a web application. Essentially, a topic is a collection of items, called categories, that can be accessed, modified or deleted by different users at different times. In this way, users can submit updates to the topic data and receive updates from other collaborating users.

A view can use multiple topics to delimit different collaboration contexts. Users linked by a topic can then share the same awareness. The topic is therefore a mechanism for sharing data as well as a context for delimiting collaboration.

Internally, topics are maps or lists that have a unique identifier within the context of the application [10]. These are created on demand and maintain the overall order of the changes produced. Following the Vaadin server execution model, physical data is shared within the JVM, avoiding data duplication between multiple connections to the same topic. Topic data is not persisted, and its state is lost after the server restarts. The framework provides an API (Application Programming Interface) to interact with the topics as a data producer and/or consumer. Upon establishing a connection in the capacity of a consumer, the individual is systematically notified whenever an update is disseminated by a producer within the pertinent topic.

3.4 CollaborationAvatarGroup

It is the component to display the avatars of the users who are collaborating in a topic. It is a User Interface (UI) component that can be added to a view and automatically updates to reflect the current presence of users in the topic. In addition to displaying avatars, it also provides a number of options to customize the display of avatars, such as size, layout, and presentation. It is also feasible to regulate the upper limit of avatars presented individually prior to their consolidation into an aggregated list.

3.5 Binder/CollaborationBinder

A binder is a programming component used to bind data between the user interface and a data model in an application. In the context of Vaadin, a binder is a tool that allows linking the fields of a form in the UI with a Java data model object. Thus, when the user interacts with the form fields, the binder automatically updates the corresponding properties of the data model object. Similarly, when data model properties are updated, the binder ensures that the UI fields are updated with the new values. This facilitates data validation, conversion and update between the UI and the data model.

The *CollaborationBinder* is the extension of the binders provided by Vaadin Collaboration Kit to allow real-time collaboration on forms. By including the *CollaborationBinder* in a form, it connects its components to a specific topic, allowing changes made to the form to be automatically propagated to other users working on the same topic. It also supports awareness of the linked components, showing both the presence and identity of the users interacting with each component.

This mechanism is the simplest to implement collaborative aspects since it allows visual components to be associated with their categories within a topic. The alternative would be to implement methods for linking the event manager of each component as producer and consumer of data in the topic category.

3.6 Migration Process

A migration process from a Java desktop application based on Swing to its web version with collaborative functionalities has been defined.

1. Analysis of the original application to determine by studying the following points:

   - Determine if it follows a client-server architecture. If so, identify what communication mechanism it uses.
   - At the form level identify if the Model View Controller (MVC) pattern is applied.
   - Determine which views are susceptible to collaboration and whether the collaboration context will be general for the entire view or a division by area is required.
   - Identify whether unit, integration or acceptance tests exist in the original application.

2. Server migration.

   - In applications with client-server architecture, it is necessary to determine whether to maintain this architecture or to integrate the two parts, taking advantage of the fact that in the new technological environment with Vaadin Flow everything is executed on the server and does not require the development of a communication layer.
   - In the absence of this architecture the most recommendable is not to implement a specific server and perform a single project following the Flow model.
   - If the server is maintained, the model layer will be maintained for database access. In the application, existing classes will also be reused or entities can be extracted from the server to a new module for import into both the server and the client. However, if the refactoring process can be deepened, the most appropriate would be to integrate client and server following the Flow model since, even extracting the entities to a new module, for efficiency and security it is a good practice to apply the DTO (Data Transfer Object) pattern to use specific objects instead of entities, for data transfer in service calls.

3. Migration of the Swing client application to its web version. The Model View Presentation (MVP) pattern will be applied.

   - Implement the views by adding the originally existing visual components. For each view it is requisite to generate three distinct files: a view interface, the presentation class and the view class.

- If MVC was applied, the original controllers must be refactored, updating the calls to the view references with the references to the new objects.
- If the original application had some type of tests, include them in the new application project and update them with respect to the new development. If there were no previous tests, it is advisable to develop unit and integration tests to validate the integration of the controllers after refactoring.

4. Inclusion of collaborative functionalities.

- If the application lacked user management, add at least basic management to identify the user.
- A topic will be created for each view or area.
- Replace the original binders with collaborative binders, associating them with their corresponding topics.
- Update existing tests.

4   Case Study

The Registry of Third Parties of a public administration (Fig. 1) is presented as a case study. The objective of this registry is to unify the persistence of users who use its telematic services, gradually integrating their existing information into other systems and applications.

For its management, a Swing desktop application in Java is used, which is proposed to be improved with a web application that allows better access and also includes collaborative functions, to improve the collaboration of users who use it from different locations. The study identified a user requirement for assistance during the form completion process. To address this, synchronous form editing was incorporated as a collaborative feature. For user coordination, an awareness presence component was introduced, facilitating the identification of active users on the same form. Finally, the integration of a chat function enabled communication among participants, enhancing their coordination and preventing potential parallel edits on the same record.

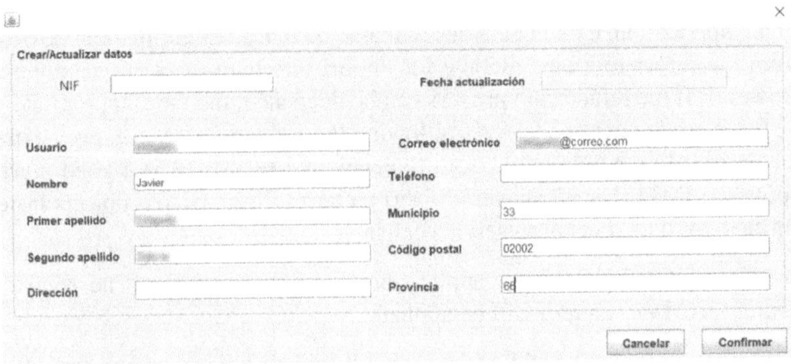

Fig. 1. Original application developed with Java Swing.

Applying the migration process, first of all, it is confirmed that the original application has a client-server architecture communicated by REST (Representational State Transfer) services. It has only five forms and applies MVC and has no test project.

It was decided to keep the client-server architecture over REST because the server endpoints used by the application to be migrated are used by other external systems. Consequently, the integration of the client and server parts was discarded. The original server entities are also reused, moving them to a new module to import it into the new client project.

Initially, the refactoring process of the original view was discarded when it was found that it was more efficient to generate a new view taking as reference the components of the original view. Other problems were also detected, such as the difference between desktop and web components. Desktop environments tends to use dialogs or small modal forms, that in web are applied more as new views or drop-down panels. This difference beyond aesthetics also implies differences in the reference of objects from the controller. Moving on to the migration of controllers, these are refactored, with changes being very limited to the parts that reference the new presentation. The change in the internal structure of a Vaadin presentation compared to a Swing form also adds more changes than expected.

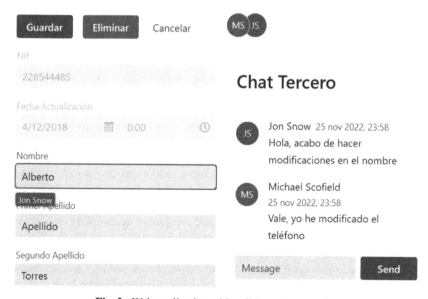

Fig. 2. Web application with collaborative aspects.

Once the migration to a functional web version is done, collaborative aspects can be added to the editing form, to include collaborative editing and awareness support in the different fields of the view (Fig. 2).

4.1 Evaluation

The migration process, complexity and degree of code reuse depends mostly on the patterns with which the original application was designed and the degree of coupling between the different layers and their components. It is also conditioned by the amount of resources to be invested in the process since, although at some points of the process there are direct migration options, it is usually advisable to perform a major refactoring, in order to obtain a higher quality maintainable development.

It has been proven that the existence of the MVC pattern facilitates the reuse of existing code, with the advantages that this entails. Thus, the controller has a high degree of reusability. On the contrary, the view layer, despite having a similar programming model between Vaadin Flow and Swing, the differences of use between components and their event handlers makes it more advisable to apply a migration process by reengineering. Moreover, in this test, the MVC pattern allowed the technological inclusion of collaborative aspects was carried out quickly. Once the application was migrated, the modifications were limited to creating the topic and changing the binder types of the components for their collaborative version associated with the created topic.

Another factor to be taken into account in the migration process and in the choice of framework is the conversion of possible technical staff responsible of maintaining legacy applications. The use of Vaadin allows the programming model to represent an evolution and not a total change, which will allow its adaptation to the new environment.

The migration from a Java Swing application to a collaborative web application represents a significant change from a Human-Computer Interaction (HCI) point of view. Changes in user interface, interactivity and collaboration lead to substantial improvements in user experience.

At the interaction level, one of the benefits of this migration is the ability to have real-time collaboration between users. The inclusion of collaborative editing in the data update views of the application, being able to see users online and their activity on the different components of the user interface, has enabled a level of collaboration that is difficult to achieve with Java Swing. Users can now work together on simultaneous tasks, with changes instantly reflected in user interfaces.

The new application follows the single page architectural approach known as SPA (Single Page Application), which provides a more fluid experience by eliminating the need to reload the page [11]. This improvement in the interactive capability of the application is especially relevant for collaborative functionalities.

In addition, the change to a PWA has opened the door to accessibility on a variety of devices. This allows users to use it whenever and wherever they want, freeing them from the limitation imposed by the need for prior installation, typical of Java Swing applications. This type of universal availability further improves usability and accessibility, key aspects of HCI [12]. PWAs can provide a user experience similar to that of native applications, even on mobile devices [13].

5   Conclusion and Future Work

In this work, a migration of Java Swing applications to collaborative web has been done using the Vaadin framework. The main element of its choice was its ability to make collaborative applications with minimal effort. The migration process to a web application was simple following the methodology proposed by Vaadin with more than 20 years of experience in this process. However, advantages were appreciated in the reengineering for the GUI (Graphical User Interface). Several limitations were identified in the Vaadin collaborative solution, the most notable being the lack of persistence of the awareness history and, by design [10], the event is not associated with the producing user. In addition, data management is limited because it is independent of the application logic. Finally, topic management of topics has weaknesses with complex data structures and nested data collections.

References

1. Murugesan, S.: Understanding web 2.0. IT Prof. **9**(4) (2007). https://doi.org/10.1109/MITP.2007.78
2. Mbarki, S., Laaz, N., Gotti, S., Gotti, Z.: ADM-based migration from Java swing to RIA applications. Int. J. Inf. Syst. Serv. Sect. **8**(2) (2016). https://doi.org/10.4018/IJISSS.2016040108
3. Lund, S., Cheng, W.L., Dua, Andre, D.S.A., Robinson, O., Sanghvi, S.: What 800 executives envision for the postpandemic workforce. Mckinsey Global Institute (2020)
4. Sneed, H.M., Verhoef, C.: Cost-driven software migration: an experience report. J. Softw.: Evol. Process **32**(7) (2020). https://doi.org/10.1002/smr.2236
5. Samir, H., Stroulia, E., Kamel, A.: Swing2Script: migration of Java-Swing applications to Ajax web applications. In: Proceedings - Working Conference on Reverse Engineering, WCRE (2007). https://doi.org/10.1109/WCRE.2007.48
6. Brings Java, JavaFX, Netbeans, Applet to browser | Webswing. https://www.webswing.org/en
7. Vaadin | Discover the Web App Framework Built for Java. https://vaadin.com/
8. Vaadin Scalability. https://vaadin.com/scalability
9. Collazos, C.A., Gutiérrez, F.L., Gallardo, J., Ortega, M., Fardoun, H.M., Molina, A.I.: Descriptive theory of awareness for groupware development. J. Ambient Intell. Humaniz. Comput. **10**(12) (2019). https://doi.org/10.1007/s12652-018-1165-9
10. Collaboration Engine architecture - summer 2021 edition vaadin/collaboration-engine Discussion #49 GitHub. https://github.com/vaadin/collaboration-engine/discussions/49
11. Mikowski, M., Powell, J.: Single Page Web Applications: JavaScript End-to-End, 1st edn. Manning Publications Co., USA (2013)
12. Shneiderman, B., Plaisant, C., Cohen, M., Jacobs, S., Elmqvist, N., Diakopoulos, N.: Designing the User Interface: Strategies for Effective Human-Computer Interaction, 6th edn. Pearson, London (2016)
13. Biørn-Hansen, A., Majchrzak, T.A., Grønli, T.M.: Progressive web apps: the possible web-native unifier for mobile development (2017). https://doi.org/10.5220/0006353703440351

Mistakes Hold the Key: Reducing Errors in a Crowdsourced Tumor Annotation Task by Optimizing the Training Strategy

Jose Alejandro Libreros[✉] , Edwin Gamboa , and Matthias Hirth

User-Centric Analysis of Multimedia Data Group, TU Ilmenau, Ehrenbergstraße 29, 98693 Ilmenau, Germany

{jose.libreros,edwin.gamboa,matthias.hirth}@tu-ilmenau.de

Abstract. Accurate tumor identification is crucial for diagnosing and treating various diseases. Nevertheless, the limited availability of expert pathologists delays reliable and timely tumor identification. Crowdsourcing can assist by taking advantage of the collective intelligence of crowdworkers through consensus-based opinion aggregation. However, the open problem of training crowdworkers rapidly for doing complex tasks poses a significant challenge, currently yielding inaccurate results. To improve the performance of crowdworkers, we present a redesign of the training strategy by addressing the errors crowdworkers face frequently. By identifying error patterns through a study, we optimize the design of the training strategy for an exemplary tumor identification crowdsourcing task.

We conduct a comparative analysis between a baseline version of the training strategy and an optimized version based on identified error patterns. Our findings demonstrate that optimizing the training strategy significantly reduces annotation mistakes during the crowdsourced tumor identification process, attributable to the increase of retention. Moreover, it provides noticeable improvements in the performance of annotation of correct tumor regions.

This research contributes to the field by testing the effectiveness of training strategy optimization in crowdsourcing tasks, specifically for tumor annotation. Addressing crowdworkers' training needs and leveraging their collective intelligence, our approach enhances tumor identification's reliability, providing alternatives for healthcare decision-making.

Keywords: Crowdsourcing · Medical Image Annotation · Optimized Training

1 Introduction

Identifying medical image abnormalities as disease biomarkers in complex cases, such as tumor identification in cancer images, is crucial for assisting healthcare professionals in symptom detection [1]. These biomarkers also enable the development of personalized patient alerts. Computational techniques like machine learning aim to automate the identification process [2]. However, these techniques represent the following challenges: 1) Many models are supervised learning models and require extensive training datasets with labeled annotations, i.e., Ground Truth (GT). Automatically generating such data remains unresolved, often requiring trained annotators [3]. 2) Limited resources for supporting the aforementioned point result in computational techniques lacking complete accuracy, thereby still requiring human labor [4]. Moreover, relying on small groups of annotators is risky since this might lead to subjective judgments and decreased accuracy due to a high workload. Furthermore, access to expert annotation sets is often limited and expensive. Crowdsourcing has emerged as an alternative that leverages a distributed community for support and helps address these challenges.

In general, crowdsourcing is an outsourcing activity via the internet to a large number of users [5]. More precisely, it describes a participative online activity with two main parties: employers and the crowdworkers. The employers offer tasks for a group of crowdworkers to complete them. A mutual benefit is expected since the crowdworkers are compensated for their labor and the employers get the work done cost- and time effectively [6]. Thus, crowdsourcing can be a valuable mechanism for training medical image annotators in a scalable and effective way. Nevertheless, skills to identify histologic patterns in cancer images are built with experience rather than a basic understanding of histology from medical education. Therefore, training crowdworkers for annotation in this context might be one of the biggest challenges since only high-reliable annotated data can be considered meaningful [7].

This paper presents an approach to training crowdworkers to annotate segment tumor regions on cancer images. The approach was developed in two stages. First, a microtask was designed (Sect. 3) to train crowdworkers on recognizing tumors in cancer images, which served to identify common error patterns done by them (Sect. 4). Second, the task instructions were optimized based on the identified patterns (Sect. 5). We present the results obtained using a comparative study of both task versions and how the optimization led to obtaining fewer erroneous results (Sect. 6).

2 Related Work

The use of crowdsourcing to compensate for the missing performance of Artificial Intelligence (AI) applications has been highlighted by Mehta et al. [8]. For instance, crowdsourcing has proven in evaluating surgical skills [9–11], particularly in fields such as urology [12] and the analysis of tissue DICOM images [13]. Studies have achieved favorable outcomes even when involving non-medical individuals [14]. Additionally, the application of crowdsourcing extends beyond the medical domain, with notable examples in the field of autonomous driving scenarios [3]. This suggests that crowdworkers can contribute to annotating images in diverse and complex domains after receiving appropriate training [1].

There is a need to train new crowdworkers or re-train the same worker after a few ratings to help them improve their ratings and make them more objective. Alternatively, implementing stricter constraints during the task can help [15].

Grote et al. [16] evaluated histological image labeling using a crowd of medical students. One of their findings is the importance of a proper training phase to obtain high-quality results. In particular they highlight the need for a precise definition of the terminology and categories. Further, they suggest that the training phase should be face-to-face or video-based teaching. However, this is not possible in microtasking use cases. Moreover, low crowd performance might be due to the quality of images rather than due to the crowd itself [4], or the wide variety of opinions [12]. Experience is only sometimes helpful in determining the expertise or performance of the crowd [9, 11]. Therefore, one option is to provide instant or close-to-instant feedback [15]. Focusing on the crowdworker training content, frustration, and incomprehension should be avoided [17, 18]. As the most crucial factor for this, the comprehensibility of the tutorial and the instructions should be ensured.

Identifying and organizing the errors done by all crowdworkers in groups of patterns might imply having optimized training content.

3 Materials and Methods

In this section, we present the dataset and the crowdsourced task that we used to design and optimize a training strategy for crowdsourced tumor annotation. We also present the two studies that we conducted to evaluate the strategy.

3.1 Dataset

The Digital Slide Archive (DSA) [2] is an online resource[1], which provides interactive access to histological Whole Slide Image (WSI)s from The Cancer Genome Atlas. The images used in this paper have been previously and collaboratively labelled with Regions of Interest (RoIs) for the classes: Tumor, Blood, Stroma, or Lymphocytic Infiltrate. The labelled data from the DSA can be used as GT data, as the coordinates of the RoIs are available online.

In this paper, we use only subregions classified as "Tumor" since the number of classes should remain low on complex annotation tasks. We further use only subregions of the images to reduce the possible workload of crowdworkers, as the images are quite large, a characteristic of multi-resolution pyramid WSIs.

Figure 1 shows the set of images used for evaluating the task and its GT. Further, we categorized the images into "Easy", "Medium", and "Hard" to annotate. The size of the tumor regions is similar in all the images. However, the contrast and the level of highlighting that a tumor has among the rest of the structures in the image, as well as the presence of other structures is different. Based on these criteria, Fig. 1a has been tagged as "Easy", Fig. 1b has been tagged as "Medium", and finally Fig. 1c and Fig. 1d have been tagged as "Hard".

3.2 Task

We ask crowdworkers to annotate tumor regions in the images presented in Fig. 1. Before starting the annotation, the crowdworkers should fill out a *demographic form* asking about gender, age, level of education, whether they are native English speakers, the motivation for doing the crowdsourcing task, whether they have seen a histological

---

[1] https://digitalslidearchive.github.io/digital_slide_archive/ Accessed Jun 2023.

image before, and if they completed a task for annotating tumors in histological images before. Then, the workers start with a *training*, in which they learn how to recognize and annotate tumors in this task. This task stage is the main focus of this paper, and the details of the two evaluated training strategies are presented in Sect. 4 and Sect. 5. After that, the crowdworkers should complete a *test* containing 3 questions (two questions "Select which image contains the tumor", and one question "Select which image is annotated correctly") to prove their understanding of the training. If they answered the three questions correctly, they can start the *annotation task*. Otherwise, they are asked to redo the training. After finishing the annotation, they receive a unique code that they can use to get paid. Figure 2 shows the task interface, which is a web element for drawing polygons while holding the left click.

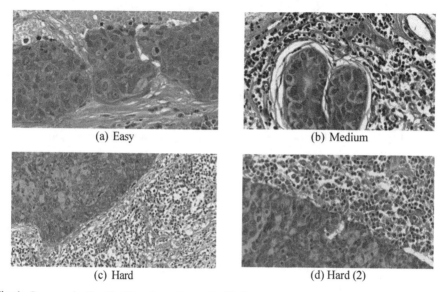

(a) Easy   (b) Medium

(c) Hard   (d) Hard (2)

Fig. 1. Image selection for Crowdsourcing task. GT for tumor area is highlighted in red, but not shown to the crowdworkers. (Color figure online)

3.3 Conducted Studies

We evaluate two versions of a strategy to train crowdworkers to recognize and segment tumors on histological images via two studies as shown in Fig. 3. In the first study, we design a baseline tutorial to show what tumors look and do not look like. We run a crowdsourcing campaign to evaluate this initial strategy and design an optimized version of the training based on identified error patterns. For this, videos of crowdworkers conducting the task while verbalizing their thoughts using the Thinking Aloud Method [19] were collected. Then, the videos were analyzed to identify optimization paths. This is described in detail in Sect. 4. In the second study, we run two parallel campaigns in which the crowdworkers were randomly assigned to one of the two versions, i.e., the baseline, with fixed technical issues, and the version with the optimized tutorial. Crowdworkers who participated in the first study are not allowed to participate in the second one to avoid adding bias to their prior training. Then, we compare the collected annotations to evaluate the effectiveness of the performed optimization. We perform two-sided hypothesis contrast to compare the quality of the tumor identification, the extent to which crowdwokers annotated error regions using mean Intersection over Union (mIoU), and the mean of the precision, recall, and F1-Score as performance metrics. The second study is detailed in Sect. 5.

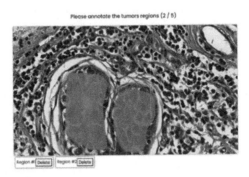

Fig. 2. Annotation task, workers should draw a polygon around tumor regions.

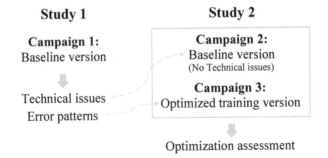

Fig. 3. Campaigns conducted under each study and their outcomes.

4   Study 1: Identification of Error Patterns

Study 1 consists of an initial campaign to validate the baseline training strategy. The campaign was published via Microworkers[2], a well-known crowdsourcing market, with positions for $n_{s1} = 30$ crowdworkers, who received a compensation of 0.30 USD for participating.

---

[2] www.microworkers.com Accessed Jun. 2023.

4.1 Training Strategy

The training strategy contains the following items:

– *General information of what the task is about*, instructions about not refreshing the window or going to the previous website using the browser.
– *The baseline version of the training*: Fig. 4 shows the training phase, which is a tutorial consisting of four animated images explaining how to annotate, what a tumor looks like, and an example of what is not a tumor.

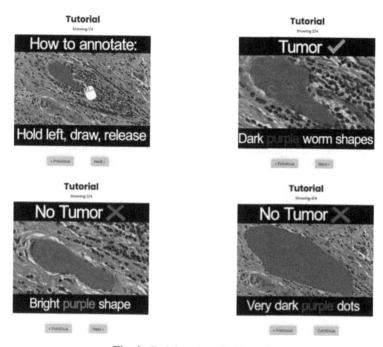

Fig. 4. Training phase in Study 1.

4.2 Findings from Study 1

The collected videos in which the crowdworkers performed that task and verbalized their thought with the Thinking Aloud Method allowed identifying some technical issues in the baseline version. First, the tutorial and test images took a long time to load, and the workers were not able to view them, so they continued without watching them. Additionally, some of the workers who could access all the images, tend to skip the training phase, thus, having to return to the tutorial after failing the test more than once.

The task design was refined base on these findings. Mechanisms were implemented to control the loading of images. Furthermore, to ensure the integral execution of the training strategy, it was necessary to implement measures to prevent skipping its main core. Specifically, a fixed countdown mechanism was put in place to restrict progress before a specific time has elapsed.

On the other hand, we observed that some workers focused on annotating only the blood cells, even when the training strategy stated that the task is related to tumor identification. Potentially, some workers pay attention to highlighted zones among others, even if those zones are not a majority.

4.3 Identified Errors

The video observation also allowed identifying the most common error patterns done by the crowdworker, which can be summarized into four categories:

- *Light purple zones (pink)*: Some crowdworkers annotated bright purple (or pink) zones, which are related to muscles or other kinds of malign tissue.
- *Dark purple zones*: Other crowdworkers annotated dark purple dots, related to the presence of lymphocytic cells in the zone. While it is true that cancer cells induce the infiltration of various immune cells that are located or distributed in different sites and play multiple roles [20], we are only interested in the explicit presence of the tumor regions.
- *Red zones*: We found annotations above red dots which belong to other type of structures.
- *White zones*: Finally, there were white regions annotated explicitly by some workers, which are related to ducts.

4.4 Optimized Training Based on Error Patterns

The optimization of the training strategy was divided into three sections, each one presented once at a time:

- *What a tumor looks like*: With two examples referring to two different zones, aiming to improve the location of tumor zones and the respect of the border of the tumor zones.
- *What a tumor does not look like*: (Based on the error patterns identified in Study 1) with clearly visible advice about not selecting light purple zones (muscle), purple dots (lymphocytes), red dot zones (blood), and white zones (not tissue), as shown in Fig. 5.
- A video *about the platform* was included, i.e., how to annotate, how to delete regions, how to proceed with the next image, and the availability of the tutorial, as shown in Fig. 6.

Furthermore, the location of the button to access the tutorial was moved close to the "next" button, to avoid workers to miss it.

5 Study 2: Evaluation of the Optimized Training Strategy

The primary objective of this Study 2 is to quantify the reduction of errors in image segmentation through the implementation of error-based learning techniques. In this section, we examine and compare two versions of the training strategy –one baseline and one optimized–, taking into consideration four key criteria that effectively summarize the aforementioned error patterns. Additionally, we have included and discussed an analysis of performance metrics specifically related to tumour identification.

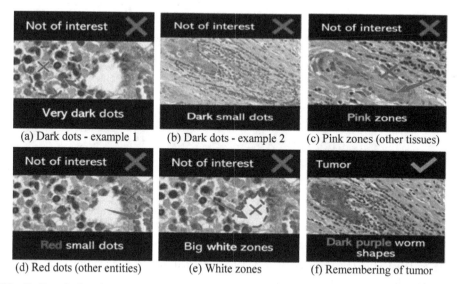

(a) Dark dots - example 1   (b) Dark dots - example 2   (c) Pink zones (other tissues)

(d) Red dots (other entities)   (e) White zones   (f) Remembering of tumor

Fig. 5. Description about each error pattern defined from Study 1, and the comparison with the tumor region in the same slide, as part of the optimized training strategy used in Study 2.

For the comparative study of the training strategies, 150 crowdworkers were recruited parallelly per training strategy version, i.e., in total $n_{baselineversion} + n_{optimizedversion} = 300$. The campaigns were published again using Microworkers. Each worker was paid 0.30 USD for completing a task.

5.1 Performance and Error Comparison Between Training Strategies

Our intention is to show the differences between the two sets of results of crowdworkers which have taken the baseline version of the training strategy and the optimized version, from different perspectives, like visual and by using the standard metrics of assessment of segmentation. In particular, Fig. 7 illustrates the heatmaps that encompass the collective responses provided by crowdworkers for each task. In addition, Table 1 shows the means of the most frequent quantitative comparison metrics used for evaluating semantic segmentation, i.e., mIoU, precision, recall, and F1-Score. The metrics were calculated for correct annotated tumor regions, as well as the segmentations metrics of the wrong zones, labelled as the categories described in Sect. 4.3.

For clarification, Table 1 presents the performance results for all the combined images (referred to as 'All'), based on different metrics. Additionally, the table provides individual performance metrics for each image: 'Image 1' representing the 'Easy' difficulty level, 'Image 2' representing the 'Medium' difficulty level, 'Image 3' representing the 'Hard' difficulty level, and 'Image 4' representing the 'Hard 2'.

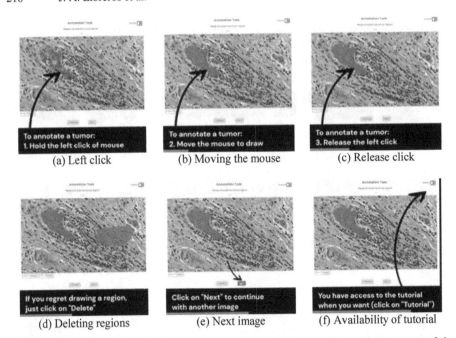

Fig. 6. Detailed instructions on how to annotate (selected frames of the video), as part of the optimized training strategy used in Study 2.

The measurements for each image encompass two aspects. Firstly, they evaluate the performance of the segmentation area for all regions associated with tumors. We anticipate observing improved segmentation performance based on these metrics. Secondly, the measurements assess the performance of regions exhibiting light purple (pink), dark dot, red, or white areas within the image. Our expectation is that these error performances will decrease when utilizing the optimized version of the training strategy.

5.2   Results and Findings

As shown in Fig. 7, the segmentation boundary extends beyond the tumor region, resulting in the annotation of numerous pixels that lie outside the desired area, resulting in some light-purple pixel zones annotated. While there are a low amount of workers who have difficulties with underperformance, we do notice that most pay more attention when clear information is presented. We see that there is no performance hit when we split the errors and create a warning for each one.

When considering the performance of crowdworkers on Image 1 (referred to as "Easy"), it is important to examine both Table 1 and Figs. 7a and 7b. We remark that there are observed improvements in a majority of the metrics related to correctly segmented regions belonging to the tumor, although did not reach statistical significance. Furthermore, there was a notable reduction in the metrics associated with incorrectly covered regions, specifically the light purple, dark purple, red dot, and white regions.

While there was a decrease in the performance of correctly identifying the tumor region in image 4, this decrease was not statistically significant. Higher mIoU values indicate better coverage of true tumor regions, while higher recall suggests fewer false negative predictions (foreground pixels omitted from the prediction).

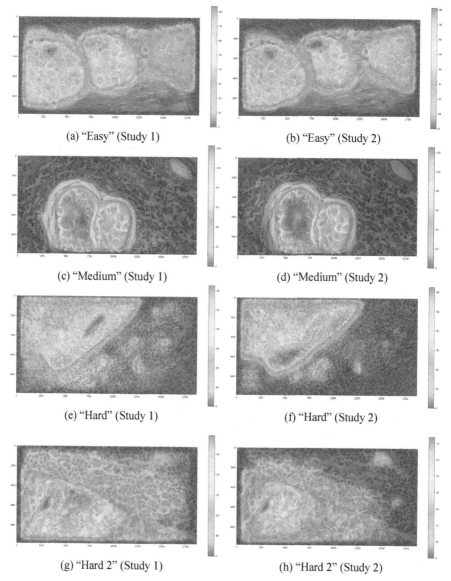

(a) "Easy" (Study 1)   (b) "Easy" (Study 2)

(c) "Medium" (Study 1)   (d) "Medium" (Study 2)

(e) "Hard" (Study 1)   (f) "Hard" (Study 2)

(g) "Hard 2" (Study 1)   (h) "Hard 2" (Study 2)

Fig. 7. Comparison between the set of answers of Study 1 and Study 2 per task image.

We assert that the absence of statistical significance might be attributed to the fact that the observed performance improvements are contingent upon intricate details and refinements. Nevertheless, our study endeavors to address these aspects and enhance the overall performance further.

On the other hand, some error rates according to the different metrics of mistakes in annotations of dark purple dots regions are statistically significantly smaller (due to the more conservative two-sided Wilcoxon test). One of the noteworthy outcomes derived from Table 1 for Study 2 is not solely the cessation of error propagation with respect to Study 1, but also the notable diminution in the annotated regions linked to dot regions. Image 2 –"Medium"– as well as Image 3 and Image 4 –"Hard"– have a huge presence of lymphocytic entities –dark dots. Surprisingly, Image 3 –"Hard"– has shown the most significant reduction in all metrics (Table 1), which can be seen in Fig. 7e and Fig. 7f.

Table 1. Comparison of metrics (mean values) in Baseline version of the training strategy (BV) and the optimized version (OV) across tumor and error regions annotated by the crowdworkers.

Metric	Image	Correct regions Tumor BV, OV	Error regions –wrongly annotated– Light purple BV, OV	Purple BV, OV	Red BV, OV	White BV, OV
mIoU	All	0.69, 0.76 *	0.03, 0.03	0.15, 0.08*	0.11, 0.04*	0.03, 0.02
	1	0.25, 0.26	0.01, 0.01	0.02, 0.01	0.01, 0.0	0.0, 0.0
	2	0.34, 0.35	0.02, 0.01	0.02, 0.02	0.04, 0.01*	0.04, 0.03
	3	0.17, 0.17	0.0, 0.0	0.02, 0.02*	0.10, 0.04*	0.0, 0.0
	4	0.17, 0.14	0.02, 0.03	0.05, 0.04	0.07, 0.03*	0.01, 0.0
Precision	All	0.69, 0.76*	0.03, 0.03	0.15, 0.08*	0.11, 0.04*	0.03, 0.02
	1	0.68, 0.70	0.05, 0.04	0.02, 0.01	0.01, 0.01	0.01, 0.0
	2	0.75, 0.80	0.04, 0.02	0.11, 0.08	0.06, 0.02*	0.07, 0.06
	3	0.71, 0.81	0.0, 0.1	0.18, 0.05*	0.22, 0.09*	0.01, 0.01
	4	0.64, 0.73*	0.03, 0.05	0.30, 0.20*	0.13, 0.04*	0.02, 0.01
Recall	All	0.26, 0.25	0.03, 0.02	0.05, 0.03	0.16, 0.09*	0.07, 0.04
	1	0.30, 0.31	0.02, 0.02	0.03, 0.01	0.03, 0.02	0.02, 0.01
	2	0.39, 0.39	0.03, 0.02	0.02, 0.03	0.15, 0.07*	0.14, 0.09
	3	0.17, 0.17	0.01, 0.0	0.04, 0.02*	0.21, 0.11*	0.02, 0.01
	4	0.18, 0.15	0.07, 0.05	0.08, 0.06	0.26, 0.18*	0.09, 0.05
F1-score	All	0.30, 0.30	0.02, 0.02	0.04, 0.03	0.08, 0.03*	0.02, 0.02
	1	0.30, 0.31	0.02, 0.02	0.03, 0.01	0.03, 0.02	0.02, 0.01
	2	0.39, 0.39	0.03, 0.02	0.02, 0.03	0.15, 0.07*	0.14, 0.09
	3	0.17, 0.17	0.01, 0.0	0.04, 0.02*	0.21, 0.11*	0.02, 0.01
	4	0.18, 0.15	0.07, 0.05	0.08, 0.06	0.26, 0.18*	0.09, 0.05

* $p < 0.05$.

Green: Version of the training strategy with better score of specific metric in tumor identification per image, when the comparison has statistical significance.

Red: Version of the training strategy that has achieved lower score of coverage of wrong region annotated, per image, when the comparison has statistical significance.

Moreover, it is noticeable when Image 3, –"Hard"–, where there are more red dot regions, Table 1 shows a reduction by around 10% in all the metrics after taking the optimized version of the training strategy. Even more, this can be seen in a practical way from Fig. 7c and Fig. 7d.

Regarding the white regions, reports of Table 1 suggest a decrease in errors with regard to the white regions, this decrease was not significant because, by itself, it was already low when using the baseline version of the training strategy.

Although, there were counterproductively few punctual decreases in the performance of correct tumor regions (e.g., the mIoU, recall and F1-Score of Image 4 – "Hard 2"), or the increment of coverage of wrong regions, e.g., increment of the recall of wrongly segmented dark purple regions in Image 2 – "Medium"–, or the mIoU of the wrongly segmented light purple regions in Image Image 4 – "Hard 2" after doing the task with the optimized version of the training strategy. However, those incidences are very few and with no statistical significance.

6 Discussion

In this section, we explore some lights and pitfalls of our study, based on the error classifications.

6.1 Error Pattern Findings

Light Purple Regions. Our results go in the same direction as [5, 12, 21, 22]. Whilst the error rates observed in both Study 1 and Study 2 are relatively minimal, achieving meticulous segmentation poses a persistent challenge due to the requirement of allocating a significantly longer duration per worker, potentially contradicting the fundamental principles of microtasking. But even though not statistically significant, our optimized training strategy managed to decrease the mean error of wrong annotations of muscle or other kind of structures.

Dark Purple Dots Regions. According to our results, we evidenced the retention of crowdworkers, as we had a special focus on the optimized training. We intended to advise to crowdworkers that they should avoid the very dark dots. Our training strategy has distinguished appropriately the differences, even with slight changes between actual tumor structures and dark purple dots. This is reflected in the decrease in the annotated regions, in both the significant decrease and the not significant ones.

Red Dot Regions. We believe that explicitly mentioned in the tutorial, it allows the workers to have the knowledge in present. The way how the advertisements were made (very impositive, using red crosses), makes the advert remain.

White Regions. We consider this criterion strategically, due to its strong presence in the upper-right area of image 2. In fact, although not statistically significant, the reduction in recall and F1-Score of annotated white regions is remarkable.

Overall Results in Correct Detection Regions. The error-based training strategy implemented resulted in both a reduction of annotated incorrect regions and an improvement in the delineation of accurate tumor regions. There were improvements in precision for both the overall images and individual images, particularly in image 4. The mIoU for all image sets showed significant enhancements, particularly in images 1, 2, and 3. Our focus has been on reducing errors, not to penalize bad performance, but rather to gain insights into the training needs of crowdworkers. By employing an optimized strategy, workers were able to identify distinct instances of failure. They shown increased attentiveness and considered multiple error criteria simultaneously, leading to a reduction in missegmented areas and an overall improvement in the identification of tumor regions.

7 Conclusion

In this paper, we addressed the challenge of effectively training crowdworkers engaged in tumor identification tasks through a redesigned training strategy. By conducting a study and identifying error patterns, we optimized the design of the training strategy for crowdsourcing tasks. We also compared the performance of a baseline training strategy with an optimized version based on the identified error patterns. The results demonstrated a significant reduction in annotation mistakes during the crowdsourced tumor identification process, and the effectiveness of the optimized training strategy.

As mentioned, this paper is a contribution to the generation of training material for crowdworkers since it allows us to understand which material provide or generate if wanted to create personalized training in the future. Personalized training in crowdsourcing should consider the errors. Regarding the use case of annotation of medical images, previous works have shown other strategies for achieving high-quality results, but the training was ineffective. In this paper, we wanted to focus on the decrease in errors as a first step. We demonstrated here that, even for complex tasks such as medical, providing training based on errors done by a few previous crowdworkers might decrease the error rates rapidly. We propose the identification of errors as the first step in the path for generating training data, possibly using AI-based schemes. AI-based collaborations in crowdsourcing should be used not only for proposing ratings (e.g., segmentations or classifications in case of images) and being validated with the crowdworkers but also for discovering the errors the workers are aggregating, and then having automatic and refined inferences as improvement of those used in this study.

Therefore, the subsequent phase in the progression of personalized training entails the development of a framework that can effectively detect and rectify general errors across various criteria in real-time, with the potential inclusion of AI-based assistance. On the other hand, in a real context, in which an image is labelled by a limited amount of workers, assuring that almost all the workers understand the task is crucial. In such a sense, as a lack of our work, some workers remain confused when presenting a totally different test before a totally different task. Then, the effect of redesigning the test before the task (by annotating very basic regions for testing the learning and letting workers who pass that test, perform the task) could be explored in the future. Other aspects not considered in this study would be valuable to experiment in combination with our proposal. For instance, exploring usability settings in the performance of crowdsourcing tasks in depth, and achieving automatic/intelligent generation of usable elements for generic tasks, or the easy design of them for very specialized tasks through small building blocks, would have a trade-off between the time to create the task from an employer, and the performance obtained by crowdworkers.

This approach enhances the opportunity for both fully human-based tumor annotation and hybrid human-AI collaboration schemes.

References

1. Amgad, M., et al.: Structured crowdsourcing enables convolutional segmentation of histology images. Bioinformatics **35**(18), 3461–3467 (2019). https://doi.org/10.1093/bioinformatics/btz083
2. Gutman, D.A., et al.: The digital slide archive: a software platform for management, integration, and analysis of histology for cancer research. Can. Res. **77**(21), e75–e78 (2017). https://doi.org/10.1158/0008-5472.CAN-17-0629
3. Gamboa, E., Libreros, A., Hirth, M., Dubiner, D.: Human-AI collaboration for improving the identification of cars for autonomous driving (2022). https://ceur-ws.org/Vol-3318/short14.pdf
4. Garcia-Molina, H., Joglekar, M., Marcus, A., Parameswaran, A., Verroios, V.: Challenges in data crowdsourcing. IEEE Trans. Knowl. Data Eng. **28**(4), 901–911 (2016). https://doi.org/10.1109/TKDE.2016.2518669
5. Hoßfeld, T., et al.: Best practices for QoE crowdtesting: QoE assessment with crowdsourcing. IEEE Trans. Multimed. **16**(2), 541–558 (2013). https://doi.org/10.1109/TMM.2013.2291663
6. Estellés-Arolas, E., González-Ladrón-De-Guevara, F.: Towards an integrated crowdsourcing definition. J. Inf. Sci. **38**(2), 189–200 (2012). https://doi.org/10.1177/0165551512437638
7. López-Pérez, M., et al.: Learning from crowds in digital pathology using scalable variational Gaussian processes. Sci. Rep. **11**(1), 11612 (2021). https://doi.org/10.1038/s41598-021-90821-3
8. Mehta, P., Sandfort, V., Gheysens, D., Braeckevelt, G.J., Berte, J., Summers, R.M.: Segmenting the kidney on CT scans via crowdsourcing. In: 16th International Symposium on Biomedical Imaging, pp. 829–832. IEEE, Venice (2019). https://doi.org/10.1109/ISBI.2019.8759240
9. Bui, M., Bourier, F., Baur, C., Milletari, F., Navab, N., Demirci, S.: Robust navigation support in lowest dose image setting. Int. J. Comput. Assist. Radiol. Surg. **14**(2), 291–300 (2019). https://doi.org/10.1007/s11548-018-1874-8
10. Goldenberg, M., Ordon, M., Honey, J.R.D., Andonian, S., Lee, J.Y.: Objective assessment and standard setting for basic flexible ureterorenoscopy skills among urology trainees using simulation-based methods. J. Endourol. **34**(4), 495–501 (2020). https://doi.org/10.1089/end.2019.0626
11. Kandala, P.A., Sivaswamy, J.: Crowdsourced annotations as an additional form of data augmentation for CAD development. In: 4th IAPR Asian Conference on Pattern Recognition, pp. 753–758. IEEE, Nanjing (2017). https://doi.org/10.1109/ACPR.2017.6
12. Conti, S.L., et al.: Crowdsourced assessment of ureteroscopy with laser lithotripsy video feed does not correlate with trainee experience. J. Endourol. **33**(1), 42–49 (2019). https://doi.org/10.1089/end.2018.0534
13. Morozov, S., et al.: A simplified cluster model and a tool adapted for collaborative labeling of lung cancer CT scans. Comput. Methods Program. Biomed. **206**, 106111 (2021). https://doi.org/10.1016/j.cmpb.2021.106111
14. Marzahl, C., et al.: Is crowd-algorithm collaboration an advanced alternative to crowdsourcing on cytology slides? In: Tolxdorff, T., Deserno, T., Handels, H., Maier, A., Maier-Hein, K., Palm, C. (eds) Bildverarbeitung für die Medizin 2020. Informatik aktuell, pp. 26–31. Springer, Wiesbaden (2020). https://doi.org/10.1007/978-3-658-29267-6_5

15. Rice, M.K., et al.: Crowdsourced assessment of inanimate biotissue drills: a valid and cost-effective way to evaluate surgical trainees. J. Surg. Educ. **76**(3), 814–823 (2019). https://doi.org/10.1016/j.jsurg.2018.10.007

16. Grote, A., Schaadt, N.S., Forestier, G., Wemmert, C., Feuerhake, F.: Crowdsourcing of histological image labeling and object delineation by medical students. IEEE Trans. Med. Imaging **38**(5), 1284–1294 (2019). https://doi.org/10.1109/TMI.2018.2883237

17. Ørting, S. N., et al.: A survey of crowdsourcing in medical image analysis. Hum. Comput. **7**(1), 1–26 (2020). https://doi.org/10.48550/arXiv.1902.09159

18. Hirth, M., Borchert, K., De Moor, K., Borst, V., Hoßfeld, T.: Personal task design preferences of crowdworkers. In: 12th International Conference on Quality of Multimedia Experience, pp. 1–6 (2020). https://doi.org/10.1109/QoMEX48832.2020.9123094

19. Gamboa, E., Galda, R., Mayas, C., Hirth, M.: The crowd thinks aloud: crowdsourcing usability testing with the thinking aloud method. In: Stephanidis, C., et al. (eds.) HCII 2021. LNCS, vol. 13094, pp. 24–39. Springer, Cham (2021). https://doi.org/10.1007/978-3-030-90238-4_3

20. Wang, J., Tian, S., Sun, J., Zhang, J., Lin, L., Hu, C.: The presence of tumour-infiltrating lymphocytes (TILs) and the ratios between different subsets serve as prognostic factors in advanced hypopharyngeal squamous cell carcinoma. BMC Cancer **20**(1), 731 (2020). https://doi.org/10.1186/s12885-020-07234-0

21. Kittur, A., Chi, E.H., Suh, B.: Crowdsourcing user studies with mechanical turk. In: SIGCHI Conference on Human Factors in Computing Systems, CHI 2008, pp. 453–456. Association for Computing Machinery, New York (2008). https://doi.org/10.1145/1357054.1357127

22. Paley, G.L., et al.: Crowdsourced assessment of surgical skill proficiency in cataract surgery. J. Surg. Educ. **78**(4), 1077–1088 (2021). https://doi.org/10.1016/j.jsurg.2021.02.004

Personalization and Accessibility in a Digital Repository

Silvana Aciar[1]([envelope]) [iD], Patricia Paderewski[2] [iD], Francisco Gutierrez-Vela[2] [iD], and Luciano Grossi[3] [iD]

[1] Instituto de Ciencias Astronómicas de la Tierra y el Espacio (ICATE – CONICET/UNSJ), San Juan, Argentina
silvana.aciar@conicet.gov.ar

[2] Dpto. de Lenguajes y Sistemas Informaticos, Universidad de Granada, Granada, Spain
{patricia,fgutierr}@ugr.es

[3] Facultad de Ciencias Exactas, Físicas y Naturales, UNSJ, San Juan, Argentina

Abstract. Developers of institutional digital repositories are committed to creating repositories that adhere to international standards and adopt metadata to ensure interoperability and open access to content. As the volume of digital objects stored in repositories increases, the implementation of customized filtering mechanisms becomes necessary to address the issue of information overload. Moreover, it is imperative that repositories remain accessible to all individuals, thus requiring the development of repository objects and interfaces that adhere to accessibility standards. This paper presents the aspects of customization and accessibility that must be considered when implementing a repository to ensure user usability, accessibility, and satisfaction. The development of a prototype learning object repository is introduced, incorporating recommendation systems as a customization mechanism, and implementing web accessibility guidelines in its interface to ensure information access for all individuals.

Keywords: Digital Repositories · Customization · Accessibility

1 Introduction

In contemporary society, Information and Communication Technologies (ICTs) have become ubiquitous, shaping the everyday experiences of people and enabling the generation and sharing of digital content [1, 2]. The inception of the Open Access initiative aims to simplify information utilization by eliminating legal and technical obstacles, thereby enabling unrestricted access to scientific, academic, and cultural resources online [3, 4]. This initiative empowers users to freely read, download, copy, distribute, and utilize such information without constraints.

Within educational institutions, it is imperative to establish the necessary resources and mechanisms to guarantee universal access to generated information. Digital repositories have emerged as expansive digital archives [5, 6], streamlining the management,

P. H. Ruiz et al. (Eds.): HCI-COLLAB 2023, CCIS 1877, pp. 225–241, 2024.
https://doi.org/10.1007/978-3-031-57982-0_18

storage, preservation, dissemination, and retrieval of the digital information they contain, referred to as digital objects. A digital object is described as "a distinct unit of information in digital form" [7].

Digital objects encompass a diverse array of types, spanning the likes of theses, conference papers, lecture materials, technical reports, multimedia content, journals, patents, regulations, software, and learning resources. Retrieving these objects requires accompanying metadata, which offers information about their content and structure [7]. As institutional repository initiatives continue to expand, a wealth of literature on software selection, architectural frameworks, standards, and repository implementation procedures has emerged [8–10]. Repositories may adopt centralized or decentralized architectures [11, 12], with popular software options including Fedora, DSpace, and Greenstone [11–14].

As previously stated, the central aim of repository creation is to facilitate resource sharing. Initiatives that consolidate and provide access to digital resources from various repositories have emerged, such as the Federated Network of Institutional Repositories of Scientific Publications, known as LA Referencia [15, 16]. This network includes repositories from eight Latin American countries, offering access to over 800,000 articles and theses from a hundred universities in the region. With this abundance of information, the challenge transitions from scarcity to managing information overload while ensuring continued accessibility to repository contents.

This paper offers solutions to these challenges by introducing a prototype learning object repository that emphasizes customization and accessibility. The structure is as follows: Sect. 2 addresses customization aspects to mitigate result overload; Sect. 3 presents accessibility guidelines for creating accessible repository contents and interfaces; Sect. 4 describes the prototype of a personalized and accessible learning object repository; Sect. 5 outlines the evaluation and validation process involving experts and end-users; and Sect. 6 offers conclusions and avenues for future research.

2 Personalization in Digital Repositories

Various initiatives aimed at establishing networks of interoperable repositories, coupled with the growing number of open-access digital objects, have significantly expanded the options available to individuals seeking information. Consider the following scenario:

Example 1: Oscar is in search of information regarding "Artificial Intelligence." He navigates through several repositories using the search engine embedded within their portals. The search yields dozens of results. Despite his efforts, Oscar can only review 15 out of over 2000 results retrieved. Due to time constraints, he is unable to continue analyzing the subsequent results.

Oscar experiences what is commonly referred to as information overload, wherein the abundance of choices makes it challenging to discern the most suitable option. With a vast array of choices available, Oscar finds it impossible to assess all options thoroughly and identify the one that best aligns with his needs. When faced with more than 100 options, tools become essential to facilitate searching, filtering, selection, and decision-making processes, assisting users in determining the most appropriate option.

Numerous challenges associated with repository usage are centered around the effectiveness of their search tools. An examination of the literature identifies three key factors influencing content searches and subsequent user satisfaction with the outcomes: interface design, search strategies, and information indexing [7, 17, 18].

Regarding interface design, repositories must feature interfaces that are intuitive, easy to navigate, and straightforward to enhance user experience. Given the vast amount of information they contain, repositories should adopt a visual architecture that presents data in a comprehensible and user-friendly manner [18–20]. Visual interfaces should be incorporated to categorize available objects visibly, thus enhancing usability. While transitioning from textual to graphical interfaces may require additional effort, integrating navigation mechanisms through conceptual maps that provide an overview of thematic areas, prominently displaying query results associated with each theme, and incorporating personalized search mechanisms tailored to individual user profiles are highly recommended.

In terms of user search strategies, they typically fall into three distinct categories: metadata-based searches, content-based object searches, and hybrid searches [19–21]. Metadata-based strategies involve correlating the words comprising the user's query with the data provided by the object's metadata. Techniques such as cosine similarity, ontology-based reasoning, fuzzy clustering, and inference rules are commonly utilized for this purpose [20, 21]. These methods rely on the internal representation of objects and user queries, which may include vector representations, ontologies, and similar structures. Content-based object search strategies are less prevalent in repositories due to the intricate nature of analyzing all object content, which can encompass various formats like images, text, video, and audio [21, 22]. However, this technique is relatively simpler to implement when dealing solely with textual objects. To address the complexities involved, various techniques such as Bayesian rule-based classifiers, support vector machine-based classifiers, decision trees, and natural language processing methods are applied [21–23]. A technique gaining traction in digital repositories to enhance response accuracy involves employing a hybrid approach between the aforementioned strategies. This approach entails mapping the user's query with metadata while also extending the search to object content. A combination of techniques from both strategies, including similarity measures and natural language processing methods, is employed to improve search effectiveness [21, 24].

Regarding information indexing, the internal architecture of a repository must consider how information is treated and organized to ensure it can be easily presented to users [18, 20]. Key instruments for knowledge representation include taxonomies, thesauri, and ontologies. In [20], the authors recommend implementing a scheme that enables proper integration of repository search tools with the internal information representation architecture. This scheme should allow for linking with interface visualization tools, incorporation of complementary terms such as synonyms and related terms, and definition of multiple search criteria.

An alternative to traditional information search, especially for filtering search results, has emerged with recommender systems. These systems are widely used in e-commerce, tourism, social networks, and other domains as a solution to information overload issues

[25–28]. The primary function of a Recommender System is to assist users in selecting products or services from a set of options [28].

In a digital repository, a recommender system's role is to automatically present materials (digital objects) according to each user's profile and needs [29–32]. To achieve their objectives, these systems encounter two significant challenges: acquiring user information to create a user profile and determining how information selection or filtering will be performed.

In creating user profiles, two methods are utilized to gather information. Explicit information collection involves users inputting preferences, such as weighting various items or completing a form detailing their likes and dislikes. Implicit information collection, on the other hand, involves the system transparently gathering data from user interactions, such as analyzing search history. The second challenge in implementing recommender systems within digital repositories lies in selecting the appropriate recommendation method to map user preferences and interests to the digital objects recommended. Researchers have categorized recommender systems into several types based on how they filter information to make recommendations. The most common classification [25] divides recommender systems into four types: collaborative filtering, content-based filtering, demographic filtering, and hybrid filtering. Collaborative filtering identifies user consumption preferences and generates recommendations based on similar behavioral patterns among users. It aims to accumulate user recommendations on items, identify similarities between users, and produce new recommendations for specific users. Content-based filtering selects new objects based on characteristics of previously consumed objects. It extends collaborative filtering by learning the user's profile from the characteristics of previously ranked objects and offering recommendations accordingly. Demographic filtering categorizes users into groups and provides recommendations based on group characteristics such as age, gender, and place of origin. Hybrid filtering combines one or more recommendation techniques and is the most complex to build but often yields the best results by maximizing advantages and minimizing disadvantages associated with different recommendation methods. The most common combination includes demographic filtering, collaborative filtering, and content-based filtering. Recent studies have integrated ontologies and text mining techniques to extract information from user comments in digital repositories for recommending digital objects, using a hybrid approach to recommendation methods [33, 34].

3   Accessibility in Digital Repositories

Given that repositories are typically accessed through web interfaces, and considering the aim of this project to develop a prototype institutional learning object repository at the National University of San Juan, Argentina, adherence to accessibility laws is crucial. In Argentina, Law 26.653 - 2010 "Accessibility of information on web pages" establishes standards to ensure web information accessibility for individuals with disabilities. It is imperative to ensure access to digital resources for all individuals, in line with these legal requirements.

In many cases, objects stored in repositories are inaccessible to individuals with special access needs. Let's consider the following scenario:

Example 2: Luis, who has a visual impairment, needs information on "neural networks." He relies on a screen reader to access online information. However, when accessing repositories, Luis encounters difficulties navigating the repository portal with his screen reader. Moreover, he is unable to access information about neural networks stored in the repository with his screen reader. In numerous repositories, objects may be inaccessible to certain individuals, or they may be designed with specific user populations in mind, rendering them inaccessible to others. In some cases, even repository interfaces are inaccessible.

Accessibility, as defined by ISO/TC 16027, is the ease and effectiveness with which a product, service, environment, or instrument can be used by individuals with diverse abilities [35–37]. Ensuring accessibility is essential to guarantee that digital resources and interfaces are usable by everyone, regardless of their abilities or disabilities.

There are several limitations that can pose barriers to accessing repositories or the content stored within them [35]:

- Hearing impairment: Difficulty locating sounds and distinguishing auditory information.
- Visual impairment: Challenges in obtaining visually presented information, using color-related information, and distinguishing different types of fonts.
- Motor impairment: Difficulty using the keyboard and mouse, handling multiple pages simultaneously, reaching objects, executing precise and swift actions, concentration and perception issues, completing tasks within time constraints, reading and understanding existing information, and understanding an object's function without subtitles.
- People with specific and diverse technologies: Compatibility issues with different browsers, utilization of slow communication or devices lacking audio output, and use of devices without a mouse.
- Environmental characteristics: Usage in noisy environments and indoors/outdoors with high brightness.

Repositories must cater to the needs of users with specific requirements while also providing benefits for everyone. Guidelines for universal design should be followed. The W3C - World Wide Web Consortium [38] has established accessibility guidelines, known as "WCAG Accessibility Guidelines" in its latest version 2.0, which measure web accessibility at three levels:

- Priority 1 or Level A: These are the points that a web development MUST meet for one or more groups of users to not find it impossible to access their website.
- Priority 2 or Level AA: These are the points that MUST be met for one or more groups of users to not encounter difficulties in accessing the site.
- Priority 3 or Level AAA: These are the points that CAN be met for one or more groups of users to not encounter "Some Difficulty" in accessing the page.

WCAG 2.0 specifies guidelines for making any web development accessible, which are also used for creating digital resources such as documents, presentations, and PDF documents in an accessible format [39–41]. To make objects accessible, they must be made perceivable, operable, and understandable for various individuals [40].

4 Repository with Personalization and Accessibility Criteria

This work presents the development of a prototype of a Digital Repository. The repository is purpose-specific, a Learning Object Repository, where learning objects are stored in SCORM format, as well as other types of digital resources used in the teaching and learning process, such as audio, images, videos, and digital documents.

The prototype was created to implement personalization and accessibility mechanisms to meet the needs of users in diverse contexts. Figure 1 presents the prototype of the Learning Object Repository, which we have named the Accessible and Personalized Learning Object Repository, hereinafter referred to as ROAAP.

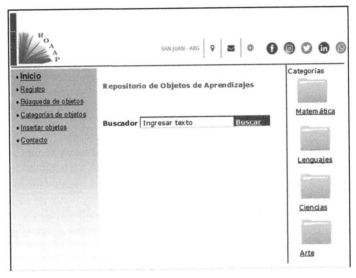

Fig. 1. Prototype of the Learning Object Repository ROAAP.

ROAAP exhibits the following characteristics:

- Search Tool: This essential function allows users to explore learning objects using diverse criteria such as title, keywords, author, target audience (teachers, students), and format type (images, audio, documents, etc.).
- Recommendation Tools: Registered users receive automatic recommendations for learning objects upon entering the repository. Recommendations are based on their profile, interests, and specific accessibility requirements.
- Accessible Interface: The repository interface adheres to WCAG 2.0 accessibility guidelines, enabling users with specific needs to navigate and access learning objects easily. Additionally, for object tagging and retrieval based on individual needs, the repository utilizes the LOM (Learning Object Metadata) educational metadata standard and IMS (IMS Learning Resource Metadata Information Model). These standards encompass metadata for various impairments such as visual, motor, and auditory impairments.

- Storage of Learning Objects: Users can upload learning objects in various formats and specify educational and specific needs metadata. Internally, the repository automatically disaggregates SCORM format learning objects, integrating them with other digital resources like images, videos, and audios into more cohesive units. These units are stored individually for easy retrieval. Learning objects are organized into collections (Science, Mathematics, Language, Art, Sports, and General Culture), further categorized into five sub-collections based on object type (Audio, Document, Video, etc.). This logical organization streamlines object search and retrieval for users across different pedagogical areas. In the repository, the presentation of learning objects is personalized according to the needs and profile of users through a recommendation system.

To create user profiles, both explicit and implicit information collection techniques are employed. Upon registration in the repository, users provide information pertinent to their profile, including their role (student or teacher), their areas of interest or field of work (educational, business, disciplines such as mathematics, language and communication, biological sciences, etc.), and any visual, auditory, or motor difficulties they may have. Implicit information collection occurs automatically and is seamless to the user. The recommender system analyzes the user's query history to infer their preferences and interests. As users interact with the repository, their profiles are dynamically updated. Leveraging this user information, the prototype utilizes two information filtering techniques to generate recommendations. Firstly, demographic filtering is applied to recommend learning objects tailored to the user's profile. For instance, if a user has indicated visual impairments and their area of interest is education, the repository suggests objects suitable for individuals with these characteristics. Through demographic filtering, the repository endeavors to encompass users with and without physical disabilities in its recommendations.

Additionally, content filtering is implemented to recommend objects similar to those the user has frequently accessed. This method ensures that users receive recommendations aligned with their preferences and browsing history. Figure 2 illustrates the recommendations presented to a registered user upon entering the ROAAP repository.

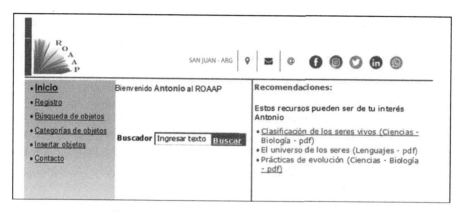

Fig. 2. Recommendations Interface in the ROAAP.

5 Evaluation of the ROAAP Prototype

Accessibility evaluations were conducted for ROAAP through both automated tools and manual assessments by international experts in accessible educational technologies. Furthermore, end users from diverse countries validated ROAAP to assess its functionalities. The accessibility evaluation is presented initially, followed by the validation process by end users.

5.1 Accessibility Evaluation

The accessibility evaluation of ROAAP was conducted based on the Web Content Accessibility Guidelines (WCAG) 2.0 established by the W3C. Two international experts were involved in the evaluation process: a professor from the National University of Colombia, specializing in accessible developments, and a professor from the Federal University of Rio Grande do Sul, an expert in accessible technologies. Both experts performed automatic evaluations using the AChecker tool (http://www.achecker.ca) and manual assessments to ensure compliance with each guideline. The repository was tested on browsers such as Mozilla Firefox and Google Chrome.

The results of the automatic evaluation revealed 6 known issues, all related to guideline 1.3 Adaptable, where a label was not associated with a text-type element. Potential issues were identified in the interface tables, where elements indicating the quantity of table items and some table captions were missing. These observations were addressed and rectified in the current version of the repository.

In the manual evaluation, both experts verified the repository's adherence to WCAG 2.0 guidelines. Table 1 provides a summary of their observations (Fig. 3).

All the observations and recommendations made during the evaluation process were implemented in the current version of the repository.

5.2 Validation with End Users

After the accessibility evaluation and the implementation of accessibility improvements suggested by experts, the repository underwent evaluation with end users.

The validation process was based on the TAM method (Technology Acceptance Model) [42]. The TAM model, proposed by author Davis, is widely recognized as a robust and validated method for ensuring the successful adoption of technologies within organizations [42, 43]. In numerous instances where the use of a specific technological tool needs understanding and validation, TAM has demonstrated its effectiveness and ability to predict technological adoption among users within organizations. The TAM model is widely accepted by researchers in Information and Communication Technologies due to its proven efficacy in predicting the use of particular technologies. This model is utilized to forecast the use of a technology, primarily based on two main attributes:

- Perceived Usefulness (PU): The extent to which an individual believes that using a particular system will enhance their job performance.
- Perceived Ease of Use (PEOU): The degree to which an individual believes that using a particular system will require minimal effort to perform their tasks.

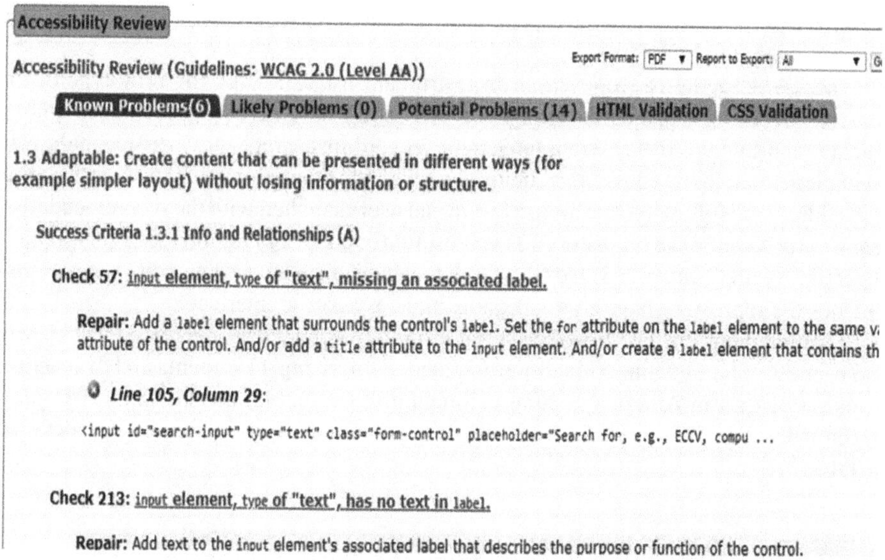

Fig. 3. Results of evaluating the accessibility of the ROAAP using the AChecker tool.

Table 1. Results of the accessibility evaluation of the ROAAP by experts in accessible educational technologies.

Guideline	Priority	Observation
1.1.1: Non-text Content	A	When exploring image-type objects, alternative text or long descriptions alternative to visual content is not provided. Alternative text should be provided for images used as input
1.4.8: Visual Presentation	AAA	The site does not have the option to change the background and foreground color
2.4.1: Bypass Blocks	A	There is no way to skip repeated blocks and go directly to the main content
3.3.6: Error Prevention	AAA	Error prevention mechanisms are not estab-lished in the form data submission, there is no way to undo or cancel the submission
3.3.2: Labels or Instructions	A	There are form elements and tables without label instructions

TAM posits that an individual's perceptions of the perceived usefulness and ease of use of an information system play a crucial role in determining their intention to use the system. Rooted in the Theory of Reasoned Action (TRA), which aims to predict people's behavior based on their attitudes and intentions, TAM establishes that the relationships between beliefs, attitude, intention, and behavior predict user acceptance of Information Technologies (IT) [42, 44].

The TAM Model is proposed as an instrument for validating the prototype of the ROAAP Learning Object Repository and evaluating the degree of acceptance among teachers and students from various universities regarding the repository as a technology to be implemented in the educational field. The objective of employing TAM for validation is to address the following questions: 1) Are end users satisfied with the recommendation features received in the repository? 2) Is it useful for end users for the repository to have accessibility mechanisms? 3) Do the search mechanisms meet user search expectations? 4) Does the repository have a user-friendly and easy-to-use interface?

To implement the TAM method, tests of the repository's use were conducted with end users. A total of 65 individuals participated, comprising 44 students and 21 teachers from various Latin American countries, including Colombia, Brazil, Chile, Uruguay, Argentina, and Paraguay. The demographic characteristics of the respondents are detailed in Table 2.

Table 2. Demographic characteristics of survey participants.

Characteristic	Category	Quantity
Gender	Male	34
	Female	31
Cuntry	Argentina	18
	Colombia	12
	Brazil	10
	Chile	11
	Uruguay	8
	Paraguay	6
Profession	Teacher	21
	Students	44
Ages	Between 15 and 20	5
	Between 21 and 30	18
	Between 31 and 40	22
	Between 41 and 50	15
	Over 50	5

As a preliminary step, a Skype session was organized to introduce the repository to the users. During this session, the users were provided with the repository's user manual. They were then instructed to undertake three activities within the repository: Storing an OVA, Tagging an OVA, and Retrieving an OVA. Subsequently, upon completing the activities, the participants were asked to respond to a questionnaire structured according to the TAM method. The questionnaire and the summarized results for each question, as provided by the 65 validation participants, are presented in Table 3.

Table 3. Results of the questionnaire to end users.

Question	Yes	No	Undecided
Interface			
1. Does the interface maintain coherence and uniformity in structures and colors?	65 63	2 1	2 1
2. Is clear and concise language used?	62		1
3. Is it friendly, familiar, and approachable?	65		
4. Are labels meaningful?	64		
5. Does it use a well-defined and clear organization system?	64		
6. Is the organization and navigation structure adequate?	65 65		
7. Has information overload been avoided?			
8. Is it a clean interface, free from visual noise?			
Searches			
9. Are objects easily found?	63	2	
10. Does it allow for multiple search criteria?	62	3	
11. Are the established criteria sufficient?	62	3	
12. Does it display search results in a comprehensible manner?	65 65		
13. Does it assist when unable to provide results for a given query?			
Accessibility			
14. Do images have alternative text?	65		1
15. Is there high contrast between font color and background?	64 63		2
16. Is the website compatible with different browsers?	65		
17. Can you enjoy all content without needing to download and install additional plu-gins?	65		
18. Did the screen reader work well when accessing the repository?			
Features and Recommendations			
19. Is the categorization of objects into areas and types appropriate?	64 65	1 2	2
20. When using ROAAP, did object recommendations help facilitate object searching?	65 63		
21. Are you satisfied with the functionality of the recommendations?	63 65		
22. Do you find the recommendations received accurate and suitable for your needs and profile?			
23. Would you use ROAAP in your academic activities?			
24. Would you recommend ROAAP to other colleagues?			

Table 4 illustrates the relationship between the TAM method criteria, the research questions, and the questionnaire items administered to the end-users. This layout facilitates the acquisition of answers to the research questions associated with each TAM criterion.

To gauge the reliability of the designed instrument, Cronbach's alpha coefficient was employed as a reliability measure, widely used to assess the reliability of the TAM

Table 4. Relationship between the TAM criteria, the research questions, and the questionnaire items to end users.

TAM criteria	Research Questions	Survey Questions
Perceived Usefulness	1. Are end users satisfied with the recommendation functionalities provided in the repository? 2. Is it beneficial for end users that the repository has accessibility mechanisms? 3. Do the search mechanisms meet users' search expectations?	20. Did using ROAAP's object recommendations help you facilitate object search? 21. Are you satisfied with the functionality of the recommendations? 22. Do you find the recommendations received accurate and suitable for your needs and profile? 23. Would you use ROAAP in your academic activities? 24. Would you recommend ROAAP to other colleagues? 7. Has information overload been avoided? 14. Do images have alternative text? 16. Is the website compatible with different browsers? 17. Can you enjoy all content without needing to download and install additional plugins? 18. Did the screen reader work well when accessing the repository? 10. Does it allow for multiple search criteria? 11. Are the established criteria sufficient? 13. Does it assist you if it cannot provide results for a given query?

(continued)

Table 4. (*continued*)

TAM criteria	Research Questions	Survey Questions
Perceived Ease of Use	4. Does the repository have a user-friendly and easy-to-use interface?	1. Does the interface maintain coherence and uniformity in structures and colors? 2. Is clear and concise language used? 3. Is it friendly, familiar, and approachable? 4. Are the labels meaningful? 5. Does it use a well-defined and clear organization system? 6. Is the organization and navigation structure adequate? 8. Is it a clean interface, without visual noise? 9. Are objects easily found? 12. Does it display search results comprehensively? 15. Is there high contrast between font color and background? 19. Is the categorization of objects into areas and types appropriate?

method. Cronbach's alpha is an index of internal consistency ranging from 0 to 1. It is utilized to ascertain whether the evaluated instrument collects flawed information, resulting in erroneous conclusions, or if it is a reliable instrument providing stable and consistent measurements. Cronbach's alpha is calculated using Eq. 1, as obtained from [45].

$$\alpha = \frac{K}{K-1}\left[1 - \frac{\sum Vt}{Vt}\right] \tag{1}$$

where α represents the Cronbach's Alpha, K denotes the number of items within the criterion under evaluation, V_i stands for the variance of each item, and V_t represents the total variance. A reliability score of 0.70 or higher is considered respectable.

Based on the data obtained, the Cronbach's coefficient for the conducted survey is: Alpha = 0.9266. This value suggests that the questionnaire is reliable, indicating that it measures what it intends to measure. Subsequently, Cronbach's alpha was also calculated for each of the TAM method criteria separately. For the Perceived Usefulness criterion, Alpha = 0.9060, and for Perceived Ease of Use, Alpha = 0.9343. These values indicate that the TAM-based questionnaire yields accurate conclusions.

Figure 4 presents the results obtained for each question graphically. As depicted in the graph, the repository boasts a user-friendly interface that is easy to navigate, with a well-defined and clear navigation structure. Accessibility responses were positively classified, even for users without physical limitations. The main functionalities of the repository, including Storage, Tagging, and Retrieval of learning objects, were satisfactorily performed by the users.

Furthermore, it can be observed that the recommendations of learning objects were widely accepted by the users. The majority agreed that the recommendations received were precise and aligned with their needs. Regarding ease of use, it garnered good acceptance overall, with most users acknowledging the simplicity of the tool and expressing their willingness to recommend it to other colleagues.

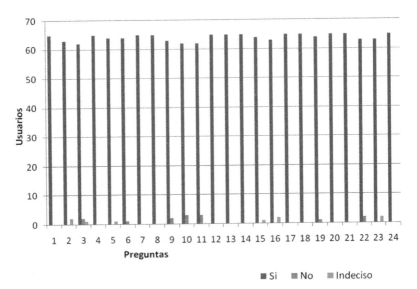

Fig. 4. Graph of the results obtained from the validation of the ROAAP by the end users.

6   Conclusions and Future Work

In this paper, we introduce the integration of personalization and accessibility mechanisms into digital object repositories. For personalization, we propose the implementation of a recommendation system that filters objects based on users' profiles and requirements. Regarding accessibility, we advocate for the adoption of the WCAG 2.0 web accessibility guidelines within the repository.

Building upon this proposal, we developed a prototype Learning Object Repository capable of storing, tagging, and retrieving learning objects across various disciplines, including Mathematics, Languages, Sciences, Arts, Sports, and General Culture. In addition to these fundamental repository functionalities, the following features were incorporated:

- A recommendation system that autonomously suggests learning objects utilizing collaborative, demographic, and content-based filtering techniques.

- Implementation of web accessibility guidelines to ensure an interface accessible to all users, including those with specific visual, motor, auditory, etc., needs.
- The prototype underwent evaluation in two phases: Accessibility assessment by international experts in accessible education technologies, resulting in positive outcomes with minor observations integrated into the current prototype version. User acceptance and functionality validation were conducted through tests involving 65 participants from diverse countries. The obtained results affirm that the prototype meets users' expectations.

For future endeavors, we propose the analysis and integration of digital preservation mechanisms into the Learning Object Repository. This initiative aims to ensure the creation and preservation of stored objects over time, enabling their retrieval and utilization irrespective of hardware or software obsolescence.

Acknowledgments. This work was carried out within the framework of the projects: Ibero-American Network to Support Teaching-Learning Processes of Professional Competencies Through Ubiquitous and Collaborative Environments - AUIP; and the FEDER/Junta de Andalucía-Consejería Transformación Económica, Industria, Conocimiento Un-iversidades/ Proyecto B-TIC-720-UGR20. This work has received financial support from the National Council for Scientific and Technical Research (CONICET).

References

1. Briz-Ponce, L., Pereira, A., Carvalho, L., Juanes-Méndez, J.A., García-Peñalvo, F.J.: Learning with mobile technologies–students' behavior. Comput. Hum. Behav. **72**, 612–620 (2017). https://doi.org/10.1016/j.chb.2016.05.027
2. Clark, R.C., Mayer, R.E.: E-Learning and the Science of Instruction: Proven Guidelines for Consumers and Designers of Multimedia Learning. Wiley, Hoboken (2016)
3. Ziotis, K.: The open access initiative: a new paradigm for scholarly communications. Inf. Technol Libr. **24**, 157–162 (2013). https://doi.org/10.6017/ital.v24i4.3378
4. Miguel, S., Bongiovani, P., Gómez, N., Bueno, B.: Prospect for development of open access in Argentina. J. Acad. Librarianship **39**(1), 1–2 (2013). https://doi.org/10.1016/j.acalib.2012
5. Yousef, M.I.: The role of open access in supporting the digital repositories activities. In: Communication, Management and Information Technology, pp. 517–524. CRC Press (2016). https://doi.org/10.1201/9781315375083
6. Webster, J. W. Digital Repositories. New Top Technologies Every Librarian Needs to Know: A LITA Guide, 153 (2019)
7. Gaona-García, P.A., Martin-Moncunill, D., Montenegro-Marin, C.E.: Trends and challenges of visual search interfaces in digital libraries and repositories. Electron. Libr. **35**(1), 69–98 (2017). https://doi.org/10.1108/EL-03-2015-0046
8. Dublin Core (DCMI). http://dublincore.org/1484.12.1-2002 - IEEE Standard for Learning Object Metadata. https://standards.ieee.org/findstds/standard/1484.12.1-2002.html
9. Plataformas de software para repositorios: https://repositorioinstitucional.wikispaces.com/Plataformas+de+software+para+Repositorios+Institucionales
10. Rudder, J., Kati, R., Smith, J.: Implementing a new Carolina Digital Repository: communities, customizations and change (2019). https://doi.org/10.17615/cmp3-kb13
11. Suleman, H.: Reflections on design principles for a digital repository in a low resource environment (2019). http://pubs.cs.uct.ac.za/id/eprint/1331

12. Joo, S., Hofman, D., Kim, Y.: Investigation of challenges in academic institutional repositories: a survey of academic librarians. Libr. Hi Tech **37**, 525–548 (2018). https://doi.org/10.1108/LHT-12-2017-0266
13. Meera, B.M., Krishnamurthy, S., Kaddipujar, M.: Institutional repository know-how of a decade in managing digital assets. In: EPJ Web of Conferences, vol. 186, p. 07001. EDP Sciences (2018). https://doi.org/10.1051/epjconf/201818607001
14. Pyrounakis, G., Nikolaidou, M.: Comparing open source digital library software. In: Theng, Y., Foo, S., Goh, D., Na, J. (eds.) Handbook of Research on Digital Libraries: Design, Development, and Impact, pp. 51–60. IGI Global (2009). https://doi.org/10.4018/978-1-59904-879-6.ch006
15. Banco Inter-Americano de Desarrollo, CLARA. Proyecto RG-T1684 Conformación de una Red Federada de Repositorios Institucionales de Documentación Científica en América Latina (2001). https://sites.google.com/site/bidclara/Inicio
16. La Referencia. http://lareferencia.redclara.net/rfr/
17. Prabhakar, S., Rani, S.V.: Benefit and perspectives of institutional repositories in academic libraries. Sch. Res. J. Humanity Sci. Engl. Lang. **5** (2018). https://doi.org/10.21922/srjhsel.v5i25.10948
18. Aljohani, M., Blustein, J.: Heuristic evaluation of university institutional repositories based on DSpace. In: Marcus, A. (ed.) DUXU 2015. LNCS, vol. 9188, pp. 119–130. Springer, Cham (2015). https://doi.org/10.1007/978-3-319-20889-3_12
19. González-Pérez, L.I., Ramirez-Montoya, M.S., García-Peñalvo, F.J.: User experience in institutional repositories: a systematic literature review. Int. J. Hum. Capital Inf. Technol. Professionals (IJHCITP) **9**(1), 70–86 (2018). https://doi.org/10.4018/978-1-7998-2463-3.ch026
20. Gaona-García, P., Montenegro-Marín, C., Gaona-García, E., Gómez-Acosta, A., Hassan-Montero, Y.: Issues of visual search methods in digital repositories. Int. J. Interact. Multimedia Artif. Intell. **5**(3) (2018). https://doi.org/10.9781/ijimai.2018.10.005
21. Osorio-Zuluaga, G.A., Duque-Mendez, N.D.: Search and selection of learning objects in repositories: a review. In: 2018 XIII Latin American Conference on Learning Technologies (LACLO), pp. 513–520. IEEE (2018). https://doi.org/10.1109/LACLO.2018.00090
22. Gordillo, A., Barra, E., Quemada, J.: A hybrid recommendation model for learning object repositories. IEEE Lat. Am. Trans. **15**(3), 462–473 (2017). https://doi.org/10.1109/TLA.2017.7867596
23. Chellatamilan, T., Suresh, R.M. Automatic classification of learning objects through dimensionality reduction and feature subset selections in an e-learning system. In: 2012 IEEE International Conference on Technology Enhanced Education (ICTEE), pp. 1–6. IEEE (2012). https://doi.org/10.1109/ICTEE.2012.6208621
24. Khattak, A.M., Ahmad, N., Mustafa, J., Pervez, Z., Latif, K., Lee, S. Y. Context-aware search in dynamic repositories of digital documents. In: 2013 IEEE 16th International Conference on Computational Science and Engineering, pp. 338–345. IEEE (2013). https://doi.org/10.1109/CSE.2013.59
25. Melville, P., Sindhwani, V.: Recommender Systems. In: Sammut, C., Webb, G.I. (eds.) Encyclopedia of Machine Learning and Data Mining, pp. 1056–1066. Springer, Boston (2017). https://doi.org/10.1007/978-1-4899-7687-1_964
26. Aggarwal, C.C.: An introduction to recommender systems. In: Recommender Systems, pp. 1–28. Springer, Cham (2016). https://doi.org/10.1007/978-3-319-29659-3_1
27. Ricci, F., Rokach, L., Shapira, B.: Recommender systems: introduction and challenges. In: Ricci, F., Rokach, L., Shapira, B. (eds.) Recommender Systems Handbook, pp. 1–34. Springer, Boston, MA (2015). https://doi.org/10.1007/978-1-4899-7637-6_1

28. Drachsler, H., Verbert, K., Santos, O.C., Manouselis, N.: Panorama of recommender systems to support learning. In: Ricci, F., Rokach, L., Shapira, B. (eds.) Recommender Systems Handbook, pp. 421–451. Springer, Boston, MA (2015). https://doi.org/10.1007/978-1-4899-7637-6_12

29. Clements, K., Pawlowski, J., Manouselis, N.: Open educational resources repositories literature review–towards a comprehensive quality approaches framework. Comput. Hum. Behav. **51**, 1098–1106 (2015). https://doi.org/10.1016/j.chb.2015.03.026

30. Rodríguez, P.A., Ovalle, D.A., Duque, N.D.: A student-centered hybrid recommender system to provide relevant learning objects from repositories. In: Zaphiris, P., Ioannou, A. (eds.) LCT 2015. LNCS, vol. 9192, pp. 291–300. Springer, Cham (2015). https://doi.org/10.1007/978-3-319-20609-7_28

31. Castro, L., Aciar, S., Reategui, E.: Learning object recommendation for teachers creating lesson plans. XX Congreso Argentino de Ciencias de la Computación. Buenos Aires (2014). http://sedici.unlp.edu.ar/handle/10915/42368

32. Aciar, S., Duque, N., Aciar, M.: Procesamiento de Opiniones de Usuarios Respecto a Objetos de Aprendizaje Basado en Ontologías y Minería de Texto. LACLO 2014. Manizales. Colombia

33. Saquicela, V., Baculima, F., Orellana, G., Piedra, N., Orellana, M., Espinoza, M.: Similarity detection among academic contents through semantic technologies and text mining. In: IWSW, pp. 1–12 (2018)

34. Méndez, A.G., Arias, E.B., Vives, J.Q.: Estimación de calidad de objetos de aprendizaje en repositorios de recursos educativos abiertos basada en las interacciones de los estudiantes. Educación XX1 **21**(1) (2018)

35. Directrices de accesibilidad. http://bid.ub.edu/17marti2.htm

36. Guía breve de accesibilidad. http://www.w3c.es/Divulgacion/GuiasBreves/Accesibilidad

37. Casanova, M.: Educación inclusiva: un modelo de futuro, p. 292. Wolters Kluwer España, Barcelona (2011). ISBN/ISSN: 978-84-9987-030-4

38. W3C - World Wide Web Consortium. http://www.w3.org/standards/webdesign/accessibility

39. Guía de contenido digital accesible. http://www.grihotools.udl.cat/mpiua/edicion-digital-sin-barreras-accesible/

40. Ponce, J.I.P.: Reflexiones sobre la accesibilidad web para el contenido educativo en los sistemas de administración de aprendizaje. REFCalE: Rev. Electrónica Formación Calidad Educativa **6**(1), 193–206 (2018). https://refcale.uleam.edu.ec/index.php/refcale/article/view/2553

41. Othamni, B., González, M.L.C., Rodrigo, C., Pérez, V.A.L.: Accesibilidad del modelo de educación a distancia para estudiantes con discapacidad visual. Rev. Educ. Inclusiva **11**(1), 25–38 (2018)

42. Elyazgi, M., Nilashi, M., Ibrahim, O., Rayhan, A., Elyazgi, S.: Evaluating the factors influencing e-book technology acceptance among school children using TOPSIS technique. **3**(2) (2016)

43. Leyton Soto, D.: Extensión al modelo de aceptación de tecnología TAM, para ser aplicado a sistemas colaborativos, en el contexto de pequeñas y medianas empresas. Departamento de ciencias de la computación, Facultad de Ciencias físicas y matemáticas, Universidad de Chile. Santiago de Chile (2013). https://repositorio.uchile.cl/handle/2250/115509

44. Chuttur, M.: Overview of the Technology Acceptance Model: Origins, Developments and Future Directions. Universidad de Indiana, EEUU (2009). https://aisel.aisnet.org/sprouts_a ll/290

45. González Alonso, J., Pazmino, M.: Cálculo e interpretación del Alfa de Cronbach para el caso de validación de la consistencia interna de un cuestionario, con dos posibles escalas tipo Likert. Rev. Publicando **2**(16) (2015). https://nbn-resolving.org/urn:nbn:de:0168-ssoar-423821

Prompt Engineering, An Alternative for Video Game Development?

Alexander Rozo-Torres[ID] and Wilson J. Sarmiento[(⊠)][ID]

Multimedia Research Group, Universidad Militar Nueva Granada, Bogotá, Colombia
{est.omar.rozo,wilson.sarmiento}@unimilitar.edu.co

Abstract. This position paper presents some relevant considerations regarding the challenges involved in the integration of *"prompt engineering"* tools into the video game development industry. The core of this work is a general framework for developing video games using *"prompt engineering"* tools, which includes incorporating them into a traditional workflow comprising pre-production, production, and post-production stages. Additionally, this paper provides an example of developing a video game with minimal intervention of prompt outputs. It showcases a recommender tool, prompt inputs, their corresponding outputs, and how they are integrated into the final product at each stage. Thus, the trends and challenges presented in this paper are based on the insights gained from this experience.

Keywords: Prompt engineering · Video game development · Artificial intelligence tools · Video game industry

1 Introduction

In the last decade, the development of video games has undergone significant changes thanks to new tools that have streamlined the process. This shift has led to a transition from requiring individuals with hard skills in computer graphics to creative individuals with softer programming skills. However, recent advancements in Artificial Intelligence (AI) tools have the potential to bring about a profound transformation in the game development industry. Today, a diverse range of tools is readily available to anyone only a single *"prompt"* away. One can obtain images, programming code, 3D models, audio, and more through natural language queries in a Large Language Models (LLMs) AI platforms. This structured and systematic use of queries is known as *"prompt engineering"*. Although its use generates some controversial arguments, it is evident that it will bring about relevant changes in computer-supported tasks.

As mentioned above, video game development is no exception; it is possible that *"prompt engineering"* is the seed of deep changes in the game development industry. This paper presents a position on this controversial discussion. In brief, this work shows how to include *"prompt engineering"* in a traditional game development workflow and proposes a general framework for this process.

The rest of this paper is organized as follows: Sect. 2 presents the background of *"prompt engineering"*, focusing on its application in audiovisual production. Section 3 proposes a general framework that incorporates *"prompt engineering"* into a traditional game development workflow. Section 4 provides an example of developing a video game using *"prompt engineering"* and the proposed framework, with minimal intervention of *"prompt"* outputs. Lastly, Sect. 5 discusses trends and challenges based on the insights gained from this experience.

2 Background

"Prompt engineering" is a new and controversial term that involves the task of querying an Artificial Intelligent (AI) tool in natural language to obtain a specific output through Large Language Models (LLMs). In this regard, ChatGPT[1] defines *"prompt engineering"* as *"the process of crafting precise instructions and context for AI systems, optimizing their performance, and aligning them with intended objectives through careful design and refinement"*. Although this concept is relatively new and unclear, its real origin, Bard[2] (Google Chat Prompt) asserts that *"the term prompt engineering was first coined by Oriol Vinyals, Mike Nielsen, and Quoc V. Le in their paper Prompt Engineering: A New Approach to Training Large Language Models (2021)"*, but it was not possible for the authors of this paper to verify this reference. Consequently, the natural question arises: Is it a reliable technology? This work does not aim to provide a definitive answer to this question. However, it is undeniably clear that *"prompt engineering"* is a current trend that requires rigorous discussion and testing by the research community. As for the application of *"prompt engineering"* in audiovisual production, including video game development, it is challenging to establish a formal discussion related to previous works. Nevertheless, this section presents some recent publications on this topic, including works published in the arXiv and IEEE Xplore repository.

The contributions of White, J. et al. [1], prompts engineering is an increasingly relevant creative skill set and an emerging discipline essential for dialogue with LLMs [2], from answering questions to generating art or code, and can be integrated into areas such as video game design and development. Defining that the quality of the results of the LLMs is directly related to the context and indications provided by the users, impacting previous interactions and the output generated from them [1, 2].

In this sense, the first input describes a catalog of *"prompt engineering"* techniques, presented in pattern form, highlighting the potential of indications and the generation of improved outputs. The prompt patterns' concept is similar to software patterns in that they provide reusable solutions for specific problems, focusing, in this case, on the context of generating output for different LLMs [1]. The prompt patterns catalog is classified for facilitate to solve common problems between users and LLMs in conversation, to improve their application in the input LLMs.

Meanwhile, for the prompt design guides the creative process, exploring through the abstract-concrete aspects, abstract-figurative subjects, proposing ingenious prompt design guidelines for interaction with LLMs [3]. Furthermore, provide a taxonomic prompt modifier used by professionals in the context of text-to-image generation, including descriptions and image prompts, style modifiers, quality boosters, repetitions, and

---

[1] ChatGPT, OpenAI, https://chat.openai.com.
[2] Bard, Google AI, https://bard.google.com.

magic terms that can be extremely useful for AI digital art professionals, providing resources to improve their creative processes and achieve higher quality results [4].

This exploration bridges the gap between language and imagination, considering a path for interactions with generative models with a strong conceptual starting point for the AI generation, that can be extremely useful for AI digital art professionals, providing them with practical guidance and resources to improve their creative processes and achieve higher quality outputs [4].

In the field of tools for *"prompt engineering"*, new tools emerge dedicated to enhancing specific areas. In the same way, Prompt Space [5], is an approach addresses the lack of a solid theoretical basis for determining optimal prompts in current prompts by using text embeddings to construct a space that represents all prompts, generating demos with questions and chains of reasoning by selecting simple and effective prompts for LLMs. PromptIDE [6] allows iterative experimentation, automating the creation and evaluation with variations of prompts, simultaneously in different models, tasks, and data sets, facilitating the optimization of the interaction with LLMs, enhancing principles-based workflow for *"prompt engineering"*, and increasing the language used to write general prompts.

Similarly, GitHub Copilot [7] is an advanced AI model for generating source code from natural language descriptions, integrates seamlessly into development environments such as Visual Studio Code, using prompts to solve specific programming problems. Generative source code generation tools, emerge as a form of human-AI interaction, promoting the development of computational thinking skills.

Regarding generative pretraining models stand out for represent from data to pixels, using Natural Language Processing (NLP) techniques [8, 9]. Through pre-training on large datasets, them achieve better performing tasks compared to other AI models such as ChatGPT and Davinci [8]. Notably, unlike models predicting pixels and learning image representations in an auto-regressive manner, generative pretraining utilizes neural network architectures that process input sequences and generate output sequences without relying on 2D or descriptive input knowledge [9].

The video game creation is a complex task due to the inherently multidisciplinary nature of the development process. It involves various disciplines intertwining with software development, which significantly contributes to the overall complexity. Some authors recommend a methodology in software engineering experience in the multiple disciplines of video games (art, design, audio, video, coding, and others). Petrillo, F. and Pimenta, M. [10], conducted research in which few software engineering studies dedicated to the video game development industry usually use agile methods such as the Waterfall, eXtreme Programming, Scrum or Agile Modeling methodology, adopting good practices in the video game development process [11].

For Kanode, C. and Haddad, H. [11] combines methods during pre-production, having an advantage to explore the video game and the interaction between the game and the user. Additionally, to using project and risk management to handle the variation of functions, changing requirements and the optimization of the multimedia assets generated and other resources are integrated into the development process.

Kristiadi et al. [12] suggests agile methodologies, especially Scrum, that can solve game development and reduce production time by following the iteration cycle itself

[11]. Proposes an integration of the Scrum in the development of the game for flexibility and adaptation to development, managing progress and involving the pre-production, production, and post-production stages. Similarly, Torres-Ferreyros, C. et al. [13] demonstrates the development of a video game with Unreal Engine showing that is possible to create a high-quality game in a short period of time using limited resources. The video game development uses a four-stage methodology: pre-production, production, testing and post-production, proposed by the International Association of Game Developers (IGDA).

Lanzi, P. and Loiacono, D. [14] propose a collaborative design framework that combines interactive evolution and LLMs, to simulate the typical human design process in the design of video games that can be described in the form of free text. The generation of ideas is based on the indications given in ChatGPT that are later taken as creative ideas. In the same way, Deckers, N. et al. [15] explores the art of *"prompt engineering"* for generative models and proposes an approach for interactive text retrieval through the *"infinite index"*, a systematic guide designed to indicate topics, terms, features, or parts of generated documents. In addition, applies the potential of this approach, creating graphics for a moodboard as a creative task of game design, using text-to-image LLMs such as DALL-E, Midjourney and Stable Diffusion.

On the other hand, Trapova, A. [16] gives a perspective on the impact of AI on video games and intellectual property rights. In the digital age, the commercial lifespan of a video game, from development to release, takes place primarily in a digital environment. In this context, property and video game interests converge on several levels and one of the most important dimensions is the management of intellectual property rights and terms of service when AI drives, although this also allows stimulating creativity.

However, to date, it has not been explored how to include *"prompt engineering"* with LLMs to facilitate the development process of a video game, which is the focus of this work than to aim incursion in this open topic.

3 Proposed Framework

In order to incorporate *"prompt engineering"* into the content creation processes of video game development using large language models (LLMs), it is necessary to establish a starting point within a well-known workflow. Figure 1. Illustrates a traditional workflow for video game development, consisting of three stages: preproduction (define the basic architecture and narrative of the video game), production (generating and iteratively developing elements) and post-production (validating, testing, and distributing the video game). The following sections include details and descriptions of what task can be performed *"prompt engineering"* in each stage.

3.1 Pre-production

The Pre-production stage is an essential stage that combines creative innovation with detailed planning. It is a critical process for exploring narrative and gameplay concepts, with the goal of establishing a solid foundation for the later stages of a project's development. This initial phase lays the foundation for a successful and well-structured production process that integrates GenAI.

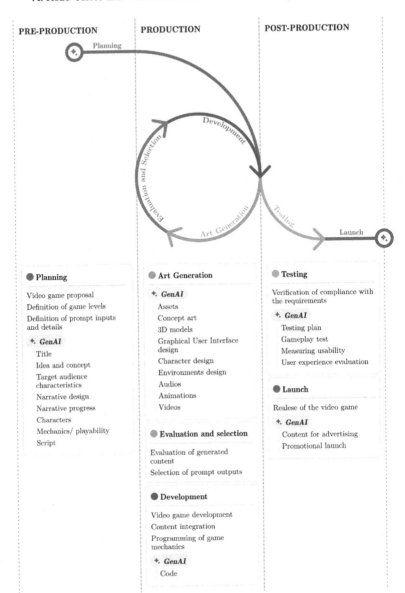

Fig. 1. A general framework to include *"prompt engineering"* of video game development. Is an extended traditional workflow where each stage has a list of proposed task reach with *"prompt engineering"*.

Planning. The game designers and developers define the video game proposal, design documents, genre, idea, main concept, determine the specific characteristics of the target audience and the game levels. Furthermore, as a fundamental part of this stage, the *"prompts"* are included that will guide the generation of content by AI generators in subsequent stages of development. These *"prompts"* are key tools that ensuring the aesthetics, narrative, and experience of the video game. Including the story, title, narrative progress, character design, costumes, settings, user interface and gameplay of the video game created from *"prompts"*.

3.2 Production

The Production stage converges artistic creativity powered by GenAI tools and video game development. Facilitating the creation of content efficiently, optimizing tasks such as asset generation, decision making and dynamic adaptation of the game in the development environment. In addition, these tools allow to focus on more creative aspects by delegating repetitive tasks to LLMs, which enhances efficiency and quality. During this process it is relevant to monitor, evaluate, integrate and improve iteratively for the overall quality and success of the game.

Art Generation. The game assets are generated by GenAI tools, including images, videos, animations, 3D models, audio, video, text, and others, which are subsequently integrated into the final video game.

Evaluation and Selection of Generated Content. The content generated by the AI tools is evaluated and selected, choosing those elements that adapt to the desired aesthetic and comply with the definition and narrative concept of the video game. The generations are analyzed considering the relevance to the video game experience.

Development. This iterative process consists of the development of the video game for the platform defined in the planning. The generated assets are integrated to create the environments, user interfaces and establish the interaction with the graphic resources. The video game is programmed and coded, ensuring the previously defined functionalities and gameplay, and errors are corrected with the support of AI for programming.

3.3 Post-Production

The final stage in video game development is Post-production. During this phase, the generated and programmed elements are integrated into an immersive experience for the players. Furthermore, a series of tests is conducted to identify and resolve bugs and adjusting visual details to achieve game balance before ultimately publishing the video game.

Testing. The testing is responsible for evaluating the video game, verifying compliance with the requirements, and performing gameplay, usability, performance, response, and interaction tests. Throughout this process, the aim is to detect potential issues and bugs that could impact the player's experience.

Launch. The launch is the last stage of the process and covers the final distribution and the generation of publicity for the video game powered by AI content generators.

4   Video Game Development Example

In **Pre-production**, the first decision of any video game developer is the genre. We have chosen the 3D Endless Runner genre for practice reasons because the game mechanics are well-known, simple to a user, and easy to implement. Then, with this in mind, a *"prompt"* dialog with ChatGPT found the main aspects of the video game as title, population target, storytelling, the main character, narrative pro and graphics concept. Below shows some relevant fragments of *"prompt"* dialog.

Developer: Act as a gaming expert. Perform the following task: Create the best narrative for an endless runner video game, where the main character is a space runner. Include the story summary, gameplay elements, and narrative progression. The response is intended for a game designer and developer.

ChatGPT: Summary of the story: In a distant future, humanity has conquered space and established colonies in various galaxies. However, a dark and mysterious force threatens to plunge the universe into chaos.

...

ChatGPT: Gameplay: The game takes place in a 3D endless runner environment, with a 3D view that allows players to enjoy the stunning space landscapes. The space runner moves automatically forward, and players must use intuitive controls to dodge obstacles,

...

ChatGPT: Narrative Progression: The game's narrative unfolds as the space runner advances on their mission. Throughout the race, fragments of an ancient prophecy are found, revealing clues about the source of the evil threatening the universe.

...

Developer: Imagine a catchy and memorable title that captures the attention of the audience for the aforementioned proposed video game.

ChatGPT: Of course! Here is a pleasant and memorable title that will capture the attention of the audience for the proposed video game:

ChatGPT: "Cosmic Run: Guardians of the Balance"

Developer: What would be the graphic design style for the previously proposed narrative?

ChatGPT: For the previously proposed narrative, the type of graphic design that would complement and enhance the game experience would be one that combines futuristic, cosmic, and space elements. Here is a description of the suitable graphic design style:

ChatGPT: Futuristic Aesthetic: The graphic design should present a modern and futuristic visual style with clean lines, geometric shapes, and a vibrant color palette. Neon colors and bright tones can be used to represent the energy and dynamism of the universe.

ChatGPT: *Cosmic Environments: The game's environments and backgrounds should reflect the vastness and beauty of space. This includes the depiction of galaxies, nebulae, star systems, and exotic planets. The backgrounds can be animated or have moving elements to create a sense of depth and spatial movement.*

...

Developer: *Describes the physical, sociological, and psychological aspects of the main character of the video game "Cosmic Run: Guardians of the Balance" Includes the design, costumes and visual elements that describe the character*

ChatGPT: *Physical aspects: The main character of the video game "Cosmic Run: Guardians of the Balance" is a brave and determined space runner. The space runner is agile and athletic, with a slender build and toned muscles. Their height is average, but their appearance denotes hidden strength and energy. Their facial features are proportionate and expressive, with penetrating and determined eyes. Their hair, with a futuristic tone, is styled in an aerodynamic shape that gives them a dynamic look even at rest.*

ChatGPT: *Sociological aspects: The space runner belongs to an elite group of space pilots dedicated to protecting cosmic balance and maintaining peace in the universe. He is revered as a symbol of hope and bravery, and their task is respected and recognized by all civilizations that depend on them for their survival. Is a visually striking and powerful character, whose futuristic design, technological attire, and visual elements convey their bravery, determination, and connection to the vast universe.*

ChatGPT: *Design and costumes: The design of the space runner is futuristic and streamlined. Their wear a tight-fitting spacesuit made of a durable yet flexible material that perfectly conforms to their figure. The suit features stylized lines and subtle technological details, such as illuminated panels that highlight their silhouette and signify their connection to the advanced technology of the game. Their helmet is sleek and aerodynamic, with a translucent visor that showcases their bright eyes and a heads-up display (HUD) that reflects vital information for their mission.*

ChatGPT: *Visual elements: The space runner emanates an aura of cosmic energy, visualized as a subtle luminosity that flows through their body and intensifies as they collect the time gems on their journey. This energy manifests as luminous lines that snake along their suit and emit bright flashes when they unleash their special abilities.*

With these elements, the process can continue with the **Production** stage. The first step is the **Art generation** for video game. The co-creation approach used a diverse set of LLMs tools (DALL-E, Midjourney, Stable Diffusion, Leonardo.AI, Adobe Firefly, Skybox AI) for the multimedia production. However, *"prompt"* input always included relevant words/sentences related to narrative and aesthetic concepts. Adobe Firefly[3], generated the texture effect for the name of the video game *"Cosmic Run"*, proposed by

---

[3] Adobe Firefly, Adobe Inc., https://www.adobe.com/products/firefly.html.

ChatGPT, with the *"prompt"* input: *"Space, fantasy, video game"*. Figure 2 shows the name for the video game.

Cosmic Run

Fig. 2. *"Cosmic Run"* Adobe Firefly text effect *"prompt"* output.

The generation of the physical environment where the main character will live the storytelling. In 3D video games, a well-known technique is a skybox, a textured (cube or sphere) surrounding the game world, creating the illusion of a distant background. We used Skybox AI[4] with *"prompt"* input: *"Generate beautiful cosmic galaxy sky with stars"*, to be consistent with the graphic concept described by ChatGPT. Figure 3 shows the four first outputs.

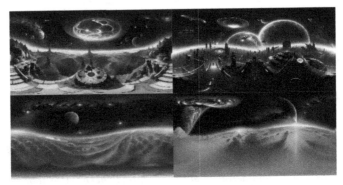

Fig. 3. Skybox alternatives generated by Skybox AI prompt.

For character design, we used the Leonardo.AI[5] for the reason of credits disposables, with *"prompt"* input: *"Full-body front-facing video game character in a form-fitting space suit, made of a strong yet flexible material that fits perfectly to his figure. The suit features sleek lines and subtle technological details, such as light-up panels that highlight your silhouette and denote your connection to the game's advanced technology. His helmet is sleek and streamlined, with a translucent visor that shows off his glowing eyes and a HUD that reflects information vital to his mission"*, to be consistent with the graphic concept and aspects described by ChatGPT. Figure 4 shows the six first outputs.

The game state generated according to the description of the cosmic environment from *"prompt"* input: *"Generate stars props for video game"*, to be consistent with the

---

[4] Skybox AI, Blockade Labs, https://skybox.blockadelabs.com.

[5] Leonardo.AI, Leonard.AI Inc., https://leonardo.ai.

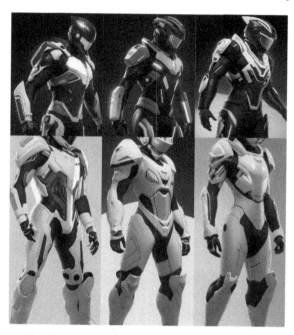

Fig. 4. First Leonardo character *"prompt"* outputs.

graphic concept and aspects described by ChatGPT. Figure 5 shows the outputs generated. Continuing with the process, the **Evaluation and selection of the contents** generated by the LLMs was conducted taking into the relation to the narrative and aesthetics of the video game, guaranteeing that the elements had a match with the environment in which the story takes place. To make the selection, aspects such as colors, visual style, environment, aesthetic, quality, dimensions, among others, were considered, integrating properly, and contributing to immersion.

Fig. 5. Images of game state generated by Leonardo to use in HUD.

With the previously selected assets, the process continues with the **Development**. The first step is to have the development platform. There are game engines such as Unity3D and Unreal that provide the tools that allow the design, creation, and publication of video games. We use Unity3D, a recognized engine and excellent support for 2D and 3D video games, and it does not require a high-quality graphics environment, using the language of programming C#. The next step is integrated the assets in the development environment to maintain them as resources, allowing the visual design of the game and the user interface. Later, programming the mechanics of the game and the interaction with the character, environment, scoring, physics and collisions in C# and fix errors. Figure 6 shows the video game in Unity3D.

Fig. 6. Screenshot of the video game ruining in Unity Editor. It is possible to see the skybox, character and HUD selected.

The process continues with the **Post-production** stage. The **Testing** detecting possible bugs or issues with the interaction in order to solve programming errors before launch. A *"prompt"* dialog with ChatGPT proposed a testing plan for experts and users.

Developer: Act as an expert in testing a 3D endless runner video game set in stunning space landscapes, where the space runner automatically moves forward and laterally. Propose a testing plan involving both experts and end users. Define the recommended number of end users and experts, along with a testing schedule. Additionally, include a proposal for using state-of-the-art validated instruments to assess usability, user experience, and gameplay.

ChatGPT: I propose the following testing plan for the 3D endless runner video game set in stunning space landscapes:

1. *Testing Objectives: a. Evaluate gameplay mechanics and controls. b. Assess level design and progression. c. Measure user engagement and satisfaction. d. Identify and address any technical issues or bugs.*
2. *Testing Participants: a. Experts: Include experienced gamers, game testers, and professionals familiar with endless runner games. b. End Users: Select a diverse group of players who represent the target audience for the game.*
3. *Number of Participants: Experts: Aim for a group of 5–10 individuals and End Users: Recruit around 20–30 players to gather diverse feedback.*

4. *Testing Schedule:*
   (a) *Phase 1: Expert Testing; Duration: 2–3 weeks, focus on evaluating core mechanics, level design, and technical performance. Regular meetings to discuss findings and provide feedback.*
   (b) *Phase 2: End User Testing; Duration: 4–6 weeks. Conduct individual and group play testing sessions. Gather feedback through surveys, interviews, and gameplay observations.*
5. *Instruments for Evaluation: a. Usability: Utilize validated tools like the System Usability Scale (SUS) to assess the game's usability and user interface design. b. User Experience: Employ questionnaires or interviews to gauge player satisfaction, immersion, and overall experience. c. Gameplay Assessment: Utilize gameplay metrics, such as completion times, scores, and player behavior analysis, to measure gameplay effectiveness and balance.*

ChatGPT: *By following this testing plan and incorporating state-of-the-art evaluation instruments, we aim to ensure the game's quality, usability, and player satisfaction.*

Developer: *Please provide me with a proposal for state-of-the-art instruments to evaluate user experience and engagement with gameplay.*

ChatGPT: *Certainly! Here's the proposal for state-of-the-art instruments to evaluate user experience and engagement with the gameplay of a video game:*

1. *User experience evaluation: Surveys, interviews, and observations.*
2. *Gameplay engagement assessment: Game metrics, play testing and heatmaps.*
3. *Biometric data collection: Eye-tracking and heart rate monitoring.*
4. *Post-game surveys and reviews: Online surveys and player reviews.*

ChatGPT: *These state-of-the-art instruments will provide valuable insights into the user experience and engagement with the gameplay of the video game, allowing for iterative improvements and enhanced player satisfaction.*

Finally, in the **Launch**, the video game is published with all the requirements and graphics for the target audience. In addition, an advertising plan is generated to evoke and attract people by demonstrating the uniqueness of the video game through campaigns on social media and online stores. A dialogue *"prompt"* with ChatGPT proposed a marketing and publicity plan for the game's release.

Developer: *Act as an expert in marketing of a 3D endless runner video game set in stunning space landscapes, where the space runner automatically moves forward and sideways. Propose a launch and advertising plan that engages a broad audience, especially lovers of action and adventure video games. Additionally, it includes a proposal for advertising on social media campaign, user reviews, ratings, community, and stores online.*

ChatGPT: *Marketing and Launch Plan for a 3D Endless Runner Video Game*

1. *Define the target audience.*

2. *Establish key messaging.*
3. *Pre-launch phase: Teaser campaign, influencer partnerships and beta testing and feedback.*
4. *Launch phase: Launch trailer, app store optimization (ASO) and cross-promotion.*
5. *Advertising on social media: Engaging content creation, targeted ad campaigns and influencer marketing.*
6. *User reviews, ratings, and community: Prompting reviews, community engagement and user-generated content.*
7. *Online store presence: Steam and other platforms.*

5   Conclusions and Final Remarks

This work is a positional paper that shows a first version of a framework to include Large Language Models (LLMs) AI tools that are currently popular, called *"prompt engineering"*. The proposed framework in brief, is an extended traditional workflow with a description of tasks that can be performed with *"prompt engineering"*. This work also presents a video game developed example that involves the stages of pre-production, production, and post-production were only sketching. The tools used in the video game developed example were ChatGPT, Leonardo.AI and Skybox AI, but for text-to-text tasks, it is possible to use other tools such as Bard, Jarvis or Replika; and for text-to-images tasks, there are alternatives such as DALL-E, Midjourney or Stable Diffusion. This work does not explore the use of LLMs specialized in programming code generation, such as GitHub Copilot, SourceAI or Replit Ghostwriter, and evaluation of this tool in a video game developed will be addressed in future work. Another tool that will be tested in future work is LLMs to generate 3D content (mesh and animations) as 3dfy.ai, Kaedim3D and DeepAI, among others. *"Prompt engineering"* is an emerging field that can cover wide areas in the design and development of 2D and 3D video games in a faster and more iterative way, mixing ideas and generating proposals between the user and LLMs. It requires creativity and detail in simple or complex *"prompt"* and that can even be extended in immersive systems, facilitating the design, and generating visual alternatives, concepts, and ideas in the future.

The experiences in the development of the example video game, and some previous test interactions, evidenced that using LLMs text-to-images tools can notably reduce the production of assets and audiovisual material necessary for video game development. However, the main challenge is to keep the same graphic concept. It was observed that separate execution in time using similar *"prompt"* inputs could have results that differ from the graphic concept to be followed. A solution is that these outputs can be used as inputs by graphic artists, who can use them to unify the visual concept. In this regard, that is the main challenge to break the barriers in the use of these technologies by professionals in the audiovisual field, who understand their benefits and do not see these developments as a threat to their work. The main challenge in using text-to-text LLMS tools is the need for more robustness in some of their outputs, but they are a good starting point for a multidisciplinary team. The integration of LLMs have great potential to transform game development through *"prompt engineering"*. However, the rapid evolution of AI raises questions about the intellectual property and copyrights of the generated content. Establishing authorship can be challenging in situations involving machines. It is essential to explore how copyright and intellectual property rights can be protected among developers, designers, creators and LLMs in the generation of images, audio, videos, 3D models, academic and research content. For this reason, several contributions of AI-generated content reference the models used, and others label the content to differentiate it from not being human creative expression.

Acknowledgements. This work is a result of IMP-ING-3407 research funded by Chancellor of Research of the *Universidad Militar Nueva Granada*.

References

1. White, J., et al.: A prompt pattern catalog to enhance prompt engineering with ChatGPT. In: Computer Science/Software Engineering (2023). arXiv:2302.11382. https://doi.org/10.48550/arXiv.2302.11382
2. Oppenlaender, J., Linder, R., Silvennoinen, J.: Prompting ai art: an investigation into the creative skill of prompt engineering. In: Computer Science/Human-Computer Interaction(2023). arXiv:2303.13534. https://doi.org/10.48550/arXiv.2303.13534
3. Liu, V., Chilton, L.B.: Design guidelines for prompt engineering text-to-image generative models. In: Proceedings of the 2022 CHI Conference on Human Factors in Computing Systems, CHI 2022. Association for Computing Machinery, New York (2022). https://doi.org/10.1145/3491102.3501825
4. Oppenlaender, J.: A taxonomy of prompt modifiers for text-to-image generation. Behav. Inf. Technol. (2023). https://doi.org/10.1080/0144929X.2023.2286532
5. Shi, F., et al.: Prompt space optimizing few-shot reasoning success with large language models. In: Computer Science/Computation and Language (2023). https://doi.org/10.48550/arXiv.2306.03799
6. Strobelt, H., et al.: Interactive and visual prompt engineering for ad-hoc task adaptation with large language models. IEEE Trans. Visual Comput. Graph. 29(1), 1146–1156 (2023). https://doi.org/10.1109/TVCG.2022.3209479
7. Denny, P., Kumar, V., Giacaman, N.: Conversing with copilot: exploring prompt engineering for solving cs1 problems using natural language. In: Proceedings of the 54th ACM Technical Symposium on Computer Science Education, SIGCSE 2023, vol. 1, pp. 1136–1142. Association for Computing Machinery, New York (2023). https://doi.org/10.1145/3545945.3569823
8. Sorensen, T., et al.: An information-theoretic approach to prompt engineering without ground truth labels. In: Proceedings of the 60th Annual Meeting of the Association for Computational Linguistics, vol. 1: Long Papers. Association for Computational Linguistics (2022). https://doi.org/10.18653/v1/2022.acllong.60
9. Chen, M., et al.: Generative pretraining from pixels. In: III, H.D., Singh, A. (eds.) Proceedings of the 37th International Conference on Machine Learning. Proceedings of Machine Learning Research, vol. 119, pp. 1691–1703. PMLR (2020). https://proceedings.mlr.press/v119/chen20s.html
10. Petrillo, F., Pimenta, M.: Is agility out there? agile practices in game development. In: SIGDOC 10: Proceedings of the 28th ACM International Conference on Design of Communication, SIGDOC 2010, pp. 9–15. Association for Computing Machinery (2010). https://doi.org/10.1145/1878450.1878453
11. Kanode, C.M., Haddad, H.M.: Software engineering challenges in game development. In: 2009 Sixth International Conference on Information Technology: New Generations, pp. 260–265 (2009). https://doi.org/10.1109/ITNG.2009.74

12. Kristiadi, D.P., Sudarto, F., Sugiarto, D., Sambera, R., Warnars, H.L.H.S., Hashimoto, K.: Game development with scrum methodology. In: 2019 International Congress on Applied Information Technology (AIT), pp. 1–6 (2019). https://doi.org/10.1109/AIT49014.2019.914 4963

13. Torres-Ferreyros, C.M., Festini-Wendorff, M.A., Shiguihara-Ju´arez, P.N.: Developing a videogame using unreal engine based on a four stages methodology. In: 2016 IEEE ANDESCON, pp. 1–4 (2016). https://doi.org/10.1109/ANDESCON.2016.7836249

14. Lanzi, P.L., Loiacono, D.: ChatGPT and other large language models as evolutionary engines for online interactive collaborative game design (2023). In: Proceedings of the Genetic and Evolutionary Computation Conference, GECCO 2023, pp. 1383–1390. Association for Computing Machinery (2023). https://doi.org/10.1145/3583131.3590351

15. Deckers, N., et al.: The infinite index: Information retrieval on generative text-to-image models. In: Proceedings of the 2023 Conference on Human Information Interaction and Retrieval, CHIIR 2023, pp. 172–186. Association for Computing Machinery, New York (2023). https://doi.org/10.1145/3576840.3578327

16. Trapova, A.: AI as a vehicle for creativity in video games–any room for flexibility via contracts? case study on AI dungeon. A case study on AI Dungeon. Forthcoming book chapter in 'Copyright contracts' (Hendrik Vanhees and Simon Geiregat) by LeA Uitgevers (2023). https://doi.org/10.2139/ssrn.4434824

Redesign of the Dashboard of a Web Telemetry System for Decision Support

Rubén Rivera-Medina⬤, Huizilopoztli Luna-García(✉) ⬤, José M. Celaya-Padilla⬤, Oscar O. Ordaz-García⬤, and Roberto Solís-Robles⬤

Laboratorio de Tecnologías Interactivas y Experiencia de Usuario (LITUX), Universidad Autónoma de Zacatecas, Jardín Juárez 147, Centro Histórico, 98000 Zacatecas, Mexico
{ruben.riveramedina,hlugar,jose.celaya,oscarordazg,
rsolis}@uaz.edu.mx

Abstract. Dashboards allow to graphically represent the behavior of systems in multiple disciplines, as well as to interpret the most important information, providing visual support and reasoning capacity to the user for a better action or decision making based on observation and analysis. However, due to their static nature, they do not provide forms of interaction with users and therefore do not satisfy their individual needs. This article takes into account the User-Centered Design as a paradigm for the design of any product and implements the stages proposed by the ISO 9241- 210:2019 standard for the design of a Telemetry Dashboard that allows the interactions required by end users based on the SLR performed by *A. Vazquez-Ingelmo, F. J. Garcia-Penalvo, and R. Theron* who use the same standard for this review.

Keywords: Dashboard · data visualization · Telemetry · User-Centered Design

1 Introduction

A Dashboard can be defined as a graphical monitoring interface in which the information of major importance for the fulfillment of specific objectives is presented, also benchmarks can be considered as indicators for decision support and metrics tracking in a large number of multidisciplinary sciences [1–4].

Among the predecessors of this interface, we can consider the so-called "control centers" in which an operator had the possibility to observe in real time the behavior of the systems and take actions or decisions based on what was observed. The objective of a Dashboard is to provide visual support, expanding the capacity of analytical reasoning by means of an interactive graphical interface [5–7].

Among the many disciplines covered by Dashboards is medicine. [8], telemetry systems, the internet of things (IoT), the social domain, and agriculture [9]. In the educational domain, Dashboard in learning analytics dashboards (LADs) are used for monitoring student performance and learning, as well as for prediction of students who may be at risk of failing the year, these analytics have shown behavioral and cognitive feedback directed to the advising process. Advisors use LADs during student counseling

© The Author(s), under exclusive license to Springer Nature Switzerland AG 2024
P. H. Ruiz et al. (Eds.): HCI-COLLAB 2023, CCIS 1877, pp. 257–270, 2024.
https://doi.org/10.1007/978-3-031-57982-0_20

to monitor students' academic progress by means of line graphs or histograms allowing modeling changes in students' motivations and self-regulated learning (SRL) [10]. LADs allow the collection of information from students and use it to improve their learning. Since 2010, the field of LAD research has increased, highlighting the Escuela Superior Politécnica del Litoral (ESPOL) in Guayaquil, Ecuador; which in 2017 joined the "LALA Erasmus +" project for the development of a LAD called LISSA, being the result of a user-centered design (UCD) with a focus on Latin America [11].

In the social sphere, Dashboards gained momentum when they were used to determine the number of population (such as the one used in the city of Boston [12]), which show a summary of the current number of inhabitants, jobs generated, economy, air quality, traffic and some general statistics, all of which provide the government with supporting data for decision making. O. Lock, et al. shows something similar in [6] where the use of Dashboard stands out for innovating in terms of interaction with citizens, which helps the collection of information taking into account the complaints and suggestions of the population.

The capabilities and scope of Dashboards through the visual representation of data for easy interpretation and implementation in multidisciplinary environments, provide support for decision making. However, there is the problem that plagues all these applications, the "cognitive saturation" that comes with having all the information available in a single interface. So far, the Dashboards that have been referred to in this work are static or read-only Dashboards, which attempt to present information to the user in an effective and efficient manner by focusing on visual features that by their static nature do not provide a form of user interaction [13, 14]. However, nowadays these present a deficiency in the representation and analysis of complex and multidimensional data at the operational level such as those obtained by telemetry systems, which are responsible for the automation of communications in remote locations and the collection of data from sensor networks that measure certain physical or chemical magnitudes, transforming this information into wireless signals for sending and subsequent processing [15, 16].

In recent years, Dashboards have been implemented that, although they meet the requirements of the companies, do not satisfy the different needs of the users, because they are developed using commercial templates that are already preset by companies such as Google Data Studio, Google Sheets, Microsoft Excel, Power BI, etc. While this is not all bad as mentioned in [14] (where a systematic literature review (SLR) methodology is followed) it can be used in favor for a simple and low-cost development by modifying the way in which it is designed, obtaining as a result of the implementation of the ISO 9241-210:2019 standard just like S. SAITO and K. OGAWA in [17].

In the present work a reformulation of the design of the Dashboard "Web Telemetry" for the presentation of a telemetry system, which was developed by the company "Desarrollos Tecnológicos en Hidráulica Aplicada" H-Tech México, is carried out [18]. The design will be based on the SLR proposed by A. Vazquez-Ingelmo, F. J. Garcia-Penalvo, and R. Theron at [14] and the user-centered design paradigm defined by the ISO9241-210:2019 standard [17]; seeking to obtain a properly configured Dashboard without the user having extensive experience in visualization environments.

2 Materials and Methods

Due to the popularity that Dashboards have gained over the years and the recent boom due to the events of the COVID 19 pandemic, the large number of topics that can be represented on a Dashboard has increased along with its popularity, however, there is no single template that can be used for all users, as a result of the fact that each user has gained experience in a different way, depending (as the name suggests) that each user has a different visualization capacity or interests [11, 14].

2.1 User-Centered Design

In general terms, UCD can be described as a process that uses the needs of the users and the context in which the Dashboard will be applied as the center or basis of the whole process.

    UCD consists of 6 phases:

- PHASE 1: UCD PLAN.
- PHASE 2. SPECIFICATION OF THE CONTEXT OF USE.
- PHASE 3: SPECIFICATION OF USER REQUIREMENTS.
- PHASE 4: CREATION AND DEVELOPMENT OF DESIGN SOLUTIONS.
- PHASE 5: EVALUATION OF THE DESIGNS.
- PHASE 6: THE DESIGNED SOLUTION MEETS THE USER'S REQUIRE-MENTS.

    UCD has the characteristic of being a process that iterates from phase 2 to phase 5 until the objective or best version of the project (in which the user's requirements are met) is achieved. UCD was created by Donald Norman in the 1980s and was defined in the ISO 9241-210:2019 standard [17, 19].

Identification of the Context of Use and Specification of Requirements

At this stage, involving the end user provides the context in which the user will use the Dashboard, allowing to identify their desires, motivations and conditions of use. To obtain this information there are several techniques or methods such as: Affinity Diagramming is a method that helps teams to collaboratively study the results obtained from research and ideas that arise in design sessions, generating strategic and visionary ideas based on the user experience (UX). The affinity diagram is commonly used in UX development and is an adaptation of the KJ diagramming method named after its author Kawakita Jir. In summary, affinity diagrams seek to organize related facts, objects or functions into distinct groups, consisting of a workshop leader and observers who are the rest of the team, the method consists of two steps:

1. The generation of sticky notes where team members individually write down ideas, facts or functions.
2. Organization of the notes in groups, after the session to generate ideas where the notes are constructed, the team has a second session where the notes are analyzed for their classification in categories, priority and the next steps in the design to be investigated are determined [20].

Stakeholder meeting is a grouping of designers, developers and users, with the objective that designers and developers share their ideas with the client or end user, and that, from the user's perspective, he/she makes his/her needs known, thus facilitating a communication channel, which, if it did not exist, the designer could divert the product towards a wrong idea and a possible confusion with what the user really needs. Having a balance or communication between the two parties allows the design of low-fidelity prototypes in early stages to high-fidelity prototypes in more advanced stages. As a result of this communication channel, the designer can make use of the scenario technique, where he/she generally describes in written form, narratives of how he/she believes the user will use the product to perform certain tasks, highlighting the objectives of the users who will use the product, what may work in the context and how the users interpret what is happening when they are using the product [21]. Once these techniques and methods were understood, a Stakeholder meeting was held to provide the first vision of the project, as well as its objectives and requirements, thus generating the prototype visible in Fig. 4.

Once feedback was obtained from the individual users, the Affinity Diagraming technique was used to obtain a global context, since it sought the opinion of the users through a consensus among them and was able to identify the types of users, their characteristics, skills, experience, education, habits and capabilities, as well as the tasks they perform [17].

Finally, for these stages, a review of the existing Dashboards in the topics mentioned in the introduction of this work was carried out, based on the SLR performed by [14] In addition, observations, ideas, sections and components resulting from this research, which will be used in the implementation of the Affinity Diagramming technique, were also raised, thus obtaining the generalities of the Dashboard and managing to generate another prototype Fig. 5.

Production of Design Solutions

To formulate a design solution, the descriptions obtained from the context of use, as well as from the requirements specification, must be taken into account, since it is essential to follow design standards while respecting the opinions of the users, helping to find a balance that will provide a better user experience. In order to produce a good design solution, it must go from the general to the particular, making this transition in response to user-centered feedback and evaluations. Including in the design the user tasks, with an interaction between the user and the system considering at all times the user experience, as explained in ISO 9241-210:2019 [17]. For this work, two low-fidelity prototypes were created with some interactions that allowed the user to obtain a vision of the requirements. It should be noted that these prototypes were designed based on the requirements and the context obtained from the users, in addition to the SLR made by [14] with the Wondershare Mockitt payment tool.

Design Evaluation

The design evaluation stage is undoubtedly an important stage, since this is where the initial objectives are manifested. However, the process does not end here, since this stage will provide new requirements that will improve the design and therefore improve the final product. A user-centered evaluation provides important feedback from the end user, obtaining valuable information about the strengths and weaknesses of the design solution from the perspective of the user [17].

As explained in [14] current Dashboards do not provide interaction with the user, so it is not frequent that the user is able to participate in the decision making for the development of the same. On the other hand, in [11] proposes evaluations made by experts who for the purposes of their research are experts in the field of learning.

The first prototype was the result of the Stakeholder meeting technique and was evaluated by users through the same technique, considering the opinions of designers, developers and users. This evaluation provided the initiative for the design and evaluation of the second prototype using a System Usability Scale (SUS) because it allowed the evaluation of "Effectiveness: can the users successfully achieve their objectives?", "Efficiency: how much effort is necessary for them to achieve those objectives?" and "Satisfaction: was the use of the system satisfactory?" [22]. Providing an overall view of the usability of the system being evaluated, in addition "SUS" can be administered quickly and easily because it consists of ten predefined questions (of which five are positive; odd questions and five negatives; even questions) that employ a Likert scale ranging from 1 to 5 from "strongly disagree" to "strongly agree". "SUS" is a questionnaire that is administered to users after they have had an opportunity to interact with the system being evaluated. The user must immediately answer the survey avoiding any discussion of the system, in order to obtain the user's opinion in a natural way. If the user is unable to answer a particular question, he/she should mark the central point of the scale. The interpretation of the results obtained is a fundamental part of this scale, so to be able to carry it out it is necessary to subtract one from the value obtained in the odd questions and add the result to the previous one, as well as subtract five from the answer obtained in the even questions and add the result. To obtain the final score the two results of the previous sums are added and multiplied by two point five (2.5) obtaining a score ranging from 0 to 100, it should be noted that the score obtained does not represent a percentage of the usability of the evaluated system, however it is a scale where if a score higher than 68 is obtained this is considered acceptable and any score below this indicates the presence of errors or aspects to be corrected [23].

3 Results

For the redesign of the "Web Telemetry" dashboard, the need was identified to improve its hierarchical structure, reduce information saturation and ease of use for users. The problem with the existing dashboard was the lack of a clear organization of the different subsystems, which made it difficult to understand the information presented. In addition, the data overload made it difficult to analyze telemetry data efficiently and quickly. To address these issues, the user-centered design paradigm was implemented to understand user needs and requirements. Based on this information, a Telemetry Dashboard prototype was developed that presents a clear hierarchy of subsystems, offers a cleaner and more visual presentation of information, and has improved interactivity. The solution sought to improve the user experience by providing an intuitive and easy-to-use interface that facilitates the understanding and analysis of telemetry data in an efficient manner.

This section presents the results obtained from this implementation for each stage.

3.1 Identification of the Context of Use

As a result of the two iterations, two types of users were identified:

- **Standard user**. - This person has a bachelor's degree, specifically in engineering, and generally works in the offices of an intermunicipal drinking water and sewerage system or a private sector company whose operations include wastewater treatment, management of water wells (from aquifers), water networks, etc.
- **Super users**. - This has the same level of education as the standard user; however, this is usually the system administrator and is in charge of the maintenance of the different sensor networks deployed by the standard user.

Once the users were identified, an analysis was made of the tasks they perform and their level of importance to be implemented in the Dashboard. These tasks were classified as:

- **Main tasks:**
  1. Login/Logout.
  2. Monitoring of the last hour of a group of sensors.
  3. Monitoring of the last hour of a specific sensor.
  4. Consultation of the data reported by a group of sensors in a given time range (previous dates).
  5. Monitoring of well pump voltage and current.
  6. Voltage and current query in a given time range (past dates).
  7. Battery voltage monitoring of devices with this feature.
  8. Monitoring of device shipment status.

- **Secondary Tasks:**
  1. System change.
  2. Display of the identifier of each device.
  3. Visualization and monitoring of test systems, such systems have the functionalities expressed in the main tasks.

It should be noted that only super users can perform the secondary tasks, so they were not taken into account for this implementation.

Its level of importance was determined by the users by means of a vote and is represented by the graph shown in Fig. 1.

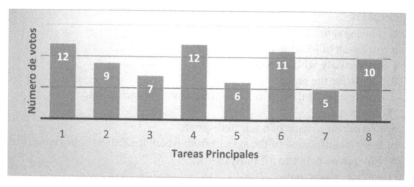

Fig. 1. Graph of votes for tasks suggested as top tasks by users.

3.2 Specification of Requirements

For the first iteration when applying the Stakeholder meeting technique, the initial needs of the users were identified, these expressed the need to monitor graphically the values collected by the sensors and not in a terminal, it was considered that there are independent systems for each intermunicipal system of drinking water and sewerage or private sector companies, these contain 3 types of subsystems (water sources, water networks and treatment plants) which in turn contain groups of sensors according to the needs of the same. Therefore, considering the above, the first prototype was designed, as shown in Fig. 4.

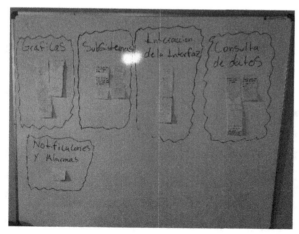

Fig. 2. Group classification resulting from the Affinity Diagramming technique applied to the users.

For the second iteration, when implementing the Affinity Diagramming technique, the result was the classification of the requirements into 5 groups, which in turn are subdivided into specific requirements for each group (process that can be seen in Fig. 3). This classification can be seen below (Fig. 2):

264   R. Rivera-Medina et al.

1. Graphics.
    a. Time graphs.
    b. Inclusion of Maximums and Minimums.
    c. Interactivity with graphics.
    d. Labels for the series.
    e. Tooltips that will display data information for each point.
2. Subsystems.
    a. List of subsystems of a selected system.
    b. Easy identification of the system from which the data is being consulted.
    c. Navigation between all subsystems.
3. Interface interaction.
    a. Margins for interfaces.
    b. Links in icons.
    c. Themes and colors according to the company.
    d. Availability.
    e. User's Guide.
    f. Icons and colors depending on the sensor.
4. Data query.
    a. Identification of sensors by ID (super Users only).
    b. Allow the selection of time periods
    c. Personalized data consultation.
5. Notifications and Alarms
    a. Alarms when maximums or minimums are exceeded.
    b. Notifications of change of shipment, connection and energy status.

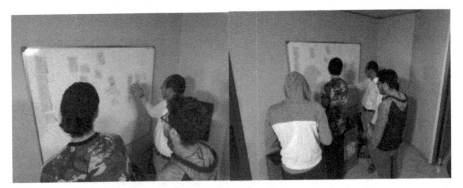

Fig. 3. Users performing the importance ranking and grouping phase belonging to the Affinity Diagramming technique.

3.3 Production of Design Solutions and Their Evaluation

Based on the characterization of the users, the requirements meeting and the identification of user needs, prototype number one was designed to provide a solution to the problems raised in the first iteration. This consists of three droplist (one for each subsystem) where the sectors that constitute each one is listed, these are located in the header next to the company's logo, the user's name and an icon that identifies it as such, the latter also having the function of a button to close assignment. The body of the prototype consists of a grid of graphs (one for each existing sensor in the selected sector) and a Date Range Picker that would allow the user to perform data queries in time ranges of interest.

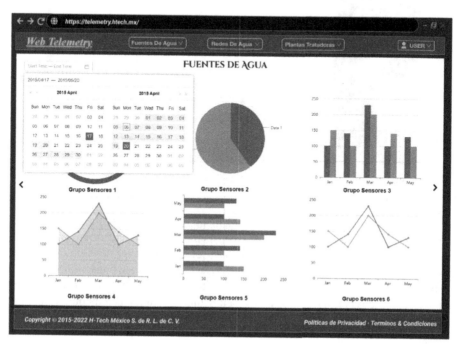

Fig. 4. Prototype version 1 of the Telemetry Dashboard "Web Telemetry".

This first prototype, when presented to the users, generated a feedback that allowed the identification of its deficiencies, some of which are as follows:

- Content saturation, which could be expressed as a cognitive overload.
- Lack of segmentation, since the separation of sensor groups was not clearly presented.
- Lack of individuality, since it is not possible to independently query a range of dates for only one specific group.
- Lack of orientation or localization within the navigation, not knowing where you are located in the navigation system.

Once this feedback was obtained, and considering it as the first evaluation of the users, a session was prepared to carry out an affinity diagramming (observable in Fig. 2 y Fig. 3) that allowed to obtain a second prototype with the correction of requirements and the integration of the feedback obtained.

Fig. 5. Prototype version 2 of the Telemetry Dashboard "Web Telemetry".

The second prototype seen in Fig. 5 has a menu bar consisting of the droplist for the subsystems that will allow navigation between them, the sectors and groups corresponding to each one in a hierarchical way. The body of this prototype consists of a second navigation bar that provides the user with the visual help to locate himself in the system (knowing in which subsystem he is in which sector and in which group of sensors) and at the same time serves as Breadcrumbs, below this navigation is a module consisting of three elements:

– Header, this is displayed:

  • On the left: an icon representing the type of graph displayed, the connection status of the device, the name of the sensor group, the device identifier (ID).
  • On the right: the option to view all the sensors data together in a single graph, a droplist with the sensors to visualize the data of the sensor of interest.

– Body, this shows the graph of the data of the selected sensor or sensors.
– Footer, this is displayed:

  • On the left side there are default options for the consultation of common date ranges, such as; last hour, day, etc. and the custom option that will allow the consultation of date ranges of interest in a personalized way.
  • On the right is the date picker range that would be activated only when the custom option is selected.

This second prototype was developed using HTML, CSS3, JavaScript and other technologies. The functionality of the main tasks listed in Sect. 3.1 was implemented.

3.1 Identification of the context of use which allowed us to perform a SUS usability evaluation. We had the participation of 12 users, each one was invited to perform the following tasks:

1. Monitoring of the last hour of a group of sensors.
2. Consultation of the data reported by any group of sensors in a given time range (previous dates).
3. Monitoring of the voltage and current of the pumps of Wells 7, 8 and 9 (which have this type of sensing).
4. Monitoring of the battery voltage of the devices that have this feature (such as those of the L. C. Sector).

Fig. 6. Users performing the SUS survey and the tasks designated for its completion.

This was done without giving previous indications on how to carry them out, which provided a first interaction of the user with the system (as shown in Fig. 6), in the Table 1. SUS survey results per user with their respective individual score and average score. The answers obtained to each question per user can be observed, these answers are according to the Likert scale mentioned in the section of **Design Evaluation.**

The last column shows the SUS scores obtained per user, obtaining an overall score of 74.791, placing the Dashboard developed in this work in the acceptable range as can be seen in Fig. 7 taking as a reference the scale mentioned in [23] where it is concluded that any score above 68, considers that the evaluated system has an acceptable overall usability.

Table 1. SUS survey results per user with their respective individual score and average score.

Temporary mark	User	Do I think I would like to use this system frequently	Did I find the system unnecessarily complex?	I thought the system was easy to use?	Do I think I would need the support of a technician to be able to use this system?	Did I find that the various functions of this system were well integrated?	I thought there was too much inconsistency in this system?	I imagine most people would learn to use this system very quickly?	Did I find the system too complicated to use?	Did I feel very safe using the system?	Did you need to learn a lot of things before you started with this system?	SUS Scores
28/10/2022 13:46:57	1	5	3	4	1	4	1	4	1	4	1	85
28/10/2022 14:14:23	2	4	1	5	2	5	1	4	1	4	3	85
14/11/2022 13:09:53	3	1	3	3	2	3	3	2	4	4	5	40
14/11/2022 13:11:25	4	3	1	3	1	5	1	1	1	5	1	80
14/11/2022 13:12:54	5	4	3	3	2	4	3	4	2	4	4	62,5
14/11/2022 13:15:19	6	4	3	3	2	3	2	4	3	3	2	62,5
14/11/2022 13:21:39	7	3	1	5	1	3	1	4	1	4	1	85
14/11/2022 13:21:47	8	5	1	4	1	4	2	4	1	4	1	87,5
14/11/2022 13:22:20	9	4	3	4	1	4	3	4	2	3	1	72,5
14/11/2022 13:22:58	10	5	3	5	1	4	1	5	1	5	1	92,5
14/11/2022 13:29:23	11	5	1	3	2	5	1	4	2	5	2	85
14/11/2022 13:42:42	12	3	3	3	4	4	1	4	1	3	4	60
											Average	74.791

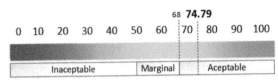

Fig. 7. Representation of the SUS scale results, based on the Net Promoter Score representation style.

4   Conclusions

Dashboards applied to different topics such as telemetry, represent a tool that supports the user in decision making through real-time monitoring of data provided by the sensor networks of such systems. With the implementation of user-centered design, an interactive Dashboard prototype was designed with a hierarchy that adapts to the structure of the systems implemented in the company Desarrollos Tecnológicos en Hidráulica Aplicada H-Tech México [18].

Through a first iteration with the users, the prototype could be evaluated by means of user feedback and corrections based on the SLR performed by A. Vazquez-Ingelmo, et al. in [14] allowing in a second iteration to reach a second prototype resulting from the implementation of affinity diagrams. This second prototype was taken to development and its evaluation was performed using a SUS system usability scale, which resulted in a score of 74.791, indicating that the Telemetry Dashboard designed in this work has an Acceptable usability as shown in Fig. 7. The Telemetry Dashboard "Web Telemetry" meets the main requirements described by the users, and incorporates the main tasks listed by the users. Although the usability of the Dashboard is in the acceptable range, the score obtained is not the highest, indicating that there are things to improve, so we intend to continue exploring usability techniques that allow us to reach the best version, implementing the secondary tasks listed by users. Regarding the final product designed in this work, it is not possible to show the final version explicitly due to data protection and the confidentiality agreement with the company Desarrollos Tecnológicos en Hidráulica Aplicada H-Tech México [18].

Acknowledgements. We wish to express our gratitude to the academic community of the Master of Science in Information Processing (MCPI) program for their important support and guidance in this work. We also express our gratitude to the Consejo Nacional de Humanidades Ciencias y Tecnologías (CONAHCYT) for their financial support, support that allows us to approach our research goals and to develop our skills.

Disclosure of Interests. The authors have no competing interests to declare that are relevant to the content of this article.

References

1. Medina, E.: Designing freedom, regulating a nation: socialist cybernetics in Allende's Chile. J. Lat. Am. Stud. **38**(3), 571–606 (2006). https://doi.org/10.1017/S0022216X06001179
2. Mattern, S.: Mission control: a history of the urban dashboard. Places J. (2015)
3. Townsend, A.M.: Smart Cities: Big Data, Civic Hackers, and the Quest for a New Utopia. W. W. Norton (2013). https://books.google.com.au/books?id=PSsGAQAAQBAJ
4. Few, S.: Clarifying the Vision. In: SwitchPoints, p. 21. John Wiley & Sons, Inc., Hoboken, NJ, USA (2015). https://doi.org/10.1002/9781119198048.part2
5. Thomas, J.J., Cook, K.A.: A visual analytics agenda. IEEE Comput. Graph. Appl. **26**(1), 10–13 (2006). https://doi.org/10.1109/MCG.2006.5
6. Lock, O., Bednarz, T., Leao, S.Z., Pettit, C.: A review and reframing of participatory urban dashboards. City Cult. Soc. **20**, 100294 (2020). https://doi.org/10.1016/j.ccs.2019.100294

7. Schintler, L.A., McNeely, C.L.: Encyclopedia of Big Data. Springer, Cham (2019). https://doi.org/10.1007/978-3-319-32010-6

8. Lahey, T., Nelson, W.: A dashboard to improve the alignment of healthcare organization decisionmaking to core values and mission statement. Camb. Q. Healthc. Ethics 29(1), 156–162 (2020). https://doi.org/10.1017/S0963180119000884

9. Ferrández-Pastor, F., García-Chamizo, J., Nieto-Hidalgo, M., Mora-Martínez, J.: Precision agriculture design method using a distributed computing architecture on internet of things context. Sensors 18(6), 1731 (2018). https://doi.org/10.3390/s18061731

10. Aguilar, S.J., Karabenick, S.A., Teasley, S.D., Baek, C.: Associations between learning analytics dashboard exposure and motivation and self-regulated learning. Comput. Educ. 162, 104085 (2021). https://doi.org/10.1016/j.compedu.2020.104085

11. De Laet, T., Millecamp, M., Ortiz-Rojas, M., Jimenez, A., Maya, R., Verbert, K.: Adoption and impact of a learning analytics dashboard supporting the advisor—Student dialogue in a higher education institute in Latin America. Br. J. Edu. Technol. 51(4), 1002–1018 (2020). https://doi.org/10.1111/bjet.12962

12. C. of Boston, Boston CityScore - Case Studies. Case Studies. https://www.boston.gov/innovation-and-technology/cityscore#case-studies

13. Nadj, M., Maedche, A., Schieder, C.: The effect of interactive analytical dashboard features on situation awareness and task performance. Decis. Support. Syst. 135, 113322 (2020). https://doi.org/10.1016/j.dss.2020.113322

14. Vazquez-Ingelmo, A., Garcia-Penalvo, F.J., Theron, R.: Information dashboards and tailoring capabilities - a systematic literature review. IEEE Access 7, 109673–109688 (2019). https://doi.org/10.1109/ACCESS.2019.2933472

15. Lopez, J.L., Sierra, J.E., Medina, B.: Telemetry system proposal for remote and real-time measurements in a multimodal transport system. J. Xi'an Univ. pf Archit. Technol. XII(Vi), 479–486 (2020)

16. Burattin, A., Eigenmann, M., Seiger, R., Weber, B.: MQTT-XES: real-time telemetry for process event data. In: CEUR Workshop Proceedings, vol. 2673, pp. 97–101 (2020)

17. Saito, S., Ogawa, K.: Ergonomics of human-system interaction. Jpn. J. Ergon. 30(1), 1–1 (1994). https://doi.org/10.5100/jje.30.1

18. H-Tech MX, "Aplicada, Desarrollos Tecnologicos en Hidraulica." https://htech.mx/

19. Anderson, N.S., Norman, D.A., Draper, S.W.: User centered system design: new perspectives on human-computer interaction. Am. J. Psychol. 101(1), 148 (1988). https://doi.org/10.2307/1422802

20. Scupin, R.: The KJ method: a technique for analyzing data derived from Japanese ethnology. Hum. Organ. 56(2), 233–237 (1997). https://doi.org/10.17730/humo.56.2.x33592351444655

21. Johansson, M., Arvola, M.: A case study of how user interface sketches, scenarios and computer prototypes structure stakeholder meetings. BCS Learn. Dev. (2007).https://doi.org/10.14236/ewic/HCI2007.18

22. Brooke, J.: SUS: a quick and dirty usability scale. In: Usability Evaluation in Industry, vol. 189, pp. 207–212. CRC Press (1996). https://doi.org/10.1201/9781498710411-35

23. Blattgerste, J., Behrends, J., Pfeiffer, T.: A web-based analysis toolkit for the system usability scale. In: The15th International Conference on PErvasive Technologies Related to Assistive Environments, pp. 237–246, ACM, New York, NY, USA, June 2022. https://doi.org/10.1145/3529190.3529216

Scenarios, Shared Understanding, and Group Decision Support to Foster Innovation Networks

Vanessa Agredo-Delgado[1,3(✉)] ⓘ, Leandro Antonelli[2] ⓘ, César A. Collazos[3] ⓘ, Alejandro Fernandez[2] ⓘ, Pascale Zaraté[4] ⓘ, Guy Camilleri[5] ⓘ, Julio Hurtado[3] ⓘ, Mario Lezoche[6] ⓘ, Regina Motz[6,7] ⓘ, Herve Paneto[6] ⓘ, and Diego Torres[2] ⓘ

[1] Corporacion Universitaria Comfacauca - Unicomfacauca, Popayan, Colombia
vagredo@unicomfacauca.edu.co
[2] Lifia - Facultad de Informática, Universidad Nacional de La Plata, La Plata, Argentina
{lanto,alejandro.fernandez}@lifia.info.unlp.edu.ar
[3] Universidad del Cauca, IDIS, Popayán, Colombia
{ccollazo,ahurtado}@unicauca.edu.co.edu.co
[4] University of Toulouse, IRIT, Université Toulouse - Capitole, Toulouse, France
Pascale.Zarate@ut-capitole.fr
[5] University of Toulouse, IRIT, Université Toulouse III - Paul Sabatier, Toulouse, France
Guy.Camilleri@irit.fr
[6] Université de Lorraine, Nancy, France
{mario.lezoche,Herve.Panetto}@univ-lorraine.fr
[7] Instituto de Computación Facultad de Ingeniería de la Universidad de la República, Montevideo, Uruguay

Abstract. Collaborative innovation is a dynamic process that involves diverse individuals and organizations pooling resources and working together to develop new ideas, products, or services. Successful collaboration in networked innovation projects is challenging due to the need to cross the knowledge boundaries that exist between organizations, disciplines, and cognitive frames. This paper proposes an approach aimed at facilitating knowledge mobilization and fostering learning in the intricate landscape of networked innovation projects. Stored in a shared repository, scenarios serve as a foundation for collaborative processes, guiding participants toward a shared understanding and the construction of mutual meaning. A pivotal aspect of this approach is the inclusive engagement of Stakeholders in a collaborative decision-making process of scenario ranking that includes identifying and negotiating comparison criteria. Although the approach is presented with examples in the domain of agriculture, where validation of the constituent elements took place, its adaptability renders it domain-independent offering a robust framework for collaborative innovation across various sectors.

Keywords: Innovation networks · Scenarios · Shared understanding · Group decision · Knowledge mobilization

P. H. Ruiz et al. (Eds.): HCI-COLLAB 2023, CCIS 1877, pp. 271–285, 2024.
https://doi.org/10.1007/978-3-031-57982-0_21

1 Introduction

Collaborative innovation refers to the process of bringing together individuals or organizations with different backgrounds, experiences, and expertise to develop new ideas, products, or services [1]. It is defined as a collaborative effort that unites diverse organizations around a shared question. Its objective is to create an inclusive environment where the exploration of alternative perspectives and the full engagement of individuals can contribute to the strengthening of both organizations and entire sectors [2].

It is increasingly recognized that including multiple perspectives and international collaboration is essential for successful innovation [3]. Countries and organizations commit to initiatives to support multinational, industry-academia collaboration. Horizon Europe, for example, is the largest research and innovation funding program of the European Union (EU) and supports international research collaborations with countries outside the EU. Diverse perspectives bring a range of ideas, experiences, and knowledge to the table, which can help to identify new opportunities and solutions. International collaboration, in particular, can be valuable in addressing complex global challenges that require a broad range of expertise and resources.

Collaboration in such networked innovation projects is challenging as it implies crossing knowledge boundaries. Knowledge boundaries arise from the differences that exist between organizations, disciplines, and cognitive frames. They constitute major barriers to knowledge mobilization and learning [4]. Therefore understanding their nature is of paramount importance to successful networked innovation. Equally important is the development of strategies to mobilize knowledge across them.

In this work, we propose an approach to support knowledge mobilization and learning in networked innovation projects. We focus specifically on the need to capture and mobilize knowledge of value to create opportunities for innovation. Scenarios, stored in a shared repository, are used to capture and share information about application and solution domains. A collaborative process guides participants to reach a shared understanding and construct shared meaning. Stakeholders engage in a collaborative decision-making process of scenario ranking that includes identifying and negotiating comparison criteria.

This article is organized as follows: Sect. 2 introduces the core background concepts, namely, knowledge boundary and boundary crossing mechanisms, scenarios, shared understanding, and multi-criteria decision-making. Section 3 discusses related work. Section 4 presents the approach by first providing an overview and then going onto the details of its three core activities. Section 5 discusses preliminary evaluation efforts. Finally, Sect. 6 discusses the article's main contributions and presents conclusions.

2 Background

2.1 Knowledge Boundaries

A knowledge boundary represents the limit between an agent's knowledge in relation to a different knowledge domain [4]. Paul Carlile [5, 6] proposed a topology of knowledge boundaries consisting of three distinctive types: syntactic boundaries, semantic boundaries, and pragmatic boundaries.

Syntactic knowledge boundaries are the easiest to cross as people have shared logic, values, and world views. Strategies to cross syntactic boundaries usually rely on knowledge transfer (mainly explicit knowledge) based on documents and information systems and using a common lexicon. In an international networked innovation project, the differences in language (e.g., French, Spanish, etc.) and vocabulary among experts from the same discipline constitute a simple example of a syntactic knowledge boundary.

In semantic knowledge boundaries, stakeholders do not have shared knowledge or a set of values but different understandings of the same knowledge. There is a need to develop sensitivity to other people's understanding. Strategies to cross semantic boundaries emphasize translation and the development of a common meaning. Differences in meaning and context specificity become important, and tacit knowledge becomes more relevant. An international networked innovation project will certainly face semantic knowledge boundaries as it involves experts and practitioners from several disciplines and organizations, each of them with a potentially different understanding of the shared endeavor. Pragmatic knowledge boundaries present different understandings and interpretations, and interests that may lead to conflict. Actors must be willing and prepared to negotiate existing practices and transform existing knowledge toward common interest. Crossing pragmatics boundaries is challenging and normally characterized as a process of "creative abrasion", negotiation, and co-creation of common ground that leads to new practices. A networked innovation project brings together academics and practitioners, suppliers and consumers, partners, and competing companies. Each stakeholder may have a different motivation to participate and a different outcome in mind.

There are well-known (boundary-spanning) mechanisms that can be applied to work across and around knowledge boundaries. We talk about a "boundary object" when boundary crossing is based on a shared object (for example, a software artifact) that sits between sides in the border and is the focus of collaboration [5, 6]. When boundaries are crossed as a result of the participation of individuals in collaborative spaces and activities, we talk about boundary practice [7].

2.2 Scenarios

A scenario [8] is an artifact that describes situations (in the world, the application, or the software domain) using natural language. It describes a specific situation that arises in a certain context to achieve some goal. There is a set of steps (the episodes) to reach that goal. In the episodes, actors use materials, tools, and data as resources to perform some specific action. Although there are many templates to describe scenarios, this work is based on the one proposed by Leite et al. [9].

To illustrate how the template is used, let's consider a situation related to the agricultural domain, where there is an infrastructure in the field to provide irrigation. The infrastructure is managed from an operations room, that is, the room that has the control to start and stop the pump. Table 1 captures the situation as a scenario.

Table 1. Scenario that describes the start of the irrigation system from an operations room.

Attribute	Description
Scenario title	Start of the irrigation system through an operations room
Goal	Protect access to the water infrastructure to ensure responsible water use
Context	The field counts with an irrigation infrastructure (pipes, tanks, pumps, and valves) to irrigate the field
Actors	expert, supervisor, operator
Resources	The checklist to determine whether it is necessary to irrigate the field The security protocol to access and operate the pump and valves
Episodes	An expert evaluates the conditions of the field to determine whether it is necessary to irrigate The expert writes a report to the supervisor with the recommendation to irrigate The supervisor authorizes the operator to start the irrigation system. The operator accesses to the operations room The operator starts the pump and opens the valves

2.3 Shared Understanding

Collaboration is an essential issue in today's interconnected and complex world. Whether it's in the workplace, academia, or any other collective endeavor, successful collaboration relies on effective communication, coordination, and, most importantly, shared understanding [10]. Shared understanding refers to the collective comprehension and agreement among individuals within a group regarding the goals, objectives, tasks, and expectations. It could be identified as the foundation for productive collaboration and enables teams to achieve remarkable outcomes.

Shared understanding could be interpreted as the bedrock of successful collaboration within groups. It enhances communication, promotes trust and cohesion, facilitates decision-making, and enables teams to adapt to change. By fostering a collective comprehension and agreement among members, shared understanding paves the way for productive collaboration and outstanding achievements [11].

There are many benefits to building shared understanding in collaborative groups, which have been investigated and proven by several authors. It allows for predicting the group's performance and obtaining better quality and quantity of products. In addition, it is more likely that the team will be successful and minimize time losses due to reprocessing [12]. Some of the main benefits of shared understanding are enhanced communication and coordination [13], trust and cohesion, improved decision-making, and better adaptation to change [14].

2.4 Multi-criteria Decision Making

Multi-criteria Decision Analysis (MCDA) is used to support decision-makers when several scenarios or alternatives are possible. These scenarios or alternatives are generally evaluated thanks to several criteria [15]. This kind of problem-solving may involve decisions on how to design the best choice or how to select the best solution from a finite set of alternatives [16].

Researchers in this area are concerned about topics on requirements of multiple decision-makers, more informed decision-making support, and formalization of actors' preferences, the ability to cope with several points in decision-making, taking into account human, organizational and social issues in decision-making [17].

Zaraté [18] wrote that to implement decision support, the techniques and methodologies used are extracted from the field of applied mathematics, such as optimization, statistics, and decision theory, as well as less formal and more multidisciplinary fields, such as organizational analysis and cognitive science. These techniques lead to two types of results: the optimum result and the satisfactory result. The satisfactory result is generally the one that guides to the best compromise among all constraints: technical, social, human, etc.

3 Related Work

Duin et al. [19] propose the Unified Collaborative Innovation Framework (UCIF), a methodological framework that aims to organize and simplify user-centered, open innovation. UCIF aims to remove scientific and linguistic obstacles and obstacles stemming from different backgrounds and perspectives that inhibit collaboration. Thus, their proposal has the same goal as ours. Nevertheless, they propose a framework with a specific technique to tackle the problem.

Greer et al. [20] review the literature studying how firms engage in collaborative innovation with individual and business customers. Their work highlights areas where research is needed for a greater understanding of the strategic issues and for managing the collaborative process. We agree with the review since our proposed approach addresses both concerns. Our proposed approach includes one step to deal with shared understanding and another step to find an agreement collaboratively.

Serrano et al. [21] discuss the possible contributions of pervasive intelligence for enhancing collaborative distributed innovation processes. They state that pervasive intelligence enables a new quality of information sharing, joint planning, joint problem-solving, integration of operations, etc. These factors will positively influence collaborative innovation processes. We think that, in some way, our proposed approach provides some kind of pervasive intelligence.

Gonzalez Benito et al. [22] analyses the role of collaboration in the contribution of innovation. A survey administered to Spanish firms from industrial, building, agriculture, and trade-service sectors measured two levels of innovation, incremental and radical, and two dimensions of collaboration, channel, and consulting advice. Small businesses take more advantage of channel collaboration, whereas large businesses rely more on consulting advice-based collaboration. Although our proposed approach focuses on small business and channel collaboration, we believe that it can also be used in the scope of large businesses with a consulting advice-based collaboration.

Ozcan et al. [23] analyze the stages of the innovation process and find three main steps: (i) input, (ii) transformation, and (iii) output. Our proposed approach matches these steps. Our capturing the knowledge step is the input since the knowledge is captured. The agreeing on the understanding is the transformation since the scenarios are described in a way to be understood by all the participants. Finally, the out is the rank of scenarios where the participants involved agree about the decision.

Khan et al. [24] report the conclusions of some innovative processes developed in Finland. They find that interdependencies are an important variable to be considered in the collaboration and innovation process. These interdependencies are also present in our proposed approach since scenarios (the artifact to capture the knowledge) are interdependent between them. So, there is also interdependence between the participants.

Bommert et al. [25] discuss the risks and advantages of innovation in the public and private sectors. They emphasize that bureaucracy is a big risk. We think that our proposed approach involving different stakeholders and pushing them to have a shared understanding of the situation can help to tackle this issue.

Ojasalo et al. [26] performed an empirical study about open innovation in smart cities, particularly the role of the actors. They have found that the cities (their government) must be orchestrators while the other actors (citizens, companies, and other cities) contribute. It is interesting these two different roles. A further revision of our approach will consider this aspect.

4   The Proposed Approach

4.1   Our Approach in a Nutshell

The proposed approach captures, in a repository of scenarios, the stakeholder's knowledge regarding the domain of innovation. Figure 1 provides an overview of the key components of the approach. In the "Capture knowledge" activity, stakeholders collaboratively write scenarios. Scenarios are kept in a shared scenario repository. Scenarios and the repository act as boundary objects. The "Reach shared understanding" activity engages stakeholders in boundary practice that aims to obtain mutually understood versions of the scenarios. This activity also results in a shared vocabulary. Collaborative work to improve the value of the scenarios repository for innovation continues as stakeholders engage to "Rank the scenarios". This improves the stakeholder's understanding of the scenarios and their contribution to innovation. As it occurs in the boundary between knowledge domains, the ranking of the scenarios is a practice that can lead to new knowledge and innovation.

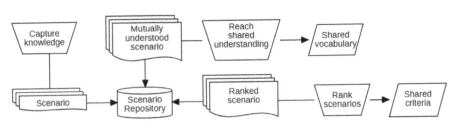

Fig. 1. Approach overview

As an example, let's consider the agricultural domain mentioned. The irrigation can be started manually by physically accessing the operations room to start the pumps as depicted in Table 1. Still, an IoT web application can also be used to do it. Table 2 describes this later alternative.

Table 2. Scenario that describes the start of the irrigation system with an IoT web application.

Attribute	Description
Scenario title	Start of the watering system
Goal	Protect access to the watering system to ensure responsible use
Context	The field counts with a watering infrastructure (pipes, tanks, pumps, and valves)
Actors	expert, supervisor
Resources	The checklist to determine whether it is necessary to water the field
Episodes	An expert evaluates the conditions of the field to determine whether it is necessary to water The expert writes a report to the supervisor with the recommendation to water The supervisor logs in to the IoT web application The supervisor starts the pump and opens the valves

Thus, scenarios described in Tables 1 and 2 are examples of scenarios obtained after the "Capture knowledge" activity. It is important to mention that both scenarios are quite similar, and they differ in the use of an IoT web application. Nevertheless, they also differ in the use of a specific word: one scenario uses the term irrigation, while the other scenario uses the term watering. This is a tiny difference, but it is an example of some difference that will be dealt with in the "Reach shared understanding" activity. This activity deals with the description of the scenarios considering the language and the style of writing and also the knowledge stated. For example, after describing both scenarios, the stakeholders involved can agree that there is only one way to start the irrigation system, and it should be done by accessing the operations room (because there is no IoT web application or because it is too dangerous to expose this control to the internet). Let's consider that both scenarios are true, and the language issue was already dealt with in both scenarios using the term irrigation. Then, the activity "Rank scenarios" deals with these two scenarios, and stakeholders decide which scenario they prefer. They can rank the scenarios in different ways. They can assess security issues, financial issues, or other different factors. Thus, "Ranking scenarios" includes determining the factors and using the agreed factors to rank the scenarios according to them.

4.2 Capture Knowledge with Scenarios

Scenarios are a simple way to describe a macro-system. The term simple denotes that scenarios are described with natural language, accessible for people without technological backgrounds. To make scenarios richer, it is important to involve a group of people with different backgrounds and different points of view (perspectives). The result of this activity of capturing the knowledge is a repository of scenarios describing the same phenomenon. These scenarios may have the same or different perspectives. Moreover, the scenarios can use different terminology (terms), for example, synonyms, hyponyms, and hypernyms.

The technique proposed for writing scenarios (based on [27]) adopts an incremental approach. One person initially describes certain attributes, which are then further elaborated upon by either the same individual or another participant. This collaborative process allows for the gradual development of scenario descriptions by incorporating multiple perspectives. Specifically, the technique proposes to describe in the first place the title, the context, and the goal of the scenario. Although the title and the goal could be enough, different contexts (starting points) can arise to obtain the same goal. Thus, it is important to start with these three attributes and then continue with describing the episodes as a second step. The third step consists in identifying actors and resources. This activity can be done independently of the episodes, but by analyzing the episodes, the identification of actors and resources will be richer. Thus, after describing every group of attributes, the complete scenario can be reviewed and improved by the previously described attributes.

For instance, let's consider a scenario to describe the start of the irrigation system. This task can be carried out in two different ways: by accessing manually to an operation room (Table 1) or by using a web app (Table 2). The title, the goal, and the context of both scenarios could be the same. In our example, the titles are different. Nevertheless, if two different people had described every scenario, it could happen that they did not realize that there are two different scenarios and the description of the attributes could be quite similar.

The following step is the description of the episodes. The episodes should be a set of steps for achieving the goal considering the context as a starting point. In our example, if people think there are two different ways of starting the irrigation system, they should include these specific aspects in the episodes. In Table 1, it is clear that an operator enters the operation room, while in Table 2, it is clear that the supervisor logs into a web application.

Since the technique is iterative and incremental, its philosophy is describing the attributes in phases and, at the same time, reviewing and improving the attributes previously described. For example, after describing the episodes, somebody can discover that the title should contain some expression that differentiates both ways of starting the irrigation system. Thus, somebody can modify the scenario title in Table 2 by adding "Start of the watering system using an Iot web application".

The following step consists of the identification of actors and resources. The identification of actors and resources should primarily stem from the episodes themselves. While it is possible to perform this identification before describing the episodes, in certain cases, identifying actors and resources from the episodes can provide valuable insights that enrich the overall narrative. Such an approach allows for identifying elements that can enhance the episodes and contribute to a more comprehensive depiction. For example, analyzing episodes of the Scenario described in Table 1 it can be concluded that there are three actors: expert, supervisor, and operator. The episodes clearly describe the interaction between the three of them. Maybe, after identifying the three actors, some experts can think about describing episodes to notify the supervisor and the expert that the task has been done. Moreover, analyzing the episodes, two resources can be identified: (i) the procedure (or checklist) to determine if it is necessary to irrigate and (ii) the security protocol to access the operation room. With these resources, some experts can realize that some episodes are missing since they show that it is necessary to follow a protocol (authorization) to access the operations room.

4.3   Reach Shared Understanding

As previously stated, shared understanding refers to "The ability to coordinate behaviors towards common goals or objectives (meaning-in-use or action perspective) of multiple agents within a group (group level) based on mutual knowledge, beliefs and assumptions (content and structure) about the task, the group, the process or the tools and technologies used (object scope/perspective) that may change throughout the group work process due to various influencing factors and impacts the processes and outcomes of group work" [28], in addition to being a prerequisite for the successful implementation of collaborative work [29], this is because the groups engaged in this type of work must have some common knowledge and understanding, which functions as a joint baseline, to be able to work productively, where everyone can speak the same language and understand the meaning of the concepts on which they are working [28].

The objective of this activity is to ensure all actors understand the scenarios defined in the previous step. Two scenarios were defined in natural language, determining that irrigation can be initiated manually by physically accessing the operations room to start the pumps. Still, also an IoT web application can be used to do so. In addition to this, the use of different words to refer to the same action was appreciated. One scenario uses the term irrigation, while the other uses watering. That is why this second step aims to standardize the concepts and/or terms so that everyone can understand the same thing without using the same words that may have different meanings/interpretations (i.e., homonyms) or using different words for actions, elements, or situations that mean the same thing (i.e., synonyms). It is important to consider that this type of event also occurs because, in the previous step, to make the descriptions of the steps richer, a group of people with different backgrounds and points of view is involved, which generates different interpretations, perceptions, ideas that must be homogenized so that there are even understandings. The idea is that at the end of this step, the previously defined scenarios can be understood, thus generating a consolidated group of scenarios that everyone understands and that, subsequently, the actions to be taken can be determined based on decision-making management.

Reaching a shared understanding of the scenarios is a collaborative process that involves several steps/activities, as depicted in Fig. 2. The process starts with the "Understand the scenarios" activity. After finishing, each of the stakeholders individually defines what they understood about each scenario ("Individual understanding"), based on the need to build tacit knowledge (that which is acquired through their own experience) and which must subsequently be made explicit at the time of materializing it in a result [30]. Each participant resolves his or her doubts about what has been socialized ("Resolution of doubts"). After this, "Sharing" takes place, where each participant inserts

Fig. 2. Reaching shared understanding of the scenarios

a meaning, tuning in with the others in the group, who actively listen and try to grasp the explanation of what each one understood about the scenarios, using them to give meaning to the situation in question [31]. "Debate" is a moment in which a mutual construction of meaning takes place, dealing with the differences of interpretation between the group participants through discussions with arguments and clarifications [32]. It is during the debate that those different words that had been given to the irrigation are clarified, determining the selection of the most appropriate word ("Conflict resolution"). After solving these differences, the group actions are reached, which is the moment in which the interpretation of meanings or actions are materialized with the support and collaboration of all the participants of the group to clearly define these discrepancies of perceptions or knowledge that had not been previously considered, the scenarios are defined again with their elements, where differences have been solved and where all the participants have put their collaboration, and all are in agreement ("Group understanding"). Finally, additional debate or conflict resolution is generated if it is the case and if it is required. As a result of reaching a shared understanding, each scenario can result in one or more alternatives so that all participants understand what has been defined with the information of each one of them and that if something is subsequently talked about or referred to in these scenarios, everyone understands what it is about.

4.4 Rank the Scenarios

During this final part of the process, the stakeholders rank the different scenarios. This ranking can be used to purge low-value or incorrect scenarios of the repository or to select scenarios for innovation initiatives. The set of Scenarios will be used as input; the output will be the ranked set of scenarios.

The ranking will be determined by considering some criteria. The participants will first decide the criteria to be used. Obtaining the set of criteria is a co-design process done by the group. Considering the two scenarios described in Tables 1 and 2, one criterion to determine which scenario should be used could be scenario precision. The scenario described in Table 1 is more precise because it specifies the irrigation mode: using an operations room. Another criterion could be the resources used for each scenario. The scenario described in Table 2 uses fewer resources than the one described in Table 1. The design of the set of criteria depends on the context of the decision to be made and on the involved stakeholders.

The group of stakeholders, having built a coherent family of criteria, will define the different alternatives to be ranked. The set of scenarios will form the set of alternatives. Some stakeholders could be attracted by a part of one scenario to be considered as an alternative. In that case, the considered part of the scenario will constitute a new scenario and, consequently, a new alternative. When the set of criteria and the set of alternatives are defined in a consensus mode, each decision maker will give his own preferences for each alternative and on the importance of criteria. Each stakeholder can consider one criterion, i.e., the precision in the previous example, as more important than the others. Finally, each decision maker will give his own preferences depending on each criterion, i.e., this scenario (Table 1) is better for me than the other (Table 2) on the criterion of resource usage.

If the stakeholders disagree on a scenario to choose, their preferences are considered, and the best consensus will be calculated by a Group Decision Support System (GDSS). In this work, we propose using the GRUS system for group decision support [33] that adheres to the previously described decision-making process. In this system, multi-criteria Decision-Making Methodologies are embedded.

5 Preliminary Evaluation

This proposal aims to support knowledge mobilization and learning in networked innovation projects. It builds upon a rich body of literature on knowledge mobilization across knowledge boundaries (as summarized in [4], Chapter 8). As boundary objects, it proposes scenarios (and a repository of scenarios) and Group Support System (GSS). As boundary processes, it proposes collaborative scenario writing, shared understanding, and collaborative multi-criteria ranking of scenarios. A complete evaluation of the whole approach is currently out of reach for the project. However, each of the constituting parts has been evaluated in comparable situations. Following, we discuss each of these evaluations.

The iterative approach described in this manuscript to capture the knowledge of the domain using Scenarios is based on a previous proposal [27]. That publication reports the evaluation of using Scenarios with an iterative and collaborative approach. The System Usability Scale (SUS) [34] was used to evaluate the usability and applicability of the approach. Although SUS is mainly used to assess the usability of software systems, it proved to be effective in assessing products and processes as well [35]. The score obtained in the evaluation was 70,53 which is considered above average (in a range from 0 to 100) according to common practice.

The approach to shared understanding presented in Sect. 4.3 is based on a previous proposal shown in [36]. This previous proposal mainly focuses on achieving shared understanding in collaborative problem-solving activities. It focuses on the ability of an individual to participate effectively in a process by which two or more agents attempt to solve a problem by sharing the understanding and effort needed to reach a solution and pooling their knowledge, skills, and efforts to reach that solution [37]. Networked innovation can be classified as a problem-solving activity where the aim is to solve a problem in the field of agriculture. Therefore, we consider that the principles of the shared understanding process presented in Sect. 4.3, evaluated [38], can be generalized to this work.

Group decision support systems support a group of decision-makers to decide collaboratively. The approach considered in this work and reported in [33] is based on Multi-Criteria Analysis. In [39], it has been shown that evaluating such systems is possible. This evaluation is based on several experiments involving students in several countries. Several sessions of decision-making problems have been conducted. In these experimental studies, the alternatives were the items to be chosen.

6 Discussion and Conclusions

In this work, we proposed an approach to support knowledge mobilization and learning in networked innovation projects. It focused primarily on the need to capture and mobilize knowledge about the potential opportunities for innovation. Scenarios, stored in a shared repository, are used to capture and share information about application and solution domains. A collaborative process guides participants to reach a shared understanding and construct shared meaning. Stakeholders engage in a collaborative decision-making process of scenario ranking that includes identifying and negotiating comparison criteria, using a GDSS. Scenarios, the shared repository of scenarios, and the GDSS act as boundary objects that keep collaboration focused and mainly serve to cross syntactic boundaries. Collaboration to reach a shared understanding and to rank scenarios constitute boundary practices that help identify and cross semantic boundaries. In addition, these two boundary practices help identify the nature and assess the magnitude of the existing pragmatic boundaries. Although the approach is well integrated and its parts have been evaluated independently, we plan to perform a case study in order to assess the usability and applicability of the whole integrated approach.

Acknowledgements. This paper is partially supported by funding provided by the STIC AmSud program, Project 22STIC-01.

References

1. Swink, M.: Building Collaborative Innovation Capability. Res.-Technol. Manage. **49**(2), 37–47 (2006). https://doi.org/10.1080/08956308.2006.11657367
2. Xie, X., Fang, L., Zeng, S.: Collaborative innovation network and knowledge transfer performance: a fsQCA approach. J. Bus. Res. **69**(11), 5210–5215 (2016). https://doi.org/10.1016/j.jbusres.2016.04.114, https://www.sciencedirect.com/science/article/pii/S01482963 16302946
3. Dutta, S., Lanvin, B., Wunsch-Vincent, S., León, L.R.: Organization W.I.P: Global innovation index (2022). Unknown (0). https://doi.org/10.34667/TIND.46596
4. Liu, S.: Knowledge Management: An Interdisciplinary Approach for Business Decisions, 1st edn. Kogan Page, London (2020)

5. Carlile, P.R.: A pragmatic view of knowledge and boundaries: boundary objects in new product development. Organ. Sci. **13**(4), 442–455 (2002). https://doi.org/10.1287/orsc.13.4.442.2953

6. Carlile, P.R.: Transferring, translating, and transforming: an integrative framework for managing knowledge across boundaries. Organ. Sci. **15**(5), 555–568 (2004). https://doi.org/10.1287/orsc.1040.0094

7. Hawkins, M.A., Rezazade, M.M.H.: Knowledge boundary spanning process: synthesizing four spanning mechanisms. Manage. Decis. **50**(10), 1800–1815 (2012). https://doi.org/10.1108/00251741211279611

8. Carrol, J.: Five reasons for scenario-based design. In: Proceedings of the 32nd Annual Hawaii International Conference on Systems Sciences. 1999. HICSS-32. Abstracts and CD-ROM of Full Papers, vol. Track3, p. 11 (1999). https://doi.org/10.1109/HICSS.1999.772890

9. do Prado Leite, J.C.S., Hadad, G.D.S., Doorn, J.H., Kaplan, G.N.: A scenario construction process. Requirements Eng. **5**, 38–61 (2000). https://doi.org/10.1007/PL00010342

10. Jonker, C.M., Treur, J.: Compositional verification of multi-agent systems: a formal analysis of pro-activeness and reactiveness. In: de Roever, W.P., Langmaack, H., Pnueli, A. (eds.) Compositionality: The Significant Difference, pp. 350–380. Springer, Berlin (1998). https://doi.org/10.1007/3-540-49213-5_13

11. Bittner, E., Leimeister, J.: Why shared understanding matters – engineering a collaboration process for shared understanding to improve collaboration effectiveness in heterogeneous teams. In: 2014 47th Hawaii International Conference on System Sciences, pp. 106–114. IEEE Computer Society, Los Alamitos (2013). https://doi.org/10.1109/HICSS.2013.608

12. Langan-Fox, J., Anglim, J., Wilson, J.R.: Mental models, team mental models, and performance: process, development, and future directions. Hum. Factors Ergon. Manuf. Serv. Ind. **14**(4), 331–352 (2004). https://doi.org/10.1002/hfm.20004

13. Kleinsmann, M., Buijs, J., Valkenburg, R.: Understanding the complexity of knowledge integration in collaborative new product development teams: a case study. J. Eng. Technol. Manage. **27**(1), 20–32 (2010). https://doi.org/10.1016/j.jengtecman.2010.03.003, https://www.sciencedirect.com/science/article/pii/S0923474810000044

14. Castañer, X., Oliveira, N.: Collaboration, coordination, and cooperation among organizations: establishing the distinctive meanings of these terms through a systematic literature review. J. Manage. **46**(6), 965–1001 (2020). https://doi.org/10.1177/0149206320901565

15. Yoon, K.P., Hwang, C.L.: Multiple Attribute Decision Making: An Introduction. Sage Publications, Thousand Oaks (1995).https://doi.org/10.4135/9781412985161

16. Marks, L., Dunn, E., Keller, J., Godsey, L.: Multiple criteria decision making (MCDM) using fuzzy logic: an innovative approach to sustainable agriculture. In: Proceedings of 3rd International Symposium on Uncertainty Modeling and Analysis and Annual Conference of the North American Fuzzy Information Processing Society, pp. 503–508. IEEE (1995)

17. Meyer, P.: Contributions au processus d'Aide Multicritère à la Décision: Méthodes, Outils et Applications. Ph.D. thesis, Dauphine recherche en Management (2013)

18. Zaraté, P.: Tools for Collaborative Decision-Making. John Wiley & Sons, Hoboken (2013)

19. Duin, H., Jaskov, J., Hesmer, A., Thoben, K.D.: Towards a framework for collaborative innovation. In: Cascini, G. (ed.) Computer-Aided Innovation (CAI), vol. 277, pp. 193–204. Springer US, Boston, MA (2008). https://doi.org/10.1007/978-0-387-09697-1_16

20. Greer, C.R., Lei, D.: Collaborative innovation with customers: a review of the literature and suggestions for future research*: collaborative innovation with customers. Int. J. Manag. Rev. **14**(1), 63–84 (2012). https://doi.org/10.1111/j.1468-2370.2011.00310.x

21. Senano, V., Fischer, T.: Contribution of pervasine intelligence to collaborative innovation processes. In: Network-Centric Collaboration and Supporting Frameworks, vol. 224, pp. 93–100. Springer US, Boston, MA (2006). https://doi.org/10.1007/978-0-387-38269-2_10. series Title: IFIP International Federation for Information Processing

22. González-Benito, Ó., Muñoz-Gallego, P.A., García-Zamora, E.: Role of collaboration in innovation success: differences for large and small businesses. J. Bus. Econ. Manage. 17(4), 645–662 (2016). https://doi.org/10.3846/16111699.2013.823103

23. Ozcan, S., Islam, N.: Analyses of collaborative innovation activities throughout the stages of innovation process. In: 2016 Portland International Conference on Management of Engineering and Technology (PICMET), pp. 446–452 (2016). https://doi.org/10.1109/PICMET.2016.7806550

24. Khan, I.S., Kauppila, O., Fatima, N., Majava, J.: Stakeholder interdependencies in a collaborative innovation project. J. Innov. Entrepreneurship 11(1), 38 (2022). https://doi.org/10.1186/s13731-022-00229-0

25. Bommert, B.: Collaborative innovation in the public sector. Int. Public Manage. Rev. 11(1), 15–33 (2014). https://ipmr.net/index.php/ipmr/article/view/73

26. Ojasalo, J., Kauppinen, H.: Collaborative innovation with external actors: an empirical study on open innovation platforms in smart cities. Technol. Innov. Manage. Rev. 6, 49–60 (2016). https://doi.org/10.22215/timreview/1041

27. Antonelli, L., Ville, J.D., Dioguardi, F., Fernández, A., Tanevitch, L., Torres, D.: An iterative and collaborative approach to specify scenarios using natural language. In: Anais do WER22 - Workshop em Engenharia de Requisitos, Natal - RN, Brazil, 23–26 August 2022. WERpapers (2022). https://doi.org/10.29327/1298262.25-2

28. Bittner, E.A.C., Leimeister, J.M.: Creating shared understanding in heterogeneous work groups: why it matters and how to achieve it. J. Manag. Inf. Syst. 31(1), 111–144 (2014)

29. Oppl, S.: Supporting the collaborative construction of a shared understanding about work with a guided conceptual modeling technique. Group Decis. Negot. 26, 247–283 (2017). https://doi.org/10.1007/s10726-016-9485-7

30. Stahl, G.: Group cognition in computer-assisted collaborative learning. J. Comput. Assist. Learn. 21(2), 79–90 (2005). https://doi.org/10.1111/j.1365-2729.2005.00115.x

31. Webb, N.M., Palincsar, A.S.: Group Processes in the Classroom. Prentice Hall International, Hoboken (1996)

32. Van den Bossche, P., Gijselaers, W., Segers, M., Woltjer, G., Kirschner, P.: Team learning: building shared mental models. Instr. Sci. 39, 283–301 (2011). https://doi.org/10.1007/s11251-010-9128-3

33. Camilleri, G., Zaraté, P.: A group multicriteria approach. In: Kilgour, D.M., Eden, C. (eds.) Handbook of Group Decision and Negotiation, pp. 1023–1048. Springer, Cham (2021). https://doi.org/10.1007/978-3-030-49629-6_17

34. Brooke, J.: "SUS-A Quick and Dirty Usability Scale." Usability Evaluation in Industry. CRC Press (1996). https://www.crcpress.com/product/isbn/9780748404605. ISBN: 9780748404605

35. Bangor, A., Kortum, P.T., Miller, J.T.: An empirical evaluation of the system usability scale. Int. J. Hum.-Comput. Interac. 24, 574–594 (2008). https://doi.org/10.1080/10447310802205776

36. Agredo-Delgado, V., Ruiz, P.H., Mon, A., Collazos, C.A., Moreira, F., Fardoun, H.M.: Validating the shared understanding construction in computer supported collaborative work in a problem-solving activity. In: Rocha, Á., Adeli, H., Reis, L., Costanzo, S., Orovic, I., Moreira, F. (eds.) Trends and Innovations in Information Systems and Technologies: Volume 3 8, pp. 203–214. Springer, Cham (2020). https://doi.org/10.1007/978-3-030-45697-9_20

37. O'Neil, H.F., Chuang, S.H., Chung, G.K.: Issues in the computer-based assessment of collaborative problem solving. Assess. Educ.: Principles, Policy Pract. 10(3), 361–373 (2003). https://doi.org/10.1080/0969594032000148190

38. Agredo-Delgado, V., Ruiz, P.H., Mon, A., Collazos, C.A., Moreira, F., Fardoun, H.M.: Applying a process for the shared understanding construction in computer supported collaborative work: an experiment. Comput. Math. Organ. Theory, 1–24 (2021). https://doi.org/10.1007/s10588-021-09326-z

39. Zaraté, P.: Multi-criteria group decision support system: multi cultural experiments. In: de Almeida, A.T., Morais, D.C. (eds.) Innovation for Systems Information and Decision. Lecture Notes in Business Information Processing, vol. 405, pp. 47–61. Springer, Cham (2020). https://doi.org/10.1007/978-3-030-64399-7_4

Social Presence and User Experience: The Influence of the Immersive Virtual Classroom in Synchronous Distance Learning

Juan Fernando Flórez Marulanda[✉] ⓘ, Cesar A. Collazos ⓘ, and Julio Ariel Hurtado ⓘ

Universidad del Cauca, 190003 Popayán, Colombia
{jflorez,ccollazo,ahurtado}@unicauca.edu.co

Abstract. Previous research has examined student preferences for specific video styles in asynchronous and synchronous courses and social presence in online virtual courses. However, only some works have examined the social presence and user experience in synchronous distance learning courses delivered in an immersive or augmented reality classroom. This case study, using a sample of 198 students examines the design of video style used in a synchronous distance learning course mediated by an immersive virtual classroom (IVC) on the professor's social presence perceived by students, including other factors such as usability, communication, and reliability. The results showed that the immersive video style of the IVC used in streaming a synchronous remote classroom strongly and reciprocally conditioned students' perceptions of the professor's social presence. The results also established that the social presence in the IVC, enhanced by a video style that allows the communication of non-verbal immediacy responses, has an important influence on the perception of reliability and communication, while usability has a significant positive influence on the perception of communication, video style design and social presence. On the other hand, the professors' experience using IVC suggests that the visual design provides a sense of immersion but that there is still a need to improve the instructor-student interaction in its audio aspect.

Keywords: Social Presence · Immersive Virtual Classroom · Synchronous Video Style

1 Introduction

The Covid pandemic 19 forced videoconferencing platforms to become the main medium for supporting working meetings and remote education worldwide. While videoconferencing offers many benefits, such as the ability to see meeting participants or share screens, it still has limitations, such as restricted social interaction [1], which are compounded by technical issues such as sound delays and limited bandwidth for participants. Technical issues often result in webcams being turned off during remote synchronous meetings and classes. Webcam off is particularly important because it prevents viewing

© The Author(s), under exclusive license to Springer Nature Switzerland AG 2024
P. H. Ruiz et al. (Eds.): HCI-COLLAB 2023, CCIS 1877, pp. 286–300, 2024.
https://doi.org/10.1007/978-3-031-57982-0_22

faces and hidden body language and disrupts the conversation flow and social interaction [2]. Previous studies have found that instructor social presence is a crucial aspect in learning environments to increase student satisfaction and perceptions of learning [3–5]; in online technology-mediated education, a strong correlation between instructor verbal [6] and nonverbal [7] immediacy behaviors with instructor' social presence among their students has been demonstrated [8]. Huang in his work, demonstrated that instructor social presence affects intrinsic and extrinsic motivation in using messaging services in virtual learning environments [9]. According to Schutt [8], it has been noted since the 1970 s that "social presence" is partly a quality of the "communication media" through which immediacy behaviors are represented, with these "media" varying in the degree of social presence they can convey. Although videoconferencing is synchronous in time, it is not immediate in a strict sense, so according to Lindemann [10], videoconferencing can be characterized as a form of "mediated immediacy".

During the Covid19 pandemic, in synchronous meetings and classes context, Matthews et al., [11] used several Extended Reality (XR)-based solutions, taking advantage of the limitations identified in videoconferencing [12]. The main concern in these XR technologies was how to improve the presence of the interlocutor, but there is not yet agreement about how to interpret both, the concept of presence in XR and how to satisfactorily address the social challenges of remote presence [11]. Nebeling and his colleagues, in their work XRstudio [13], identified and solved some of the limitations associated with the high technical requirements and low usability of current XR educational technologies, aimed both at generating audiovisual educational resources and at conducting synchronous classes in XR. In the design of XRstudio, authors studied the design taxonomies in video styles that should be included in their proposal. However, they omitted the aspect of instructor social presence from their specifications [13]. This aspect, among others, will be the main barrier that XR solutions must overcome to spread this technology. An experiment developed during the Covid19 pandemic at the HCI laboratory of the University of Bremen showed the relevance of social presence, evaluating the perception of four virtual reality platforms against a videoconferencing platform over a four months period for selecting a collaborative meeting tool to be used further on [14]. Findings showed that the HCI researchers chose videoconferencing because it provided a more immersive experience by allowing them to see the faces and emotions of the people they were talking to, among other improvements in participation and co-presence. The inability to see the "real" faces and emotions of their peers was one of the critical factors in the decision of many participants in the experiment [14].

In the above context, this paper proposes to evaluate the perception of social presence of a professor in an Immersive Virtual Classroom (IVC) used during synchronous online classes among college students of the Universidad of Cauca-Colombia. IVC is an augmented reality videoconferencing environment for instructors that allows a synchronous online class with full HD transmission of a specific video style while students and instructor maintain an audio interaction as in a standard videoconference [15]. To the best of our knowledge, studies of social presence in augmented reality videoconferencing platforms in synchronous remote classrooms are scarce.

2 Background

A key aspect of videoconferencing is the design of the video style. This design feature was studied in asynchronous videos of recorded video lectures in MOOC (Massive Online Open Courses) courses context, in order to propose taxonomies of the different video designs used in MOOCs. The design of the video style is a relevant area of research in recent years, especially for asynchronous learning, where two taxonomies are currently proposed [13] and [16]. Among the review of multiple video styles described by Nebeling et al., in [13] and the research on video style satisfaction and learning gathered by Choe et al., in [16], there are more than sixteen video styles used in MOOC courses, summarized in this paper as eight:

1. Talking head (i.e., the miniature video of an instructor's torso next to the shared screen, typical of videoconferencing platforms) [13, 16],
2. Recording a live classroom lecture (i.e., recording a lecture from a student's perspective) [13, 16],
3. Interview (recording of a dialogue between two people) [13, 16],
4. Slides (slides of a lecture with narration) [13, 16],
5. Professor writing on a whiteboard (i.e., a sequence of an instructor drawing freehand on a surface) [13],
6. Screen recording (i.e., the computer screen sequence of an instructor explaining his or her lesson) [13],
7. Lightboard (recording of an instructor writing behind a transparent board) [16] and
8. Miscellaneous (e.g., custom animations, demo recordings, writing on slides with tablets, filming on location, etc.) [13, 16].

One conclusion from the research conducted by Choe et al., [16] is that students have strong preferences for certain video styles, even though their learning outcomes are the same. Video styles described by Choe et al., as impersonal, and unfamiliar were rated low, while those described as personal, engaging, and evoking positive affective responses were rated high [16]. Research measuring satisfaction with live video streaming styles in synchronous learning is still lacking. At the Universidad of Cauca, we evaluated four video styles used in synchronous distance learning: a) talking head, b) speaker next to slide, c) speaker inside slide, and d) lightboard [17]. One finding in [17] is that styles c) and d) were the most satisfying to students and recommended for use in synchronous sessions. Style c) Speaker inside slide is a streaming video for synchronous sessions; it is particularly remarkable because it involves a live composition of the instructor's video with modified slides of the material being taught, with the instructor appearing behind the slides [17]. Thanks to the visual feedback of this composition, the instructor can interact with the material on the slides and experience a sense of "immersion" in the material being taught, which allows this type of video to be interpreted as a form of augmented reality [15].

2.1 Immersive Virtual Classroom - IVC

IVC is a videoconferencing platform that incorporates an augmented reality component into the material used by a lecturer in a synchronous session, allowing the production of educational instructional videos. It does not require any post-production time and was developed during the Covid19 pandemic at the University of Cauca [15] (see Fig. 1).

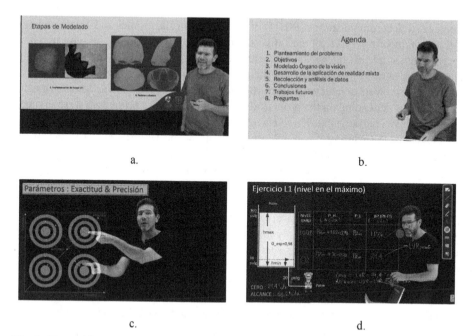

a.

b.

c.

d.

Fig. 1. Type of live streaming video in IVC: a) Speaker next to slide, b) Speaker in front of slide, c) Speaker inside slide, d) Speaker writing on slides.

IVC performs a live composition of the slides' audiovisual material with the instructor's video, allowing the instructor interacts via online with the material being taught through a feedback monitor. Simultaneously, students see the instructor live in full HD quality (1920 x 1080 pixels) and interact with him via audio using a conventional videoconferencing platform.

Four characteristics determine the functionality of IVC in a synchronous remote classroom between an instructor and their students: a) interactions, b) IVC modes, c) live streaming architecture, and d) video style used [15]. IVC has four live streaming video layouts: a) speaker next to the slide, b) speaker in front of the slide, c) speaker behind the slide, and d) speaker writing on the slides (see Fig. 1). Each design style presents different levels of interaction and augmented reality, and requires different levels of audiovisual conditioning.

3 Method

The study included the evaluation of twelve synchronous classes delivered in IVC on the part of inviting participants, who complete a questionnaire after each class. A mixed methods approach was used to collect quantitative and qualitative data to explore participants' perceptions of each IVC experience and their observations.

3.1 Courses and Participants

The study extended students and professors from twelve courses of different semesters of three engineering programs (Industrial Automation (PIAI), Systems (PIS), and Electronics & Telecommunications (PIET)) of the Faculty of Electronics and Telecommunications Engineering (FIET) of the Universidad of Cauca (Colombia). This gave us a heterogeneous sample of college students with previous experience with videoconferencing platforms or currently using them for their synchronous classes.

The classes were conducted by lecture-based courses, with slight variations in teaching dynamics depending on the professor's style. Sixteen FIET professors were invited, of whom eleven participated. These eleven professors performed twelve distance learning classes in IVC during a compulsory virtuality at the Universidad of Cauca from Tuesday 16 May, to Tuesday 6 June due a to a chickenpox outbreak. The professors (two women and nine men) have an average age of 40.82 (with a standard deviation - SD 9.43) years and an average of experience of 13.27 (SD 7.75) years. Each evaluated lesson of the twelve courses conducted in IVC had an average duration of 59.17 (SD 13.44) minutes and presented an average of 23.08 (SD 7.25) students (see Table 1). All participating courses set as typically taught in a traditional classroom had a duration of ten weeks of face-to-face (F2F) instruction. All professors had previous experience with videoconferencing platforms to support their synchronous teaching due to the Covid19 pandemic.

Each professor decided the course as part of the test, who agreed to teach a distance lesson in IVC. However, completion of the survey was voluntary for students. The survey collected relevant demographic data such as age and gender: the average age of the students who responded to the survey is 21.48 (SD 3.68) years, 18.18% are female, and 81.82% are male. Students indicated their previous experience with videoconferencing platforms. There were 277 participants, with 198 different students responding to the survey. Each class had a minimum of eleven and a maximum of 33 students. The total population of FIET students in the first semester of 2023 was 1785.

3.2 Procedure and Questionnaire

We designed and delivered an instructor's manual and an interaction protocol for students in IVC. A few days before the synchronous IVC lesson, each professor explained to their students the interaction protocol to be used in IVC. In this protocol, professor gave instruction to the students for watching the live streaming on a computer/laptop with a suitable size monitor/screen, to use a hands-free device, to ask questions freely during the lesson, to keep their webcam turned off, and not to leave their microphone open during the lesson. Each professor given a 30-min IVC introduction before the lesson so that he could interact with the teaching material, position himself spatially in the context of the slides, and know how to use the feedback monitor. Finally, professors are advised to look at the video camera regularly, especially when students ask questions.

After each lesson, the professor shared a link to an online questionnaire with the students via the videoconferencing platform chat (or sent an email). Each receiver could decide whether to participate in the survey, resulting in an average response rate of

Table 1. Summary of the twelve synchronous online classes performed in IVC.

Cod	Participating course	Program	Students	Answers	Class duration [min]
C1	*Sistemas de Control Continuo A*	PIET	29	24	53
C2	*Máquinas Eléctricas*	PIAI	22	17	54
C3	*Comunicaciones Móviles*	PIET	11	10	67
C4	*Teoría de la Computación*	PIS	33	29	50
C5	*Ingeniería de Software II*	PIS	29	13	55
C6	*Circuitos Analógicos III*	PIET	19	11	58
C7	*Sistemas de Control Continuo B*	PIET	21	15	98
C8	*Programación Orientada a Objetos A*	PIS	31	13	62
C9	*Programación Orientada a Objetos B*	PIS	25	21	62
C10	*Sistemas Avanzados de Manufactura*	PIAI	28	18	50
C11	*Ingeniería de Producto*	PIAI	16	14	50
C12	*Cálculo Vectorial*	PIET	13	13	51

71.48%. Students were not pressured to complete the survey to avoid negative consequences for insincere responses. The questionnaire began with an informed consent. Then the questionnaire asked about previous experience with videoconferencing platforms, which 90.9% of the participants had. Next question was about the devices they used to view the course in IVC, revealing that 56.06% viewed on a PC with a monitor smaller than 20 inches, 29.80% on a PC with a monitor larger than 20 inches, 9.59% on a smartphone, 4.04% on a smart TV, and 0.51% on a laptop.

The study used an instrument that collected quantitative data for evaluating the acceptance of a virtual leaning environment based on Moodle validated by Santana et al., [18] and developed by Ruiz and Romero [19]. The instrument included five factors: communication, design, usability, general aspects, and reliability, with fifteen items, three for each factor. Adapting the instrument for augmented reality videoconferencing platforms in synchronous remote classrooms retains the communication, design, usability, and reliability factors, with the wording of each item modified or adapted to the IVC (see Table 2). We discard the General Aspects factor and add the Social Presence factor. To determine the three items associated with the new factor, we conducted a review of the high immediacy behaviors (video, audio, and text) suggested by Schutt et al., in [8] for specifically selecting the video immediacy behaviors to be mapped into three items for the IVC-mediated social presence factor (see Table 2). A seven-point Likert scale (1-Totally Disagree, 2-Significantly Disagree, 3-Disagree, 4-Neutral, 5-Agree, 6-Significantly Agree, 7-Totally Agree) was used to answer each of the fifteen items.

Table 2. Latent factors and items used to assess IVC in synchronous classes.

Communication (C)	I find that IVC facilitates communication between professor and student
	I think IVC facilitates communication between students
	All the digital tools (YouTube, Meet, Classroom) used in IVC are valuable
Design of Video Style (D)	Seeing the professor next to the slides was helpful for the class
	The size of the slides and the space occupied by the professor are adequate
	Full HD quality transmissions were helpful for the class
Usability (U)	I find IVC easy to use
	I find the IVC communication protocol to be intuitive
	The professor-student interaction provided by IVC is acceptable and helpful to the learning process
Social presence (S)	During the lesson, the professor was able to express emotions
	With IVC, it is possible to see the different gestures made by the professor during the lesson
	During the lesson, the professor physically highlighted interesting information
Reliability (R)	I had connection problems during the development of the IVC class
	I had audio problems during the IVC class
	I got through the whole class without any technical problems

In addition, the questionnaire includes open-ended questions about observations about the advantages and disadvantages of remote instruction in IVC compared to traditional F2F or remote instruction on a traditional videoconferencing platform.

3.3 Data Analysis

The study ran twelve remote synchronous lessons in IVC during an unexpected period of virtuality at the Universidad of Cauca. Therefore, from all possible combinations of the four IVC characteristics, we set values that would allow the participation of the greatest number of professors (speaker next to slide) and the geographical dispersion of students during that period (distributed) (see Table 3).

The support platforms in IVC during the twelve classes the study used: YouTube for streaming, Google Meets for traditional videoconferencing, and Google Forms for survey.

In addition to demographic information, the survey collected quantitative data in fifteen questions (see Table 2) and qualitative information (responses to open-ended questions) in four questions. The quantitative data were analyzed using a modified and

Table 3. Features configured to evaluate IVC in the twelve synchronous remote classes.

IVC Feature	Value
Interaction	Instructor-taught material and Instructor-Student
IVC mode	Distributed (webcams off)
Live streaming architecture	Video server: one-to-many
Video style	Speaker next to slide

reduced structural equation model proposed by Santana-Mancilla et al., in [18] (see Fig. 2 a). In this model, the factor Social Presence (S) is highlighted to determine its perception of the factors: Usability (U), Communication (C), Design of Video Style (D) and Reliability (R). The questionnaire's qualitative data were analyzed using thematic analysis by identifying similarities and inductively creating word clouds. The study collected one hundred ninety-eight responses with qualitative data and the questionnaire items. The structural equation model (see Fig. 2 a) proposes to research and analyze the following hypotheses in IVC:

H1. **U** influences students' perceived **C**.
H2. **D** influences students' perceived **C**.
H3. The instructor's **S** influences students' perceived **C**.
H4. **R** influences students' perceived **C**.
H5. **U** influences **D**.
H6. Students' perceived **C** influences **D**.
H7. **R** influences **D**.
H8. The instructor's **S** influences **D**.
H9. **U** influences **R**.
H10. Students' perceived **C** influences **R**.
H11. The instructor's **S** influences **R**.
H12. **D** influences **R**.
H13. **U** influences the instructor's **S**.
H14. Students' perceived **C** influences the instructor's **S**.
H15. **R** influences the instructor's **S**.
H16. Instructor's **S** is influenced by **D**.

We ran a statistical processing of the quantitative data and the graphical processing of the open-ended questions performed using the R program, for building the structural model to support the hypotheses, while we used the word clouds for providing a graphical summary of answers to the open-ended questions.

4 Results and Discussion

The 15-question questionnaire obtained a Cronbach's alpha coefficient of 0.890, indicating high reliability of the students' answers. The resampling of the data by bootstrapping (generation of 5000 subsamples) allows a statistical analysis of the data and the verification of the proposed hypotheses. The arc weights obtained from the proposed structural model (see Fig. 2 b) and the p-value obtained for each hypothesis (see Table 4) with an alpha of 0.05 show that all sixteen hypotheses are accepted. In each factor, one arc has a higher weight than the others.

According to findings (see Fig. 2 b), in the communication factor, there is a significant positive effect of usability (H1, $\beta = 0.7912$), social presence (H3, $\beta = 0.5926$) and style design (H2, $\beta = 0.4572$) on the perception of communication. The result related to H1 is an already known relationship, as mentioned by Redish in [20], where he gives an account of the mutual influence between usability and communication. Similarly, the work of Yammiyavar et al., [21] illustrates the relationship between social presence and communication.

Table 4. Arcs with their IVC structural equation model weights

Arc	Weight (β)	SD	t-stat	P-Value	Confidence Interval 95%
C~U	0.7912	0.0859	9.2142	>0.0001	[0.6592;0.8222]
C~D	0.4572	0.0095	48.0936	>0.0001	[0.1550;0.1723]
C~R	0.2059	0.0607	3.3918	0.0007	[0.0848;0.1992]
C~S	0.5926	0.0991	5.9800	>0.0001	[0.1213;0.2968]
D~U	0.7653	0.0239	31.9560	>0.0001	[0.7379;0.7812]
D~C	0.4158	0.0282	14.7555	>0.0001	[0.1242;0.1709]
D~R	0.2067	0.0200	10.3454	>0.0001	[0.0550;0.0880]
D~S	0.8913	0.1408	6.3319	>0.0001	[0.2557;0.5179]
R~U	0.3571	0.0701	5.0930	>0.0001	[0.2323;0.3648]
R~C	0.5090	0.1023	4.9744	>0.0001	[0.2155;0.3950]
R~D	0.5618	0.0650	8.6393	>0.0001	[0.1086;0.2321]
R~S	0.7735	0.0824	9.3850	>0.0001	[0.4020;0.5551]
S~U	0.7374	0.0763	9.6665	>0.0001	[0.6548;0.7924]
S~C	0.5387	0.0962	5.6012	>0.0001	[0.1013;0.2827]
S~D	0.8909	0.1135	7.8483	>0.0001	[0.2895;0.4960]
S~R	0.2845	0.0604	4.7094	>0.0001	[0.1806;0.2950]

In the perception of video style design, the results confirmed a significant positive effect of social presence (H8, $\beta = 0.8913$), usability (H5, $\beta = 0.7653$), and communication (H6, $\beta = 0.4158$) on the perception of video style design. A result supporting hypothesis H8 is presented in the work of Choe et al., [16] when it is indicated that those video styles described as engaging and evoke positive affective responses score high. A similar result in support of H8 is found in [17] when the "lightboard and speaker inside slide" video styles were the preferred by students.

The results confirmed a significant positive effect of social presence (H11, $\beta = 0.7735$), video style design (H12, $\beta = 0.5618$), and communication (H10, $\beta = 0.5090$) on perceived trustworthiness. Similarly, the results confirmed a significant positive effect of video style design (H16, β = 0.8909), usability (H13, β = 0.7374), and communication (H14, β = 0.5387) on perceived social presence.

Hypothesis H8 (β = 0.8913) and H16 (β = 0.8909) form the highest weighted arcs of the model, confirming a strong perceived mutual relationship between social presence and video style design used. Hypothesis H11 (β = 0.7735) indicates that social presence has a strong positive influence on the perceived reliability of IVC, but also on video style design (H12, β = 0.5618) and communication (H10, β = 0.5090). Finally, hypotheses H1 (β = 0.7912), H5 (β = 0.7653), and H13 (β = 0.7374) indicate that usability in IVC has a significant positive impact on perceptions of communication, video style design, and social presence.

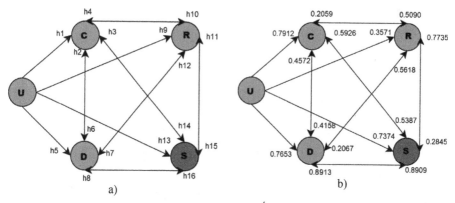

Fig. 2. Structural equation model for IVC of five latent factors: U (Usability), D (Design of Video style), S (Social presence), C (Communication) and R (Reliability) with a) arcs evaluated and b) arcs with their weights.

Analyzing the word clouds of students' open-ended responses regarding the perceived disadvantages of IVC compared to F2F classroom (see Fig. 3 a) and traditional virtual classroom (see Fig. 3 b), the general disadvantage of IVC is the audio delay that hinders student-instructor interaction. Another disadvantage of IVC compared to the F2F classroom (see Fig. 3 a) is the poor Internet connection, which directly affects the quality of student-instructor interaction. On the other hand, regarding the disadvantages of IVC compared to the conventional virtual classroom (see Fig. 3 b), most students emphasize that there is no disadvantage.

When analyzing the word clouds of students' open-ended responses regarding the perceived advantages of IVC over F2F and traditional virtual classrooms (see Fig. 4), the general advantage is "seeing" the professor. Two other perceived advantages of IVC over F2F classroom (see Fig. 4 a) are instructor interaction with slides and recording of lectures. On the other hand, regarding the advantages of IVC over conventional virtual classroom (see Fig. 4 b), most students emphasize the video quality and perceive the "gestures" of the professor.

Regarding the user experience of the professors participating in IVC, their students were not forced to turn on their webcams in any course (during the Covid19 pandemic this was common practice at the Universidad of Cauca to avoid connection problems),

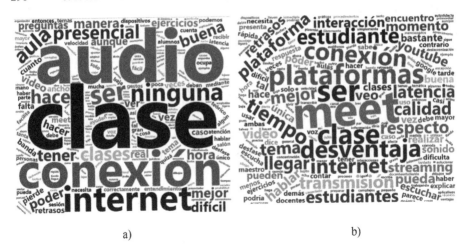

a)   b)

Fig. 3. Disadvantages IVC with a) F2F classroom and b) Conventional virtual classroom

a)   b)

Fig. 4. Advantages IVC with a) F2F classroom and b) Conventional virtual classroom

so during this period of virtuality it was not required either. This meant that there was no video feedback from the students to the professor, but he could see the matrix window of the videoconferencing platform on a second monitor and hear them over a speaker system. Although researchers encouraged to professors to motivate their students to ask questions during the lecture, most limited themselves to a typical lecture. At the end of the lecture, each professor asked if there were any doubts, and for achieving an instructor-student interaction; however, there were some cases when students sporadically activated their microphones to ask questions, where the professor stopped his lecture to answer the question.

In the professors' user experience with IVC, the analysis of their answers to the fifteen questions identified aspects related to usability (questions 7, 8, and 9), visual design (questions 4, 5, and 6), and interaction design (questions 1, 2, 3, 9, and 14) (see Fig. 5). In terms of usability, the trend in the heat map is positive, although this is an aspect that needs further work, along with improving the communication protocol. Over 50% of professors felt that IVC-mediated instructor-student interaction was at an acceptable level. Regarding the visual design, they consider that the technology allows a level of immersion and, together with the full HD transmission, both were useful for their teaching. In terms of interaction design, it is unclear to them whether IVC allows for student-student interaction. However, they agree that it facilitates instructor-student interaction, although the audio delay aspect needs to be improved.

Finally, from the analysis of the open-ended responses of the professors regarding the advantages of IVC, the use of corporal language during the virtual class is highlighted, which is related to hypotheses H8 and H16. Professors also mention that IVC is a novel method that motivates students. On the other hand, regarding the disadvantages of IVC, they mention that there is "more" social interaction in a F2F classroom. Also, the Internet connection for students to participate in IVC and the software and hardware resources needed to run an IVC class are perceived as disadvantages.

Likert Scale	Question 1	Question 2	Question 3	Question 4	Question 5	Question 6	Question 7	Question 8	Question 9	Question 10	Question 11	Question 12	Question 13	Question 14	Question 15
	IVC facilitates T-S communication	IVC facilitates S-S communication	Youtube, Meet and Classroom are valuable for IVC	Immersion in the slides is useful for the classroom	Slide size and teacher space facilitates immersion	Full HD transmission is useful for the lecture	IVC is easy to use	IVC communication protocol is intuitive	T-S interaction is acceptable	I expressed emotions in my class	I manifested gestures in my class	I highlighted information bodily	I experienced connection problems in the lecture	I experienced audio problems in the lecture	I experienced technical problems in the lecture
TD	0,0	0,0	0,0	0,0	0,0	0,0	0,0	0,0	0,0	0,0	0,0	0,0	45,5	45,5	0,0
SD	9,1	9,1	0,0	0,0	0,0	0,0	0,0	0,0	0,0	0,0	0,0	0,0	9,1	18,2	0,0
D	0,0	9,1	0,0	0,0	0,0	0,0	0,0	0,0	0,0	0,0	0,0	0,0	27,3	9,1	0,0
NT	0,0	36,4	0,0	0,0	18,2	9,1	0,0	9,1	9,1	9,1	0,0	0,0	9,1	9,1	0,0
A	27,3	9,1	0,0	18,2	18,2	18,2	36,4	27,3	54,5	27,3	18,2	9,1	9,1	18,2	18,2
SA	45,5	27,3	45,5	27,3	45,5	9,1	36,4	27,3	18,2	36,4	45,5	45,5	0,0	0,0	27,3
TA	18,2	9,1	54,5	54,5	18,2	63,6	27,3	36,4	18,2	27,3	36,4	45,5	0,0	0,0	54,5

Fig. 5. Heat map of professors' percentage responses to quantitative questions about their user experience in IVC.

5   Conclusions, Limitations, and Further Work

This study provides valuable information about the user experiences of students and professors who used an augmented reality videoconferencing platform in a synchronous online class. Questionnaires were used to collect responses to closed-ended Likert-scale and open-ended questions related to usability, communication, design of video style, reliability, social presence, and pros and cons concerning web videoconferencing and F2F teaching.

The quantitative analysis confirms that the design of the video style used in the synchronous remote classroom streaming with IVC strongly and reciprocally conditions the students' perception of the professor's social presence. Furthermore, the social presence enhanced by a video style that allows for the communication of nonverbal immediacy responses has an important influence on perceptions of reliability and communication. IVC usability significantly influences perceptions of communication, video style design, and social presence. The qualitative analysis of the students' responses shows that the main disadvantage compared to the F2F classroom is that the audio delay affects the instructor-student interaction in IVC. In contrast, there are no perceived disadvantages compared to the traditional virtual classroom delivered via videoconferencing. On the other hand, IVC has advantages over traditional videoconferencing: "seeing" the professor, "perceiving" his gestures, interacting in augmented reality with slides and high-quality video generated, and regarding the F2F classroom, students identify as advantages of IVC: the interaction with slides and the recording of lectures.

Professors' experience with IVC shows that more than half of them find the instructor-student interaction via IVC acceptable, but that audio delays should be addressed. According to the heat map, usability shows a positive trend but needs to be improved. In terms of visual design, they feel that IVC provides a sense of immersion in the slides, and that this and full HD transmission are two useful features for a synchronous remote class. A general benefit of IVC identified by professors is the use of corporal language in the online classroom. Interestingly, professors indicate that there is more social interaction in the F2F classroom. However, the practice conducted in IVC was mostly a typical lecture, with limited or no instructor-student interaction during most of the time devoted to the online class. This common practice suggests that instructor-student interaction, mediated or not by technology in general, is also influenced by professors' practices, regardless of the type of classroom in which the class is held.

This study there are some limitations. First, the study examined students' perceptions of their professor's social presence mediated by the IVC. The researchers in this study developed the technology during the COVID19 pandemic and evaluated perceptions based on feedback from students in three engineering programs. However, the technology has not yet been evaluated by experts outside the university. Second, the study did not randomly select students, nor were the participating courses homogeneously distributed across semesters. Third, the primary method for the study was survey research. The high number of participants across twelve courses, good survey-response rate, the novelty effect and both quantitative and qualitative data could have raised the likelihood that the student responses are a useful outcome variable in this study. Nonetheless, the doubts about the reliability of student surveys imply that others assessment measures ought to corroborate our findings. Finally, we have not yet examined how students' perceptions of their teacher's social presence mediated by an IVC affect their learning performance.

The study shows the importance of explicitly identifying the distinctive characteristics involved in designing technologies such as IVC to ensure a good user experience for professors and students. The results indicate the need to redesign IVC using user-centered design approaches, considering their characteristics, and defining appropriate profiles for students and professors. A next step to improve is to conduct formal usability measurements and integrate the student Social Presence component into IVC.

Empirical studies of the impact of immersive technologies such as IVC on learning outcomes are currently needed. These studies should determine not only which technological features, but also which synchronous and asynchronous teaching-learning processes have the best impact on learning outcomes. Finally, it is envisioned to implement future experimental designs where concepts such as instructor-student social presence, engagement, awareness, and augmented reality are integrated into IVC to better impact learning outcomes.

References

1. Bauman, O., Sander, L.: 5 reasons why Zoom meetings are so exhausting. The Conversation. https://theconversation.com/5-reasons-why-zoom-meetings-are-so-exhausting-137404
2. Venter, E.: Challenges for meaningful interpersonal communication in a digital era. HTS Teol. Stud. **75**(1), 1–6 (2019). https://doi.org/10.4102/hts.v75i1.5339
3. Gunawardena, C.N., Zittle, F.J.: Social presence as a predictor of satisfaction within a computer-mediated conferencing environment. Am. J. Distance Educ. **11**(3), 8–26 (1997). https://doi.org/10.1080/08923649709526970
4. Picciano, A.G.: Beyond student perceptions: issues of interaction, presence, and performance in an online course. J. Asynchronous Learn. Netw. **6**(1), 21–40 (2002)
5. Richardson, J.C., Swan, K.: Examining social presence in online courses in relation to students' perceived learning and satisfaction, no. 1. State University of New York at Albany (2001)
6. Gorham, J.: The relationship between verbal teacher immediacy behaviors and student learning. Commun. Educ. **37**(1), 40–53 (1988). https://doi.org/10.1080/03634528809378702
7. Richmond, V.P., Gorham, J.S., McCroskey, J.C.: The relationship between selected immediacy behaviors and cognitive learning. Ann. Int. Commun. Assoc. **10**(1), 574–590 (1987). https://doi.org/10.1080/23808985.1987.11678663
8. Schutt, M., Allen, B.S., Laumakis, M.A.: The effects of instructor immediacy behaviors in online learning environments. Q. Rev. Distance Educ. **10**(2), 135 (2009)
9. Huang, Y.M.: Exploring students' acceptance of team messaging services: the roles of social presence and motivation. Br. J. Educ. Technol. **48**(4), 1047–1061 (2017). https://doi.org/10.1111/bjet.12468
10. Lindemann, G., Schünemann, D.: Presence in digital spaces. A phenomenological concept of presence in mediatized communication. Hum. Stud. **43**(4), 627–651 (2020). https://doi.org/10.1007/s10746-020-09567-y
11. Matthews, B., See, Z.S., Day, J.: Crisis and extended realities: remote presence in the time of COVID-19. Media Int. Aust. **178**(1), 198–209 (2021). https://doi.org/10.1177/1329878X20967165
12. Aagaard, J.: On the dynamics of Zoom fatigue. Convergence **28**(6), 1878–1891 (2022). https://doi.org/10.1177/13548565221099711
13. Nebeling, M., Rajaram, S., Wu, L., Cheng, Y., Herskovitz, J.: Xrstudio: a virtual production and live streaming system for immersive instructional experiences. In: Proceedings of the 2021 CHI Conference on Human Factors in Computing Systems, pp. 1–12 (2021). https://api.semanticscholar.org/CorpusID:233986933
14. Bonfert, M., et al.: Seeing the faces is so important—experiences from online team meetings on commercial virtual reality platforms. Front. Virtual Real. **3**, 945791 (2023). https://doi.org/10.3389/frvir.2022.945791

15. Marulanda, J.F.F.: Modelo de Aula Virtual Inmersiva para un Ambiente de Aprendizaje Sincrónico Mixto. In: Libro de actas TAEE 2022 XV Congreso de Tecnología, Aprendizaje y Enseñanza de la Electrónica: Livro de procedimentos TAEE 2022 XV Conferência em Tecnologia, Aprendizagem e Ensino da Eletrónica= Proceedings book TAEE 2022 XV International Conference of Technology, Learning and Teaching of Electronics (p. 93). Escuela Universitaria Politécnica de Teruel (2022)

16. Choe, R.C., et al.: Student satisfaction and learning outcomes in asynchronous online lecture videos. CBE Life Sci. Educ. 18(4), ar55 (2019). https://doi.org/10.1187/cbe.18-08-0171

17. Marulanda, J.F.F.: Student satisfaction pilot experience with synchronous classroom live streaming styles during the COVID-19 pandemic. IEEE Rev. Iberoam. Tecnol. Aprendiz. 17(3), 301–306 (2022). https://api.semanticscholar.org/CorpusID:250567627

18. Santana-Mancilla, P.C., Montesinos-López, O.A., Garcia-Ruiz, M.A., Contreras-Castillo, J.J., Gaytan-Lugo, L.S.: Validación de un instrumento para medir la aceptación tecnológica de un entorno virtual de aprendizaje. Acta Universitaria 29 (2019). https://doi.org/10.15174/au.2019.1796

19. Ruiz, I., Romero, S.: Moodle: una herramienta eficaz aplicada a la enseñanza de las prácticas, en el área de electrónica y arquitectura de los computadores. In: VIII Congreso de Tecnologías Aplicadas a la Enseñanza de la Electrónica, p. 165 (2008)

20. Redish, J.: Technical communication and usability: intertwined strands and mutual influences. IEEE Trans. Prof. Commun. 53(3), 191–201 (2010). https://doi.org/10.1109/TPC.2010.2052861

21. Yammiyavar, P., Clemmensen, T., Kumar, J.: Influence of cultural background on non-verbal communication in a usability testing situation. Int. J. Des. 2(2), 31–40 (2008). www.ijdesign.org

The Adoption of Industry 4.0 Practices for Small and Medium-Sized Companies: A Systematic Mapping Study

Gabriel Batista Cristiano[1] [ID], Fabio Tanikawa[1] [ID], Huizilopoztli Luna García[2] [ID], and Maria Amelia Eliseo[1]([✉]) [ID]

[1] Laboratório de Tecnologias Interativas (TecInt), Universidade Presbiteriana Mackenzie, São Paulo, SP 01239-001, Brazil
`gabriel.cristiano@mackenzista.com.br,`
`mariaamelia.eliseo@mackenzie.br`
[2] Laboratorio de Tecnologías Interactivas y Experiencia de Usuario (LITUX), Universidad Autónoma de Zacatecas, Jardín Juárez 147, Centro Histórico, 98000 Zacatecas, Mexico
`hlugar@uaz.edu.mx`

Abstract. Small and medium-sized companies play a very important role in the Brazilian productive sector, covering around 98% of the total number of companies, being responsible for the advancement of the economy and the employability of the urban population. However, Brazilian small and medium-sized companies have little support to survive and develop and are still unaware of the digital transformation promoted by industry 4.0, which often leaves them at a competitive disadvantage. This article systematically maps the literature regarding the adoption of Industry 4.0 practices by small and medium-sized companies. The article analyzes journals, identifies and evaluates studies on Industry 4.0. The research was carried out in some stages, starting with the definition of the research question, bibliographic research, selection of studies and data extraction, analysis and synthesis of results. Finally, procedures are indicated to guide the transformation process of these companies through technological solutions, employee training, integrated management systems and skills development. The study resulted in the selection of nineteen articles, which indicate that, when it comes to Industry 4.0 studies and best practice reports, there is still a lack of relevant publications in the white literature and even in the gray literature.

Keywords: industry 4.0 · small and medium-sized companies · systematic mapping · adoption of practices · reference guide

1 Introduction

With the advancement of technology and the digitization of products and services, the way of doing business and consuming has also changed in recent years and, this update of the means of production became known as the fourth industrial revolution or Industry 4.0. Since then, a series of studies have been carried out to understand Industry 4.0

and its impacts on companies that adopt this new production model. Although industry 4.0 is superficially known for the adoption of recent technologies such as Internet of Things (IoT), cloud computing, big data, Artificial Intelligence (AI), digital twins, sensors, among others, it is bigger than that; a better definition of the term is presented by Palmeira et al. (2022) who define Industry 4.0 as an ecosystem built by the set of various interconnected multidisciplinary technological systems and innovations, capable of sending and receiving information quickly, promoting the automation of the decision-making process and, consequently, highlighting the multidisciplinary character of Industry 4.0.

In Brazil, industry 4.0 is still in the development phase, "being far behind compared to other countries" (Passos, 2020). According to the Brazilian Agency for Industrial Development (ABDI, 2021), less than 2% of companies are immersed in Industry 4.0, and 40% of Brazilian companies do not have a defined budget for the implementation of IT (Information Technology) projects. However, a survey by the Federation of Industries of the State of São Paulo (FIESP, 2018) indicates that the degree of knowledge of companies with an industrial focus on the concept of era 4.0 is increasing (TOTVS, 2022).

When analyzing the panorama of Brazilian production, we see that small businesses were responsible for 27% of the national Gross Domestic Product (GDP), according to a survey carried out by the Brazilian Support Service for Micro and Small Companies (SEBRAE, 2021). In addition, in 2021, around 4 million new ventures were opened, breaking the record for this historical series (SEBRAE, 2021). Therefore, the importance of the participation of small businesses in the Brazilian economy is evident, whether through the value generated or the opportunities for job openings. It is also important to promote the digital transformation of these companies so that they are not alienated from the innovations promoted by industry 4.0 and become even more relevant and competitive in the Brazilian market. For this, small and medium-sized companies need to know the potential of adopting new technologies and acquire the necessary knowledge to implement the enabled initiatives of the Industry 4.0 ecosystem. Thus, the objective of this article is to show the results of a literature mapping that shows the panorama of existing guides and guidelines that indicate ways for the adoption of new technologies in different sectors of the company, so that, in the future, to offer to Small and Medium Companies (SMEs) an explanatory guide to start and manage the Industry 4.0 adoption process. With this, SMEs can increase their competitiveness, operational efficiency and have sustainable growth.

This article is warranted as follows: Sect. 2 introduces tools and work related to the topic of the article. Section 3 presents a detailed explanation of the systematic mapping process. Section 4 presents the results achieved by the work. Section 5 shows the research limitations, and the last Sect. 6 presents the conclusion of this work.

2   Theoretical Reference

This section presents the definitions and concepts used in the construction of this work.

2.1 Industry 4.0 and the Situation of Small and Medium-Sized Companies in Brazil

According to Laurent and Monsone (2019), industry 4.0 should be seen as a complex and dynamic ecosystem, composed of different actors and interconnected elements. Industry 4.0 emerged to face the competitiveness of Asian industry, it was probably proposed by the German government in 2011, to promote the digitization of manufacturing and leverage European industry. This represents the fourth industrial revolution. Within the industry 4.0 ecosystem, all involved technologies and individuals are capable of generating and disseminating data, managing information, and optimizing technological resources, ultimately fostering a novel culture of innovation. Also, according to Laurent and Monsone (2019), the vision of the Industry 4.0 ecosystem can help overcome the challenges of digital transformation and the integration of automation and Artificial Intelligence to improve daily tasks.

Palmeira et al. (2022) and Hidayatno et al. (2019), define industry 4.0 as a phase of revolution and transformation, defined by connectivity, digitization, allowing easy access to data, and consequently the automation of the decision-making process. This industry would be formed by the combination of several technologies, such as cyber-physical systems, IoT, and Big data, for example. The problem that Palmeira et al. (2022) sets out to understand is the transformation process of legacy industries, those industries with production models prior to the innovations of Industry 4.0, towards the fourth industrial revolution. Industry 4.0 is also characterized by rapid communication in production itself, as company data can be sent and received from anywhere in the factory. With this, the migration of legacy companies can occur with or without changes in the production line.

Digital transformation has become a relevant topic in discussions about innovation and business management. It refers to the process by which organizations adopt and integrate digital technologies into their operations, seeking to improve efficiency, competitiveness, and value creation (Brasil, 2023). While digital transformation offers opportunities for businesses, its implementation also faces significant challenges. A study carried out by Gaspar (2022) in the hotel sector of São Luís-MA highlights the obstacles and challenges faced by managers of small companies in this process. Among the challenges identified are resistance to change, lack of technical knowledge and limited financial resources.

Eliseo et al. (2022) consider that "[…] the means and small companies are responsible for a large part of production in Brazil and which, inversely proportional, use little or no technology" which compromises the potential of these companies to become even more relevant on the national scene. Eliseo et al. (2022) also points out that to encourage the digital transformation of these companies requires a joint effort between public and private entities and the participation of professionals in the area to guide the approach to small and medium-sized entrepreneurs on the journey of digital maturity.

2.2 Literature Mapping

Systematic mapping is a research methodology that seeks to provide an overview of a research area, through the identification and categorization of the amount and types of research and available results (Petersen et al. 2008). Getting the picture of a research area is done through a five-step guideline. Each step generates a result that leads to the next phase of the process.

The relationship between the steps of the Systematic Mapping (SM) process and the results generated in each phase performed in this article is established according to the Fig. 1, based on the Petersen (2008) systematic mapping representation.

Process steps

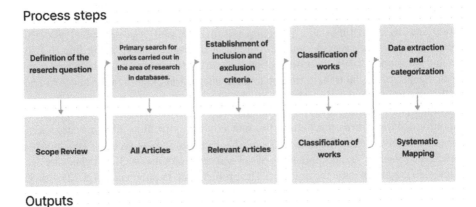

Outputs

Fig. 1. Process Steps of Systematic Mapping. Adapted from Petersen (2008).

Falbo (2018) highlights that systematic mapping is a high-quality classification methodology. However, one must be aware that, if not familiar with this technique, SM can become a time-consuming process. He also recommends the involvement of multiple researchers during the classification and evaluation of works related to the research topic, as this methodology is subject to varying classifications for the same research topic, depending on the researchers involved.

2.3 Related Works

Among the references used in this work, the contribution of Eliseo et al. (2022) stands out, which provides a starting point by carrying out an analysis of the available literature on the development of Industry 4.0 within the scope of small and medium-sized companies in Brazil. Eliseo et al. (2022) report that the development of industry 4.0 in Brazil is still in its initial phase, still restricted to the reality of large companies, however, when analyzing the country's productive context, it highlights the role played by small and large companies, and that promoting digital transformation in these companies is to ensure that they are updated in relation to the global market, making them more competitive. The authors also argue that in order to overcome the barriers present in the insertion of small and medium-sized companies in the 4.0 Industry, such as the high costs of technologies and the lack of knowledge about the benefits of adopting Industry 4.0 practices by small and medium-sized companies entrepreneurs, it is necessary to create joint initiatives between public and private organizations, and professionals in the area of computing, management and even in the area of Human-Computer Interaction (HCI) to prepare and guide these companies in their transformation.

The work by Silva and Campos (2019) proposes a systematic review of the literature on Industry 4.0, in order to identify its main discoveries, trends and applications. The methodology used involved the search for scientific articles in relevant databases, the careful selection of studies that met the inclusion criteria and the analysis of results. The authors highlight the main findings found, such as the integration of production systems, the use of technologies such as the Internet of Things (IoT) and artificial intelligence, and the associated benefits, such as increased efficiency, cost reduction and quality improvement. In addition, emerging trends in Industry 4.0 are identified, such as mass personalization, human-machine collaboration, and the adoption of platform-based business models. The results of the study provide a comprehensive and up-to-date view of Industry 4.0, helping researchers, professionals and decision makers to understand and apply this concept in various industry sectors.

Passos (2020) addresses the foundations and impacts of Industry 4.0 on the Brazilian economy. The purpose of this work is to analyze how Industry 4.0 is being implemented in the Brazilian context and what are the main expected impacts. The study discusses key Industry 4.0 concepts, such as the Internet of Things (IoT), artificial intelligence and cloud computing, and explores how these technologies are transforming production processes and the economy in general. The results highlight that Industry 4.0 has the potential to boost productivity, efficiency and innovation in Brazilian industries, in addition to promoting the creation of new business models and the generation of qualified jobs. However, the challenges and obstacles that may arise during the adoption of Industry 4.0 are also discussed, such as the need for investments in technological infrastructure and workforce training. This analysis offers important insights for managers and policy makers interested in understanding and taking advantage of the benefits of Industry 4.0 in the Brazilian economy.

While the present study employs references with similar themes and methodologies as the works mentioned above to support its development, it also distinguishes itself by examining references and recommendations concerning the adoption of Industry 4.0 practices across various domains within a company, irrespective of its field of operation.

3 Research Method

This section is dedicated to reporting the Systematic Mapping process used for the development of the work. For the Systematic Mapping process, we consider the observation of Falbo (2018) who says that we should not consider general search engines such as standard Google search and Duck Duck Go for example, but due to the research area having many more publications in the so-called gray papers, we chose to use these search engines to consider these types of work as well. The steps of the systematic mapping process used to build this study were:

1) Definition of the research question.
2) Primary search for works carried out in the research area in databases.
3) Establishment of inclusion and exclusion criteria.
4) Classification of works.

Exclusion criteria play an important role in the process of selecting articles in a Systematic Mapping. These criteria are established to identify and remove articles that do not meet the requirements or quality standards established for the review. In all databases in which the surveys of papers were carried out, they were organized by relevance. The steps of data extraction and categorization, and the number of selected works are represented in Fig. 2.

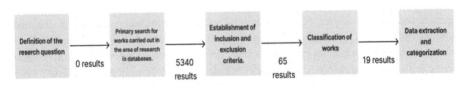

Fig. 2. Systematic Mapping description

3.1 Definition of the Research Question

The research question guides the entire process of searching and selecting relevant studies for systematic mapping. Therefore, the following research question was established:

Q1: What are the guidelines or procedures for small and medium-sized enterprises to undergo transformation into Industry 4.0?

3.2 Primary Search in Databases

"Finding possible relevant publications to answer the research question requires creating an appropriate search string and selecting relevant databases" (Wortmann; Combemale; Barais 2017). If the search strings are well elaborated, it is possible to optimize time and efforts in the search for articles. The strings allow the search to quickly identify relevant studies, filtering out irrelevant results or those not related to the search topic. Based on this assumption, we define the following search string:

((Methodology OR Processes OR "Best practices" OR Guide OR recommendation) AND ("small companies" AND "medium companies") AND ("industry 4.0" OR "Digital transformation")).

As the search progressed, the search strings have been adjusted and refined, allowing the inclusion of additional terms, the exclusion of irrelevant terms and the refinement of the search criteria for more accurate and meaningful results. According to Wortmann, Combemale and Barais (2017), the choice of research bases is also relevant to the research context. Thus, the following databases were considered:

1) Accessible: to facilitate the process of finding data without differentiating its literature (gray or white), broad search bases such as Google Scholar, Google standard search and Duck Duck Go were used.
2) National: to find articles with Brazilian initiatives, the specific Brazilian database Periódicos CAPES was included.

3.3   Establishment of Inclusion and Exclusion Criteria

The search exclusion criteria were:

EC1 - By relevance: So that the search is not too extensive, the first 300 articles found will be considered, as previously mentioned, they will be organized by relevance.

EC2 - By title: The title was read, considering the context of the question: What are the guidelines or procedures for SMEs to transform themselves, considering industry 4.0 and the chosen keywords.

EC3 - Non-primary articles: Articles that do not present primary studies (such as editorials, summaries of keynote lectures, tutorials, literature reviews).

EC4 - Non-duplicated articles: Articles not duplicated.

EC5 - By abstract: In this criterion, the abstract of the article was read, considering ideas/goals adhering to the context of our research and question.

EC6 - Articles with error: Often, the title and abstract were removed from the page of the research bases, if, when opening the article for the next stage, it presents errors and/or does not open, it was disregarded in this criterion.

EC7 - Full reading: In this criterion, all articles have been fully read. This criterion was made to complement the previous step and thus confirm the articles in which they are adherent to the context of our research and question.

EC8 - Initiatives in the Brazilian context: Articles within the Brazilian context. This step is contained in the previous steps.

EC9 - Review of Excluded Articles: A review of articles that may still be relevant to the context but were excluded by the previous steps.

EC10 - Summary of Resulting Articles: A review of the final selection of articles.

As Almeira (2022) states, it is important to clearly define and document the exclusion criteria before starting the article selection process. In addition, it is recommended that the exclusion of articles be performed by at least two independent reviewers, to ensure objectivity and minimize bias. Any divergence in the exclusion of articles can be resolved through discussions and consensus among reviewers or through a third reviewer, if necessary. This contributes to the reliability and transparency of the selection process.

3.4   Classification of Works

In this phase of the systematic mapping, the inclusion and exclusion criteria are applied to the repository of articles extracted from the selected databases, after that, the remaining works undergo two evaluation criteria: reading the title and reading the article abstract, thus, the articles still considered adherent to the research question by the researchers are finally used as a reference to answer the research question.

For a better view of the Papers being "sifted" by the exclusion criteria and evaluated by reading the title and abstract, a Table 1 was created with the aim of organizing the previously defined exclusion criteria in a structured way.

Each row in the Table 1 represents the exclusion criteria used, and the columns represent the bases on which the articles were extracted. When applying the exclusion criteria, the articles sifted and accepted by each exclusion criterion were marked in the table, this increases the transparency and consistency in the article selection process. After applying the inclusion and exclusion criteria, 19 articles were selected, as shown in Table 2.

Table 1. Sifted Articles

Exclusion Criteria	Duck Duck Go	Google	Capes	Scholar	Total
Starting quantity (<2018)	37	8	315	4980	5340
By relevance (>300)	37	8	300	300	645
By title	1	8	27	33	69
Non-primary articles	1	8	27	33	69
Non-duplicated articles	1	8	27	29	65
Abstract reading	1	6	16	22	45
Full article reading	0	6	6	7	19
Review of articles	–	6	6	7	19
Accepted articles	–	6	6	7	19

Table 2. List of selected Articles

Accepted Articles	Authors	Search plataform
Soluções tecnológicas da Industria 4.0 para micro, pequenas e médias empresas do setor de transformação digital	Dutra (2022)	Google
O guia completo de transformação digital para pequenas empresas	Pires (2024)	Google
Como promover a transformação digital em pequenas empresas? Saiba!	Pix Comunicação (2024)	Google
Indústria 4.0: como preparar pequenas e médias empresas	Polímeros (2019)	Google
Guia de referência para atuação em Gestão da Inovação com foco em Transformação Digital	Brasil 2023	Google
Indústria 4.0 e suas interfaces em uma empresa de pequeno porte no interior da Bahia	Santos (2021)	Google
Processo de transformação ágil em uma empresa brasileira de Telecom	Gonçalves et al. (2021)	CAPES
Digital transformation with agility: The emerging dynamic capability of complementary services	Andrade et al. (2023)	CAPES

(*continued*)

Table 2. (*continued*)

Accepted Articles	Authors	Search plataform
A percepção de gestores acerca das competências necessárias no contexto da indústria 4.0	Barbosa et al. (2021)	CAPES
Indústria 4.0 e transformação digital: Uma discussão conceitual, sob a perspectiva neoschumpeteriana, que inclui políticas de CT&I e CATCH UP	Cintra et al. (2019)	CAPES
Inovação em modelo de negócios através do uso de tecnologias da indústria 4.0 em pequenas e médias empresas	Fassini (2021)	CAPES
Implicações da transformação digital nos pequenos negócios do ramo alimentício diante da pandemia COVID-19	Costa et al. (2021)	CAPES
Industria 4.0 para pequenas e médias empresas	Pereira (2018)	Scholar
Análise da adoção de tecnologias da indústria 4.0 por pequenas e medias empresas do setor de usinagem	Baio Junior et al. (2022)	Scholar
Transformação digital no setor hoteleiro de São Luís-MA: entraves e desafios para gestores de pequenas empresas	(Gaspar, 2022)	Scholar
Transformação digital de modelo de negócio tradicional de lavanderias: uma proposta de framework	Machado (2021)	Scholar
Modelo de maturidade para indústria 4.0 para PME's brasileira: um estudo de caso em uma indústria de ração animal	Oliveira Júnior (2018)	Scholar
Processo de inovação no contexto de transformação digital: framework para gestão da inovação	Oliveira, Oliveira and Ziviani (2021)	Scholar
Transformação digital: como adquirir as habilidades certas para esse movimento	Forbes (2024)	Scholar

3.5 Data Extraction and Categorization

"To obtain a quality systematic mapping, it is essential to have a reliable and well-defined classification scheme" (Falbo, 2018). For this article, the works selected for theoretical basis were categorized according to the database (Fig. 3), the year of publication (Fig. 4), the type of research (Fig. 5) and the general themes of the works (Fig. 6), in order to create an overview for understanding the area of study covered by the research question.

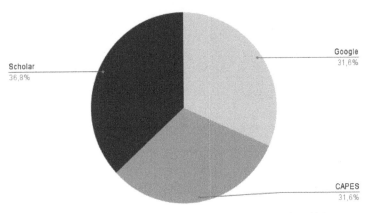

Fig. 3. Graph of the Search Platform count (own authorship)

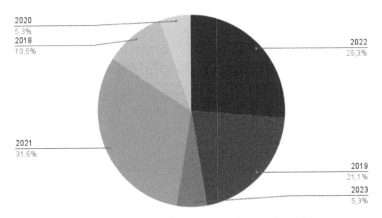

Fig. 4. Graph of publication years (own authorship)

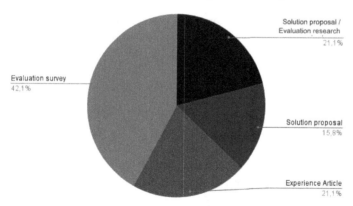

Fig. 5. Graph of search type classification (own authorship)

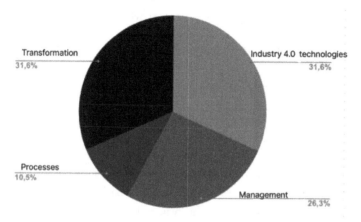

Fig. 6. Graph of general themes of the works (own authorship)

4 Results

Based on the systematic mapping process, it was possible to list the following information on the research topic.

The transformation towards Industry 4.0 for small and medium-sized companies requires the adoption of specific guidelines and procedures. Several articles and guides highlight some recommendations to assist in this process. A survey carried out in a small company in the interior of Bahia identified that employee training is essential, either through internal or external training, aimed at developing skills related to Industry 4.0 technologies and processes (Santos, 2021).

The Reference Guide for Innovation Management with a focus on (Brasil, 2023) Digital Transformation, highlights the importance of committed and engaged leadership, capable of fostering innovation and stimulating the adoption of disruptive technologies. In addition, the need to map and understand the company's internal processes is highlighted, identifying opportunities for improvement and optimization through digitization and automation. Table 3 list some questions that comprise the organizational structure and culture of the company, which can be applied in order to generate the necessary material to establish the vision and direction of the business in the process of innovation (Brasil, 2023).

Table 3. Questions to consider for developing the company's vision and direction (Brasil, 2023).

Number	Question
1	What is the organization's level of ambition regarding innovation?
2	How does the company map and evaluate the impact of new technologies on its business?
3	How will innovation efforts and results be measured and tracked?
4	What is the company's legacy, what keeps it, not as an anchor, but as a lever?
5	What is the purpose of the company's heat, why does it exist? Does this purpose need to be redefined?
6	How does leadership behave in relation to encouraging tis employees to suggest new ideas?
7	How does leadership recognize the importance of innovation for the future of the company?
8	How much of leadership decision are based on data?
9	Is there a mechanism for assessing and coding the company's learning? How does it work?
10	How does the organization introduce new tools and/or tecno-alloys?
11	Does the organization deal well with mistakes and failures?
12	Does the organization value diversity in the innovation ecosystem?
13	Does the organization relate to the innovation ecosystem?
14	How does the organization conduct change processes?
15	How are employees encouraged to plan/think about changes in the work environment?
16	What is the level of confidence of employees in developing their own initiatives in the company?
17	How is the entrepreneurial profile of employees valued in the company?
18	Is the recognition policy for efforts and results in line with employee's expectations?

With these questions addressed, it is expected that the SME management understands how innovation can help its business and is able to visualize the operation of the enterprise transformed by the adoption of innovative measures.

It is worth noting that digital transformation goes beyond the simple adoption of technologies, and it is essential to rethink the business model. A proposed framework for innovation management highlights the importance of identifying new business opportunities, creating innovative value propositions and developing sustainable revenue models. It follows a framework model for monitoring the process and innovation management, inspired by the framework provided by Oliveira, Oliveira and Ziviani (2021) (Fig. 7).

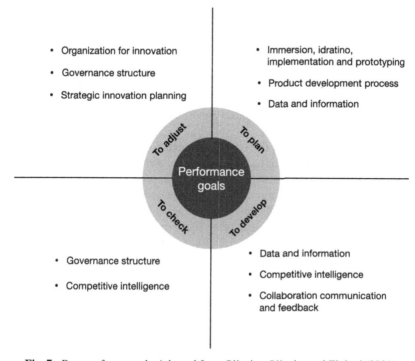

Fig. 7. Process framework. Adapted from Oliveira, Oliveira and Ziviani (2021)

A complete guide to digital transformation for small businesses highlights the importance of a well-defined strategy, with clear objectives and measurable goals. In addition, it is recommended to analyze the market and the target audience, seeking to identify the technological demands and trends relevant to the business. The choice of sustained suppliers and the establishment of strategic partnerships are also relevant aspects in the digital transformation process.

In the context of digital transformation, Dutra (2022) highlights the importance of identifying the specific needs of the sector and seeking appropriate technological solutions. This may involve the implementation of technologies such as the Internet of Things (IoT), big data, robotics and 3D printing, adapted to the demands and capabilities of smaller companies (Dutra, 2022).

Another relevant aspect is the implementation of integrated management systems (ERP) in small companies. The use of these tools contributes to improving the efficiency and optimization of internal processes, allowing better management of resources, in addition to providing strategic information for decision-making. Therefore, investing in technology and management systems is essential for companies that wish to become more efficient and competitive (Silva et al., 2020).

Additionally, a study carried out on the perception of managers about the skills needed in the context of Industry 4.0 highlights the importance of developing technical skills and knowledge related to new technologies. Training employees in areas such as artificial intelligence, data analysis and automation are essential for companies to make the most of the benefits provided by digital transformation (Barbosa et al., 2021).

However, it is important to highlight that digital transformation is not without its challenges. A study carried out in the hotel sector of São Luís - MA highlights that small companies face obstacles and challenges in the digital transformation process, such as lack of financial resources, employees' resistance to change and lack of knowledge about available technologies. Therefore, it is essential that companies are prepared to face these challenges and seek technical support and training to ensure the success of the transformation (Gaspar, 2022).

In short, the works selected through the systematic mapping process indicate that the guidelines and procedures for transforming small and medium-sized companies into Industry 4.0 involve training employees, identifying appropriate technological solutions for the sector, implementing integrated management systems, developing skills related to new technologies, facing challenges and seeking technical support. Digital transformation is a complex process, but it can bring significant benefits to the competitiveness and growth of smaller companies.

5   Research Limitations

This study suffers from some limitations, among which we can mention the difficulty of finding a substantial amount of work in the white or gray literature referring to the Brazilian scenario. It is also worth mentioning that there are not many contributions that propose to teach how to adopt industry 4.0 practices, which means that the present work presents a group of more generic recommendations and lacks more detailed guidelines for small and medium-sized entrepreneurs who could potentially use the reference guide prepared here.

6   Conclusion and Discussion

This work aimed to identify and select a set of practices and recommendations to support the digital transformation process of SMEs and the adoption of Industry 4.0 practices through a Systematic Mapping. The study resulted in the understanding that when dealing with Industry 4.0 studies and reports of best practices, there is still a lack of relevant publications in the white literature and even in the gray literature. However, it is understood that digital transformation has been shown to be a key element to drive innovation in companies, especially through the adoption of Industry 4.0 technologies.

Innovation management requires the use of appropriate frameworks, consideration of the necessary skills of managers, and overcoming the specific challenges faced by small companies. Digital transformation represents an opportunity for companies to improve their efficiency, competitiveness, and value creation through the adoption of digital technologies. Digital maturity, in turn, is a crucial aspect for the success of digital transformation, as it indicates the organization's degree of capacity and readiness to fully leverage the benefits of these technologies.

As a proposal for future work, the elaboration of a guide to help small and medium-sized Brazilian companies to adopt appropriate technologies for their businesses towards Industry 4.0 are suggested.

Acknowledgement. This work was supported by MackPesquisa (Mackenzie Research and Innovation Fund [Fundo Mackenzie de Pesquisa e Inovação]), Project number 221006.

References

ABDI. Agência Brasileira de Desenvolvimento Industrial: Conectividade e Indústria - Aplicação e inserção digital (2021). https://api.abdi.com.br/file-manager/upload/files/Instituto_FSB_Pesquisa_-_ABDI_-_Conectividade_VF__2___1_.pdf. Accessed 02 Feb 2024

Andrade, C.R.O., Gonçalo, C.R., Santos, A.M.: Digital transformation with agility: the emerging dynamic capability of complementary services. Rev. Adm. Mackenzie **23**, eRAMD220063 (2023). https://doi.org/10.1590/1678-6971/eRAMD220063.en

Baio Junior, A., Carrer, M.J.: A. Análise da adoção de tecnologias da Indústria 4.0 por pequenas e médias empresas do setor de usinagem. In: Gestão e Produção, vol. 29, p. e122. UFSCAR, São Carlos (2022). https://doi.org/10.1590/1806-9649-2022v29e122

Barbosa, V.D.S., Firmino, T.T., Amorim, A.F.A.: A percepção de gestores acerca das competências necessárias no contexto da indústria 4.0. Rev. Tecnol. Soc. **17**, 118–132 (2021). https://doi.org/10.3895/rts.v17n49.13631

Brasil. Ministério da Ciência, Tecnologia, Inovações e Comunicações: Guia de Referência para atuação em Gestão da Inovação com foco em Transformação Digital (2023). https://www.portaldaindustria.com.br/publicacoes/2023/1/guia-de-referencia-para-atuacao-em-gestao-da-inovacao-com-foco-emtransformacao-digital/. Accessed 28 May 2023

Cintra, L.P., et al.: Indústria 4.0 e transformação digital: uma discussão conceitual, sob a perspectiva neoschumpeteriana, que inclui políticas de CT&I e CATCH UP. Revista Economia & Gestão, vol. 19, pp. 114–132. UFMG, Belo Horizonte (2019). https://doi.org/10.5752/P.1984-6606.2019v19n54p114-132

Costa, J.T., de Souza Barbosa, M.A., Lima, A.C.N., Caldas, A.V.S.: Implicações da transformação digital nos pequenos negócios do ramo alimentício diante da pandemia covid-19. Rev. Gestão. Org. **19**(2), 197–217 (2021). https://doi.org/10.51359/1679-1827.2021.252703

Dutra, C.C. Soluções tecnológicas da Indústria 4.0 para micro, pequenas e médias empresas do setor de transformação industrial, 2nd edn. Núcleo de Engenharia Organizacional; Ministério da Economia, Porto Alegre (2022). https://lume.ufrgs.br/handle/10183/252948

Eliseo, M.A., et al.: An overview of brazilian companies on the adoption of industry 4.0 practices. In: Agredo-Delgado, V., Ruiz, P.H., Correa-Madrigal, O. (eds.) HCI-COLLAB 2022. Communications in Computer and Information Science, vol. 1707, pp. 15–27. Springer, Cham (2022). https://doi.org/10.1007/978-3-031-24709-5_2

Falbo, R.D.A.: Mapeamento Sistemático, vol. 7 (2018) http://claudiaboeres.pbworks.com/w/file/fetch/133747116/Mapeamento%20Sistemático%20-%20v1.0.pdf

Fassini, R.: Inovação em modelo de negócios através do uso de tecnologias da indústria 4.0 em pequenas e médias empresas. TEDE. Pontifícia Universidade Católica do Rio Grande do Sul, Porto Alegre (2021). https://tede2.pucrs.br/tede2/handle/tede/9893

FIESP homepage. Federação das Indústrias do Estado de São Paulo.: Fiesp Identifica Desafios da Indústria 4.0 no Brasil e Apresenta Propostas. https://www.fiesp.com.br/noticias/fiesp-identi fica-desafios-da-industria-4-0-no-brasil-e-apresenta-propostas/. Accessed 02 Feb 2024

Forbes Website.: Transformação digital: como adquirir as habilidades certas para esse movimento, https://forbes.com.br/carreira/2022/03/infomercial-pmi-transformacao-digital-como-adquirir-as-habilidades-certas-para-esse-movimento/. Accessed 02 Feb 2024

Gaspar, L.S.: Transformação digital no setor hoteleiro de São Luís – MA: entraves e desafios para gestores de pequenas empresas. Universidade Federal do Maranhão, São Luis (2022). http://hdl.handle.net/123456789/5779

Gonçalves, M.L.D.A., da Silva, R.A.C., Silva, E.A.C., Penha, R.: Processo de transformação ágil em uma empresa brasileira de Telecom. Rev. Gestão Proj. 12(1), 70–94 (2021). https://doi.org/10.5585/gep.v12i1.17801

Hidayatno, A., Rahman, I., Rahmadhani, A.: Understanding the systemic relationship of industry 4.0 adoption in the Indonesian food and beverage industry. In: Proceedings of the 5th International Conference on Industrial and Business Engineering, vol. 19, pp. 344–348. Association for Computing Machinery, New York (2019). https://doi.org/10.1145/3364335.3364352

TOTVS Website.: Indústria 4.0: guia completo. https://www.totvs.com/blog/gestao-industrial/ind ustria-4-0/. Accessed 02 Feb 2024

Laurent, E.M., Monsone, C.R.: Ecosystems of industry 4.0: combining technology and human power. In: Proceedings of the 11th International Conference on Management of Digital Ecosystems, New York, vol. 1 pp.115–119 (2019). https://doi.org/10.1145/3297662.3365793

Machado, D.A.D.S.: Transformação digital de modelo de negócio tradicional de lavanderias: uma proposta de framework. UNINOVE, São Paulo (2021). http://bibliotecatede.uninove.br/han dle/tede/2897

Mais Polímeros Website: Indústria 4.0: como preparar pequenas e médias empresas (2019). https://maispolimeros.com.br/2019/07/05/industria-4-0-como-preparar/. Accessed 02 Feb 2024

Oliveira Júnior, L.: Modelo de maturidade para a indústria 4.0 para PME's brasileiras: um estudo de caso em uma indústria de ração animal. UTFP, Pato Branco (2018). http://repositorio.utfpr.edu.br/jspui/handle/1/4067

Oliveira, R.R., Oliveira, R.R., Ziviani, F.: Processo de inovação no contexto de transformação digital: framework para gestão da inovação. Perspect. Gestão Conhecimento 11(3), 2–15 (2021). https://periodicos.ufpb.br/index.php/pgc/article/view/61766

Palmeira J., Coelho G., Carvalho, A., Carvalhal P., Cardoso, P.: Migrating legacy production lines into an industry 4.0 ecosystem. In: 20th International Conference on Industrial Informatics, pp. 429–434. INDIN, Perth (2022). https://doi.org/10.1109/INDIN51773.2022.9976084

Passos, L.H.S.: A indústria 4.0: fundamentos e principais impactos na economia brasileira. Rev. Adm. Negócios Amazônia 12(2), 53–63 (2020). https://doi.org/10.18361/2176-8366/rara.v12 n2p53-63

Pereira, K.C.C.L.: Indústria 4.0 para pequenas e médias empresas. Centro Universitário do Estado do Pará, Belém (2018). http://repositorio.cesupa.br:8080/jspui/handle/prefix/148

Petersen, K., Feldt, R., Mujtaba, R., Mattsson, M.: Systematic mapping studies in software engineering. In: Proceedings of the 12th international conference on Evaluation and Assessment in Software Engineering, EASE 2008, pp. 68–77. BCS Learning & Development Ltd., Swindon (2008). https://dl.acm.org/doi/10.5555/2227115.2227123

Pires, L.O.: Guia completo de transformação digital para pequenas empresas. https://www.sensio.com.br/blog/transformacao-digital-pequenas-empresas. Accessed 02 Feb 2024

Pix Comunicação Website: Como promover a transformação digital em pequenas empresas? saiba! https://blog.pix.com.br/pequenas-empresas/. Accessed 02 Feb 2024

Santos, A.O.: Indústria 4.0 e suas interfaces em uma empresa de pequeno porte no interior da Bahia. Estudo de Caso. USSC, Santa Catarina (2021). https://repositorio.animaeducacao.com.br/handle/ANIMA/17753

SEBRAE (ed.): Micro e pequenas empresas geram 27% do PIB do Brasil (2021). https://seb rae.com.br/sites/PortalSebrae/ufs/mt/noticias/micro-e-pequenas-empresas-geram-27-do-pib-do-brasil,ad0fc706464674l0VgnVCM2000003c740l0aRCRD#:~:text=Bras%C3%ADlia% 20%2D%20Os%20pequenos%20neg%C3%B3cios%20respondem,presidente%20do%20S ebrae%2C%20Luiz%20Barretto. Accessed 02 Feb 2024

Silva, B.D., de Campos, F.C.: Indústria 4.0: revisão sistemática da literatura 2008–2018, achados, tendências e aplicações. In: IX Congresso Brasileiro de Engenharia de Produção. conBRe-pro, Ponta Grossa (2019). https://aprepro.org.br/conbrepro/2019/anais/arquivos/08262019_ 100820_5d63e2acb438b.pdf. Accessed 02 Feb 2024

Ds Silva, C.M., Lemos, F.A.M., Gama, G.M., Alves, G.R.: Implantação de sistemas integrados de gestão (ERP) em pequenas empresas. In: Repositório Institucional do Conhecimento. Fac-uldade de Tecnologia Deputado, Jundiaí (2020). http://ric.cps.sp.gov.br/handle/123456789/ 4652. Accessed 02 Feb 2024

Wortmann, A., Combemale, B., Barais, O.: A systematic mapping study on modeling for industry 4.0. In: 20th International Conference on Model Driven Engineering Languages and Systems, Austin, TX, vol. 17, pp. 281–291 (2017). https://doi.org/10.1109/MODELS.2017.14

Author Index

© The Editor(s) (if applicable) and The Author(s), under exclusive license
to Springer Nature Switzerland AG 2024
P. H. Ruiz et al. (Eds.): HCI-COLLAB 2023, CCIS 1877, pp. 319–320, 2024.
https://doi.org/10.1007/978-3-031-57982-0

Printed in the United States
by Baker & Taylor Publisher Services